BEYOND THE REVOLUTION

BEYOND THE REVOLUTION

*A History of American Thought
from Paine to Pragmatism*

WILLIAM H. GOETZMANN

BASIC
BOOKS

A MEMBER OF THE PERSEUS BOOKS GROUP
NEW YORK

Designed by Timm Bryson

Library of Congress Cataloging-in-Publication Data
Goetzmann, William H.
    Beyond the Revolution : a history of American thought from Paine
to pragmatism / William H. Goetzmann.
        p. cm.
    Includes bibliographical references.
    ISBN 978-0-465-00495-9
    1. United States—Intellectual life. 2. Philosophy, American—
History. 3. Political science—United States—History. 4.
Intellectuals—United States—Biography. 5. Philosophers—United
States—Biography. 6. Political scientists—United States—Biography.
I. Title.
    E169.1.G55 2009
    973—dc22
                                                    2008025590

10 9 8 7 6 5 4 3 2

This book is dedicated to my grandchildren:

RUSTY, ZOË, GRIFFIN, SOPHIE, AND WELLS

CONTENTS

INTRODUCTION

This book is the story of the search by American intellectuals for cultural self-definition. In some sense it is intended to be a kind of existential epic with those very special people—the intellectuals—as protagonists engaged in the Sisyphean task of forever confronting the new and making it meaningful to society. Intellectuals pursue their tasks—often esoteric and wildly impractical to the common man—because they feel "cultural anxiety," or a compulsion constantly to redefine the context of reality in which they find themselves. They assume the burden of first sensing, then grappling with, and finally organizing the new, which is of value to civilization itself. More than mere custodians of knowledge, they stand for most of their lives face to face with the terrors and ambiguities of ultimate reality. And as such, in Henry James's terms, they are the "hard core creators of culture."

In the United States the role of the intellectual currently is not much appreciated. On both the political right and the political left, intellectuals are deemed to be "elitists." They are members of an elite only in the sense that relatively few people have the talent, sensibility, intelligence, and especially the inclination to worry about the culture as a whole. Most Americans prefer to remain caught up in the everyday concerns of living a "normal life," pursuing limited if special interests, and advocating causes whose origin and meaning they scarcely question. Recently the social history of such people has come to fascinate historians. This is particularly ironic because of all nations, the United States is and has been from the beginning the product of intellectuals. As F. Scott Fitzgerald observed, in contrast to France, which was a land, and England, which was a people,

America always had about it "the quality of an idea." At a certain point in time, 1776, it emerged as a concept from the minds of a particular group of Founding Fathers who were nothing if not intellectuals. As intellectuals and Founding Fathers, these men in varying ways all shared a special vision of the future based in part on their studies of the past. This vision and its adventures or misadventures—even its universality—forms my theme, but by no means my only concern, in this narrative of American thought and consciousness.

My theme, of course, is the American quest for the climactic model of world civilization that not only would incorporate the best ideas, the best lifestyles, and the most profound spiritual values, but also would forever remain free and open to the new. It would be the world's first truly cosmopolitan civilization—a "nation of nations," as Walt Whitman put it, with the "course of universal being" flowing through it. Since the American Revolution the quest has proven to be an exciting one, though the results—certainly as of 1900, the formative period during which America passed through its first major crises—have perhaps remained inconclusive; hence, the existential nature of this narrative.

My study of American intellectual history has itself raised large questions that cannot be ignored. The first of these concerns is the role of information and its relationship to what we call cultures and civilizations, for it was, after all, information with which the "hard core creators of culture" were grappling. So important, therefore, is this question that it forms a major theme of my narrative. It suggests an underlying interpretation of intellectual and cultural history in the form of several related questions, which run as follows: what is civilization as opposed to a culture, what functions do intellectuals perform in both contexts, how do we know when we have a truly significant civilization, and why is the study of America especially significant in any case?

Most studies of civilizations and cultures use the terms interchangeably as ways of referring to those clearly delineated structures of interrelated institutions, language, ideas, values, myths, and symbols that give form and meaning to societal behavior. Often civilization is seen as simply a more advanced or complex culture made so by the emergence of one or more distinctive traits such as religion, art, or law that seem to characterize the Judeo-Christian, Byzantine, Roman, Greek, Oriental, and Islamic civilizations, respectively. This has led to some confusion and, in my opinion, great and possibly dangerous superficialities.

Cultures are structures of interrelated institutions, languages, ideas, values, myths, and symbols. They tend to be exclusive, even tribal. Civilizations, on the other hand, are open to new customs and ideas. They are syncretistic, chaotic, and often confusing societal information mechanisms. They continue to grow in the richness, variety, and complexity of societal experience as it is brought before the people by intellectuals, politicians, artists, writers, technologists, and scientists from all parts of the then-known world. Civilization advances beyond the set prescriptions of culture into a broader eclecticism, and to identify both the individual and the social is harder to discern. It is possibly too subtle, too kaleidoscopic, too demanding, though also swirling and adventuresome for all of its elusiveness.

Civilization, as such, however, is also deceptive, because beneath the surface of apparent chaos and contradiction lies great efficiency in absorbing, organizing, and distributing the world's information. Human beings, individually and collectively, by the nature of their biological makeup, cannot help but be sensors of the world's data. They must forever puzzle over and account for—organize in some fashion—this experience that gradually becomes knowledge for better or for worse. Cultures and systems of ideas are then, figuratively speaking, temporary bulwarks, stopping places, organizational makeshifts in the path of on-rushing civilizations that are the inevitable products of history in the same sense that learning is the inevitable product of individual experience. The question then becomes almost quantitative, as early advocates of mass education, such as Thomas Jefferson, dimly realized. Is that civilization best or highest that incorporates or makes relevant to its people the maximum of the world's data? Does it crest at a point of maximum learning activity? And does it recede into folk culture status when new information is shut out by conscious political and cultural proscriptions—when real intellectuals no longer have a vital role to play and the totalitarians, politicians, traffic directors, bureaucrats, drill-masters, and fascists take over?

America, it appears, had almost no choice from the outset. It began as a palimpsest of world experience—its lineage ringingly articulated in the writings of the Founding Fathers. And as waves of immigration swept over the new land and the citizens of the United States had ever-increasing access to the world's ideas, inventions, and varieties of consciousness, it became ever more eclectic—cosmopolitan, not in spite of, but because of itself, in that it had its beginnings in the conscious ideal of eighteenth-century cosmopolitan reason. The United States is unique, therefore, only in having a clearly discernible beginning; unlike that of so many other nations, its revolution led to a unique independence. In this book I am concerned with the multifaceted role of the intellectuals as they have given shape to our civilization in its crucial formative period. My objectives should consequently be clear. In the course of my narrative I propose:

1. To describe the evolution and growth of a utopian and cosmopolitan American civilization, with all the evidences of progress, regress, doubt, and failures to live up to the ideal.
2. To see this evolutionary growth as a kind of gigantic, ongoing information mechanism.
3. To describe and analyze various major intellectual, scientific, and artistic structures or configurations for dealing with data coming not only from the experiences of the New World but also from Europe and all parts of the globe.
4. To examine and characterize American intellectuals, artists, and scientists as sensors of realities and purveyors of information and opinions as well as dreams to a civilization they were defining by means of their consciousness and interpretations.
5. To delineate as much as possible the social and cultural matrix in which America's intellectuals functioned.

It should be clear that my overall interpretation runs counter to Frederick Jackson Turner's attempt to isolate American uniqueness and to characterize American culture as one owing to the existence of a vast frontier to the west. In my view American civilization was not only a product of the frontier, the pioneer, and even nature. Democracy and a whole host of other American values did not emerge "stark and strong: from out of the forest" in a kind of virgin birth. Rather, civilization in the United States was the product of the world's ideas put to the service of the North American people on one level by those "hard core creators of culture"—the intellectuals—who transmitted, transformed, and ultimately made attractive to our citizens

BOOK I

WORLD HISTORY IS
AMERICAN HISTORY

whatever the world had to offer. American civilization was thus always a de-rivative and syncretistic civilization. In my opinion, there is honor in ac-knowledging this fact, and folly in the reductionist search for the one quintessentially unique American factor in our global civilization. This is an interdependent world, and there is no better time than now to acknowledge this fact and to build upon it. If this book does nothing more than serve as a parable illustrating and defending this proposition, it will have served its purpose.

CHAPTER ONE

Tom Paine's Vision

"The Birthday of a new world is at hand," proclaimed citizen Tom Paine on July 10, 1776. "We have it in our power to begin the world over again!" Paine, a ragged but independent refugee from the slums of London, seemed to personify the promise of America as a "new world." The best years of his youth he had spent as a half-starved corset maker—a trade he detested so much that only the solace of Gin Lane made it bearable. He had seen one wife die amid London's squalor, and another deserted him because he was a failure at everything he tried. Stout, ugly, habitually unshaven, dirty, and described by everyone who saw him as a man with "twisted eyes," Paine was a piece of the world's flotsam when he arrived in America in 1774 bearing a crumpled letter of introduction from Benjamin Franklin. The letter secured him a position as editor of Robert Aitken's *Pennsylvania Magazine*, where he taught himself the craft with rugged determination, and within a year achieved some distinction as a writer. However, the British attack at Lexington and Concord in April 1775 and the subsequent assembling of the First Continental Congress in Philadelphia fired his revolutionary imagination, and he abandoned his editorial duties in summer and fall 1775 to scratch out *Common Sense*, his immortal two-shilling pamphlet that swept revolutionary America by storm.

In *Common Sense* he forcefully articulated the moral possibilities of colonial America and formulated them into a persuasive ideology of world revolution that captured the imagination of thousands. "The cause of America is in great measure the cause of all mankind," Paine insisted. "'Tis not the affair of a city, a county, a province, or a kingdom, but of a continent—of at least one eighth part of the habitable globe. Tis not the concern of a day, a year, or an age; posterity are virtually involved in the contest, and will be more or less affected, even to the end of time, by the proceedings now. Now is the seed-time of continental union, faith and honor." Paine's message went out to people on both sides of the Atlantic by the hundreds of thousands. Carried along by more than ringing rhetoric, his homely argument made him into a prophet—the prophet of reason who saw clearly into the millennial future for which North America had been preparing itself for nearly two centuries.

Even while Paine's pamphlet was hitting the streets of Philadelphia, a Second Continental Congress, made up of representatives of all thirteen colonies, was meeting in that city to consider the question of independence, war, and the possibilities for European cooperation that might eventually lead to the formation of a new nation in America. Paine's pamphlet removed the frames of time and space from this discussion. Focusing on the basic nature of man everywhere, Paine unveiled a transcendent and global drama in which America and the American stood at center stage, the symbol of mankind's hopes for a future of harmony and liberty. Drawing upon all peoples from all places, America stood at the meridian—the first potentially cosmopolitan civilization where man and man's reason and man's rights might prevail. Paine declared, "Freedom hath been hunted round the globe. Asia, and Africa, have long expelled her—Europe regards her like a stranger, and England hath given her warning to depart. Oh receive the fugitive and prepare in time an asylum for mankind."

Paine enunciated three essential functions in the formation of American thought and culture. He served as a profound myth-maker. He made clear some of the basic relationships of man, society, and government upon which the future republic was to rest. And he made the revolutionary heritage of America so overt as to be unmistakable for all future generations.

As myth-maker, Paine, in *Common Sense*, wove together powerful emotive strands to create enduring myths about American size, uniqueness, open-mindedness, and goodness—America's fundamental difference from the rest of the world. Drawing upon American pride in the size and sublime immensity of the continent, not to mention the endless abundance of nature that supplied resources for world trade, Paine appealed to a kind of Newtonian geography. "There is something very absurd," he wrote, "in supposing a continent to be perpetually governed by an island. In no instance hath nature made the satellite larger than its primary planet. . . . " Then there were the American people. According to Paine, they were not, as was commonly supposed, all freeborn Englishmen and therefore held by cultural ties to the Mother Country. For "Mother" he substituted the "melting pot" parent. Europe, not just England, was the parent country of America. "This new world hath been the asylum for the persecuted lovers of civil and religious liberty from *every part* of Europe." But if the people in America were "lovers of civilization and religious liberty," they stood in stark contrast to the oppressed of England and Europe who remained behind, victims of a "monster" civilization. This—the contrast theme—was central to his argument. America was a free, abundant asylum of nature and plenty. Europe was encrusted with wicked, corrupt, and degrading institutions, such as monarchies, condemned even in the Bible, which enfeebled her population and stifled freedom. The contrast theme Paine presented became basic to defining America.

In one grand synthesis, Paine captured the implicit millennialism of a vast spectrum of American believers, including not only hopeful tradesmen, farmers, newly arrived immigrants, and scientifically minded devotees of progress, but also Calvinists of all persuasions, who for over a century had impatiently looked toward the coming of Christ's kingdom in the New World. According to Paine, America was God's country of the future. The spirit of revival, constant regeneration, and future-oriented habits of pragmatic thinking had already become basic to American thought. Paine, as myth-maker, used it to build an intercolonial self-identity intended to bind the colonies together in a common cause and a new utopian nation.

Paine's social and political thought had even wider scope. Considering himself a citizen of the world, he was not concerned solely with America, but first with mankind, and then America as it offered an experiment or model to the rest of the world. Like most eighteenth-century thinkers, he

was Newtonian and believed in models as they reflected the basic principles of nature, yet stood off from it as an observer, possessed of special
powers of reason and the senses that English philosopher John Locke had
clearly described. Man's task was to use his reason to bring himself into
ever-closer harmony with nature, for to be in harmony with nature meant
that one was possessed of its secrets and most fully assumed his natural
dignity in the universe. But for Paine, contrary to Locke, man did not
start out with a mental tabula rasa. Rather, following the Scottish Common Sense philosophers, Paine preferred to believe, like Thomas Jefferson, that man possessed an innate sense of morality and sociability that
made naturally for brotherhood. "Let us suppose a small number of persons settled in some sequestered part of the earth, unconnected with the
rest," he wrote. "In this state of natural liberty, society will be their first
thought." Man in a state of nature thus seeks harmony, brotherhood, cooperation, and sociability rather than ruthless competition. The sole object of government is to enable him to achieve these objectives by
preserving his freedom. Thus Paine drew a clear distinction between society and government. "Society is produced by our wants, and government
by our wickedness; the former promotes our happiness positively by unit-
ing our affections, the latter negatively by restraining our vices. The one
encourages intercourse, the other creates distinctions. . . . Government
like dress is the badge of lost innocence."

The problem arose, however, when simplicity, like innocence, vanished
before complexity created by ever-increasing numbers of people with conflicting aims. For all his belief in innate reason and morality, Paine also saw
irrationality and wickedness generated out of complex and overly populous
societies. Hence the sad necessity for government. America, for him,
clearly represented the last best instance of underpopulation and hence of
Adamic innocence that made true liberty and brotherly individualism possible. Thus the tone of strident urgency in *Common Sense*. There was, in
Paine's view, very little time left for man to slough off the corruptions of
Europe and get back on the natural path of unfettered harmony and freedom. The significance of the revolutionary crisis was for him whether
America could resist the encroachments of a corrupt monarchy and thus
reverse the depressing tide of tyranny in the nick of time.

In advocating revolution and independence Paine was also assailing the past and the centuries of corruption that had come to fetter European freedom. Unlike Locke, also a believer in the contract theory of government, he took no solace in the venerable British Constitution or historic English traditions said to guarantee "the rights of freeborn Englishmen." He had seen too much corruption in the Britain of his day. Instead he wished America to begin anew—to embark on a venture in true utopianism. The aim of the revolution, as Paine saw it, was to wipe away the stain of the past and to found, through the rational common sense of men, a completely new society dedicated to an ideology of brotherly individualism in which the rights to life, liberty, property, equality, and the pursuit of happiness were the axioms and postulates of man's existence. Moreover, he sought to guarantee the security of these rights by means of a representative republican government with a written constitution in which the maximum democratic participation was encouraged to ensure minimum governmental interference with man's basic rights. Society was more important than government. The individual, in whom Paine ultimately placed his faith, was more important than the state and certainly any ruler. Paine thus proposed to found a revolutionary government upon rationally derived ideas, not traditions, upon an ideological model rather than existing institutions. His was a blueprint drawn from the world of reason and experience that he hoped would take shape in a written constitution that would come to serve all men, including the Americans. Remarkably enough, in the winter of 1776, he found himself in the main among like-minded cosmopolitan men at Valley Forge, who were also conscious of their role on a global and timeless stage. In July of that year, the Continental Congress produced in the Declaration of Independence, addressed specifically to a "candid world," what Paine must have regarded as a gloss upon his text.

Paine's vision of a new society that would embrace and absorb all the people of the earth was, of course, merely a secularized eighteenth-century version of a prophetic and millennial dream that had fascinated peoples for over a thousand years. The meeting of the Continental Congress in Philadelphia in 1776 that launched the colonies on their revolutionary course and the subsequent creation of a unique constitutional government in 1787 meant to form the basis of a great cosmopolitan experiment were the products of a certain group of people at a certain time and place in human history. Other utopian dreams had failed—at times tragically—in the New World. But somehow the New World invariably beckoned and offered future promise down through time to people of millennial vision and imagination. As two hundred years of America's history opened on such a note of promise, the question remained: would the dream be fulfilled?

CHAPTER TWO

The Complex Road to an Independent Civilization

Though often it did not seem so, the main theme of colonial experience in North America had been a quest for liberty, as floods of settlers interpreted it. But the achievements of that end were not so easy. In fact, the road to independence was a complex journey. First the Pilgrims, then the Puritans, came seeking religious liberty in their own peculiar fashion. To the south, on the Chesapeake River, the one thing the proprietors of the Virginia Company learned was the folly of attempting to attract plantation workers without giving them some chance to own land in the vastness of America. As the Middle Colonies developed, Pennsylvania prospered on its climate of tolerance—religious, economic, and even ethnic—which attracted thousands of settlers and not only made Philadelphia the most prosperous city in the colonies and the most tolerant, but also opened up the backcountry to rich, free settlement. The proprietary Jerseys were so in name only, as the newly arrived did pretty much as they pleased since the lordly owners were in absentia, taking the waters somewhere in Britain. And in New York, not only had the Hudson River patroon system failed and Manhattan become a polyglot city of all sorts of people, religions, and occupations, but it was so recognized by British authorities who, when they captured it from the Dutch, allowed most indigenous institutions to stand. Indeed, a main theme of British North American imperialism seems to have been the population of the colonies with whatever people seemed available and willing. Governed largely by mercantilistic theories, British sovereigns, merchant adventurers, and Parliament seemed most concerned with exploiting the resources of the new continent as fast as possible, getting rid of overpopulation or malcontents at home, and creating a large new market for British goods. For well over one hundred years, the British government's attention to the colonies was largely confined to militarily combating Dutch, French, and Spanish designs on its New World possessions and regulating commerce in the interests of the Mother Country through a series of navigation acts or trade regulations.

Religion at times became an issue because British rulers lived in an age when the spirit of the Reformation reinforced a natural imperial competition with Catholic France and Spain. Consequently, they endorsed, even at times enthusiastically, the holy aspects of the English mission to North America. But when intense religious conflicts arose in the mid-seventeenth century, the reaction of Britain's rulers was always toward broadened toleration, from neglect of Roger Williams's accusations against New England and Charles II's ordering of religious toleration in Massachusetts, his granting charters of toleration to Williams in Rhode Island and Penn in Pennsylvania, to the broad application of William and Mary's Toleration Act of 1689 over all their North American colonies. In the meantime throughout the colonies, little by little, locally dominated political institutions began to develop, from the famous Virginia House of Burgesses to the New England town meetings built upon the bases of religious congregationalism.

This whole broad imperial outlook on the part of Britain has been termed a policy of "salutary neglect," but, on the contrary, it would be more accurate to say that it was a policy of headlong, opportunistic imperial development in which large numbers of grateful, loyal, functioning citizens were seen to be England's best resource in the competition with Spain, France, and Holland. To achieve this strength in the shortest possible time, within the broad outlines of a traditional mercantilist design, a middle-class laissez-faire policy that even countenanced indentured servitude and slavery prevailed. Americans came to equate this policy, even as it ignored slavery, with liberty, which they believed to be traditional not only in their own long colonial experience, but also traditional in the rights of Englishmen under the British Constitution. Eventually American philosophers, following John Locke, traced the natural right to liberty—or laissez-faire—back through the best times in ancient history to the mythical origins of man in a state of nature. Through a process of historicism they made such rights fundamental to the nature of man himself and the never-ending quest for these rights as something holy.

The striking fact about all this is that, for such a very long time, with minor exceptions, the interests of Britain and its North American colonies seemed to coincide. The bitterest struggles seemed to take place within the colonies themselves—partially due to growing pains that continually jostled, threatened, or at times replaced the status of colonial elites or leadership groups. The struggle of the Puritan orthodoxy to retain absolute control over its "visible saints" in the face of worldly alternatives was one such example. The bitter war waged by the Awakeners against the so-called Arminians was another. These struggles were fought out in the pulpits of intellectualism, in contrast to Major General James Wolfe's more mundane French and Indian War conflict with Louis-Joseph, the Marquis de Montcalm de Saint-Véran, on the Plains of Abraham.

By the Peace of Paris in 1763, which ended the French and Indian War, however, in North America itself a new status revolution had taken place fully as profound as the ousting of the French from the backwoods heartlands of America. Religion per se had lost its monopoly on the definition of the "good life" in America. The Great Awakening had subsided for a time like a sudden storm blown out to sea and with it had gone the minister's authority in the vanguard of continental leadership. Instead new men ruled—merchants made rich on war profits, lawyers made rich on merchants' profits and squabbles, and most important of all, a new intellectual class that gained great sway over the minds of Americans through the media of newspapers, almanacs, circulated letters, politically oriented sermons, manifestoes, and pamphlets. Such figures as Samuel Adams, Benjamin Franklin, James Otis, Patrick Henry, John Dickinson, Thomas Jefferson, and Tom Paine immediately spring to mind. In place of the minister's struggles over freedom of conscience and the merits or demerits of private revelation, these new men—the American philosophes—directed their energies to defining and arguing, using every basic strand of traditional western thought, the nature of human liberty in this world rather than the next.

But why had they arisen as contenders and leaders at all? Why did they feel compelled to precipitate a crisis within what seemed to be a harmonious British empire governed by their own admission under the most enlightened constitution and set of laws western man had ever devised? Economic motives were not the most important. The Navigation Acts, with the exception of controls over sugar and molasses, were largely beneficial to the colonists. And these acts were so loosely enforced as to make smuggling take on the character of legitimate business enterprise. The king seemed to have nothing but goodwill for his colonies and even made an American, Benjamin West, his court painter. Both King and Parliament were proud of their new-won North American empire, and glory probably should have been enough.

Parliament was hardly a united body, but rather a collection of local representatives bound up with a limited set of constituents, parochial concerns, and the game or sport of jockeying for status and glory within the confines of the Houses themselves. Such a piece of witty one-upmanship as Horace Walpole's judgment of Charles Townshend—"He had almost every great talent . . . if he had had but common truth, common sincerity, common honesty, common modesty, common steadiness, common courage and common sense"—may have seemed at the time more important than a wise and farsighted policy for the North American colonies. In short, despite the great names of Parliament handed down to us by British historians, despite the striking personalities of Walpole, Pitt, Fox, Burke, Townshend, North, Grenville, et al., the British Parliament seems really to have differed little in its instincts from the Virginia House of Burgesses or a Massachusetts assembly. It was excessively local in character. At a time when worldwide intellectual currents were sweeping through western civilization and Britain itself had acquired a global empire, Parliament seemed almost testy at the inconvenience of interrupting its sport and attending to the responsibilities of its new empire. And so it delegated its responsibilities to a series of second-rate ministers who lasted but a short while in office and whose policies often conflicted, sometimes canceled one another out, and were invariably impulsive. It was almost as if they believed that God, not Adam Smith, had devised an invisible hand to run world affairs for their landowner or merchant clients' benefits, and active political participation in world affairs of state was asking just a bit much for all but the most fanatical opportunist or the lesser members who simply had to make their mark.

The best way out was to delegate authority, and by 1763, as relates to foreign policy, Britain had the largest, most cumbersome bureaucracy of its time—a major triumph of spoilsmanship and shrewd obfuscation in the eyes of some. As Esmond Wright has written, "The following all had some control over the colonies: The Secretary of State for the Southern Department, the Board of Trade and Plantations (made up of merchants), the Treasury, the Surveyor and Auditor-General of the Colonies, the Commissioner of Customs, the Secretary-at-War, the Admiralty, the Admiralty Courts, the Surveyor-General of the King's Woods, the Postmaster General and the Bishop of London. The Admiralty alone had fifteen branches scattered in all parts of the town, from Whitehall to Cheapside; the Board sat in Whitehall, but the Navy Office was in Seething Lane, the Victualling Office in East Smithfield, the Ordnance in the Tower." And one might have added that the ships were docked along the Thames and the Royal Observatory, which furnished the sailing charts and was administered by the Admiralty, was located up the Thames at Greenwich. Clearly Washington, D.C.'s current "foggy bottom" originated long ago in eighteenth-century London.

Beyond this, the experience of the French and Indian War fastened a permanent hostile bureaucracy on America. To a man, the British commanders who participated in that campaign—John Campbell, Earl of Loudoun, Lord Jeffrey Amherst, Henry Bouquet, Sir William Johnson, and General Thomas Gage—had nothing but contempt for the continentals. Most colonies had furnished supplies and men only with the greatest reluctance. And all the successful campaigns in the vast war of forest and lakes were mounted by common British redcoats whose lobsterbacks alone had reflected imperial glory from the wild Mohawk Valley to the unscalable heights of Quebec. Accordingly, General Gage was appointed commander-in-chief for North America to watch over the immense hinterland and to guard against the unruly Americans. In 1763 a new strategy was launched, which Gage enthusiastically carried out until 1774 when he was relieved. American settlers were to be kept out of the interior—the backcountry of

Pennsylvania and the Ohio River country. So, too, were British regulars to avoid becoming enmeshed in another vast land war in the wilderness. Troops were to be stationed around the fringes of the frontier to keep the settlers out and to protect the Indians so they might continue to furnish furs to British manufacturers. Because of its strategic location vis-à-vis the Hudson River Valley, New York was selected as the main headquarters of the British army, and great numbers of troops were to be quartered there and sent out as reinforcements to frontier garrisons. Along with this, Britain sent its own agents among the Indians seeking trade and pacification so as to avoid another war. And finally in 1763 a royal proclamation was issued forbidding Americans to cross over and settle beyond the Alleghenies. This offended thousands of would-be American settlers as well as groups of land speculators in the seaboard towns who had hoped to profit by dealing in the greatly extended territories won by the British soldiers.

Beyond all this, Parliament suddenly became aware—doubtless prompted by taxpaying clients from the landholding sections of the realm—that the war and the keeping of the peace had become very expensive. Revenue acts taxing the colonies for what after all could be construed as a war in their interests seemed essential. Unfortunately, the primary act passed for securing revenue was the Stamp Act of 1765. This act fell most heavily on exactly the wrong group in America—the new elite of merchants, lawyers, publicists, and philosophes whose every document from newspapers and pamphlets to wills, cargo manifests, and land deeds had to bear the king's stamp. This directly threatened the most intelligent, aggressive, and recently triumphant elite in the colonies. In addition, this group had increasingly felt threatened not only by the rising military establishment and its pretentious if not contemptuous officer class but also by still another British bureaucracy fastened upon America. These were the ever-growing numbers of customs agents, revenue collectors, English factors, insurance agents, bondsmen, inspectors, Vice-Admiralty Court officers, royal governors, and their growing staffs of agents and spies to which now were to be added a legion of stamp sellers and an armada of revenue cutters and patrol boats. In addition to the artificial status enjoyed by these new parliamentary favorites, colonial businessmen, farmers, shippers, and the publicists bitterly resented the habitual extortion, overzealousness, and racketeering that was common practice among those who swelled the

wealth, the Crown's men on the spot not only glossed over their own countless peccadilloes, dishonesties, and examples of bad judgment, but they also failed to face up to the obvious. Such a policy meant civil war, an expensive conflict that Britain, should France be drawn into it, just might lose—along with its northern American empire. This overreliance upon the expert, the civil servant, the man on the spot, the Tory colonial, seems almost an inescapable "precondition for takeoff" into a disastrous imperial war. More than any other factor, this proconsul strategy of offending the civil leaders and needlessly showing military, economic, and bureaucratic coercion seems to have led to the American Revolution.

In any case, British strategy failed. Besides organizing the colonists as never before, it brought to the front the natural leaders in America. Further, it so mobilized the intellectual talents of these leaders as to generate a new kind of revolution—an ideological revolution. By 1776, the war, which had already begun in April 1775 at Lexington and Concord, had turned into something quite different from a legal struggle. It had become the philosopher's war, an ideological conflict that was made to represent the culmination of the Enlightenment struggle for the rights of man in a better environment shorn of the last vestiges of decadent feudalism. What better place than America—"Nature's Nation"—for the opening struggle in the great cause of liberty that Paine so optimistically declared "the birthday of a new world." The American Revolution as it developed through seven long years of war had become an adventure of the mind and a scene of creation, as well as a grim struggle of body against body.

I

When the American philosophers turned to the task of the formulation of ideological revolution and the creation of a secular world utopia they were self-consciously aware of being a part of the Enlightenment. From the beginning theirs was not a limited but a worldwide vision that took its cue from the mathematical generalities of the Scientific Revolution and the new social sciences generated by such men as John Locke, Montesquieu, David Hume, Beccaria, and hundreds of others from all over Europe. They were worldly philosophers, but they also paid close attention to an

emergent anthropology, a sociology of the common man, moral philosophy stemming mainly from the Scottish Enlightenment, the wisdom of the
classical writers, and the lessons of a recent history.

History, both ancient and modern, was most important to them. Observing through Edward Gibbon's eyes, they could see how the Roman Republic collapsed because of venality and immorality, which led to public
laxness and a vulnerability to emperors and tyrants. Robert Molesworth's
account of the subversion of Denmark brought the same lesson even closer
to their own times. And Paine's historical urgency in *Common Sense* convinced them that if the secular millennium was to be achieved, time was
running short. From what they could observe of conditions in England and
France, not to mention those of the Crown's agents in America, reason, individualism, morality, and true liberty might well vanish from the earth if
they failed to create a model state for the world. The Revolution had come
at the precise moment when belief in reason, balance, and individual natural rights had reached a crest in the western world. By the French Revolution in 1789, romantic emotionalism and the concept of mass man had
begun to replace reason and individualism.

The leaders of the American revolutionary generation, then, despite
their self-conscious awareness of the ideological experiment to which they
were pledging their lives, their fortunes, and their sacred honor, made no
pretense to originality. Their real genius lay in being forcefully dedicated
but characteristic men of their time who put to work the best the Enlightenment had to offer before their world disappeared forever. Their ideas
were a palimpsest—a synthesis of the best of the world's knowledge up to
1776. Thanks to their efforts, certain Enlightenment qualities or habits of
mind became traditional American values. Among these were a reverence
for principles, particularly individual liberty, a dedication to reason and the
rational solution, a belief in order and at the same time constant change, a
talent for practicality and down-to-earth political organization, a faith in
learning, a sense of world responsibility and mission, and perhaps most important of all, an extreme and sensitive receptivity to new ideas, and a confidence in intellect. This receptivity to novelty and confidence in the
utilitarian power of intellect best sustained the American philosophes on
the road to revolution.

Professor Bernard Bailyn in *The Ideological Origins of the American Revolution* has convincingly described the American receptivity to ideas. Speaking of the revolutionary generation pamphlet literature, he asserted, "To judge simply from an ennumeration of the colonists' citations, they had at their finger tips, and made use of, a large portion of the inheritance of Western culture, from Aristotle to Moliere, from Cicero to Phileleutherus Lipsiensis [Richard Bently], from Vergil to Shakespeare, Ramus, Samuel Pufendorf, Jonathan Swift, and Jean-Jacques Rousseau." Bailyn then offers a broad classification of these borrowed ideas that serves to underscore not only the cosmopolitan sources of revolutionary thought, but the marked degree to which the Revolution was ideologically inspired.

A product of their formal education, the tradition of classical antiquity was basic to the thought of the revolutionary leaders. However, in their numerous references to antiquity, revolutionary thinkers relied most heavily upon the literature of the Roman Republic and the writings of authors, primarily Plutarch, Livy, Cicero, Sallust, and Tacitus, who lamented the collapse of their republic in the face of social and political corruption and the rise of tyrannical emperors. The analogy with the eighteenth-century British Empire, of course, was obvious, as Patrick Henry made clear when opposing the Stamp Act. He declared, "Caesar had his Brutus—Charles the first, his Cromwell—and George the third—may profit by their example." As Bailyn points out, "Britain, it would soon become clear, was to America 'what Caesar was to Rome.'" American visitors to England, such as Benjamin Franklin and John Dickinson, continually saw this analogy in the corruption and venality of English life, about which they wrote home in letters to friends. As early as 1758, during the Seven Years' War, Franklin wrote to Joseph Galloway, "The Nation . . . knows and feels itself so universally corrupt and rotten from Head to Foot, that it has little Confidence in any publick Men or publick Measures." Ten years later he quoted with horror Beckford's bland question to the House of Commons: "'Pray does that gentleman imagine there is *any member of this House that does not Know what corruption is?*'" Franklin added, "which occasioned only a roar of laughter, for they are so hardened in the practice, that they are very little ashamed of it. All the members are now in their counties and boroughs among their drunken electors; much confusion and disorder in many places, and such profusion of money as never was known before on any similar occasion." England, he concluded in another letter to John Ross in 1768, was "intent on nothing but luxury, licentiousness, power, places, pensions and plunder." John Dickinson, while a law student in London in 1754, was appalled at the utter corruption of Parliament. "Boroughs were bought for 200 guineas," and the opposing voter was "made dead drunk and kept in that state, never heard of by his family or friends till all is over and he can do no harm." The young Pennsylvanian concluded, "I think the character of Rome will equally suit this nation: 'Easy to be bought, if there was but a purchaser.'"

At the same time, too, steeped in classical writers and reared on Latin and Greek, American intellectuals came to identify personally with heroic figures of the Roman Republic rather than the Empire. Young John Adams declaimed Cicero aloud in his room at night, and the reasoned style of the Republican orators, to a marked degree, governed the thought of American intellectuals. The image of corrupt and collapsing Rome was a powerful one to early Americans but so, too, was the stylistic medium in which it was conveyed, which perhaps explains why so many revolutionary tracts were signed "Agricola," "Publicans," "Cato," and "Poplicola."

A second important source of inspiration, and one not strictly confined to the lawyer class, was the English legal tradition. For a long time the colonists believed in the precedent-derived common law of the British Constitution that, though never written down, was very real to them. They believed it guaranteed their rights as "freeborn Englishmen" through the ages. As a consequence they made frequent reference to such English authorities on the common law as Sir Edward Coke, Sir Francis Bacon, Sir Matthew Hale, Sir John Vaughan, Sir John Holt, and William Blackstone. The latter's *Commentaries on the Laws of England*, after his first volume was published in 1765, became the standard treatise on English common law.

Parliament often overrode precedent. In 1761, arguing against illegal search and seizure, authorized by the Writs of Assistance, before the Superior Court in Boston, James Otis rested his case on "the constitutional doctrines of Coke and Hale." "An act against the Constitution is void," he asserted, "an act against national equity is void." The common law and natural law were superior to acts of Parliament. Samuel Adams, protesting the Stamp Act in 1765, took the same legalistic and constitutional tack: "The leading principles of the British Constitution have their foundation in the Laws of Nature and universal Reason. Hence . . . British Rights are in great measure, unalienably, the Rights of the colonists, and of all Men else." Since Parliament and all colonial assemblies derived their authorities from the Constitution, they could pass no laws contrary to the Constitution without "destroying their own foundations." The stamp tax, which, in Adams's view, violated the colonists' natural rights as Englishmen, was just such an act. John Dickinson's *Letters from a Farmer in Pennsylvania*, a widely distributed protest against the Townshend duties levied in 1767, denied Parliament's power to tax the colonists at all and instead proclaimed that King and Parliament could regulate only trade. Dickinson based his case largely on Coke's *Second and Fourth Institutes of English Law*, though he made frequent reference to Plutarch, Tacitus, and Livy as well. Alexander Hamilton, writing in defense of the "natural rights of mankind" and on the right of revolution in February 1775, after the passage of the Intolerable Acts, quoted Blackstone on the transcendent importance of the law of nature, "which being coeval with mankind, and dictated by God Himself, is, of course superior in obligations to any other. It is binding over all the globe, in all countries, and at all times. No human laws are of any validity, if contrary to this."

The English legal tradition, like classical antiquity, was the vast "country of the past" in which the American revolutionaries felt at home, because to them the history of the best part of western civilization was also the history of American civilization. They could ransack the limitless past to test the validity of their Enlightenment hypothesis, to buttress their arguments, to derive some sense of common identity, and to provide stern lessons on what had been right and could go wrong. John Adams made this clear in his first widely distributed address in 1765, *A Dissertation on the Canon and Feudal Law*. Declaring that all men had rights "antecedent to all earthly government," Adams traced the subversion of human rights to feudal laws and "Romish policy," their resurrection by the Puritans, and their present subversion of the government of Britain and its minions in North America. "Have not some generals from England treated us like servants, nay, more like slaves than like Britons? Have we not been under the most ignominious contribution, the most abject submission, the most supercilious insults, of some customhouse officers? . . . Are we not children of Great

Britain any more than the cities of London, Exeter, and Bath?" he cried
out. All his life Adams remained a close student of history, continually using it to buttress his legal and political arguments, but King and Parliament
had the power until the Revolution.

Meanwhile, to the south, Thomas Jefferson, as a young law student at
the College of William and Mary between 1760 and 1764, was developing
an even more systematic and elaborate interpretation of history to justify
American rights. At the time, as Jefferson candidly admitted, he could get
no one but his legal mentor and Raleigh Tavern drinking companion
George Wythe to agree with him. But eventually his early theory formed
the broad theoretical basis upon which he rested the preamble to the Declaration of Independence. His argument went as follows: frontier America
was at present a culture roughly equivalent to the later stages of Saxon culture that emerged from the German forests to conquer and settle ancient
Britain. And just as the Saxons came to Britain of their own volition and
created their own free government in a state of nature, claiming the land by
right of conquest and use, so, too, had men out of Britain freely embarked
across the ocean to wild America to form their own free commonwealth.
"No circumstance has occurred to distinguish materially, the British from
the Saxon migration," he wrote in his *Commonplace Book*. "America was
conquered, and her settlements made firmly established at the expense of
individuals, and not of the British public." Thus America owed nothing to
King or Parliament. The rights and privileges of its citizens derived from
their freely taken individual excursions into the state of nature. In wild
America, as in the Saxon woodlands, individual conquest, occupation, and
freely delegated authority yielded sovereignty.

According to Bailyn, the law "was a repository of experience in human
dealings embodying the principles of justice, equity, and rights; above all it
was a form of history . . . and, as history, it helped explain the movement of
events and the meaning of the present." The canons of English law served
two further functions: to constantly remind the colonists of their rights as
individuals, and to make revolution, especially for the relatively established
classes, as at Runneymede, seem nothing more than rightful restoration.
The latter was a common theme in English as well as European history and
it fit in well with the classical tradition. Indeed the recurrence of periodic

episodes of restoration revolutions throughout European and English history forced many Enlightenment intellectuals on both sides of the Atlantic to accept a cyclical theory of history. They could square this theory in their minds only with the seemingly contradictory but popular idea of progress derived from scientistic modes of thought, by believing that every revolutionary cycle was a step in the direction of inevitable progress because it drew man back from his artificial follies into an ever-closer relationship with nature and God's natural laws. Corruption, error, and a tendency toward "artificiality" were man's weaknesses, but his reason and his innate moral sense were more powerful in the long run, and through periodic revolutions (or restorations), sometimes even violent revolutions, man got back on the right track and continued his pilgrim's progress toward perfection and harmony with God.

II

Puritan thought was a third profound component of the American revolutionary mind. The Puritan, taking his cue from the Bible and John Bunyan (*Pilgrim's Progress*), believed that man's purpose, or at least his hope, no matter how wicked he might be, was to achieve redemption, which meant unity with God. The drama of Christian existence for religious Americans consisted of a series of restoratory revolutions—there could be no other kind of revolution because God's world had begun in perfection. Only man was vile. God's covenant with Abraham, changing the course of Adam's descendents from the miserable to the hopeful, Christ's miraculous coming, Paul's conversion and new morality, the triumph of Christianity over wicked Rome, the violent cleansing of the Reformation, and the inspired removal to the purity of the New World were all major Restoration revolutions in the religious mind, holy because they were evidence that God was still concerned with man's eventual happiness. His concern had been visible most recently in the Great Awakening where the violent return to evangelical and fundamental Calvinism had drawn together masses of colonists in a great revolution of purification. As Jonathan Edwards so confidently expected, that revolution clearly heralded a coming millennium of moral brotherhood—the restoration of God's kingdom, first as a new "city upon a hill" in North America, then as a "new model" society for mankind.

The Protestant worldview, like that of the Enlightenment thinkers, was a cosmic view. All mankind and all human events, past and present, were of a piece—part of the mind of God, which existed infinitely beyond the arbitrary confinements of space and time. Hence the covenant theology and the independent relationship of man to God, though founded upon a specific event in the past—God's bargain with Abraham—had continuing and vital meaning for everyday life in the present. And though Edwards and his evangelical followers had largely rejected the covenant theology (if man properly worshiped God, God in turn would save man) in favor of a return to fundamental Calvinism, the covenant habit linked with the idea of individual responsibility for salvation persisted as fundamental rights in the minds and emotions of the clergy and their congregations. The evangelicals stoutly defended these rights against the Church of England and worldly Arminians alike. Indeed, the congregation and the churches themselves were covenants or compacts between the individual believers and the ministers they called.

The threat to this right of independent choice in covenanting together and in choosing a minister, posed by the rumors of the impending imposition of an Anglican bishopric on New England from 1750 onward, aroused the clergy of nearly all persuasions, except Anglicans, and turned them against England. The extension to Puritan Boston of the Anglican Society for the Propagation of the Gospel in Foreign Parts, rather than among the heathens in the wilderness, smacked of British tyranny. It threatened not only the Puritan Orthodox establishment but also backcountry evangelicals whom the high church Tory leader, Sir William Johnson of New York, arrogantly called "stupid Bigots" and "Independent firebrands." The Awakeners and independents thus joined the liberal clergy and defended with a vengeance this assault on their religious freedom.

In 1766, representatives of almost every dissenting religious faction met in New Haven, Connecticut, at the urging of the Reverend Ezra Stiles, to devise a united defense against the threat of episcopacy. For once, the evangelicals suspended their incessant war against Arminianism and worldly church materialism to face the threat from without. In a Thanksgiving sermon of that year, a New Light clergyman expressed the group's sentiments:

They looked upon it as the darkest day New England ever saw. They considered also the near connection there is between our civil and religious privileges, and every true lover of Zion began to tremble for *the ark of God*. For they saw, while our civil liberties were openly threatened, our religions shook; after taking away the liberty of taxing ourselves, and breaking in upon our charters, they feared the breaking in upon the act of *toleration*, the taking-away of liberty to choose our own ministers, and then imposing whom they pleased upon us for spiritual guides, largely taxing us to support the pride and vanity of diocesan Bishops and it may be by and by making us tributary to the See of Rome.

This complex of themes carried forward from 1766 to 1776 by the majority of American clergymen served to link American Calvinism from New England Congregationalism to Scottish Presbyterianism with the revolutionary cause. Though in the course of events the Liberal clergy became more concerned with the abstract Enlightenment values of life, liberty, and property, evangelicals fired up their zeal to a fever pitch after 1774, when the Quebec Act promised toleration for hated Roman Catholics.

III

In a sense, the revolutionary ideological themes the colonists drew from the classical tradition, English common law, and Calvinism represented a resort to "the country of the past," a reference to ancient authority culled from the history of men in all times and all places. These themes were given a sharper and more immediate focus in the minds of the revolutionary generation by events and tracts of the more recent past, most notably the tradition of Whig political dissent that grew ever more prominent in 1690 England. This formed a fourth theme of revolutionary ideology.

The Glorious Revolution of 1688 had proved to be a sore disappointment to many British intellectuals. Parliamentary supremacy, as it evolved into ministerial government, came to be even more tyrannical than the monarchy and, insofar as greater numbers were involved, the wickedness and corruption became more obvious and widespread. By the mid-eighteenth century virtually every Whig cause célèbre and every sordid Tory machination was broadcast over America and linked to the shrill warnings of English dissent literature. As Bailyn has put it, "To say simply that this tradition of opposition thought was quickly transmitted to America and widely appreciated there is to understate the fact. Opposition thought, in the form it acquired at the turn of the seventeenth century and in the early eighteenth century, was devoured by the colonists. From the earliest years of the century it nourished their political thought and semi-liberties. There never seems to have been a time after the Hanoverian succession when these writings were not central to American political expression or absent from polemical politics." During this period, American intellectuals acquired what amounted to a five-foot shelf of opposition classics. John Milton's *Eikonoklastes* and *The Tenure of Kings ad Magistrates;* James Harrington's *Oceana;* Algernon Sidney's *Discourses Concerning Government;* Benjamin Hoadley's *The Original Institution of Civil Government Discussed* and *The Measures of Submission to the Civil Magistrates Considered;* Henry St. John, Viscount Bolingbroke's weekly issues of the *Craftsman,* which from 1726 to 1736 unmercifully attacked Walpole's ministry; and *Cato's Letters* by John Trenchard and Thomas Gordon all were standard references for American dissidents. These works were the mainstay and production of "coffeehouse radicals" and opposition politicians, spokesmen for the anti-court independents within Parliament and the disaffected without, draftsmen of a "'country' vision of English politics that would persist throughout the eighteenth century."

Of all these works perhaps the most influential was Trenchard and Gordon's *Cato's Letters.* Written in response to the disastrous collapse of the government-promoted public investment scheme known popularly as the South Sea Bubble, *Cato's Letters* came out serially in the *London Journal* and then in book form in 1720. As such, they incorporated virtually every indictment that could be made of English society and ministerial government, denouncing particular politicians, standing armies, the fleecing of widows and orphans by government speculators, and the quashing of religious freedom by the Anglican Church. They formed a running sarcastic commentary on the social sources of what they regarded as the threats to political liberty in England and, by implication, anywhere in the world.

Thus, along with the opposition literature, such as Bolingbroke's *Crafts-man*, they demolished in America, if direct observation of the Crown's corrupt minions in the colonies had not already done so, the image of British society and British parliamentary government as the last, best hope of liberty in a despotic world. Within eleven months after the publication of the first Cato letter, James Franklin began running them in his Boston newspaper, the *New England Courant*, and his brother Benjamin incorporated them into his "Silence Dogood" letters. They were also reprinted in New York, Philadelphia, and as far south as Savannah, Georgia, while other eager readers ordered them sent straight from England by the fastest packet boat. There was little time lag in the spread of the culture of scandal, and Americans were never behind times in their appreciation of such "new ideas."

The effect of the dissemination in America of these indictments of British life was to create a Catonic image of the downfall of a once virtuous nation. And as travelers' accounts confirmed those of Trenchard and Gordon, and British schemes of taxation and episcopacy began to threaten the colonies, more and more Americans, besides being disenchanted with the Mother Country, began to see in all British policy a conspiracy of wickedness directed at the colonies. By 1774 even such a sober citizen as George Washington saw in English policy a "regular, systematic plan" in which Britain was "endeavoring by every piece of art and despotism to fix the shackles of slavery upon us." Almost none of the key American revolutionary figures—Franklin, Dickinson, both Adamses, Otis, Paine, Henry, Jefferson, Dulaney, Mayhew—were uninfluenced by the Catonic image the Whig opposition tradition generated. Even news of such "current events" as the refusal to seat the liberal John Wilkes in Parliament and the "London Massacre" shooting of a street boy during a Wilkes demonstration in 1768 (two years before the Boston Massacre) had a powerful effect on the American revolutionary mind.

As they did with the noble Romans, Americans identified with these relatively recent heroes of English liberty. *The Last Will and Testament* of Boston firebrand Josiah Quincy Jr. in 1774 perhaps says it most simply: "I give to my son, when he shall arrive at the age of fifteen years, Algernon Sidney's *works*—John Locke's *works*,—Lord Bacon's *works*,—Gordon's *Tacitus*,—and *Cato's Letters*. May the spirit of liberty rest upon him!"

IV

Though much of American revolutionary ideology was derived from a "usable past," the cast of mind that enabled intellectuals to approach the past—and the present—in the way they did stemmed from what must be termed "new" in the western world. This was, of course, the Scientific Revolution symbolized by Newton's model of the universe. Equally important, it was characterized by that experimental habit of mind that gloried in abstract thinking derived from the Scientific Revolution's triumphs of mathematics. Concreteness and "felt life" were far less important than the recognition of general laws that lay behind mere appearances and governed the relationships of things. This was the great age of order, utility, and faith in reason.

The scientists who unlocked the secrets of the universe were heroes of western culture: Newton, LaPlace, Descartes, Leibnitz, in the most abstract endeavors of all, mathematics and celestial mechanics; Avogadro, Gassendi, Boyle, and Lavoisier in chemistry; Franklin in electricity; Harvey in medicine; Cuvier in zoology; and Linneus in botany, to name a few. All of these men and hundreds of lesser lights believed in the Chain of Being connecting all things in the universe, from the lowest forms up to man and God. Man lived in an ordered universe, but because they knew the universe was ordered they were interested primarily in what could be done with it given the explosion of new knowledge visible at every hand. It mattered not whether one was of the Lockian, and hence inductive, persuasion, or the Cartesian, and hence deductive, persuasion. Both viewed nature as essentially an abstraction, subject to reason and experimentation because all phenomena were governed by fundamental laws, and, like phenomena in any part of the world, behaved in similar fashion, each according to its general place in the Chain of Being. Moreover, the cosmic model of Newton and the concept of the Chain of Being suggested that the universe and everything in it was fixed. With the techniques of reason, mathematics, and careful experimentation, theoretically it would be possible to know all there was to know about the great world machine. The rapid increase in such knowledge could result only in human progress. Hence what was most important and really new about the Age of Reason was the sublime confidence of the intellectuals and societal leaders in the powers of man's reason in understanding not just the cosmos but the world around them.

This was, of course, why the past was really usable. Careful hypotheses about the past based on abstract models would yield useful generalizations for the present just as did similar inquiries into nature. Viewed in this light, the past was not really the past in any case. It was part of a continuous present, of which man was rapidly becoming the master. And when he viewed himself, as did, say, Benjamin Franklin, he saw himself as an archetype—an anthropological model of the common man, who, exempt from the corrupt incrustations of past superstitions, had much in common with all men everywhere. This included those exotic creatures at the ends of the earth, which in the eighteenth century were being described by Louis-Antoine de Bougainville, Captain James Cook, and countless other explorers. Human nature, like all other nature, was a constant that yielded to rational inquiry. It was this faith in order, commonality, and method generated by the successes of the Scientific Revolution that made the Enlightenment and its intellectual "activist," the "philosopher," possible. It was what made theory to the eighteenth century eminently practical. And, as such, it was what gave the American revolutionaries the temerity to begin a whole new society and a new nation in the interest of mankind.

The cultural and political ideas of Locke and the philosophers that followed him were clearly another of the major ideological sources of the American Revolution. But behind them stood the more subtle influence of the Scientific Revolution. No inquiry into the intellectual history of the American revolutionary generation, however, can afford to overlook the influence of Locke and other giants of the Enlightenment. As Josiah Quincy's will suggested, Locke was central to American thinkers. In 1689, the same year he published *An Essay Concerning Human Understanding*, Locke also produced *Two Treatises on Government*, in which he outlined the nature of a new society and a new government that became a fundamental myth of America. Man existed hypothetically as an individual in a state of nature possessed of certain inalienable rights, specifically the rights to life, liberty, and property. Property provided him with security for life and liberty and enabled him to maintain the benefits of his own labor. According to Locke, all men are naturally in "a state of perfect freedom to order their actions and dispose of their possessions and persons, as they think fit, within the bounds of the law of nature." They are also in "a state . . . of equality, wherein all power and jurisdiction is reciprocal, no one having more than another." All are subject to the law of reason. With respect to government, Locke declared:

> Men being . . . all free, equal, and independent, no one can be put out of his estate, and subjected to the political power of another, without his consent. The only way, whereby anyone divests himself of his liberty, and puts on the bonds of civil society, is by agreeing with other men to join and unite into a community, for their comfortable, safe, and peaceable living one amongst another, in a secure enjoyment of their properties, and a greater security against any, that are not of it. . . . When any number of men have so consented to make one community or government, they are thereby presently incorporated, and make one body politic, wherein the majority have a right to act and include the rest.

And insofar as Locke was writing to justify the English constitutional monarchy of 1688, he asserted that (1) all government was subject to the moral law of nature; (2) since authority for government is derived from the people and from nature, they have a right to resist any government that abuses its designated powers; (3) a government with powers so designated by the people cannot delegate these powers without the consent of the people; and (4) even designated power should not be monopolized, but divided or balanced between legislative and administrative powers. Hence, in contrast to Thomas Hobbes and Robert Filmer, who believed that man derived no rights naturally but gained them from society and his sovereign, Locke did not see the king or any other power as supreme except that of the people in whom sovereignty rests within the bounds of reason and their compact. Locke's theories were widely accepted by the American revolutionary generation, even by the "black legion" of radical ministers who paradoxically also believed in original sin and innate depravity, and passed into the political language as commonplace axioms of society and government.

A multitude of other Enlightenment thinkers also influenced American ideology. Montesquieu's *The Spirit of the Laws* (1748) argued that laws must be adapted scientifically to the particular circumstance and habits of a people and a particular time and place. The revolutionaries, especially John Dickinson and John Adams, found Montesquieu's work extremely useful but limited in defending North American rights against a system at best imperfectly adapted even to Britain. Montesquieu, however, believed that democracy would work only in small states. Voltaire was valued for his civilized wit, his criticism of existing European authoritarian governments based on his belief in Lockean values, and especially for his contempt for established churches. The Baron von Pufendorf's work, along with that of Locke, convinced Americans of the validity of natural law as early as 1717, when John Wise cited him as a primary authority. Beccaria, the Italian criminologist, stressed environmentalism in the formation of human character, especially criminals, and, as such, reinforced American belief that old and corrupt institutions such as the Parliament and the monarchy must be swept away in America so as to promote a natural and healthy society. Vattel's application of natural law doctrine to diplomatic relations between nations and peoples offered a moral reference point for dealings between the colonies and Britain. And Delolome's analysis of the character of British liberty appealed especially to John Adams, while Rousseau's contradictory arguments for the supremacy of the general will and the natural rights of man to be free were largely rejected by the American ideologues who, with Locke, believed that individual rights preceded and superseded the state or any sweeping consensus. The vast array of European and English sources for American revolutionary ideology more than adequately demonstrates the cosmopolitan as well as the scientific nature of colonial revolutionary inspiration. However, above all it was to Locke that Americans turned in the time of revolutionary crisis when they hoped to achieve Utopia in the world's last real state of nature.

To summarize, far from being a narrow legalistic or pragmatic struggle within the British Empire, the American Revolution was the product of wide-ranging and profound thought about the fundamental nature of man and the world. The revolutionaries drew upon (1) the history of classical antiquity, (2) the English legal tradition, (3) Calvinistic thought of all shades, (4) a Catonic image derived from contemporary British political and social dissenters, (5) the fundamental ideas and methodology of the Scientific Revolution, (6) the writings of John Locke, and (7) a full spectrum of Enlightenment thought stemming from all over continental Europe and Scotland as well as Britain. These currents of thought ran so deep in the American mind that they served, along with taxation and condescension to the colonists, as the motivating force behind the Revolution. They did not come as last-minute rationalization for decisions made on other grounds. Rather, the widespread acceptance throughout the eighteenth century of values derived from these currents of thought convinced the colonists that they indeed had serious grievances with the Mother Country. Without a widespread belief in individual natural rights, without an ingrained tradition of religious independence, there could have been no strong feelings about British encroachments on American "liberties." Moreover, without the subtle psychological identification of patriot leaders with the heroes of the Roman Republic and the English Whig dissenters, no class of responsible revolutionary leaders would have developed—particularly since economic and social interests varied so widely from colony to colony and were so complex and conflicting within each colony. And without the dramatic expansion in all forms of knowledge generated by the Scientific Revolution, there would not have been that confidence in reason and abstract models that allowed the revolutionaries to really believe that they could replace the most powerful empire on earth with a rationally derived utopia.

CHAPTER THREE

A New Government
and a New Culture

In the Declaration of Independence, Thomas Jefferson cast the whole
range of patriot principles and ideologies into concise and tangible form.
Chosen as principal writer by his colleagues on the drafting committee of
the Continental Congress—Franklin, Adams, Sherman, and Livingston—
Jefferson produced a document that was the capstone of revolutionary
thought and perhaps the major document of eighteenth-century world revolution. As he saw it, his task was not to be original but rather to sum up
nearly a century of colonial grievances and present them as arguments on
an ideological plane. His aim, as he put it, was:

> not to find out new principles, or new arguments, never before
> thought of, not merely to say things which had never been said be-
> fore; but to place before mankind the common sense of the subject, in
> terms so plain and firm as to command their assent. . . . Neither aim-
> ing at originality of principles or sentiments, nor yet copied from any
> particular and previous writing, it was intended to be an expression of
> the American mind. . . . All its authority rests on the harmonizing sen-
> timents of the day, whether expressed in conversation, in letters,

printed essays, or the elementary books of public right, as Aristotle, Cicero, Locke, Sidney, etc.

As such, it was written to argue the justice of a course of action already decided upon by the Continental Congress when it accepted Richard Henry Lee's resolution for independence on July 2, 1776. The final draft of the Declaration was not engrossed and signed until August 2, and then only after seven crucial revisions.

The striking thing about the Declaration, however, was its ideological orientation and its sense of the "usable past" as part of a continuous present that applied to all mankind. Historian Carl Becker correctly pointed out the significant division of the Declaration into two parts. The first part, curiously like the text of a Puritan sermon, was by far the most important because it was the more transcendent. It outlined an American social and political philosophy gleaned from Locke and supported by most of the other liberal thinkers on both sides of the Atlantic, from Sir Edward Coke to Tom Paine.

> We hold these truths to be self-evident, That all men are created equal, that they are endowed by their creator with certain unalienable rights; that among these are life, liberty, and the pursuit of happiness; that to secure these rights governments are instituted among men, deriving their just powers from the consent of the governed; that whenever any form of government becomes destructive of these ends it is the right of the people to alter or to abolish it, and to institute a new government, laying its foundation on such principles and organizing its powers in such form, as to them shall seem most likely to effect their safety and happiness.

In the second part of the Declaration, Jefferson proceeded, again in sermon fashion, to his "proofs." He used the past in adducing a list of specific colonial grievances against the king—not Parliament, for the revolutionary leaders had long since come to agree that Parliament had no authority over them whatever. The colonial charters were, after all, authorized by the king (and even these in Jefferson's private view were of less significance than the right of ownership through voluntary migration from England). Previous debates concerning Parliament's powers within the empire had come to be looked upon simply as honest efforts to meet Britain halfway—to avoid separation from the Mother Country if it were at all possible, to accommodate British ambitions within the structure of traditional principles. A review of the colonial protest writing clearly indicates that Jefferson's interpretation was not at all inconsistent with the facts. As the previous sections of this narrative indicate, principle had been paramount on all occasions.

Like many great masterpieces, however, the Declaration was flawed. The sincere men who pledged their lives, their fortunes, and their sacred honor in support of what they believed was to be a new and better society on earth failed to extend their lofty principles far enough. The Continental Congress as a whole, not the drafting committee, deleted Jefferson's impassioned indictment of the king for having encouraged slavery and the slave trade in the New World. To have included Jefferson's passage would, of course, have been hypocritical, since many of the Northern and Southern patriots felt that African slavery was justified and had before them images of Greek and Roman "democracy," where slavery was traditional. Jefferson himself in *Notes on the State of Virginia* (1784), while calling slavery a "great political and moral evil" that he wished stopped, was so ambivalent about blacks that he declared, "This unfortunate difference of color, and perhaps of faculty, is a powerful obstacle to the emancipation of these people." Like others of his day, he viewed blacks as a natural curiosity and he advanced it as "a suspicion only, that the blacks, whether originally a distinct race, or made distinct by time and circumstances, are inferior to the whites in the endowments of both body and mind."

It would have been far better, however, to have extended the principles of the first part of the Declaration to include agreement upon the abolition of slavery as part of the "birthday of a New World." As events subsequently indicated, many well-meaning intellectuals remained genuinely puzzled as to the true nature and status of blacks and American Indians on the Great Chain of Being. Their perplexities and indecision carried over into the Constitution and beyond, through the first half of the nineteenth century, and allowed men with a decisive economic commitment to the "peculiar institution" to carry the day. English legal precedent, which said nothing about blacks and slavery, was no help at all. Nor were the precedents from antiquity and the Bible helpful because they were either ambiguous or outright condoned slavery. Aristotle, for example, believed that some men were natural slaves, and the story of Ham in the Bible makes blacks the symbol of God's wrath. Moreover, the most advanced scientific research from 1790 to 1860 tended to underscore the inferior status of blacks and Indians, which today offers an ironic comment on the nature of some science. And so the revolutionary generation sat, like Hamlet, "sicklied o'er with the pale cast of thought," while the opportunity for achieving a truly liberated nation, including blacks, Indians, and women, faded before them. Thus, disaster was implanted in the new nation from the beginning.

I

As the writing of Tom Paine and Thomas Jefferson had suggested, American independence rested not only on the rejection of an old government in favor of a new one, but also on the vision of a whole new society that would govern all of men's relations with one another. This vision derived from the values of English Whiggery, but in America it came to be called republicanism. As such, it formed the heart of an American revolutionary and utopian ideology that was intended to know no bounds except for the aforesaid blacks, Indians, and women.

Basically the Republican ideologues believed, with Locke, that man existed hypothetically in a state of nature and that society in this state preceded government. This society was composed of individuals who, if left uncrowded in nature, through reason would engage in "individualistic cooperation," as Paine pointed out. As individuals, they all possessed inalienable equal rights and the liberty to do as they pleased so long as they did not injure one another. However, all of the revolutionary Republicans envisioned the inevitable formation of a government—that "badge of lost innocence," as Paine would have it. The object of government would be to represent the cooperative wishes of the people—to enable them to carry out those larger enterprises that men could not do individually. As such, it would be a res publica—a "public thing" or, more accurately, a "thing" or "creature" of the public (i.e., people) and nothing more.

But to create the res publica, the society upon which it rested would have to adhere to certain values that today seem so simple and commonplace that they are more often than not overlooked or scorned. For one thing, equality of rights was paramount. Reason rather than passion was indispensable. All the classical and Puritan virtues—prudence, temperance, industry, frugality, simplicity, and charity—were axioms and postulates, as were a belief in austerity and a scorn for the kind of luxury that had destroyed not only Britain but the noble Roman Republic as well. The Republican social ideal, as Sam Adams saw it, was to create "a Christian Sparta," free of licentiousness, effeminacy, and artificiality in the form of greed and special privilege. The dire emergency of the Revolution itself served to heighten this feeling.

As John Adams said, "All things must give way to the public." "Each individual," wrote Benjamin Rush, "gives up all private interest that is not consistent with the general good." Out of this would come the moral society and hence the moral state in which men were linked to one another in harmony and benevolence and common strength for the common good. Once society adhered to these values it could then proceed to delegate authority to some of its equal members, commonly envisioned as simple farmers or mechanics, to carry out the larger tasks of government as the faithful and responsible representatives of a free people. Republicanism thus came to mean a representative government freely elected by the people as equals and responsible to them. Today all of this seems hypothetical, an abstraction or utopian model far removed from reality, but to the men of the eighteenth century it seemed eminently practical, indeed hardheaded and concrete when one looked at aristocratic and bureaucratically enfeebled Britain or all the failed European atrocities of the past. To them utopian regeneration was a dire necessity that could and must be achieved. And the beauty of it all was that the salvation of mankind would be achieved through the subversion of the satanic society of corrupt Europe. Puritanism in somewhat altered form had at last emerged from its "errand into the wilderness."

Perhaps the one who best expressed the revolutionary implications of republicanism was Benjamin Franklin. His *Autobiography* was a concrete dramatization of that archetypal person termed by Hector St. John de Crevecoeur in *Letters from an American Farmer* (1787) "this new man, the American." Essentially Franklin's *Autobiography*, the story of a plain but shrewd American who achieved success in a New World land of opportunity where no ancient institutions of privilege or aristocracy blocked the way to success, contrasted sharply with the stories of military heroes, English sea dogs, kings, courtesans, and tales of backstairs court intrigue.

But Franklin's story had another dimension. Like most men of the Enlightenment, he was an environmentalist and this meant not only that he continually pointed to American abundance, which made all things possible, but also that he focused sharply on institutions that could be formed and made to work for the practical public good. His descriptions of his formation of a fire company, a hospital, and a city watch or police force were all examples of what practical men working together (individualistic cooperation) could do for themselves, even in an urban setting. They could solve social problems by working together in a spirit of community—of participatory democracy. Moreover, they could make institutions, including especially government, work for them instead of the reverse, as was clearly the case in Europe. Just as in his scientific experiments, in which nature served man, in his social experiments Franklin made society work for man. And by implication, with a little self-discipline, every American, indeed every man, could do the same. If he did so, government itself would be no problem because it was placed in proper societal perspective. Such was the essence of revolutionary republicanism, and no one embodied its subtle values better than Franklin in his actions and in his writings, which, taken together, might be considered one long didactic Puritan sermon tempered with Augustan wit and Enlightenment cosmopolitan urbanity.

II

The years after the Declaration of Independence until the framing of the Constitution in 1787 formed, in a sense, an era of heightened democracy. The exigencies of war, of course, forced upon the colonies something of the aura of Sam Adams's "Christian Sparta" as the Continental Army under George Washington's austere leadership went through "the times that try men's souls," while the evangelical clergy preached the wonders of millennial regeneration that would result from adversity, purgation, and eventual moral triumph. More important, the common man was made to feel a part of the astounding revolutionary changes that were taking place. Nowhere was this more evident than when the people of the colonies suddenly be-

came aware that they were to be truly independent and hence actually responsible for forming their own governments based upon their own Republican assumptions as to the ideas about the nature of the good society.

During the late 1770s and early 1780s, each of the colonies turned itself
to the task of government-making. In 1781 the Continental Congress gave
way to a continental confederation in which each former colony, under the
Articles of Confederation, was equally represented by one vote, and all, except certain very limited powers, were lodged with the states. Out of this
situation certain major concepts and dilemmas emerged. The revolutionary
struggle against Britain had, at base, represented a conflict between power
and liberty. As this struggle had been conceptualized in the Declaration of
Independence, the idea of power became embodied in the king, his ministers, and his royal governors and appointees in the colonies. Hence, the
primary thrust of most attempts at forming governments within the states
was toward preserving liberty through resisting anything like executive or
magistratical power. The obvious remedy was thus to limit power in an assembly or legislature that was composed of, or represented, the people. But
this raised further questions. If the legislature was to represent the people,
how could the people ensure that it was truly representative and held their
interests uppermost, that it would not be simply a copy of the corrupt and
profligate English Parliament? And beyond this, how, with a weak executive, could the state assembly enforce decisions, commonly arrived at, upon
dissenting minorities whose own local interests seemed jeopardized? No
matter how one looked at it, power flew in the face of liberty, which the
Republican revolutionaries held most dear.

Still another group of men, among whom John Adams of Massachusetts
was prominently numbered, were concerned that the state should be ruled
by the best and most able men. They worried incessantly about the question of aristocracy or who would form the talented leadership that would
have the good of the whole state in mind rather than certain local vested
interests when making governmental decisions. For Adams, such men
would not necessarily have to be rich, though they ought to have some
propertied stake in society. Rather, they should be educated, experienced,
and broad-minded cosmopolitans and not local adventurers or rotten bor-
ough masters. Adams and such like-minded men generally had before
them the vision of an English hierarchical society in which they implicitly

believed, even while resisting a corrupt English government. A belief in hi-
erarchy and deference in society was related to the cosmological belief in
the chain of being, though at bottom it was simply a habitual way of thinking that derived from perhaps too much experience with Parliamentary history and English politics.

But in the late 1770s revolutionary democracy, rather than measured republicanism, seemed to run rampant. In the spirit of Paine and Franklin,
every man was a fit participant in government and local affairs, and local liberties not only were deemed most important but they also were being perforce defined by a democratic general will. The spirit of community per se
and disinterested public service was less important. Most of the states had
very broad suffrage, as recent research has shown, and when the local towns
or districts (if they could define themselves in the face of petty quarrels) sent
representatives to assemblies, these delegates usually went with strict instructions as to what to vote for. They were as tightly bound as any royal
governor ever was. And even then the people suspected and mistrusted the
assemblies. Western Massachusetts, for example, was in a perpetual state of
revolt if not anarchy, culminating in 1786 with Daniel Shay's rebellion. In
1778, Massachusetts rejected the whole idea of a government created by its
legislature and demanded instead a written constitution created by a special
constitutional convention elected by all the people of the state in a referen-
dum. Thus emerged two very important American governmental concepts:
the idea of a written constitution as opposed to the unwritten evolving
British constitution, and the idea of a constitutional convention that came
together for the sole purpose of forming a government and then dissolved
itself. Such a specially designated convention not only would represent the
people, but also, being only a temporary body, could have no interest in en-
trenching itself or its members in power—in contrast to using an existing
legislative assembly to draw up a state constitution, for example. Moreover,
a constitutional convention would be less bound to represent those local geographical interests that so parochialized and bound the hands of the regular assemblymen. The result of this innovation in New England was the
stormy passage of the Massachusetts Constitution of 1780, largely written
by John Adams and to an extent based upon the British model of three estates in society: the magistracy, the aristocracy, and the commons but no executive. Though other state constitutions, such as Pennsylvania's, which

lodged all power in a single assembly, varied, Massachusetts's constitution became a model for many other states and, like Virginia's, a precedent for the eventual formation of the American Constitution of 1787.

Still, however, throughout the Confederation period, most power was lodged in the legislative assemblies, and those elected to the assemblies were by no means the best men nor did they often seem interested at all in the commonwealth. Stay laws passed in favor of debtors ruined the credit if not the entire economies of states. Land rings formed for the purpose of using the government to promote speculative ventures. Territorial and boundary disputes were commonplace. Farmers fought tradesmen. Producers fought carriers, and everyone turned on the few Indians left in their own states while supporting the idea of pushing them west and guaranteeing their rights somewhere way out on the frontiers of the Northwest Territory. Tom Paine's idea of individualistic cooperation quickly became transformed into unrestrained individualism that appeared to be leading to chaos.

The creation of stable, responsible, and fair-minded governments within the states seemed virtually impossible to achieve, even though all the colonies found themselves in the midst of an economic boom that promised potential wealth for all. On the continental level, the Articles of Confederation government found itself powerless to do much of anything, except with respect to the western lands where it succeeded in passing the Ordinance of 1785 and then the Northwest Ordinance of 1787, which solved one major problem Britain could never solve, by providing for the creation of territories and then additional states to be admitted to the Confederacy on equal footing with the original thirteen. It also abolished slavery in these new territories and eventual states north of 36° 30′. Aside from these major achievements, the Confederation Congress could do little more than mediate disputes between states, make hopeful suggestions to them, and try to cope with the problems of international diplomacy where foreign powers tended to openly dismiss the new nation.

To many of the revolutionary leaders, the situation as it related to both government and society was deplorable. "Have we fought for this?" asked Washington. "Was it with these expectations that we launched into a sea of trouble and have bravely struggled through the most threatening dangers?" And in 1783 historian David Ramsay, writing to Benjamin Rush, declared, "This revolution has introduced so much anarchy that it will take half a century to irradicate the licentiousness of the people. . . . *The pulling down of government tends to produce a settled and habitual contempt of authority in the people.*" Inevitably, a reaction against the excesses of opportunism set in. This reaction, led by some of the ablest men in the country—Adams, Madison, Wilson, Hamilton, Washington—came to be called Federalism, and it culminated in the formation of a higher authority over the contentious states, the Constitution of 1787.

Essentially the problem was where to locate power or sovereignty so as not to vitiate the people's hard-won liberties, but at the same time to prevent the tyranny of the majority and to bring the multitudinous factions of the states under control. Most theorists, and especially Adams, still thinking of the English experience, advocated bicameralism, with one house representing the people at large and the other house being composed of the "natural aristocrats," or men of real talent and experience. Inevitably, though reluctantly, men who followed this lead were forced into accepting some form of wealth or propertied qualification for service in the upper house. Even Madison slowly came to this conclusion, though neither he nor Adams precluded the possibility of the brilliant poor man being eligible for such service.

However, working together the Federalists gradually began to fashion a model of government that fit their vision of the ideal state. In part, this theory grew out of debate with local-minded men intensely jealous of their liberties, the anti-Federalists. Once the Federalists had engineered significant sentiment for a reformation of the Articles of Confederation, through Adams's and Madison's models, the debate began. Both sides accepted the idea of a written constitution. Both sides also accepted Montesquieu's dictum of separation of powers, especially between the executive and the upper and lower houses, and perhaps the judiciary. They clashed, however, on several points: the need for an upper house, its composition, its powers, and the powers of the executive. More basically they clashed over the question of granting a national government any direct sovereignty over the states and the people. The Federalists saw clearly that without real power in certain areas over the states and their people, a national government could not function at all.

However, out of the debates of 1786–1789 the well-organized Federalists managed to bring about what historian Gordon Wood described as a

"Federalist Revolution." They accomplished this by accepting the basic logic of republicanism and declaring that all sovereignty lay in the people and nowhere else. They argued that unlike the British, Americans no longer had to wrest power from an existing sovereign as had the barons at Runnymede. They had only to delegate it as they chose. Thus a people could make a government that was both national and local, delegating certain powers to the central government and certain powers to the state governments and reserving the rest strictly for the people. If the people wished, they could delegate direct power over themselves to a national government without fear because it was they themselves who had done so and they who could withdraw it. The same applied to the states, which were not sacred institutions but rather creatures of the people—res publica. Thus whatever institution could best accomplish the wishes of the people, a national or state government, could be granted the necessary power. As to the fear that factions would rule a national government, Madison in his Federalist Paper 10—one of eighty-five articles published by Hamilton, Madison, and Jay in the New York press in 1787 urging ratification of the new Constitution—falling back on David Hume declared that there was safety in numbers. The larger the country and its government, the more numerous and varied the factions, and hence no one faction could become dominant. The national government could thus rise above factions in a way state and local governments alone could not.

On the issue of bicameralism, the upper house, and the recruiting of talented leadership, the Federalists asked only that the upper house be smaller in number but based on the same electorate. They believed that in this way, with fewer representatives from each state, that talent naturally would be filtered—that the people would choose more carefully. And though in the Constitutional Convention they opposed the Patterson or small state plan of equal representation by state in a single assembly, when they were forced to compromise, they actually won their basic principle—perhaps in a better way than they themselves envisioned. Each state would have only two senators, chosen by the state legislature to serve six-year terms. This, they believed, would result in a careful screening process so that only the best men would be selected for the upper house.

By carrying their logic of the people's sovereignty even further, the Federalists were also able to restore the executive to somewhat greater power, since his election and his powers, though indirectly because he was chosen by electors, were based upon the people's voice. And by acceding to the strictest separation of powers, the presidential powers as well as eventually those of the judiciary became immeasurably strengthened. The addition of a Bill of Rights demanded by the anti-Federalists also played into Federalists' hands as they saw it and as even they could not foresee it. They argued at the time that such enumeration of rights was merely limiting, since all powers not specifically delegated to national or state governments rested in the hands of the people in any case. To specify rights was to limit them. At the same time, the Bill of Rights immeasurably strengthened the centralizing power of the judiciary branch, as Americans since the Civil War have come to realize, until today the judiciary branch stands as the most important focus of power in American government.

And so, out of the Constitutional Convention of 1787 and the subsequent ratifying conventions, the "Federalist Revolution" carried the day. Turning the revolutionary Republican ideology to their advantage, the Federalists managed to create a powerful national government for a large and potentially prosperous nation that was nonetheless something quite new in world experience. It was a government based on the people that, while divided, balanced and yet almost concealed the power that was delegated on many levels and for specific purposes. They had created a government that was intended to rise above faction but would in the end generate large, effective, and sometime-warring national parties. They had created a government of potential checks and balances resembling a Newtonian world machine, but one that nonetheless contained within itself the mechanism of amendment, change, and almost organic growth. As one writer has pointed out, it "marked an end of the classical conception of politics and the beginning of . . . a romantic view of politics."

In its adaptability and its flexibility the Federalist government, based as it was on a series of compromises—the large state, small state plan, the three-fifths compromise, which counted each slave as three-fifths of a person in computing the number of representatives for each state, etc.— appeared to have something for everyone except blacks, Indians, and women. This was its chief strength, but it was also its weakness, for it was above all a characteristically American compromise by combination, a grafting of Federalist structures onto Republican ideology in such a way as to bring about consensus. Thus at the beginning consensus became a paramount objective of American government and political parties, if not American life, which has tended to obscure basic but deeply felt ideological differences. Or, as in the case of the Constitution's treatment of slavery—the three-fifths compromise and the twenty-year extension of the slave trade—it postponed resolution of these ideological differences until it was too late and violent civil war resulted.

III

Nonetheless, by 1789 the pragmatic blueprint for a secular utopia explicitly separating church and state in the Bill of Rights seemed virtually complete. Americans had made good on their revolutionary promise to create a new society with new institutions and a new government that could serve as a model for the world. And once in power, the Federalists did their best, which was perhaps not always good enough, to make the engine of government run properly.

Washington, as the first president, set an example of austere, Republican simplicity and made clear his disdain for titles of nobility. He also took pains to define the subordinate role of the military in the new civil state lest it acquire power beyond the control of the people. Tired of war, the Federalists tried desperately, though unsuccessfully (in view of the undeclared Naval War with France and Jay's Treaty, which polarized Federalists and Republicans into national parties), to steer a strict course of neutrality in foreign relations.

Alexander Hamilton, the brilliant young Federalist revolutionary, sought to enhance the powers of the new federal government with his financial plans for funding the national debt, creating a unified system of coinage and a national bank, and in fostering an infant manufacturing industry through tariffs and bounties he brought about a sophisticated economy. But he was not motivated primarily by the "stake in society" theory, though he clearly wished to involve the monied classes in the government as much as possible to ensure their support and prevent the flight of already limited capital from the country. Rather, he was concerned primarily with making America self-sufficient through the creation of a balanced economy and strengthened world credit. In this role, whatever his personal political ambitions, he prefigured countless national planners of today's newly emergent nations who wish to gain economic as well as political independence of the world's great powers.

Hamilton, however, perhaps went too far too fast in his plans for the future because in so doing he underscored rather than underplayed, as Washington had done, the "Federalist Revolution." He needlessly polarized political opinion and played a part in creating the very champion and party—Jefferson and the Republicans—that would take on the Federalists, thereby threatening to break down the fragile consensus of the Constitution. Moreover, his own political ambition split the Federalists, undermined John Adams's presidency, and caused a failure of nerve among the once well-organized Federalists.

A bitter political feud developed between and within the emerging parties that threatened to break apart the nation. The Federalists especially feared the radical ideas of the French Revolution. Adams's panicky reaction to the situation resulted in the Alien and Sedition Acts, excluding immigration and unconstitutionally forbidding public criticism of the government, which confirmed the worst Republican fears for the liberty of the people under a national government. These not only alienated Madison and a large number of earlier Federalist supporters, but they also brought forth the Virginia and Kentucky Resolutions of 1798, which, in declaring that a state could nullify a federal law, threatened then and there to shatter the new constitutional government. Thus it was perhaps fortunate that the Republicans triumphed in the national election of 1800, which swept Thomas Jefferson into office. The Federalists had done their work, and since they were able to do so only by appealing to the basic democratic principles of republicanism, the election afforded them an opportunity to demonstrate that they truly believed in these principles. With their peaceful acquiescence in Jefferson's election, the American government, which they had designed, was vindicated. The revolution at last was complete and once again the world had witnessed something relatively rare—a bloodless transfer of power within the structure of a constitutional and representative democratic government. The triumph of the Republican, the Federalist, and the American revolutions is perhaps nowhere better illustrated than in Jefferson's inaugural address, in which as leader of the incoming opposition party he strongly avowed the basic principles for which all the men of the revolutionary generation had fought:

> We are all Republicans, we are all Federalists. If there be any among
> us who would wish to dissolve this Union or to change its republican
> form, let them stand undisturbed as monuments of the safety with
> which error of opinion may be tolerated where reason is left free to
> combat it. I know, indeed, that some honest men fear that a republi-
> can government cannot be strong. . . . I believe this on the contrary,
> the strongest government on earth. I believe it the only one where
> every man, at the call of the law, would fly to the standard of the law,
> and would meet invasions of the public order as his own personal con-
> cern. Sometimes it is said that man cannot be trusted with the govern-
> ment of himself. Can he, then, be trusted with the government of
> others? Or have we found angels in the form of kings to govern him?
> Let history answer this question.

While Jefferson was resolving political differences, a whole new culture was developing along lines Paine might approve. According to English traveler to the United States Harriet Martineau, "America was meant to be everything. . . . There are many soils and many climates included within the boundary line of the United States; many countries; and one rule cannot be laid down for all." America in 1801 was a country of diversity and vastness and, according to at least one modern historian, vagueness, which became a strength because it forced Americans to constantly redefine themselves in search of an ideal—freedom. This continual search has been a principal ingredient in the constantly revolutionary nature of American thought and culture.

In America, however, revolution has taken place by means of a peculiar process, that of absorption through selection—of people, of ideas, of images, of experiences, of things. Europe was at first an obvious source of inspiration because of its antique heritage, which made American history seem to be part of European, or "world," history. Very quickly, thanks to the sea traders of the Atlantic coastline, America's inspiration became global, and the world itself acted as a gigantic museum from which Americans derived their education in self-identity. This process, stemming from the enlightened habit of empiricism, requiring constant redefinition of America's physical orientation in terms of changing concepts of global geography and a multitudinous observation of world lifestyles and values, has never ceased. America always has been, in Marshall McLuhan's terms, part of a "global village." Today, however, thanks to the overpowering generation of information via the mass media, we are more acutely aware of that fact than were Americans of previous generations who, even while absorbing aspects of world culture at a great rate, proclaimed the lineaments of American character in terms of contrast rather than combination, which was more accurate.

This irony was never clearer than in the early days of the republic. Proud Americans called for a new language, even a whole new race in North America, while at the same time working to make English a common language, concealing a pluralistic society of Frenchmen, Germans, Swedes, Scots, Dutchmen, Irishmen, Spaniards, Africans, and Indians. In their haste to form a national culture and hence to achieve status through the approbation of older nations, Americans resorted to an incredible eclecticism, which to many Europeans before Alexis de Tocqueville, the Frenchman who traveled through America and wrote the classic *Democracy in America*, gave the United States the appearance of having no sophisticated culture at all but in reality formed the basis for a truly modern civilization. Lacking a history and a character, Americans almost inadvertently created them early in the nineteenth century out of world history, world lifestyles, and world ideas.

This is not so surprising, because Americans had spent nearly two hundred years as a colonial people, who by definition are absorbers from the dominant culture. It was valuable experience, too easily dismissed by prophets of nation-building, both then and now. Moreover, America achieved its independence and went through its formative years on the rising tide of the Enlightenment—a scientific and philosophical revolution that, broadly speaking, was an informational revolution focused on the new and the novel wherever it was to be found, whether in the green jungles of the Amazon, the laboratories of Priestly and Lavoisier, the medical savants of Edinburgh, or the classical buried cities of Herculaneum and Pompeii.

In addition, as Harriet Martineau pointed out, America began as a diverse country geographically with many kinds of people who had different customs and interests. As we have seen, the Founding Fathers clearly recognized this fact in the formation of the Constitution (which like the dimensions of the nation it would govern is also vague). It was a "compromise by combination" that held out something for every class, culture, interest, and section. Most important, it tended to downplay the traditional ideal of an English-oriented class model in favor of a geographically oriented federal model resting upon the solid foundation of a common republican ideology. Colonies became states; the vast west became potential states. No two documents of the time make the compromise by combination theme clearer than Federalist Papers 39 and 10. The former outlined at great length the specific national and local characteristics of the new government, while the latter saw national strength arising from the multiplicity of factions or immediate local interests because no one faction, special interest, or class could become predominant. As it was with government, so it was with the emerging culture and the ethnic cosmopolitan national character, which grew out of the multiplicity and conflict of the eighteenth century.

While the contrast theme, which saw Europe as an "antiquated and corrupt system" and America as a "holy ground for the cultivation of pure truth," ran through the Fourth of July oratory of the early republic, and such rabid nationalists as novelist James K. Paulding called for American artists and thinkers to free themselves from the "habit of servile imitation" of European models, an equally strong identification with cosmopolitanism and world destiny braced the American mind and gave it confidence and courage in the nation's formative period. Hand in hand with the rejection of corrupt European aristocracies went the acceptance of European ideas and people associated with the principles of liberty and an identification with the fortunes of all mankind. As late as 1823, novelist Hugh Swinton Legaré, for example, speaking in Charleston, South Carolina, on the Fourth of July, warmly lauded Milton, Sydney, Byron, the Puritans, and other apostles of English liberty along with the French Huguenots, who had resisted France's authoritarian tyrants. In his view, these people and their ideas were very much a part of America, the refuge of all free men. The triumph of America, he asserted, is "greeted with the most cordial sympathy of the cosmopolite and the philanthropist; and the good and the wise all round the globe give us back the echo of our acclamations." According to Legaré, America's mission was a world mission, and "the fortunes of the species, are thus, in some degree identified with those of the *Republic*—and if our experiment fails, there is no hope for man on this side of the grave." America's unity and national character arose, from a generous, indeed limitless, cosmopolitanism that embraced men and ideas from all nations.

CHAPTER FOUR

The Scottish Enlightenment and the Minds of Early America

Although the ideas of John Locke, the English Whigs, and republican thinkers from both Britain and France formed the basis for revolution, the broadest philosophical foundation for the new nation derived from another culture and another people situated on the fringe of the British Empire— Scotland. Like the Americans, the Scots, feeling remote from London, drew upon ideas from Germany, France, and the Low Countries starting in the seventeenth century and in so doing created the Scottish Enlightenment, which had a profound influence on America.

Many of the leading Scottish thinkers, conscious of their country's comparatively recent subjugation by Britain, espoused the cause of revolution against an unjust monarch, but Scottish society was innately conservative. This conservative mix of ideas that characterized the Scottish Enlightenment seemed most useful to nation-builders in postrevolutionary America. The Scots had succeeded in generating a remarkable concentration of intellectual energy that took full advantage of the new sciences of the day, yet without abandoning a number of traditional values they greatly esteemed.

Among these values were Common Sense practicality, an innate feeling for the empirically observed–fact characteristic of a rural society, a sense of order and rectitude, and a devotion to Presbyterian Calvinism. Unlike the French and the English Deists, the Scots, in their enthusiasm for Enlightenment ideas, did not revert to the varieties of paganism that historian Peter Gay has found so characteristic of the Continental Enlightenment. In Scotland, science went hand in hand with Presbyterian religion, which was one of its primary appeals to Americans, who viewed themselves as members of a Christian civilization to which deism and atheism were anathema. The strong reaction of American intellectuals to the French Revolution and the postwar rejection of Tom Paine for his "atheistical" ideas were indicative of the dominant tides of American thought in the new republic, even after the election of Thomas Jefferson in 1800.

Beyond the model of an enlightened Christian civilization that Scotland represented, Americans also admired Scots' sense of order—an obvious priority in fashioning a new nation out of many nations or states made up out of diverse peoples. And perhaps most of all, Americans found appealing the way in which Scottish men of ideas derived practical and universal but "Common Sensical" principles out of a very clever ongoing inquiry into the facts of nature. The new knowledge they were producing in such fields as geology, natural history, medicine, and the work-yielding properties of steam, as well as their scientific insights into human nature, fascinated Americans from the early eighteenth century until the latter decades of the nineteenth century. Even more so than Scotland, America was nature's nation, and any thinking person welcomed all of the insights into nature's workings the Scots provided—especially the simply organized, practical, nonmetaphysical way in which these insights were presented. Moreover, considering the variety of peoples who swelled the new nation, the Scots' prolonged search for general principles, especially moral principles, common to all mankind was especially welcome to American intellectuals concerned with creating a civilization they hoped would be congruent with the nation. Without a continuing, informed, and updated sense of the nature of those general principles common to all mankind, America's global experiment was doomed. Thus the Scottish Enlightenment, above all other versions of that western world intellectual phenomenon, took on a heightened significance in the fashioning of the early republic. The story of the rise of

BOOK II

THE GREATER ENLIGHTENMENT FORMS THE NATIONAL CONSCIOUSNESS

Nationalism is a state of mind, permeating the large majority of a people and claiming to permeate all its members; it recognizes the nation-state as the ideal form of political organization and the nationality as the source of all creative cultural energy and of economic well-being. The supreme loyalty of man is therefore due to his nationality, as his own life is supposedly rooted in and made possible by its welfare. Nationality is formed by the decision to form a nationality.

HANS KOHN, *The Idea of Nationalism*

the Scottish Enlightenment and the transmission of its ideas to America is fundamental to the history of American thought.

Enlightenment in Scotland did not come easy, nor did it "just happen." As in many nations of the western world it grew out of the importation of new information and a corresponding clash between the old and the new ways. But the Scottish revolution in ideas was managed from the outset not by democratic philosophies but by the existing establishment.

Presbyterianism reigned supreme in Scotland. Anglicanism made inroads only with difficulty due to the prevailing spirit of Scottish nationalism and cultural self-awareness. But by the turn of the eighteenth century, the new learning of the Enlightenment had begun to challenge the Calvinistic fundamentalists of the Scottish church. Within Presbyterianism a moderate faction came to assume power—not without a struggle resembling that between the liberals and evangelicals in America.

In large measure the transformation in Scottish religion and thought was achieved through the medium of an educated elite of lawyers, educators, and practical scientists. Large landholders, tradesmen, scientists, doctors, and learned clergymen banded together in city clubs such as the Medical Society of Edinburgh, later renamed the Philosophical Society. Feeling, like the Americans, very much on the fringes of civilization, the Scottish intellectual clubs were self-conscious and close-knit organizations. As such they had maximum impact upon the five Scottish universities: St. Andrews, Aberdeen, Glasgow, New Aberdeen, and Edinburgh. In a relatively short time, they made these centers of learning among the most advanced in the European world because they looked outward to such continental universities as Leyden, Louvain, Göttingen, Halle, and Paris, where many of their faculty studied medicine, law, and even theology. The Scottish universities also deliberately avoided the model of Oxford and Cambridge. Recognizing very early that science required specialization, the Scottish universities abandoned the regenting, or tutorial teaching, system in favor of departments of specialization headed by professors in individual fields whose knowledge was both deep and practical. The cultural centrality of the Scottish universities derived primarily from two main functions. They served as a means of conserving Scottish religious values by meeting, mastering, and co-opting the new science in the interest of preserving traditional religion. And they served as practical information agencies for a colony aspiring to full participation in the commercial world of the eighteenth century, which prompted Adam Smith to publish his classic, *The Wealth of Nations* (1776).

Behind the transformation of Scottish thought lay a dramatic story of men and ideas. As we have seen, since the first decades of the eighteenth century, Americans had been steeped in Enlightenment thought derived from the scientific revolution, which had rediscovered natural law. Newton's mighty *Principia*, along with updated versions of the Great Chain of Being, presented vivid mental images of nature's ordered and rational cosmology. The same was true for the Scots. Like eighteenth-century Americans, they were relatively certain that they knew what the world looked like. Similarly, John Locke's *Essay Concerning Human Understanding* seemed to provide a straightforward way of perceiving the world and of storing away these perceptions in the mind in accordance with the innate dictates of reason that every man possessed. And since knowledge was derived from the senses, knowledge was bound to be orderly because nature itself was orderly. If they followed nature closely and adhered to reason, men could create a new and potentially perfect environment. Locke's philosophy seemed to point the way.

And yet from the beginning, as Locke himself and a number of American intellectuals recognized, his philosophy was shot through with ambiguities. If man was born with no innate ideas—a tabula rasa—where did reason itself originate? What was the source of man's moral sense of right and wrong, and where did his power of judgment come from, his free will and hence his liberty, which the colonists so strongly believed to be man's natural right? And from where did man acquire consciousness of his selfhood and of God? In short, how was man different from the animals he so carefully studied out in the state of nature? Such questions worried the Deists and the atheists scarcely at all. In America Deist writers like Ethan Allen in *Reason the Only Oracle of Man* (1784) and Joseph Priestly in his *Disquisition Relating to Matter and Spirit* (1777) were thoroughly naturalistic and tended to see man as simply the "reasoning animal" set down in a kind of continuous mechanistic and ecological present, like kudus and lions on some vast, untended Serengeti Plain. Other thinkers, such as the Anglican

Bishop George Berkeley and Scotland's amiable David Hume, probed more deeply into Locke's thought with the opposite result. Berkeley came to believe there was no objectively real world outside the mind of man. Instead, reality was a continuous set of sensations implanted in the human mind by God.

Hume, the eminent Scottish skeptic, also concluded that the world could be only a mental construct. To him, this meant that such mainstays of apparent natural law as cause and effect existed only in the minds of individuals who believed in them because of associations formed from the memory of sequences of prior experiences. For many, after Hume published his *Treatise on Human Nature* in 1738, unadulterated Lockean empiricism made no sense at all. Nature could well be nothing more than a multitudinous series of mental impressions. In Hume's view, religion was impossible because there was no "first cause" or any cause and effect at all. Similarly, science, which depended on the idea of cause and effect and laws of predictability, was also impossible.

At this point, with God himself in potential eclipse, a group of Hume's countrymen—for the most part Scottish Presbyterian moralists, led by Francis Hutcheson, Thomas Reid, James Beattie, Adam Ferguson, Dugald Stewart, John Witherspoon, and Thomas Brown—took time off from their Paisley parishes, their rambles through the Highland heather, their Edinburgh Philosophical Club meetings, and their eccentric golf matches on the heaths hard by the North Sea to begin a counterattack in the name of religious orthodoxy against their renegade countryman. In so doing they created Scottish Common Sense Realism—a powerful philosophy that reformulated Locke's ideas so as to rescue orthodox Presbyterianism.

With the Scottish and Scotch-Irish mass immigration to America in the 1730s came Common Sense Realism. It, rather than Lockeanism per se, became the "official" American philosophy and the fountainhead of theology for nearly 150 years. As it invaded American seminaries, academies, and colleges, starting with the founding of Princeton in 1777, Common Sense Realism formed the substance of virtually every president's or headmaster's edifying course of lectures on moral philosophy—especially those of the Reverend John Witherspoon, who became president of Princeton University in 1759. As late as 1883, Yale President Noah Porter's *The Human Intellect*, a classic of Scottish Realism, served as the major text in moral philosophy. In fact, headstrong minister-sociologist William Graham Sumner created a major crisis at Yale College by using a text by upstart Englishman Herbert Spencer. The Scots yielded to no man in Scotland—or in America, upon which they made an indelible impression. Once again cosmopolitanism had shown the way; borrowing from Scotland, Americans had acquired a national philosophy.

In attacking Berkeley's idealism and Hume's skepticism, the Scottish philosophers took their cue from Locke and based their ideas solidly upon a dualistic view of the world. They believed reality was divided into "mind" and "matter" and that both existed in such forms as to be comprehended— even studied closely—by reasoning individuals who followed the inductive, or Baconian, method. They claimed, however, that Locke had not gone far enough. Empiricism could be carried far beyond simple sensation and nature studies into the mental kingdoms of reason and reflection. Taking Baconian induction as a methodological given, the Scottish thinkers focused their studies first upon observations of how the human mind worked when it engaged in the processes of reasoning, reflection, inference, and judgment. Their objective was to seek out the natural laws of thought and morality and then apply them to human behavior in the perfect social and political world system, which could reflect only the wishes or workings of God himself.

The two major Scottish figures in this endeavor were Francis Hutcheson of Edinburgh University and Thomas Reid of Aberdeen, who coined the term Common Sense. Hutcheson, a disciple of Anthony Ashley Cooper, Lord Shaftesbury, grandson of Locke's patron, applied the empirical method of study to the whole range of human behavior in the social environment. He examined institutions such as family life, the origins of society and government, political economics, and the law. In all his works he was interested primarily in discerning common principles that would provide concrete solutions to the everyday problems of life. Among other things, like several of his Scottish compatriots, Hutcheson argued the right of revolution against unjust rulers. Most profoundly, however, Hutcheson asserted that the human mind was guided by benevolent social affections, which stemmed from an innate moral sense that was as real as the sense of beauty or taste to which he compared it. This point was picked up by Jonathan Edwards as early as 1755 in *The Nature of True Virtue*. Seeking to co-opt the Scottish Enlightenment thinker, much as he had done with

Locke, Edwards saw the moral sense as an implantation by God that directed the human will. In contrast to Edwards, and in concert with all other Scottish moralists, Hutcheson believed in free will and hence moral accountability. At the heart of Hutcheson's philosophy was a revision of Locke's theory of the tabula rasa. The mind was not inert but was composed of innate faculties such as reason, the moral sense, the judging sense, taste, and the intuitive ability to recognize beauty. With respect to moral questions, conscience was every man's guide. In the realm of beauty, taste provided the innate common denominator.

Thomas Reid carried the faculty psychology even further and with perhaps more sophistication. Jarred strongly by Hume's work, Reid conceded that the mind does not simply copy sensations. Rather, he asserted that the mind is active in perception. Grammatically speaking, mental faculties had a gerundive function. They were judging, tasting, and selecting experiences in such a way that there was no sharp distinction between the external world and the internal experience of the perceiving self. Reality was a continuing stream of thought and experience in which the mind selected sensations in reference to purposes that stemmed from the innate faculty of judgment. Reid's confidence in the existence of the latter faculty, as in his belief in the existence of an external world, was simply an article of faith. Like most of the Scottish Realists, he assumed what he was attempting to prove. However, his strong belief in the faculty of judgment and in the concept of the subject subtending its object out of the stream of sensations led him very close to the ideas of modern Pragmatism, and a view of probalistic truth testable only by experience. To this Dugald Stewart added a sense of statistical probability for truth, which led Scottish philosophy into the domain of mathematical abstraction, and morals back into the area of the "hedonistic calculus" and utilitarianism. In his analysis of the mind, Thomas Brown sought in physiology the location of the innate faculties, a theme soon to be congenial to the phrenologists. In all, following Hutcheson and Reid, some fifty-one major Scottish thinkers wrestled with the abstruse problems of faculty psychology. In the history of philosophy they can be seen preparing the way for Kantian idealism, Hegelianism, American Pragmatism, and twentieth-century modernism. However, their role in the context of early American history was to provide a scientific avant garde worldview, grounded in morality and principle that enabled old-time religion to be modern and allied with republican virtue at the same time. An example of this is the writings of Scottish philosopher Alexander Bain, whose ideas directly inspired American Pragmatism.

Though Scottish thought is generally believed to have come to America with John Witherspoon, it preceded that worthy's arrival by at least a generation. It formed part of the Great Awakening, as religious leaders in America were in constant contact with Scottish thinkers. The Reverend Jonathan Edwards himself corresponded with a number of Scottish clergymen, the most important of whom was John Erskine. In addition, Edwards carefully read the works of the leading Scottish philosophers. Presbyterian ministers often went to Scotland to receive church orders or to beg donations for American "kirks" and the numerous church academies that were springing up as a result of the Great Awakening. Scores of young men traveled to Scotland to study at its universities, whose renown in medicine and law soon surpassed those of English and continental universities. The famous naturalist circle that developed in Philadelphia by the mid-eighteenth century, making it the scientific capital of the colonies, was largely the product of Scottish influence.

Two members of the Philadelphia naturalist circle stood out as early progenitors of Scottish Enlightenment thought in America. Francis Alison, a protégé of Benjamin Franklin and colleague of the plant collector William Bartram, joined with Anglican minister William Smith to found the College of Pennsylvania in 1755. Alison was a Presbyterian minister, thoroughly familiar with Scottish thought, while Smith, though Anglican, had attended King's College at Aberdeen for four years (1743–1747). Smith, due to the fact that he set down the curricular reforms he had observed at Aberdeen in an imaginative utopian educational pamphlet titled *A General Idea of the College of Miranda*, became provost of the new college while Alison became vice provost and professor of moral philosophy. The two men fought bitterly for years over Anglican versus Presbyterian questions, with Alison ever fearful that Smith would sell out colonial American religious freedom to establishment Anglicanism. At the same time, both educators worked together to make the College of Pennsylvania a bastion of Scottish Enlightenment learning in America.

Alison's course in moral philosophy was almost entirely derived from Hutcheson's Scottish lectures. According to historian Douglas Sloan, "Through the teachings of Francis Alison the full sweep of the reconstruction of moral philosophy, in which Hutcheson played such an important initial role, entered the American college at a very early date." Since Alison published almost nothing, it is difficult to recapture the full sweep of the Alison-Hutcheson "reconstruction of moral philosophy." But starting with Hutcheson's extensive emendations on Locke's *Inquiry Concerning Human Understanding*, Alison took his students through the new ontology and epistemology, dissected the mind and its faculties, and established general principles derived from these dissections, which he then applied to virtually every societal institution, attempting to evaluate their efficacy by empirical examination of factual situations. Students generally copied his lecture notes, then either recited or responded to questions or statements the professor had made in class, much in the manner of a modern-day law school. As Sloan put it, "Alison was able to make his own presence at the College of Pennsylvania a primary source of resistance—against Anglicanism, and, eventually, against the British government." One surviving fragment of Alison's writing indicated something of the way he applied his Common Sense philosophy to the pressing issue of late eighteenth-century life—political liberty:

> While the public interests are tolerably secured and consulted it is unjustifiable in any people to have recourse to civil wars and force for lighter causes: but when the public liberty and safety cannot be otherwise secured it is lawful and honorable to make strong efforts for a change of government.

Scottish Realism became an even more powerful force in American thought when the Reverend John Witherspoon arrived from Scotland in 1768 to assume the presidency of Princeton. The college had been founded in 1746 as a result of the split between New Light and Old Light Presbyterians during the Great Awakening. Its founders were followers of William Tennent and his Log College New Light evangelical Presbyterianism. By 1768, when the doughty Witherspoon arrived, a refugee from an ongoing series of theological and political confrontations in Scotland,

Princeton already had a history of short-lived presidents and religious backsliding. Thus his errand into the New Jersey wilderness was precarious from the outset. The learned Scot found most of his students and faculty caught up in the subtle coils of Berkeleyan idealism, and he was forced to turn them straightaway toward the path of Scottish orthodoxy. In this perilous labor he was overwhelmingly successful. He turned out not only a generation of learned ministers steeped in the Scottish philosophy, but also a generation of political leaders who were instrumental in founding the republic according to their values.

Witherspoon had studied with Thomas Reid and John Stevenson at Edinburgh, but his famous course on moral philosophy seems to have been based entirely upon Francis Hutcheson. From the outset, in the process of stamping out Berkeleyan idealism, Witherspoon emphasized two main themes: Reason and revelation are not antithetical, and empirical observation is the best test of any principle. He felt that not only could mind and nature be examined inductively, but also society and the Bible. All, he believed, would in the end prove "agreeing." Witherspoon declared:

> At first sight it appears that authors differ much more, and more essentially on the principles of moral than natural philosophy. Yet perhaps a time may come when men, treating moral philosophy, as Newton and his successors have done natural, may arrive at a greater precision.

Thus, as a convinced Newtonian as well as a Presbyterian divine, Witherspoon taught science and the Bible as fact subject to inductive examination. His three themes were the literal truth of the Bible, man's innate moral nature, and the value of experience. In the end, his was an ethic of biblical utilitarianism but not a thoroughgoing pragmatism because Witherspoon clung to traditional interpretations of revelation; he believed in sin, and, like Edwards, he believed the moral faculty represented the continuous working of God in the individual.

Witherspoon is perhaps most famous for his pronouncements on government. He favored opposition to tyranny, signed the Declaration of Independence, and was the most active American clergyman in the American Revolution. He also espoused a theory of government derived from Hutcheson and possibly Montesquieu that declared: "The concrete task of the statesman and the political theorist was to devise forms of government that would keep man's antisocial tendencies in bounds and allow his social nature some freedom of expression." He favored written constitutions, limited government, and a system of checks and balances. Two of his favorite pupils, James Madison and James Wilson, incorporated these principles into the drafting of the U.S. Constitution. As Sloan concluded, "Witherspoon linked the demands of the new nation with the requirements of his own political-religious convictions and drew the church and its colleges directly into the task of nation-building."

In the realm of philosophy, perhaps the most interesting of Witherspoon's protégés was his son-in-law, the Reverend Samuel Stanhope Smith, who became Witherspoon's successor as president of Princeton during the college's most unruly era. Smith was one of the most profound and imaginative of the school of Scottish philosophers. A tall, elegant man who was such a master of pulpit oratory as to earn himself the sobriquet "velvet mouth," Smith had seen long and varied service by the time he assumed his role as Princeton's intellectual leader in 1795. He had graduated from the college, become a minister and missionary to the wild, brawling Scotch-Irish frontiersmen of western Virginia and Kentucky, founded Hampton-Sidney Institute for blacks in Virginia, and taught moral philosophy at Princeton for sixteen years. Though his years as Princeton's president were punctuated by continual riots among the rebellious postwar student generation, which alienated the trustees and nearly bankrupted the college, Smith somehow remained a favorite with students and faculty alike through all those grim times. Perhaps it was because he spoke their language. He had a wide-ranging scientific curiosity and dabbled in anthropology to the extent that he denied the doctrine of man's total depravity and confidently declared to the students that "polygamy and concubinage were not necessarily moral evils."

In 1787 he published an address to the American Philosophical Society, *An Essay on the Causes of the Variety of Complexion and Figure in the Human Species*, which flatly declared that blacks and Indians were members of the human family after all. He boldly espoused the evolutionary doctrines of the inheritance of acquired characteristics that came to be associated with the infidel Jean Baptiste Lamarck, and saw all mankind evolving from a common human family with a common moral sense, subject to the common moral law, and differing only by virtue of their exposure to different climates and environments. A black person's life after many generations under the long, hot sunshine of the tropics had caused him to have dark skin, which Smith called "an universal freckle." This was in sharp contrast to Thomas Jefferson's doubts as to whether a black person was a man at all, and Benjamin Rush's theory that he had been the victim of some strange variety of leprosy. To Smith, of course, the inclusion of the Indian in the human family was not remarkable. It was simply logical and necessary. If there was more than one species of man, then the moral law would be relative, and the Great Chain of Being potentially wasteful. From observation he knew the moral law to be common and universal; ergo, there was only one species of man. Ever a devotee of science, Smith sought to bring the new learning to the service of religion whenever he could. As such, his views, except in special instances, reflected almost perfectly the merger of Enlightenment ideas and religious orthodoxy that made up the mainstream of philosophical thought in the new republic.

Like that of all Scottish philosophers, Smith's main objective was the accurate delineation of the moral law. To this end, he was a critic of early Enlightenment naturalism. He followed the Scots in believing that inductive science had not been carried far enough. It had discovered laws underlying natural phenomena, but it had not gone sufficiently into the realm of human consciousness, leaving Locke's work incomplete. And neither Hume's skepticism nor Berkeley's idealism had done anything to aid the cause of true inductive inquiry into the human mind. Thus, like the other realists, he called for accurate observation of man's behavior, thought processes, reflections, and knowledge-gathering activities. In insisting that the empirical methods of science be carried into the study of man's mind, Smith was searching for the common laws of behavior—mental and moral truths upon which generalizations could be made with sufficiently verifiable certainty as to be the basis for moral action. This was the meaning of "common" in the Common Sense philosophy.

In pursuing his study of the common sense of all mankind, Smith laid down five rules:

1. That no law should be admitted on hypothesis, but should rest solely on an induction of facts.

2. That laws collected from an ample and accurate induction of facts should be deemed universal, till other facts occur to invalidate, or limit, the conclusions that have been drawn from them.

3. That laws founded on a partial induction of facts should not be extended beyond the limits to which they are certainly known to apply.

4. That similar appearance should, because of the uniformity of nature, be referred as far as possible to the same causes.

5. That the testimony of our senses and of all our simple perceptions ought to be admitted as true, and no ulterior evidence be required of the reality, or the nature of the facts they confirm.

His rules depended upon a doctrine of uniformitarianism. Long before most geologists realized that by observing the nature and pace of processes in the present, one could reconstruct the geologic past and to an extent predict the future, the Scottish Realists had come to the same conclusion about man. Also, in a true spirit of scientific sophistication, they grasped the idea of limited but useful truth. Their search for common or uniform principles would never really be finished. Some ninety-five years after Smith wrote, latter-day Scottish Realist James McCosh was still proclaiming:

> It should be freely admitted that the Scottish school has not discovered all truth, nor even all discoverable truth, in philosophy; that it does not pretend to have done so is one of its excellencies.
>
> ... Let them [the Scots] acknowledge that they have proceeded in time past in the patient method of induction, and announce openly, and without shame, that they mean to do so in time to come. Let it be their claim, that if they have not discovered all truth, they have discovered and settled some truth.

In such a spirit of inquiry, and in the idea expressed by most of the Realists that the truth is what one is prepared to act upon as if it is scientifically or morally verifiable, lay the basis of American Pragmatism and the concept of the open-ended universe.

Smith and other thinkers of the Scottish school also touched upon such modern concepts as the calculus of scientific probabilities—"perhaps, we ought to rest satisfied with only probable evidence" and a definition of free will involving the ability to select or self-determine one's own motive, or sequence of internal and external sensations from all those that continually flow through the mind as it perceives reality. The latter, of course, flew in the face of Calvinism, which denied man's free will. Smith's theology looked instead toward the romantic perfectionism or optimism of a new generation of Presbyterian evangelists, while at the same time his philosophy anticipated the "stream of consciousness" and individualistic pragmatism of William James, as late as 1890.

Convinced of the existential and comprehensible reality of the external world, which distinguished them from idealists like Berkeley, Hume, and Kant, Smith and his fellow Scottish Realists nonetheless devoted their major attention to the hidden wellsprings of true morality in every man's innate common moral sense. The latter, indeed, was perhaps the main thrust of their philosophy as they sought to buttress orthodox religion and at the same time standardize right conduct in the new republic. Smith considered the entire corpus of his famous *Lectures on Moral and Political Philosophy* (1812) as a "volume of moral experiment."

One of their number was perhaps America's first "mental hygienist." About the time Diderot became interested in Rameau's crazy nephew, Dr. Benjamin Rush of Philadelphia, a Scottish-trained physician, began to relate the faculty psychology to cases of mental disorder he had observed. Rush was nothing if not dogmatic, though he believed himself to be something of an empiricist as well as a rationalist. In combining the two, Rush believed he had modified the moral philosophy for the better. He flatly rejected pure induction in favor of hypothesis, declaring that most of Newton's discoveries "were the result of pre-conceived hypotheses." And he asserted, "To observe is to think and to think is to reason in medicine," thus emphasizing the critical and judgmental faculties that other Realists such as James Beattie had also noted. History has not been kind (perhaps appropriately enough) to Rush's theory of physical disease, to which he attributed a single cause—"vascular convulsion"—and prescribed only a pair of remedies—bleeding and purging. But his theory of mental illness has proven more interesting as an application of the Common Sense philosophy to the abnormal. He first enumerated nine mental faculties: understanding, memory, imagination, passions, the principle of faith, will, the moral faculty, conscience, and the sense of the deity. Then he argued that "the cause of madness is seated primarily in the blood vessels of the brain, and it depends upon the same kind of morbid and irregular actions that constitute other arterial diseases." Thus if in one section of the brain there was a vascular or arterial malfunction, then the faculty or faculties located in that section would also malfunction, causing what is termed madness. For Rush, "derangement" was clearly not sin, demonic possession, or crime, but an illness resulting from vascular malfunction that was related to every part of the body. Such illness stemming from physical causes and bad environment could result in extinguishing or blocking the faculties, including the moral faculties, thus causing lying, kleptomania, drunkenness, suicide, and murder—behavior not conventionally linked to madness. For Rush, moral turpitude was, or could be, a form of insanity. But this, in turn, was a function of the body and the physical, social, and political environment, which had caused the excitement and the "vascular constriction in the first place."

An ardent revolutionary who had recommended the title for the pamphlet *Common Sense* to his friend Tom Paine, Rush was, like Paine, essentially a moral utopian. A "born again" republic with free institutions, such as Rush envisioned for America, was crucial to mental as well as moral health. For him, they were the same thing. As important as the hospitals and medical schools, which he helped to found, were representative governments and free presses, which, as he put it, "serve like chimneys in a house, to conduct for the individual and public mind, all the discontents, vexation, and resentment which have been generated in the passions by real or supposed evils."

At about the same time Rush was using the faculty psychology to diagnose individual and societal ills, far to the north in Cambridge, Massachusetts, the Unitarian Conscience was born. Growing out of liberal religion of the sort espoused by Jonathan Mayhew and Charles Chauncey, the Scottish philosophy had first been upheld at Harvard by David Tappan, a moderate Calvinist who held the Hollis Professorship of Divinity for thirteen years. In 1803, upon his death, he was succeeded after a bitter political struggle by Henry Ware, a Unitarian. Soon afterward, Harvard had a Unitarian president in Samuel Webber, and following on this the new Alford Chair of Moral Philosophy received the first in a long line of Scottish Realists—Levi Frisbie. As the nineteenth century opened, Harvard had been delivered into the hands of rational religion. From that point on, each holder of the Chair of Moral Philosophy—Levi Frisbie, Levi Hedge, James Walker (also president of Harvard), and Francis Bowen—was a devotee of rational Christianity and an avid disciple of Thomas Reid and the Scottish moralists.

By 1820, it must have seemed as if the whole nation had turned to Common Sense. As far as Cambridge was concerned, however, a new orthodoxy had been born, buttressed by the rational, scientifically derived principles of Scottish Realism. It seduced New England's greats—Elizabeth Palmer Peabody, Andrews Norton, William Ellery Channing—and came to represent the institutionalized aspects of the collective conscience of New England's elite. As such it formed the foundation for the first phase of the region's literary renaissance, as well as Federalism, Whiggery, and the genteel aspects of the antislavery movement. Perhaps it is most famous, however, as the foil for the Transcendentalist movement that was to include Ralph Waldo Emerson, Henry Thoreau, Theodore Parker, George Ripley, Margaret Fuller, and a number of New England's great romantics. It was to be a fascinating struggle over consciousness, perception, and the moral nature of America, in which the knights of Germany stood forth against the champions of Scotland and English Latitudinarianism, and the outcome of the battle has to this day remained inconclusive.

Despite the flowering of the Scottish philosophy in America, when he made his celebrated visit to the United States in 1835, Count Alexis de Tocqueville concluded that in no part of the civilized world was less attention paid to philosophy than in this country.

That he missed the widespread impact of Scottish philosophy on American thought is not entirely surprising. Fundamentally the Scottish philosophy was laissez-faire. Ontologically it posited a dualistic world of mind and matter, but epistemologically, beyond its worship of the scientific method of induction from observable facts, Scottish philosophy was a knowledge-processing structure that was open-ended and flexible. It could lead anywhere the facts took it and hence took on a great variety of forms and sub-forms reinforcing evangelicalism and Unitarianism alike. The same phenomenon occurred in Scotland itself. In his monumental treatise on the Scottish philosophy, President James McCosh of Princeton had analyzed the work of the major Scottish thinkers, each differing to some degree from the other. So it was in America: William Smith and Francis Alison at Pennsylvania College frequently quarreled, and their ideas differed greatly from those of Eliphalet Nott of Union Seminary, Francis Wayland of Brown, Noah Porter of Yale, and Levi Hedge of Harvard. Though all subscribed to religion and the moral law, some investigators stressed passion and intuition over reason and the careful calculus of probabilities. Infinite adaptability was a weakness of Scottish Realism, but also its strength.

Scottish Realism officially eschewed esoteric, metaphysical system-building, but each philosopher was ultimately forced to build his own, often out of parts borrowed from the Scottish "prophets" or emerging continental eclectics, such as Victor Cousin, whose something-for-everyone amalgam drawn from the English, Scots, and Germans he forthrightly named the Eclectic Philosophy. Some standard elements emerged, however. The course on moral philosophy that appeared in every college, academy, and seminary gradually established moral philosophy as a regular profession in America, where a gentleman, even if he were not of the cloth, could make a career. Along with the professionalization of philosophy, textbooks appeared. The most widely used of all was Francis Wayland's *Elements of Moral Science*, which sold more than two hundred thousand copies. It was published in 1835, the very year that Tocqueville could find no American interest in philosophy. Literary and artistic taste, too, became somewhat standardized as Scottish rhetoric books, with their emphasis on classical verities, became standard fare in American colleges and schools.

The appeal of Scottish Realism thus was not only its scientific modernity—the way in which it stated the "old truths of the heart" in newer, more comprehensible language. It was also the disarming reliance on apparent fact—the tangible, the convincing, the common sense rather than the airy, elitist metaphysics of the Idealist or Platonist, who was forced to create his own language to describe a vast, comprehensive system nearly impossible to grasp in its entirety. And in restoring God to his heaven, in proving the enduring value of the old moralistic truths, in coming out foursquare for free will and instrumentalism, in joining the army of hope and the march of progress in the New World, as the Edinburgh Circle had done in the Scotland of the Industrial Revolution of Matthew Boulton, James Watts, and Adam Smith, the American Scottish Realists caught perfectly the spirit and optimism of the new utopian republic. If they raised questions they never answered, so too had America, whose canals, then being built, as Perry Miller has reminded us, all "flowed into the future."

Though the philosophers seemed high-minded, one cannot resist pointing out that the Scots and Scotch-Irish were also among the first frontiersmen. They were continually moving west through the Carolinas and over the Appalachian Mountains. Drawing upon their constant combat with the English lords, they became great Indian-fighters and for that matter duelists, family feudists, and just plain unruly. They were called rednecks, but they brought the Pennsylvania log cabin to backwoods America and invented bourbon and rye whiskey based on corn and rye, which were native to the country. And as Arthur Herman noted, they often changed the language: "neckid," "widder," "critter," and children as "little shits." Local streams or landmarks were sometimes named Cutthroat Gap, Tickle Cunt Branch, or Fucking Creek. Captain William Lynch of Virginia became famous because of his invention—lynching. Yet the "rednecks" or "crackers" produced such distinguished men as Daniel Boone, James K. Polk, Thomas Hart Benton, and Sam Houston, as well as William Tennent, Yale man and founder of the famous Log College in the backwoods of western Pennsylvania, where many fiery Presbyterian ministers "growed up" and set out on their evangelical missions.

CHAPTER FIVE

Nationalism and the Varieties of Capitalistic Experience

America's founding fathers were forced, from the outset of the Revolution to the achievement of political independence, to grapple with securing economic independence as well. We have come to know this as the characteristic problem of all emergent nations. In the new United States this involved not only addressing the question of international competition but also solving the many regional economic problems endemic to a vast and diverse frontier nation. Every intelligent man knew the immense backcountry held great promise for the future, but by the same token if the diverse economic needs of each new state and region were not somehow met—and made to harmonize—then the nation would divide, and in dividing lose its independence as, one by one, the Balkanized states fell back into the hands of European imperialist powers.

Among the most important thinkers in early America was an emerging group of men who turned their attention to the political economy. Some thought most directly about the production and exchange of goods and services and hotly debated the true nature of a nation's wealth. Others looked to the more basic process and impact of invention and comparative technological advantage. And there were those whose main concern was stability and justice under the law, which very often had a direct bearing on economic matters. All related to securing the people's allegiance to the new nation, without which there could be no nation at all.

In early America, these three classes of thinkers had several things in common: They consistently borrowed ideas from Europe; they believed in America as a republican experiment; and they operated almost to a man on the basis of Enlightenment assumptions about the commonality of mankind, the validity of general laws, the importance of environmentalism, the centrality of reason, the limitless potential of man, and the value of individual liberties and property. In virtually all ways they were cosmopolitan nationalists—typical products of the Enlightenment.

I

Let us turn to the political economists first. Their reasoning and their motivations were often complex, but for a time the broad lines were clear. Fixated on the concepts of isolation from the "entanglements of Europe" and the abundance of free, rich land—not to mention the image of the happy, self-sufficient yeoman so vividly mythologized by Crevecoeur in his *Letters from an American Farmer*—such thinkers as Jefferson, William Randolph, and John Taylor of Caroline saw America's future as a self-contained agricultural society where economic well-being stemmed directly from nature and the honest labor of those who worked the soil. Jefferson's famous statement "Those who labor in the earth are the chosen people of God" keynoted this whole viewpoint. Cities were, in Jefferson's terms, "sores on the body politic." Banks, paper, credit, even manufacturing were artificial, unwholesome, almost blasphemous, and certainly contrary to American spiritual values. For Jefferson, who grudgingly came to admit their necessity, they were at best "a badge of lost innocence." The Virginia school and indeed, throughout the period down to the Civil War, the Southern thinkers as a group were content to be "hewers of wood and drawers of water" for the industries of Europe, though they were happy enough to let the slaves do most of the actual hewing and drawing. Much of their thinking, conditioned by an Enlightenment view of the harmonious world of nature and the soil as a source of spiritual values, in large measure also grew out of a local assessment of their situation with which, at least for a time due to its stability, they were content. However, Jefferson owed little or no debt to French physiocratic thinkers, such as Pierre Quesnay, and it is doubtful that John Taylor did either. Cosmopolitan though he was in most things— science, learning, architecture, appreciation of the arts—in economics Jefferson and his followers were staunch localists.

Hamilton, on the other hand, recognized that true independence was not possible without at least some measure of economic self-sufficiency in a world context. His plans for establishing sound national credit in all money markets of the world, creating a national bank and a stable currency, and legislating tariff and governmental support for infant industries pursued this aim. Long-term risk capital from abroad would be needed if the country was to achieve a balanced economy. Hence sound credit was an absolute necessity. Foreign nations that were to supply the funds for American development needed to be assured of the stability and honesty of the new country. At the same time, foreign loans could be used to make capital investments in public works, such as roads, harbors, and canals, that were beyond the reach of local entrepreneurs. Meanwhile, through tariffs, through bounties, and even by means of federal corporations such as the fur trade factories in the Northwest, the government would become a partner with business in encouraging the growth of a balanced economy.

This was Hamilton's great blueprint for an underdeveloped nation and it still retains obvious implications for today. In any case, even though Hamilton himself was a controversial political figure, both Federalists and Republicans saw merit in his blueprint for a planned or at least managed economy in the national interest. That the Federalist Hamilton's ideas had gained limited assent from both political parties is clear from the Republican Albert Gallatin's espousal of a national bank, support for manufacturing, and his elaborate plans for internal improvements at governmental expense.

In proposing a managed economy in the national interest, American thinkers ran distinctly counter to the prevailing economic thought and, to some extent, even the basic philosophy of the period. Most of the economists who dominated European and American thought were British or Scottish, and their writings principally formed a rationalization for Britain's emerging dominance of world trade and industry. Because they claimed to base their ideas on a series of universal natural laws that applied everywhere and in every situation, and because they advocated universal free trade, these economists were referred to as the cosmopolitan school. The chief spokesmen for the cosmopolitan school were Adam Smith, J. B. Say, David Ricardo, and Thomas R. Malthus. Together they formed a quadrivium that based Britain's ascendance the world over on the inexorable determinism of natural law.

The best known of the group was Adam Smith, the Scottish political economist whose *Wealth of Nations* was published in 1776 and generated a revolution of its own in economic, if not social, thinking. In *Wealth of Nations*, Smith deplored the mercantilist policies that had accounted for Britain's ascendancy and called instead for world free trade and a laissez-faire policy of minimal governmental interference in the economy. In addition, he extolled the theories of division of labor and comparative advantage whereby each nation does what it can do best and exchanges those goods and services for others performed by nations with different skills. As the most advanced technological and mercantile country in the world, Britain would fabricate and ship the world's products. Other nations would supply the raw materials. Smith saw no real disadvantage to nations whose economic role subordinated them to the British technological center. Indeed, he believed that no other course was really possible because, try as one might, there was no getting around the natural laws of supply and demand and comparative advantage. For Smith, all was controlled by the invisible hand of economic man, who always made his choices according to reason and to the best advantage of his individual economic balance sheet. Nations were simply collections of rationally functioning individual economic men and women. Their wealth depended upon how rationally or prudently all of them functioned.

Smith's disciples, J. B. Say and David Ricardo, were nearly as influential as he was in American thought. Their textbooks on political economy were standard fare in most early American colleges. They were used, for example, at Harvard, Yale, Columbia, Pennsylvania, William and Mary, Virginia, and South Carolina. The doctrine of comparative advantage was especially appealing to those regions, which were just beginning to specialize, as were New England in shipping and the South in cotton and sugar farming.

Some of Ricardo's ideas particularly appealed to the Jeffersonians—specifically the theory that the only true wealth arises as rent from the land. Another formula of Ricardo's especially appealed to agrarians and would have a profound effect upon later Jacksonian thinking. He saw all economic life in terms of a clash of interests over control of fixed resources. Nature itself demanded not harmony but conflict between landowners, capitalists, and wage-earners. Since the supply of resources, or the world's goods, was limited, the economy was not infinitely expandable; what one group received, the other lost. The only rapidly expanding group was city and factory wage-earners, and for them he laid down the "iron law of wages"—the more people, the lower the wages. It was a simple application of the law of supply and demand, and to tamper with it was irrational and probably immoral. It was nature's law, and nature could do no wrong.

Ricardo's dicta were reinforced by Thomas R. Malthus's gloomy, mathematical *Essay on Population*, published in 1798, just as Eli Whitney was perfecting the principle of interchangeable parts. Malthus, like some modern-day population-explosion Cassandra, focused on the man-land ratio (apparently thinking of England and not the vast, empty North American continent) and carefully calculated the ratio of people to the food supply, concluding that inevitably, according to natural law, a certain percentage of people were destined to die of starvation. Nothing could, or for that matter should, be done about it. To tamper with nature was to tamper with the Creator. Indeed, in their conclusions Smith, Say, Ricardo, and Malthus appeared to represent the very incarnation of an Enlightenment version of the biblical Four Horsemen of the Apocalypse.

Against these men were pitted the "old-fashioned" followers of Hamilton's "artificial" economics who were antideterministic and appealed to common sense intelligence and rational planning in the national interest. The foremost of Hamilton's successors was Matthew C. Carey, the very archetype of the emergent-nation revolutionary. Carey, an Irish Catholic, began his public career as a youthful rabble-rouser against British rule of Ireland, from which he was forced to flee to France in 1782 when only twenty-two years old. In Paris he became Ben Franklin's personal printer and helped distribute his underground propaganda leaflets. As a result of his association with Franklin, Carey became even more enthusiastic about republican revolution and about America. In 1784 he returned to Ireland for one more try, where he was caught and imprisoned. Released on bail, he escaped to America, where Lafayette set him up as editor of the Jacobin, pro-French *Pennsylvania Evening Herald*. Three years later, in 1787, he established the *American Museum*, the first successful American magazine. Though it was an eclectic publication, the *American Museum* strongly supported the Federalist cause and the Scottish philosophy of Alexander Hamilton's manufacturing-oriented, mercantilist economics.

Carey thus began his career in America as a republican propagandist and a confirmed Anglophobe but, at the same time, an admirer of Hamilton (whom he probably never met). What he appreciated most about Hamilton was his series of concrete plans for freeing America from British economic imperialism. Like Hamilton, Carey became an economic nationalist. After 1815, facing the grim realities of British economic domination and cognizant of the diverse needs of a vast sectional republic, Carey served as the chief theoretician of what came to be known as the American System. Along with Henry Clay of Kentucky, Daniel Raymond of Baltimore, and Friedrich Liszt, an immigrant German economist, he advocated a protective tariff to keep out British goods, federal and state-funded internal improvements, a national bank, and cheap or free land distribution in the West. Like the classical economists whom he opposed, Carey also rested his case on natural law. In direct contradiction of Ricardo, Carey saw nature as harmonious rather than inherently competitive, and the American System was an attempt to enhance harmony in the new nation by providing something for everyone. It was, once again, compromise by combination, this time in the interests of sectional and economic harmony. The tariff encouraged manufacturing. Internal improvements paid for by the revenue from the tariff were an aid to western farmers and landowners as well as Southern cotton planters who could ship their products north as an alternative to selling in an English buyers' market. Expanded capital, managed carefully by a national bank, provided relatively cheap but solid money whose value did not fluctuate wildly either on foreign markets or in working men's pockets. And the encouragement of all industrial pursuits made for an increased demand for labor and drove all wages up. In this way America could capitalize on its vast natural advantage, develop an immense home market, and thus be self-sufficient. Free trade, such as Smith, Say, and Ricardo advocated, was good only if you were the technologically dominant nation and could undersell all others. Nobody at the time considered the importance of cheap labor except to capitalize on it.

Carey held to two further doctrines that are interesting examples of the fusion of Republican and Federalist thinking. Though by 1819 he had become a rich man, the leading publisher in America, he still held the individual worker to be most important. Thus he argued that wages must increase at a greater ratio than profits, for both the good of the business and the good of the country. He was also concerned with the question of qualitative economic freedom. In an agricultural country, youths had little choice but to continue in the family tradition and become farmers. And with the abolition of laws of entail and primogeniture, which held land inheritance intact for the eldest son, the chances were that, as the land was parceled out through inheritance, descendants would work smaller and smaller sections. Only in a balanced and complex economy that afforded economic alternatives could a young man realize his full potential. "There can be no truth more clear than this," Carey wrote in 1824, "the greater the variety of occupations in a community, the greater the scope for ingenuity and talent, the reward for industry, the higher the grade of individual and general prosperity."

Carey's ideas were paralleled by those of Baltimore lawyer Daniel Raymond, whose book *Thoughts on Political Economy* (1820) was a pioneering textbook of the nationalist school. Besides advocating the American System, Raymond encouraged active governmental participation in the economy. The main burden of his book was an attack on Adam Smith's idea that a nation is simply a collection of individual balance sheets. Raymond declared that what was good for a nation and what was good for a particular individual at a certain time and place were not the same. Indeed, he went so far as to question the "sacred" right to private property itself if it interfered with the nation's collective good. This sort of doctrine went largely unheeded throughout most of the nineteenth century in America.

Carey's two principal disciples, besides the politician Henry Clay, were the German immigrant Friedrich Liszt and Carey's own son Henry C. Carey. Liszt's *Outline of American Political Economy* (1827) was a powerful argument for a nationalistic protective tariff and economic and governmental planning. He carried these ideas back with him to Germany, where in 1841 he incorporated them in his *National System of Political Economy*. In this and other works, he created a formula for emergent nations, such as the Germany that soon began to coalesce out of a collection of dukedoms and principalities.

Henry Carey, building on his father's ideas, stressed over and over again the harmony in nature. There was, in his view, no inherent opposition between capital, labor, farming, manufacturing, producers, carriers, etc. He also denied the Ricardan theory of rent from the land as the only real value. "Rent begins," he declared, "because by the application of capital, the land has been raised from an inferior soil to a superior one." He went on to add that labor applied to the land also increased its value and, hence, he developed a labor *and* capital theory of value, about the time that Karl Marx was preoccupied with the simpler labor theory of value and the class struggle. Carey declared, "The interests of the capitalist and the laborer are in perfect harmony with each other, as each derives advantage from every measure that tends to facilitate the growth of capital and to render labor productive, while every measure that tends to produce the opposite effect is injurious to both." Both Careys basically asserted that in America there was no class struggle—nor any reason under the sun for it. In the true Republican tradition, from Benjamin Franklin onward, they were enthusiastic spokesmen for the mobile middle class, whose welfare demanded not subservience to the "invisible hand" *or* the "iron law of wages," but a positive state that was bold and independent enough to act in its own interests.

Clearly the American System grew out of the desperate situation following the collapse of the American economy after the Treaty of Ghent, which ended the War of 1812. In a series of desperate measures, the Bank of the United States was rechartered under James Madison in 1816, and a tariff bill passed, as did a bill for internal improvements, but still the depression of 1819–1820 ensued. The measures had come too late and by 1820 were received with varying degrees of enthusiasm, especially in the South and West. By 1825, when John Quincy Adams in his inaugural address advocated government aid to a national university as well as a series of astronomical observatories, the American System had ceased to hold charms for the American people. The country had righted itself, and any check on the new economic boom, any significant appearance of government management of economic affairs, appeared to be menacing rather than helpful. And so in 1828 Andrew Jackson, alleged man of the soil, Southern planter, slaveholder, and hater of banks and other forms of "artificial property," carried the day, and with him came, for better or for worse, Adam Smith's open-ended economics.

In many ways the American System had served its purpose by pointing the way to economic and, hence, real independence. Its programs were carried out all over the country on both federal and state levels—the Erie Canal is the most prominent example—and for a time it keynoted, through its doctrine of harmony, the thrust toward nationalism in the new nation. Advocates of the American System were indeed "all Republicans and all Federalists." More important, in its blueprint for achieving national independence, it created a formula that looked not just to Britain for guidance. In this, and in their ability to make clear the applicability of their blueprint for all emergent nations, perhaps with certain modifications, the advocates of the American System were more cosmopolitan than their opponents who bore that label.

It should be obvious to twenty-first-century observers of the collapse of communism and totalitarian folly that the intricacies of planning on a vast scale for an entire nation are a special talent. In America in the nineteenth century, the country simply outgrew the initial plan and until several decades into the twentieth century did without one. By the age of Jackson, America had reached the stage of economic takeoff. In the hard panic of 1837, it did not crash severely enough to call for another plan until 1929. That was a new age that demanded a new plan, the New Deal, in which one might still detect echoes of Hamilton, the Careys, Raymond, Liszt, and Marx interspersed with the rhetoric of Jefferson just as it was in the early days of the republic when the nation was trying desperately to find itself.

One further aspect of the clash of early American economic ideologies, however, is the large and simple fact that both the Jeffersonians and the advocates of the American System agreed on certain fundamental principles. Though at times anxious about the nation's immediate future, both sides implicitly or explicitly believed in America's long-term growth and prosperity. More important, both sides believed in private property as a natural right, even while disagreeing as to what constituted legitimate property. Moreover, they believed in a marketplace economy on a world scale built on the belief in private property—something that in recent times has been threatened by phony political taking for the ostensible public good. In short, both sides believed in capitalism and took for granted the emergence of a prosperous, economically mobile middle class based on the American work ethic and ingenuity. This shared belief is of the greatest importance because, of course, it ensured that the United States would for a long time be a capitalist nation geared to the marketplace; even the balanced overcorrections of the American System, which involved manipulating tariffs, looked toward that objective. And the ultimate belief in the marketplace meant the United States in the long run would compete both internally and internationally and, in so competing, throw itself open to the world's best goods and services whether home produced or of foreign origin. Capitalism was cosmopolitan economics. And as a vast home market based on a network of transportation and communications grew up in the early nineteenth century, it was almost inevitable that freewheeling Jacksonian economics would prevail. America was a country, even in the marketplace, of infinite possibilities.

II

A neglected branch of economic thought that contributed most significantly to the development of the early republic as well as symbolizing dramatically its spirit of nationalism was technology. Latter-day British economic historian H. J. Habakuk has argued persuasively that since labor was relatively scarce and expensive in the United States, Americans turned enthusiastically to labor-saving inventions. The inventor of a new device, or the successful adapter of a previously invented European or Asian device, became in many respects an early American hero. In the most practical sense he fostered progress, prosperity, economic independence, and the glories of plain republican nationalism.

Because of Jefferson's oft-quoted statement "Those who labor in the earth are the chosen people of God" and his deprecation of cities as "sores on the body politic," it has often been assumed that republicanism and a technological ideology were incompatible in the early republic. Nothing could be further from the truth. Though the free-trade agrarians struggled with early manufacturers over tariffs, neither the Federalists nor the Democratic Republicans opposed technology per se as a means of republican progress. When Hamilton promulgated his *Report on Manufactures* in 1791, his program was simply the culmination of twenty-five years of agitation for aid to infant American industries suffering from unfair British competition.

New Englanders avidly urged adoption of modern technology beginning with the establishment of wartime iron works and the erecting of Eli Whitney's cotton gin factory by George Cabot in 1787. Only the year before, the Massachusetts legislature had imported two Scotsmen to act as instructors in the use of spinning and carding machinery. The Philadelphia circle, including Franklin, Benjamin Rush, Matthew Carey, and Tench Coxe, strongly urged the adoption of the useful mechanical arts wherever possible. As early as 1775, Rush took the lead in founding the United Company of Philadelphia for Promoting American Manufacture. In the South no one scorned the cotton gin. And even Jefferson yielded ground. Upon his temporary retirement to Monticello in 1794, he established a nail factory employing ten black youths who turned out ten thousand nails a day. Following this, he built a grist mill, a manufacturing mill, and a textile mill on his various properties. Thus the Sage of Monticello gradually came to see that adopting mechanical labor-saving devices could enhance republicanism and individual liberty by spawning a dispersed cottage industry that would make every man comparatively more independent—both domestically and with respect to freedom from the necessity of importing foreign luxuries.

Nothing contributed to the optimism and pride in America more than the rapid advance of American technology. "American industry and enterprise guided by American ingenuity and intellect," read a report on the Patent Office for 1836, "have achieved in thirty years what would have taken Europe a century to accomplish." In the eyes of the average American it was not the more subtle disciplines that had worked miracles, but rather the work of practical men of "genius"—the inventors, engineers, and design entrepreneurs who seemed in the forefront of the battle with nature. These down-to-earth, businesslike, practical men had by midcentury largely conquered the most pressing problems of wilderness and space.

In 1829 Jacob Bigelow, a young popular lecturer at Harvard, resurrected the long-forgotten word "technology" and applied it to American achievement. He was the first to use the term in America and he used it most deliberately to denote "the principles, processes, and nomenclatures of the more conspicuous arts, particularly those which involve applications of science, and which may be considered useful, by promoting the benefit of society, together with the emolument of those who pursue them." Implicit in Bigelow's definition of technology was a distinction between science as contemplative—the process by which nature and its laws were observed and discoveries made—and art or artifice as the active manipulation of nature for the betterment of man. According to Bigelow, the discoveries of science must be put to the practical use of every man. Nature's principles must be made to work so the common man might have a better life of leisure and comfort. To be of real value science should be, in latter-day pragmatic terms, instrumental.

Bigelow's thought was the aggressive nineteenth-century embodiment of the early ideals of the American Philosophical Society in Philadelphia for the Promotion of Useful Knowledge, which, of course, had brought the value of science home to the common man in the eighteenth century. In so doing, it established a clear connection in the popular mind between science, progress, and democracy, of which the Franklin Institute in Philadelphia stands as a monument. The international exhibitions, such as the American pavilion at the Crystal Palace in London in 1851, also spurred national pride in machines and justified the organized and mechanized exploitation of the continent in the name of progress. The saga of science and progress along with the subjugation of the frontier became the second American epic.

The development of early American technology, despite the nationalistic mythologizing of prominent figures, proceeded in a fashion entirely consistent with other institutions of culture in the new republic. For the most part, American invention derived from the Industrial Revolution in Europe, particularly that of Britain and France—a movement that took its cue from an earlier scientific revolution and inspired so much of the Enlightenment ideology of rationalism and progress. In their development of technology, Americans simply stood on the shoulders of an earlier European generation and reached the confident stage of what twentieth-century economist Walt Whitman Rostow has termed economic takeoff that much sooner as a result of starting from a comparatively advanced and sophisticated base. In large measure Americans could take advantage of existing scientific principles, European machines that wanted refinement and cried out for ingenuous application to other industries, and advanced industrial processes that had been obscured in tradition-bound societies across the Atlantic.

Everywhere one looks in the history of early American invention, one finds this trans-Atlantic relationship to be the governing factor, from Samuel Slater's first transportation of the closely guarded principles of Sir Richard Arkwright's Spinning Jenny from England to Pawtucket in 1789, to the repeated employment of Boulton and Watt's steam engine in virtually every manufacturing and transportation enterprise throughout the early nineteenth century.

Perhaps the archetypal representative of this relationship was Robert Fulton, the "American Archimedes," as Henry Clay called him. Fulton spent twenty years in Europe, longer even than his fellow expatriate Washington Irving, working first as an artist, then as an inventor and engineer. During this time, he absorbed the most advanced ideas and techniques of British and French industrial or applied science. Occasionally he contributed important original ideas of his own—such as the use of the inclined plane instead of locks in constructing canals, a new technique for building cast-iron bridges in huge prefabricated sections, a workable submarine, and an effective underwater torpedo (which, fortunately, failed to impress the rulers of Britain and France to whom he tried to sell the idea). For the most part, however, Fulton drew upon European knowledge. His important *Treatise on the Improvement of Canal Navigation* (1796), which did so much to influence American canal-building, was based primarily upon his observation of English works. And most significant of all, his development of a practical steamboat depended not only on Boulton and Watt's steam engine (and the scientific research on gases and heat that lay behind it), but also on Charnock's *Table of the Resistance of Bodies Moved Through Water*, published serially by the British Society for the Encouragement of Naval Architecture between 1793 and 1798. Of all our early inventors, Fulton perhaps was the most obviously cosmopolitan in his life and thought. But virtually all the early pioneers of steam transportation—John Fitch, Oliver Evans, Joel Barlow, John Stevens, and J. H. B. Latrobe—depended at the outset on British technology. Perhaps only Eli Whitney and Henry

Shreve, who invented the flat-bottom river steamer of the West, were dealing in what some have loosely called the vernacular arts, or empirically derived folk invention.

Meanwhile, the age of the steamboat had come to America's western waters in 1811. Fulton's steamboat, with Nicholas Roosevelt as supercargo, had steamed from Pittsburgh down the Ohio and right through the New Madrid earthquake, down the Mississippi to New Orleans. Soon after, Pittsburgh boat maker Henry Shreve's flat-bottom steamboats—actually a throwback to Fulton's first flat-bottom steam barge, which he had demonstrated on the Seine in Paris—began to cover the western rivers. Deliberately built to last only five years because ever-advancing technology would make them obsolete, steamboats were the transportation marvel of the age and a symbol not only of republican ingenuity but also of national pride.

The European roots of Yankee ingenuity were, however, only one aspect of the technological revolution's relevance for American thought. Most fundamentally important was Americans' extraordinary receptivity to the Industrial Revolution. In this respect the Jeffersonian agrarians were swept aside in a tide of enthusiasm. In the South, Eli Whitney's cotton gin had made invention more than respectable, to such an extent that Charles Fraser of Charleston, South Carolina, actually delivered an address on "The Moral Influence of Steam." John Pendleton Kennedy, author of *Swallow Barn*, a sleepy novel of life on the old plantation, upon contemplating the steamboat said that "vast enginery, this infinite complication of wheels, this exquisite adjustment of parts, and this sure, steady, and invariable result shown in the operation of the perfect machine" was "lost in admiration of the genius that masters the whole." In the North, the country was also lost in the worship of steam power. Samuel Tyler declared:

> It is on the ocean, it is on the rivers, it is on the mountains, it is in the valleys, it is at the bottom of mines, it is in the shops, it is everywhere at work. It propels the ship, it rows the boat, it cuts, it pumps, it hammers, it cords, it spins, it weaves, it washes, it prints, and releases man of nearly all bodily toil.

With gun manufacturer Eli Whitney's exploitation of the principle of interchangeable parts and the development of a crude milling assembly line by Oliver Evans, inventor of the balloon-frame house, early assembly-line meatpackers in Cincinnati, and the creation of the utopian industrial village at Lowell, Massachusetts, by Nathan Appleton Lowell, the nation began to worship the factory as well. Efficiency, organization, standardization, interchangeability (of men and machines), speed, and productivity began to assume incredible importance in America. And far from seeming unnatural, the well-organized factory could be seen to have been derived from the secret processes of nature itself. The Industrial Revolution, based upon the application of science, which was, after all, the study of nature's laws, was seen simply as a more enlightened understanding of the way nature was meant to work. Everything, just as in the Great Chain of Being, had its place and was functioning according to its destined use. If Deacon William Paley's watch discovered by him accidentally in a woodland path denoted the mysterious artificer of nature, nature itself demanded the manufacturing of Paley's watch. Americans absorbed so eagerly the technology that came from European minds or sprang from the minds of its own great men because technology fitted in comfortably with their basic worldview and because, due to the scarcity of labor, it was an absolute necessity in developing and exploiting the continent. Beyond being necessary, technology was also holy in early America. Just as John D. Rockefeller, the wizard of Standard Oil, later could solemnly announce, "The good God gave me my money," so too could the "American Leonardo," Samuel F. B. Morse, neglecting the subtle contribution of Joseph Henry, send that famous message across his newly invented telegraph, "What hath God wrought?"

The net effect of the Industrial Revolution upon America—of steam, electricity, the cotton gin, mechanized agriculture, efficient tools, the factory, and rapid transportation—was paradoxical. Much of American life became extremely standardized and by the same token less provincial. Yet at the same time Americans became increasingly divided. Instead of "binding America together by a system of roads and canals," as John C. Calhoun hoped in 1819 when he voted enthusiastically for the internal improvement bill, the industrial and transportation revolutions caused whole sections of the country to specialize. A massive division of labor took place as the North turned almost exclusively to manufacturing, shipping, and trade, the South to cotton, timbering, and sugar and tobacco planting, and the West to farming, raising cattle on a large scale, and such extractive industries as mining and timbering.

Technology borrowed from Europe had promised the means for developing strong national spirits by giving Americans the means to span the whole continent with standardized ideas and values. Instead, it acted in the long run as a divisive force due to the sectional division of labor, especially slavery. But in the early days of the Republic few could foresee this result. Instead science and progress seemed to open up a Manifest Destiny for America. Our Whitneys, Lowells, Lawrences, Fultons, Morses, and McCormicks became giants of public esteem, a second generation of Founding Fathers who appeared to give practical reality to the common-man rhetoric of an earlier tie-wigged generation of Enlightenment futurists.

III

Still another basic means of promoting American nationalism intimately connected with economic development was the law. In the words of legal historian Robert McCloskey, "From 1789 until the Civil War, the dominant interest of the Supreme Court was in that greatest of all questions left unanswered by the founders—the nation-state relationship. And the dominant judicial value, underlying the drift of decisions in widely different areas, was the value of preserving the American Union."

At the same time, while the Supreme Court was slowly fashioning a constitutional philosophy, if not a tradition, of nationalism, legal scholars and practicing lawyers all over the country were struggling mightily to establish a system of everyday civil and criminal law that would be uniform yet functional in widely differing regional contexts. The nationalizing process thus, as far as the law was concerned, took place on two planes: in the high courts of the federal government, and within the legal profession itself, practiced largely on the state and local levels. Insofar as the nationalizing process of the law contributed to forming a national character, it too followed a pattern of cosmopolitanism as lawyers and justices, while rejecting outright transposition of English legal theory to America, nonetheless looked for broad principles that spanned the nation and had direct links to the international laws and traditions of all nations wherever they were.

American legal thought, as it had done for more than one hundred years, drew upon world legal thought—from Justinian, Samuel Pufendorf, Hugo Grotius, and Emmerich Vattel—as well as the English tradition from Sir Edward Coke and Edward Vaughn to Blackstone. As the *Pennsylvania Law Journal* of 1846 put it, Americans had none of "that prejudice against foreign systems of law, merely because they are foreign, which is all-powerful in England." And William Wetmore Storey, describing his father's legal philosophy, declared, "As America takes to itself and naturalizes the people of all nations, who seek its protection, thereby creating a composite people," so Associate Justice Joseph Storey thought "it should be cosmopolitan in its jurisprudence, and embody into its law all good rules and principles, whatever might be their birthplace."

Much of the Supreme Court's rise to prominence as an arbiter of union is well known. Resting on the ambiguities of Article III of the Constitution, which left it largely at the mercy of Congress and the executive branch, the Court only gradually attained power. And yet, beginning with the passage of the Judiciary Act of 1789, it survived the crises arising out of the Alien and Sedition Acts, such as the impeachment trial of Justice Samuel Chase, the midnight Federalist appointment of judges that led to *Marbury v. Madison* in 1803, and the treason trial of Aaron Burr, whose acquittal incurred the wrath of President Jefferson. Gradually, and with the utmost caution, the Court established itself as an independent branch of the government charged with interpreting the traditions of the law.

In large measure this achievement was due to the efforts of John Marshall, a Virginia lawyer and Federalist, appointed Chief Justice at the last moment by outgoing president John Adams. His fellow Virginian, Jefferson, hated Marshall. Nobody ever took office under less auspicious conditions, and yet through an almost miraculous combination of forcefulness, restraint, and sheer personality, Marshall from 1801 to 1835 made the Court a powerful vehicle of nationalism. A plain but charming man who liked to pitch quoits and drink home brew on the green at Richmond, Marshall nonetheless possessed a keen intellect. He was a wise selector of associate justices, a clever and sophisticated legal stylist, and a man unflinchingly dedicated to the Union.

In a memorable series of cases including *Marbury v. Madison* (1803), *McCullough v. Maryland* (1819), *The Cohens v. Virginia* (1825) and *Gibbons v.*

Ogden (1825), Marshall and the Court established the principle of judicial review and, most important, the supremacy of the federal government over the state governments in matters where the Constitution had assigned authority for "necessary and proper" action to the federal government. In these matters, Marshall's basic principles were as follows:

1. The Federal government derives its authority from the people, not from the states (the prime Federalist Party principle). Thus the Constitution is not a compact of states but an ordinance of the people.
2. The Constitution must be interpreted with a view to securing a beneficial use of the powers the federal government has been granted, not for the purpose of safeguarding state sovereignty.
3. The Constitution is a document for all times and thus must be flexible enough to meet the demands of the future; therefore it may be broadly interpreted.
4. Though the government under the Constitution is one of enumerated powers, it is nonetheless sovereign as to these powers, and in all things pertaining to the implementation of those powers.
5. The power of Congress to regulate commerce is an exclusive power; no state may interfere.

Thus Marshall contributed immeasurably to strengthening the power of the central government through his legal philosophy. In addition, through his protection of the right of private contract in such cases as *Fletcher v. Peck* (1810) and the *Dartmouth College Case* (1819), Marshall went far toward securing the allegiance of the rapidly growing landed and commercial classes to the federal government, since it guaranteed property rights under the law.

Most of Marshall's decisions were negative. That is, they prevented states, monopolists, and other powerful institutional groups from interfering with the federal government, which he saw as the guardian of the people. By arguing for broader federal powers to aid in the growth of the republic, he expressed thoughts that coincided with those of Hamilton, the Careys, and others who saw government and business as a partnership. And by striking down interference with the right of commerce and contract, Marshall helped fashion the law to promote free entrepreneurship on the broadest scale. This was to be characteristic of American legal thought on all levels until well into the twentieth century. The law thus was not passive in nineteenth-century America but instead became an active instrument of free and legal economic growth.

Beyond this, Marshall had a distinctly cosmopolitan outlook on the law itself. A highly competent legal scholar, well versed in international law, he looked first for a set of absolute principles that underlie each individual question, then proceeded to relate the situational or substantive features of the case to the personal statement principle, basing his decisions on a syllogistic logic that was, however, consistent with his overall nationalistic aims. Thus, in his view, each individual decision was based on a logic so sound that it would have held up in any court under any legal system in any country or culture. Given this devotion to the syllogism and a Newtonian structure of logic, it is almost paradoxical that Marshall also saw the Constitution as an evolving, flexible instrument that looked toward the future. Almost paradoxical—but not quite, because for Marshall, as for most other legal scholars of the time, the law took its cue from science, and science, since at least the days of Newton and Franklin, consisted of seeking out the underlying principles of nature, then using them to construct a hypothesis with which to manipulate nature. If man could thus manipulate nature, he could bring about change, progress, and societal growth. Like Franklin, Marshall was no Burkean conservative, but an Enlightenment-bred believer in science and progress.

This same scientific spirit prevailed on all levels of the law and the emerging legal profession. Tapping Reeve and James Gould, founders of the first American law school, at Litchfield, Connecticut, in 1784, regarded the law as "a system of connected rational principles"—in short, a "science." So did all the other formidable legal scholars who taught law at Harvard, William and Mary, Columbia, and Yale. Perhaps the most outstanding of all these men who conducted "the search for a 'national law' [that] actually brought a national law into being" was Joseph Storey. An Associate Justice of the Supreme Court and close friend of John Marshall's, Storey was also the first professor of law at Harvard. His works were many—volumes on the law of bailments, partnership, agency, bills of exchange, promissory notes, equity pleading to constitutional law, conflict of laws, and equity jurisprudence—but his philosophy was simple and much like Marshall's. He based his research on English common law and found usable principles in the thousands of English cases he could apply to new American situations—or any situation, for that matter, because the law was a science and part of nature. Once one located the basic classificatory principles of nature, all species of problems fit into proper categories. It was as simple as Linnaeus's botanical system.

Following such pioneers as Nathan Dane, whose eight-volume *General Abridgement and Digest of American Law* (1823) was the comprehensive survey of law for the new nation, scholars such as Joseph Storey and especially New York Chancellor James Kent did massive research into all forms of law and derived the general national legal principles by which Americans lived. Kent, for example, in his monumental, four-volume *Commentaries on American Law* (1823–1830), included not only a survey of English and American precedents, but also those from the ancient world and the Code Napoleon as well. All of these works were essentially the products of Enlightenment cosmopolitanism, with its affinity for the general principle and its assumption that men everywhere were very much alike.

During this Jacksonian period of the early republic, a bitter struggle ensued between the legal scholars, who wished to derive precedents from existing English common law and European statutes, and the Jeffersonian Republicans, who believed that common law and ancient precedent should be cast aside in favor of "codification," or starting anew, like the Constitution-makers. Jefferson was one of the most vehement of "codifiers." In a letter to Edmund Randolph in 1799, he wrote, "Of all the doctrines which have ever been broached by the Federal government this novel one of the Common Law being in force and cognizable as an existing law in their [the Federalists'] courts, is to me the most formidable." The real irony was that basically they were both on the same side. The legal scholars did not wish to slavishly imitate foreign practice. They were simply being inductive and sorting through the data for principles applicable to America. Likewise, when they turned their hand to it, as did David Dudley Field of New York with his mammoth *New York State Code of Procedure* (1849), the codifiers came out in the same place. What they were up against, of course, was the nature of the law itself—a regularizing procedure that guaranteed people that governmental conditions would, as much as possible, be the same tomorrow as they were today. Their objective, whether scholars or codifiers, was to avoid the whim or caprice government of monarchy or anarchy, or special interests, so that each common man knew where he stood. The converse, monarchy or special private interests, was to both parties "unnatural."

As it turned out, the common law scholars generally triumphed out of sheer industry, and with their triumph came a "science of the law," relative uniformity, and an enormously flexible, some would say pragmatic, instrument for use in the development of the nation. Once ascertained, principles could be wheeled in any direction. The best example of this was the work of Lemuel Shaw, Chief Justice of Massachusetts. Shaw, an incredible worker, delivered 2,200 opinions in his lifetime and "made the common law a strong ally of industrial progress" between 1830 and 1860. His most important contributions related to the problem posed by the new steam railroads. Since the trains enjoyed a monopoly of the tracks, they were unlike any previously existing common carrier. If they were to succeed, they had to proceed cross-country without obstruction.

In *Boston Water Power Co. v. Boston and Worcester Railroad* (1835), Shaw ruled that the State of Massachusetts had a right to grant the railroad a charter to cross the property of the Boston Water Power Co. even though the latter had been granted the right to its property by the same state legislature. In so ruling, Shaw invoked the principle of eminent domain. He ruled that the railroads, just the same as the power company, were public utilities, and both had been granted their contract or charters because they were projects in the public interest. The ruling in this and a subsequent case, *Fuller v. Dane* (1836), greatly broadened the state's role in the regulation of all property, and it represented a new view of contracts. Whereas Marshall's court had tended to view charters and contracts as sacred and inviolable, as in the *Dartmouth College Case* (1819), Shaw, on the state level, saw them as much more derivative of the state assemblies. Thus if it were in the public interest, the state could appropriate property already held under contract by private individuals or publicly chartered service corporations. For Shaw, the "general welfare," a slippery special-interest term, was the prime concern, and as American society became more complex, he believed it necessary that the law become more tolerant and legislatures have more freedom to promote the general good as politicians, often paid by special interests, even today, saw it. Under his tenure, all sorts of state functions expanded, including the power to regulate banks, shipping docks, liquor traffic, and houses of prostitution. Indeed, Shaw believed in social experimentation. In the important case of *Commonwealth v. Hunt* (1842), he adduced a principle from the common law that found the Boston Journeymen Bootmakers Society not guilty of criminal conspiracy in restraint of trade.

In short, Shaw discovered many new kinds of property ranging from the eminent domain of common carriers to the right to property in one's own labor, possessed by the Boston Bootmakers. But he also continually related to the public interest the legitimacy of property and the contracts that supported them. Contracts, though solemn and important, were not sacred or immutable. In going along with the state legislature, however, Shaw, even more than Marshall, Storey, Kent, et al., tended to encourage the granting of more and more charters of incorporation, which in turn—by the state court's very lack of interference—tended to promote galloping entrepreneurship in early America. State assemblies could grant as many charters, rights of eminent domain, etc., as they wished. They could also regulate these in the public interest and, if they were farsighted, include provisions for amendment or extinction for poor performance. Few legislatures—which were the creatures of lobbies—did the latter. Instead they multiplied corporations, duplicated public utilities, and chartered banks and transportation lines with reckless and ruthless abandon, as well as "regulating" practically everything. By 1835, however, the economy, with the courts largely passive, was booming. Andrew Jackson professed to oppose such excesses—especially favored chartered corpor0ations and the "artificial property" they engendered. The ambiguity of this stance was never better illustrated than in the *Charles River Bridge Case* (1830–1836), decided by Jackson Chief Justice Roger B. Taney. Here Massachusetts had granted one group exclusive rights to bridge transportation across the Charles River because it was in the public interest to promote the building of such a bridge. Later a second group built another bridge across the Charles, and a long and difficult lawsuit followed. Ultimately Taney and the U.S. Supreme Court ruled in favor of the second group because a second bridge was in the public interest. No charter, however sacred, could block the public interest. Thus, ironically, in view of Jackson's principles, the Taney Court, just as Shaw's state court rulings had done, threw open incorporation to vastly increased numbers of would-be entrepreneurs.

By the age of Jackson, economic and technological developments had become so complex that charters and contracts were extremely ambiguous legal concepts, though all continued to pay homage to them as corner-stones of the republic. Though Shaw could write in 1854 that "the common law consists in a few broad and comprehensive principles, founded on reason, natural justice, and enlightened public policy, modified and adopted to the circumstances of all the particular cases that fall within it," he knew full well that the "go-getters" and the politicos had prevailed over the rigidities of the Enlightenment rules of property. Individual case law and its precedents entered the American legal system. More and more men saw the possibilities of gaining through politics and legal toleration a "stake in society." This greatly enhanced their allegiance to the American experiment under the modified "broad principles" from which they prospered—or hoped to prosper.

CHAPTER SIX

Reform, New Religions, and Nativism

A general ferment in American life swept over the northern states from 1820 to the Civil War. For many people, the heritage of the American Revolution, if it had ever been forgotten, rose strikingly to the fore as masses of immigrants entered the country and ever-larger cities sprouted up. The extraordinarily rapid growth and complication of society at all times seemed to confront the citizen of a new America, and with this process came serious and depressing social problems never dreamed of by the Founding Fathers, who lived in an essentially agrarian society. Charles Loring Brace, an early reformer, vividly remembered his impressions of the "centers of crime and misery" in old New York. As he strolled about the city, he was aghast at the "rag-pickers den" along Pitt and Willard streets, where children became "outcasts and thieves," or Cherry and Water streets, where little girls entered prostitution at an early age. In the city's lower wards stood rows of "thieves' lodging houses," schools for crime where the old taught the young in real-life heartbreaking Dickensian dramas. Sixteenth and Seventeenth streets were widely known as Poverty Lane and accepted as such by the inhabitants with all the nonchalance and docility of a stereotypical African slave. And the newest immigrants were, of course, the lowest and most displaced of all. Dutch Hill on the East Side around Forty-second Street and Corlear's Hook housed the newly arrived Germans, whose specialty was copper-picking and wood-thievery. The Italians congregated in the Sixth Ward, their produce carts lining streets heavy with poverty, which was lightened occasionally by the sound of the street organ, the concertina, and the spontaneous aria—vestiges of the rich culture they had left behind that was little understood in the New World their countrymen had found.

Such scenes could be multiplied all along the eastern seaboard from Baltimore to Boston, and on a smaller scale in western New York's Erie Canal towns, in Pittsburgh and Cincinnati and the rising metropolises of Chicago, St. Louis, and New Orleans. To many Americans, progress was a culture shock, and in large measure the striking predominance of evangelical religion, romantic nature philosophy, and Jacksonian egalitarian politics in the period can be attributed to a reaction to the rise of complexity and the mercantile-technological growth that produced it. Rural and agricultural life was rapidly breaking down in the East. Towns were becoming cities. Large masses of people clustered together and ministered to a rising business civilization. And people found it more and more difficult to deal with all their problems as a family, or even as a church congregation oriented toward the charismatic minister in a personal way. The failure of Charles G. Finney's Broadway Tabernacle church in 1837 was symbolic of this social process. Relationships were becoming increasingly impersonal and tangential.

And so Americans resurrected some of the techniques and outlooks of the eighteenth century that arose out of English life during a similar period in that country's evolution. They adopted a philosophy of environmentalism and set about creating new institutions to replace what they regarded as the outworn or pernicious institutions they saw around them. The thought process was simple and Lockean—change the institutions, change the environment, change the person. Thus, while romanticism provided critiques and transcendental ideals, and evangelism supplied the fervor, whipping up visions of America's soon-to-be realized millennial destiny, to a large degree business organizations provided the model for reform, especially after Andrew Jackson removed the odium of monopoly from corporations and business combinations. Like members of corporations, reformers could come together voluntarily in institutions to solve social problems without invariably becoming professionals in the field. As they

did so, reform inevitably became more secularized. The ex-Puritan, bourgeois eighteenth-century printer Benjamin Franklin illustrated the process.
In Philadelphia, one recalls, he organized different groups of people to
found a free library, a college, a hospital, a firefighting company, an insurance company, a cultural club, and a world-famous scientific society. He
was also interested in using the agencies of government to further these
ends. For example, the American Philosophical Society itself was a chartered corporation. Observing the tremendous drive toward the creation of
such reform institutions in the Jacksonian era, Tocqueville, sent to examine
the American prison system, remarked, "In a democracy, where everyone is
relatively weak such organizations were essential to accomplish anything of
significance." That such institutionalized reform movements had become
paramount in American life by the Civil War is attested to in a somewhat
disdainful manner by British novelist Anthony Trollope as he recorded his
travels in America in 1862:

> "Have you seen any of our great institutions, sir?" That of course is a
> question that is put to every Englishman who has visited New York,
> and the Englishman who intends to say that he has seen New York,
> should visit many of them. I went to schools, hospitals, lunatic asy-
> lums, institutes for deaf and dumb, water works, historical societies,
> telegraph offices, and large commercial establishments. I rather think
> I did my work in a thorough and conscientious manner.

Though to Trollope this seemed a somewhat trying experience, to
Americans, as the quotation implies, institutional reform was exciting. It
was an action reflective of the basic scientific rhythm of an American society that looked always toward building, toward the future, toward perfection, and in those days toward the millennium.

I

In the early nineteenth-century "age of reform," American thinkers also
turned to the problem of children. Horace Bushnell, the Transcendentalist
clergyman from Hartford, Connecticut, in his influential book *Christian*

Nurture (1847), took a Rousseauian view of the importance of early child-hood in the development of the adult, and urged parents to inculcate proper Christian values in the child by means of the family. To Bushnell no instruction was quite as important as family instruction, and much of it consisted of developing the intuitive sense of right and wrong that tran-scended the rote learning of the school and the institutionally derived training. If the young learned right from wrong early and without institu-tional fetter, they would become good Christians.

In contrast to Bushnell stood Horace Mann of Massachusetts. As a boy Horace Mann had been nurtured in poverty, dullness, and terror—poverty at home, dullness at school, and terror on Sunday, when the Congregation-alist minister frightened him to death with fire-and-brimstone sermons promising perdition to all. It is no wonder that all his life he stood staunchly opposed to such idle amusements as lotteries, liquor, profanity, smoking, and ballet dancing. Despite all of these early disadvantages, Mann graduated from Brown University with highest honors in three years and then distinguished himself at the Litchfield Law School. By 1827, eight years after he graduated from college, Mann was a member of the Massa-chusetts Senate and pushed through a bill creating the Massachusetts State Board of Education, an instrument for reforming the schools of the Bay State. So interested was Mann in the project that he resigned from the Sen-ate and accepted the secretaryship of the Board of Education, thus begin-ning the reform career for which he is justly famous.

Over a twelve-year period, Mann transformed the Massachusetts school system into a model for most other states to follow. In effect, the world his-tory of public education begins with Mann. In detail, his were the most im-portant educational ideas before the coming of William Torrey Harris and John Dewey. Mann's philosophy was essentially simple Jeffersonianism. He believed that an educated citizenry was essential to democracy and that the more people were educated, the greater the informed participation in af-fairs of public concern. He also believed very strongly that the Bible should be read in the schools, either as a piece of literature or with no comment whatsoever. Thus seeing the school as a powerful lever for transforming society, he also sought, in the highly religious state of Massachusetts, to bring about the secularization of education. This was in direct contrast to traditional practice and the Christian nurture ideas of Bushnell.

Essentially, though he wrote a series of highly influential annual reports, Mann's ideas, as befitted a zealous reformer, were best reflected in his actions. He first rallied public opinion, organizing annual education conventions that, besides professionalizing teaching, also served to inform the public as to the purposes, needs, and value of public education. He established teachers' colleges, or normal schools, emphasizing teacher training and the professional status of the teacher. This resulted in a 62 percent raise in teachers' salaries and helped him secure their cooperation. At the same time he established the *Common School Journal* to broadcast the ideas of professional educators, thereby starting what may well be an irreversible trend.

With regard to the schools themselves, Mann successfully accomplished their secularization, the Bible notwithstanding. He also pushed through a compulsory minimum school year of six months for all children, thereby bringing into being the new institution of truant officer and putting another crime on the books. He revived the idea of the high school and established fifty throughout the state while doubling the annual education budget. Quiet and unspectacular but effective, Mann accomplished these fundamental educational changes: he secularized the schools, he created mass public education and made it compulsory, and he organized and professionalized the role of the teacher. On the latter count alone he deserved the immortality accorded him by professional educators and teachers' college presidents everywhere. Teaching now promised to be the professional equal of law, medicine, and theology. It remained only to develop a scientific technique of its own.

It is impossible to overestimate the impact of Mann's ideas and work. Such men as Henry Barnard of Connecticut followed in his footsteps, as did his successor in Massachusetts, Samuel Reed Hall. Trained teachers from these state systems spread out all over the country, spawning a craze for normal schools, professionalism, compulsory education, and truant officers of the kind that would so plague Huckleberry Finn and his friend Tom Sawyer. New England's Protestant ethic, shorn of particular religious connotations, was broadcast on a mass scale. In some ways the transformation of the schools and the creation for the first time in world history of mass free public education in mid-nineteenth-century America did more to create a common national spirit than all the literary and oratorical rhetoric.

But while Mann was dealing with normal schools and normal children, Charles Loring Brace of Litchfield, Connecticut, and Yale University could never forget the waifs and potential Oliver Twists of Corlear's Hook, Dutch Hill, and Poverty Row. After studying in Berlin, taking a walking trip through Europe, and briefly being incarcerated in Hungary as a result of his support of the defeated revolutionary patriot Louis Kossuth, Brace came back to turn his attention to the mass problem of juvenile delinquency. He became the most effective reformer in the nineteenth century in this difficult field.

Brace, however, was not the first to enter the field, and the early history of American society's response to its delinquent children is a case study in American cosmopolitanism both ways across the Atlantic. A pioneer in the treatment of the problem was John Griscom of New York, a chemistry teacher who had observed juvenile reform institutions at Hoxton, England, and at Hofwyl, Switzerland. While rejecting the elitism of the Upper School at Hofwyl, Griscom became enamored of the trade school for reform where problem children of the lower classes were placed. He returned to New York convinced that juvenile offenders and vagrants should not be housed with hardened criminals but, in Beccarian fashion, should be placed in a separate institution where they could be reformed, rescued through retraining in a gainful occupation.

By 1823 he had joined forces with Isaac Collins, who had also studied the English experiment, and James W. Garard, a crusading young lawyer interested in children. Together they persuaded the city and state governments of New York to create the New York House of Refuge in 1824, modeled after the English and Swiss experiments. It was the beginning of juvenile reform in America. By 1826 Massachusetts had followed suit and passed a law requiring orphan children to be placed in the House of Refuge, hoping to prevent juvenile crime before it happened. By 1828 Philadelphia also had imitated the New York model. On their tour through America, Gustave de Beaumont and Alexis de Tocqueville studied especially these institutions for reforming juveniles and making them useful members of society. In 1833 while on a trip to England, Joseph Tuckerman, a minister at large to the poor in Massachusetts, aroused the enthusiasm of Mary Carpenter, who in 1846 opened the first "ragged school" in England at Bristol. This led to the Ragged School Union in 1848 and eventually to the creation of the first government-sponsored system of public education in England, authorized by the Forster Education Act of 1870. Carpenter's *Reformatory Schools for the Children of the Perishing and Dangerous Classes, and for Juvenile Offenders* (1851) in turn had a marked effect on American thinking about the problem of abandoned and wayward children. She thus handed America's contribution back again with interest. In 1853, influenced by Carpenter and by his own religious inclinations, Brace founded the New York Children's Aid Society. Backed by the city's wealthiest people, this institution persisted from that day onward and was doubtless visited by Anthony Trollope while "doing his duty" on his American tour. Brace began by opening a school and a meeting house for orphan and slum children right in the heart of the slum area. He also enlisted the aid of volunteer teacher missionaries to recruit and interest wayward children in his school. Brace's plan was to prevent delinquency through rescuing the destitute. His philosophy was "self-help is the best help." He invariably tried to teach the children a useful trade. Along these lines he organized the famous Newsboys Lodging Houses where the homeless boys, who earned a living by selling newspapers, could live, self-sufficiently, by paying a token sum for room and board. Moreover, they were educated and instructed in moral principles. There also lived Horatio Alger, who gathered material for his widely popular rags-to-riches success stories that did perhaps more than anything to help the New York Children's Aid Society. His stories also provided moral roads to success for the newsboys as well as encouragement.

In addition to the lodging house, Brace also established industrial schools, night schools, special schools for wayward girls, sanctuaries for sick children, and summer camps—the forerunners of today's Fresh Air Camps—that brought children out of the crowded city and its occasions of sin into clean "transcendental" nature. In this way he anticipated the Boy Scouts by a number of years, and his operation was coeducational.

The most spectacular and yet controversial of Brace's projects stemmed from his conversations with Horace Bushnell. Convinced by Bushnell that the family was the ideal unit for reform and rehabilitation of orphaned and delinquent children, Brace placed thousands of children in foster homes. Beyond this, he sent them west under the care of agents to frontier families in great numbers, and in so doing he generated a juvenile westward movement approaching in magnitude the California Gold Rush. All this was done in the implicit belief that the frontier and a new life out in nature would be especially beneficial to the children. He had anticipated the ideas of Frederick Jackson Turner by nearly half a century, and his operation was living proof of the safety-valve theory in action (lessening the evils of crowded cities by sending the poor to the uncrowded West), though Turner apparently never knew of its existence.

For starting a "children's cavalcade to the West," Brace was severely attacked. Some westerners accused him of dumping undesirables and criminals in God's country. Others implied that he sold them as a source of cheap labor, while the Catholic Church and other denominations berated him for forcing the young away from their traditional church into alien, pagan, or heretical environments. Still Brace persisted, and some one hundred thousand children went west in frontier history's least publicized mass migration.

An enormously creative, dedicated, and energetic man, Brace also managed to write at least three books that are worth remembering: *The Best Method of Disposing of Our Pauper and Vagrant Children* (1859), *Short Sermons to Newsboys* (1866), and *The Dangerous Classes of New York* (1872). Bourgeois in his values, patrician in his bearing and outlook on life, Brace represented still another dimension of American reform that rapidly came to the fore in the nineteenth century—private philanthropy on a significant scale. Such private philanthropy has been unmatched by any country in the world. It is the other side of the capitalism coin.

In addition to the crusades for children's rights, prison reform, peace, octagon-shaped houses touted by the phrenologist Orson Fowler for healthier living, and Sylvester Graham's one-man health-food mission, which resulted in the invention of the graham cracker, another institutional reform that captivated the masses in the antebellum period was temperance. This crusade was spearheaded by the Washingtonian Movement, which began in a curious way. On April 2, 1840, six convivial souls were enjoying themselves at Chases' Tavern in Baltimore when they were accosted by a temperance lecturer. According to one account, the barkeep was rude and sarcastic to the temperance man, whereupon the happy six had a change of heart. They befriended the underdog, listened to what he had to say, took his reform message to heart, and formed the Washingtonian Temperance Society. They were almost immediately successful. Employing reformed drunkards as speakers and charging twenty-five cents a head to hear them and join the society, by the end of 1840 the Washingtonian Society had nearly one thousand members in Baltimore alone. The movement spread rapidly to other states, and in the same year, they signed up two thousand people in New York and three thousand in hard-drinking Boston.

Chapters of the Temperance Society, heavily populated with female reformers and blacks, formed all over the North. Their meetings were like city revivals with all the fervor of an evangelical camp meeting. The same people were often involved, and the same process of public confession of sin and public redemption took place. In one sense, the temperance revival took the place of ordinary evangelism in the big cities. Its issue was more visceral, so to speak. Psychologically the temperance revival had a quasireligious function. Secular though it was, it involved a moral catharsis for the reformed drunkard.

By 1843 the Washingtonian Movement numbered half a million members. It linked up with the Reverend Thomas Hunt's children's crusade, founded in 1839. Hunt's periodical, the *Cold Water Army*, sustained the campaign with stirring poems, such as the following:

> We do not think
> We'll ever drink
> Whiskey or Gin
> Brandy or Rum or anything
> That'll Make Drunk Come.

This was supplemented in 1845 by a songbook, the *Washington Teetotalers Minstrel*, featuring such songs as "Dear Father, Drink No More," "Mother Dry that Flowing Tear," and "The Rum Sellers' Lament." In 1845 the Washingtonians signed up hundreds of soldiers bound for the front in the Mexican War. Something of their impact can be gained from the following letter written by one of those soldiers:

> They have a Temperance Reading Room here, and I allow it was more for the sake of reading the papers than anything else that I have for the first time in my life joined a Washington Total Abstinence Society, but the pledge I have taken and mean to the end of my time [to]

keep sacred. The importance of keeping from drinking hard in this climate was strongly impressed in my mind the other day just after I came to the hospital. A man [who] had been on guard duty and had been drinking to excess for several days was brought into the hospital in a fit of delirium tremens from the effects of drinking so much in this hot climate. His bowels were in a state of mortification. After he was bled freely, he came to his reason. The doctors told him he must die. He made his will, and soon after he was raving in delirium. He had a strong constitution, and he struggled fearfully with death. All that night and the next day he was cursing and trying [to] leap out of his bed; it took four men to hold him down. At sun-down he came to his reason and begged for something to eat; it was Death knawing [*sic*] at his vitals. One hour more—he was raving; in another—he was dead.

Most important, the Washingtonian crusade had its effect on public policy in the form of laws. Between 1841 and 1852 no liquor licenses were granted in Boston and no liquor was sold in one hundred towns in the state. In 1846 Maine passed the first statewide Prohibition Act. Vermont followed suit in 1852, as did Rhode Island, Michigan, and the Minnesota Territory. In 1854–1855, New York, Connecticut, New Hampshire, Tennessee, Delaware, Illinois, Indiana, Iowa, and Wisconsin voted to climb aboard the cold-water wagon. Though the Civil War and its enforced excitement soon ended Prohibition, the short history of the Washingtonian Movement made one thing clear: such mass pressure groups could and did have a decided effect on public policy. By 1880 Timothy Shay Arthur had published the *Uncle Tom's Cabin* of the Temperance Movement: *Ten Nights in a Bar-Room and What I Saw There.*

No longer was the state, especially in the North, a static system of checks and balances that existed within the limits of prescriptive society. Rather, the federal government itself became involved in national reform perhaps more clearly than any other development in the early republic. Could a nation dedicated to liberty and a culture built on the mingling of lifestyles long endure if the lifestyles seemed antithetical to the nation's primacy and the quantity of new people threatened a virtual transfusion of the country's blood and spirit? Or would America prove large enough to contain all these multitudes, and would its culture be the richer for the complex dimensions Catholicism introduced?

II

The earliest Catholic clergy in America were Jesuits, one of whom visited the Separatist outpost at Salem during the time of evangelist Roger Williams. For a time when Lord Baltimore ruled Maryland, priests were of course a fairly common sight in that colony. But by 1784 only a band of ex-Jesuits, not even acknowledged by the Pope, formed the backbone of faith in America. Six years later, in 1790, however, the Reverend John Carroll, a cousin of the Founding Father, was named the first official Catholic bishop in the new United States. By that time there were about twenty-five thousand Roman Catholics in America. In 1791 the ex-Jesuits, with Carroll's help, founded Georgetown University. At the outset, however, for the first decades of the nineteenth century, most Catholic clergy were not native Americans. Rather, they were Frenchmen, primarily of the Saint Sulpician Order. Some of them had fled the French Revolution, while others had simply been sent to America in response to urgent pleas from Carroll and his small band of successors. By and large, the French clergy were extremely energetic and hence successful in establishing the Church in an America that once saw its darkest day looming at the threat of even an Anglican episcopacy in the New World. Such men as William Duboury, Ambrose Morichal, Benedict Flaget, Jean Dubois, and Jean-Louis Lefevre de Cheverus became rectors of colleges and bishops of newly formed dioceses as Catholicism spread out of Maryland to Philadelphia, New Orleans, Boston, St. Louis, Bardstown, Kentucky, and most generally throughout the Old Northwest and eastern seaboard. Duboury founded a seminary that became St. Louis University, while an American woman, Elizabeth Seton, turned from Episcopalianism to Roman Catholicism, where she founded female academies and the Sisters of Charity, who began to staff a rapidly developing system of parochial schools. She came to be called Mother Seton and is regarded by many as America's first Catholic saint.

By 1808 there were about eighty thousand Roman Catholics in America, just as the great German and Irish immigrations began. In 1829 Bishop

James Whitfield convoked the first American Provincial Council to try to coordinate church matters in the new country. At that time there were six seminaries; nine colleges, three of which were universities; thirty-three monasteries and convents; and houses for Dominicans, Jesuits, Sulpicians, and the Congregation of the Mission, all ministering to some two hundred thousand faithful. Thanks to the Irish immigration, by 1850 there were some 1.75 million Catholics in America and it had become the country's largest organized religion.

This phenomenal growth, of course, was tied to ethnicity, and it made the Church seem a foreign religion since it was governed by the Roman pope. And certainly mass ethnicity predominated in the Church. But before the Civil War there were also some eight hundred thousand converts from the more nativist religions. Unlike so many of the Protestant denominations, Catholicism was not exclusivist. It welcomed and indeed eagerly proselytized one and all. The religion's theological structure made this relatively easy. One did not have to have a "conversion experience"; he did not have to see God or pass through the ecstasies of the jerks, the barks, and the catatonic trances; he did not have to publicly confess his sinful unworthiness and grovel before ministers, congregation, and God; and he did not have to base his religious conversion on a sense of everlasting guilt or extremely precarious innocence. The sacramental ladder, which included nonimmersion baptism, confirmation, the Lord's Supper, penance, holy orders, matrimony, and the last rites of "extreme unction," at no point freighted the individual with unpardonable guilt—or even public humiliation. Penance, in particular, afforded the Roman Catholic who sinned a chance to start over without suffering the severe psychological traumas of the fundamentalists. It is perhaps not surprising that Roman Catholics appeared to be more happy-go-lucky than most religious people, and that the religion, which was one of hope, attracted so many converts. Certainly there was something just a bit incongruous about people coming to the abundant land of opportunity and then embracing a religious faith that counseled despair and fostered guilt—two qualities that yet remain characteristic of a Protestant America that modern theologian Reinhold Niebuhr has labeled "the children of light and the children of darkness."

But insofar as Roman Catholicism and its growth in America was so intimately bound with ethnicity, it suffered severe problems. Within the

Church, it soon became apparent that German Catholics were scornful of Irish Catholics and vice versa, while both groups resented domination by the French clergy. Bishop John Hughes, consecrated in New York in 1837, outspoken though he was, proved to be perhaps the most widely admired and politically powerful clergyman in the country by 1850. Gradually, however, the Church sorted out its ethnic problems—the Irish gained their Irish clergy, the Germans, their German clergy, and a new breed of American-born clergy rose to the fore. All the while, of course, all members of the faith were made aware that they belonged to a universal—a cosmopolitan church that by its very doctrine could really observe no national boundaries or nationalities. The latter, however, at the same time continually raised another basic question that Catholics in America have never completely solved. How could they square their religious faith with the demand that they be "good Americans"? From the beginning, foreign clergymen struggled with local church trustees over control of parishes and dioceses, with the latter group concerned primarily with keeping power vested in the local congregation of the faithful.

The First Plenary Council, which assembled in Baltimore in 1852, addressed itself directly to the Church and state on the Americanization question, declaring, "Obey the public authorities, not only for wrath but for conscience sake. Show your attachment to the institutions of our beloved country." It was an amplification of Christ's injunction to "render unto Caesar the things that are Caesar's and to God the things that are God's." American Church leaders also recognized the immense potential the constitutional doctrine of separation of church and state afforded. Their major confrontation with Protestants came over what was deemed to be lack of adherence to this doctrine in such things as the Protestantizing of public education. Out of the First Plenary Council of 1852, however, came not only a policy concerning relations between church and state, but also a reorganizing and restructuring of the church and even a clarification of the faith in America. The latter was symbolized by the blue-backed Baltimore Catechism, perhaps the most widely distributed and influential religious book in America next to the Bible.

In the 1840s and '50s, the Church began to attract to its ranks men of real vision and intellectual power. Bishop Hughes of New York, sensitive to the Latin culture of Mexico, served as an American negotiator and adviser

during the Mexican War, placing a chain wherever he could on the Democratic Party's war dogs of Manifest Destiny. Powerful Transcendentalist
preacher Orestes Brownson joined the Church in 1844, seeing in it not
only an institution that ministered to his beloved working classes, but also a
profoundly based theology that, thanks to the doctrine of Pierre Leroux, a
Saint Simonean, seemed to square with his transcendentalist leanings. Leroux's doctrine was pure romanticism. Man was both "subject and object,"
and his well-being depended upon a universal mystical communion with
God, nature, and his fellow men. This was, of course, the meaning of the
Lord's Supper. Brownson was further influenced by the Italian Vincenzo
Gioberti, who convinced him to abandon the German language in favor of
"ontology," which he declared enabled man to intuit his own being, which
was God. This was not far from Ralph Waldo Emerson's belief that men
could become "part or parcel of God" and certainly close to Johann Got-
tlieb Fichte's identification of man's will with God's will, had Gioberti only
known it. To Brownson, of course, such transcendental ideas rang true, and
his conversion also brought some institutionalized order to what had been
only a vague Concord inspiration.

   Isaac Hecker, a German baker and veteran of the Brook Farm and Fruitlands utopias, also followed Brownson's path. He, too, converted to Catholicism and founded the Paulist Order, which specially ministered to the poor.
He wrote several important books, such as *Questions of the Soul* (1855) and
Aspirations of Nature (1857), which Professor Sydney Ahlstrom (the leading
authority on American religions) has characterized as "genuinely persuasive
portrayal[s] of Catholicism as an answer to man's spiritual dilemmas and as a
fulfillment and guarantee of democracy's highest ideals." It was relatively
easy for the transcendentalist Hecker to relate Church doctrine that each
man is made "in the image and likeness of God" and possesses the same immortal soul to the American faith in democracy and individualism.

   In the 1840s and '50s, however, the rest of America seemed scarcely inclined to agree with Hecker's statements. Instead a virulent nativist movement arose in reaction to the "Catholic invasion." In part the nativist
movement reflected an Anglo-Saxon racial contempt for the "bog-trotting"
Irish that, like many other things in early America, aped English convention. It was also a product of class warfare, in which the upper- and middle-
class elite felt threatened by the "mudsill" masses and resented the

possibility that they too might climb the social ladder. In all of this fear and resentment, the Church was regarded as the agent provocateur of social and racial revolution—the overthrow of the Anglo-Saxon Protestant middle-class establishment. Usually the struggle pitted Whigs against Democrats, who drew their strength, according to Professor Lee Benson's study, from the Irish immigrant class.

At first the nativist campaign was a paper war. The *New York Observer,* the *Protestant,* and the *Protestant Vindicator* were founded for the purpose of lashing the Pope's legions. Catholics retaliated with the *United States Catholic Miscellany, Brownson's Quarterly,* and the *Catholic Tract Society.* Lyman Beecher, that mighty evangelist, got so carried away with the Catholic threat to seize the West that in 1834 he stopped berating Boston Unitarians long enough to write *A Plea for the West* (1834), to raise funds for the Lane Theological Seminary in Cincinnati as the only bulwark against Catholic usurpation of the entire Mississippi Valley. In the same year Samuel F. B. Morse, who was a successful painter and who invented the telegraph, also entered the lists against the Pope—reportedly because someone knocked off his hat as he gazed at a religious procession in Rome. Morse's volume was titled *Foreign Conspiracy against the Liberties of the United States* (1841). In 1836 he was defeated as a nativist candidate for New York City mayor.

Far more interesting than the diatribes of Beecher and Morse, however, was the nativist "horror literature." Rebecca Theresa Reed, a well-known woman of Boston, wrote *Six Months in a Convent* (1835), which became a lurid best seller. An even more widely known work was Maria Monk's *Awful Disclosures of the Hotel Dieu Nunnery of Montreal* (1836), which was published and partly written by anti-Catholic clerics and lawyers in New York City. This successful work naturally was followed up by *Further Disclosures* in 1837 and a competing publication, *The Escape of Sainte Frances Patrick, Another Nun from the Hotel Dieu Nunnery of Montreal* (1836). Monk herself was arrested for picking the pocket of a fellow inmate in a New York house of ill fame and died in prison. The appeal of the "horror books" was, of course, due as much to their relatively open "prurient interest" in a Victorian age as it was to the instincts of religious bigotry. If one wrote about seduction, rape, etc., in the guise of a religious exposé, such a work had sufficient socially redeeming special qualities as to receive the applause of the Watch and Ward Society. The first Maria Monk book sold three hundred thousand copies.

The cold war in the public prints, however, soon turned a hot war of violent persecution. In August 1834 a citizen's group burned the Ursuline Convent of Charlestown, near Boston. The arsonists were acclaimed public heroes and promptly acquitted. For three days in May 1844, open warfare broke out in Philadelphia as mobs burned Catholic homes and two churches while militiamen turned their rifles on the Catholic rabble and cannons on Saint Philip Neri Church. The bishop suspended worship until the hostilities died down. In New York, however, Bishop Hughes stationed armed guards around his churches, and violence was prevented.

So appealing had nativism become, however, that it erupted into the Know-Nothing Party in 1852. By 1854 the party sent seventy-five men to the U.S. Congress. It also dominated all state offices in Massachusetts, "the cradle of liberty," and many in thirteen other states, including most of New England, New York, Pennsylvania, and the South. In 1856 they ran the Honorable Millard Fillmore for president—a likely candidate. But somehow Fillmore, Whiggery, and Know-Nothingism got lost in the fast-rising blizzard of abolitionism, the Free Soil Party, and the emerging Republican Party, which took away enough of its strength to elect the doughface James Buchanan president.

The abolitionist crusade and the Civil War overshadowed but did not entirely obscure the war between Irish Catholics and the righteous establishment as the bloody New York Draft Riots during the Civil War attest. But in the Civil War so many Catholics rose to prominence—such men as Ben Butler and George B. McClellan—that Know-Nothingism either went underground as it did in New England among the "Old Yankee" stock or turned its biblical, barefoot wrath on blacks, as well as Catholics, as it did in the South under the homemade hoods and masks of the Ku Klux Klan.

By the mid-nineteenth century, then, Catholics, the Irish, and the Germans appeared to be cast as serpents in an Anglo-Saxon Eden of liberty. If this was the case, then what of the dream of a free society? The answer, of course, is that the cosmopolitan dream, the large syncretic impulse, was stronger than nativism and bigotry. For most people there was room enough for all. As Sydney Ahlstrom observed, "One of the most remarkable facts about America's Nativism was its inability to obtain significant supporting legislation. When successive showdowns came, the force of the movement proved illusory. Too many Americans, it seemed, always loved—or needed—the 'foreigners.'"

And yet the whole nativist episode, the continued embattled stance of the Catholic Church—down through the KKK revivals of the 1920s, the immigration restriction laws, the 1928 defeat of Al Smith for U.S. president, and the doubts about John F. Kennedy's "suitability" for the presidency—suggests that though the dream of tolerance has in large measure prevailed in American history, by the same token it has endured much from those who would be "orthodox." Still, in nineteenth-century America there was room for many dreams and many roles.

CHAPTER SEVEN

The Diffusion of Education

A philosophy, and for that matter a theology, based upon scientific acquisition of knowledge had little value if there were to be no agencies for its diffusion among the people. Fortunately, the Americans who sought opportunity and salvation in the new land had always placed great value on education. From the passage of the Massachusetts School Act of 1647, designed to alert pious youth to the snares of "that old deluder Satan," to the eve of the Revolution when nine colonial colleges helped produce leaders for "Church and Civil State," Americans had considered some form of education basic to developing a moral and hence successful society.

Leaders of the new nation over and over again proclaimed the importance of education. As early as 1749 Franklin laid plans for an academy that eventually became the College of Pennsylvania. Dr. Benjamin Rush, one of Franklin's Philadelphia friends, planned a national school system and founded Dickinson College in Carlisle, Pennsylvania. In *Education Agreeable to a Republican Form of Government* (1786), Rush declared, "Without learning, men are incapable of knowing their rights, and where learning is confined to a few, liberty can be neither equal nor universal." John Jay, James Madison, Tom Paine, Charles Pinckney, Joel Barlow, and John Adams echoed these sentiments. Adams believed that the nation itself should take responsibility for educating its people "in every fund of knowledge that can be of use to them in their moral duties as men, citizens and Christians." Even Washington in his farewell address of 1796 asserted that "in proportion as the structure of a government gives force to public opinion, it is essential that public opinion should be enlightened."

Perhaps the leading exponent of education as the cornerstone for the republic was Thomas Jefferson. In 1779 he submitted four bills to the Virginia Assembly, all bearing on education: a "Bill for the More General Diffusion of Knowledge" to set up a public grammar school system; a "Bill for Amending the Constitution of the College of William and Mary" to broaden its curriculum; a measure calling for a public library at Richmond; and a "Bill for Establishing Religious Freedom," thereby freeing education from church dominance. He occupied the last years of his life designing the curriculum and the architecture of his greatest monument, the University of Virginia. Jefferson declared, "Those persons, whom nature hath endowed with genius and virtue, should be rendered by liberal education worthy to receive, and able to guard the sacred deposit of the rights and liberties of their fellow citizens." He stressed the role of history in a republican education, adding, "Knowledge of those facts, which history exhibited, that, possessed thereby of the experience of other ages and countries, they [the educated citizenry] may be enabled to know ambition under all its shapes, and prompt to exert their natural powers to defeat its purposes." The Sage of Monticello cared for no greater epitaph than "Sponsor of the Bill for Religious Freedom and Founder of the University of Virginia."

Meanwhile, Jefferson's handiwork extended even beyond the boundaries of the original thirteen states. Thanks to his efforts, the Northwest Ordinance governing the vast Ohio Country beyond the Appalachians provided land grants for pioneer schools—grants that eventually ran to millions of acres as the Old Northwest filled up rapidly with settlers. Older states— Pennsylvania, Massachusetts, North Carolina, Vermont, New Hampshire, and Delaware—also passed public education bills before 1800. And between 1782 and 1802, nineteen colleges still in existence today were chartered in the new republic. In the decades to come, many more would follow. By 1840, most states had some form of public school system, and the landscape was dotted with grammar schools, academies, military institutes, and college preparatory schools readying students for matriculation in seventy-eight permanent colleges. As one authority has remarked, "College-founding in the nineteenth century was undertaken in the same spirit as canal-building, cotton-ginning, farming, and gold-mining." On the eve of the Civil War, America had some 250 colleges, and Absalom Peters was not far wrong when he proclaimed in 1851, "Our country is to be a land of colleges!"

I

Institutionally and politically, the development of education in early America reflected many of the confusions and the growing pains of the young republic itself. The Founding Fathers, most of them philosophers of a sort, were in essential agreement as to the importance and value of education in creating an enlightened electorate and a new leadership class of "natural aristocrats" who could one day take their places in guiding the nation's destiny. They also agreed on the desirability of training the masses in the basic skills of reading, writing, and arithmetic to make the people and hence the country economically and socially self-reliant. And as such men as Franklin, Smith, Rush, and Jefferson drew up plans for educating the republic, there was an explicit faith in the cultural efficiency to be derived from a utilitarian education, in addition to their inherent faith in the right reason of the common man. Nature itself was a machine to be exploited, and only with trained intelligence could man get the most out of it. In 1798, speaking of politics and education, Rush declared his aim to "convert men into republican machines . . . to perform their parts properly in the great machine of government of the state."

But these pioneer educational planners, like the framers of the Constitution, which many of them were, seemed to many citizens to advocate an over-rationalization, an overorganization of society that did not take into account the regional, religious, social, and economic variety of the people as a whole throughout the vast reaches of the continental nation. In short, they seemed overly ambitious, often simplistic, and what one today might term reductionist. Beyond this, the philosophe planners of education for the new nation, fairly or unfairly, came to be labeled infidels, atheists, and French rationalists just at a time when, released from all bondage to the

Church of England, a mounting wave of religious revivalism began to crest into the Second Great Awakening. With this burst of fervor came a heightened pride in church-affiliated education as the real key to the moral development of good citizens, which took precedence over intellectual development.

At the center of this reaction stood the New England churches and the New Light Presbyterian strongholds. As historian Russell Nye has observed, by 1840 "of seventy-five college presidents . . . thirty-six were Yale men and twenty-two Princeton." The Yale College Report of 1828, in which President Jeremiah Day unequivocally placed disciplined religious and moral education over the development of the mind, became the manifesto of the proliferating forces of conservatism in education.

In a sense, the religious reaction was no different from the reaction of local political forces against the substitution of one overarching system of government for another as a final result of the Revolution. Many religious leaders and educators were equivalent to Daniel Shays and his western Pennsylvania partisans of the Whiskey Rebellion. They reflected the enormous desire of each region in each newly independent state to run its own affairs to its best advantage. Thus in education they represented the same centrifugal force the Constitution-makers had to contend with in securing ratification of a truly national government they hoped would appeal to all the people. It was the same problem faced by Hamilton and the economic planners and by those who hoped to make a science of the law. Of all values in the early republic, liberty, in all its varieties, was still the most dear.

Clearly, then, the development of education in the United States was hardly the unhindered march of science and progress. Rather it was and has been to the present day the result of a running debate covering many issues, some of them unforeseeable at the time. Thus perhaps the best way to analyze the history of education in the early republic is in terms of its problems and contradictions. As suggested above, a fundamental problem was bound up in the clash between national or even state planning authority and the laissez-faire local spirit of the times. Most national plans, including several for a national university, were rejected. And as state boards or commissions of education slowly came into being, these too were resisted in the same spirit that Virginians rejected Jefferson's comprehensive education plan for Virginia, forcing him to concentrate on the university. Generally the grounds for objection to state plans even in New England were: (1) It promised a loss of local liberty, (2) it militated against privately supported academies and colleges, (3) it increased taxation, (4) it was elitist and impractical and tended to degrade such manual labor occupations as those of the farmer and the mechanic, (5) it interfered with the religious functions of schools and led to secularization, thus sapping the nation's Protestant moral fiber, (6) it interfered with the already admirable efforts of privately organized charitable agencies, such as the Public School Society of New York, (7) popular agencies such as lyceums could do the job better, cheaper, and more democratically, (8) it foisted Northern values onto Southern society, (9) it raised the question of racial equality, and (10) it introduced subversive foreign ideas into the minds of innocent children, thus bringing confusion and corruption and destroying traditional patriotic and religious values. All in all these made up a formidable bill of attainder against public educational system–building.

Perhaps two examples will suffice to capture the flavor of the ongoing debates. One—the Dartmouth College Case—is by now so familiar to students of history that its original significance has been forgotten. In 1815, President John Wheelock, son of Dartmouth founder Eleazar Wheelock, became so embattled with the college's trustees that he turned to the Republican Party of New Hampshire to get the state to alter the original charter in his favor against the trustees. The issue became the popular political question of the day, and the Republicans gained control of the state government on the strength of their stand on behalf of Wheelock, pictured as fighting the rich, greedy, elitist trustees. In June 1816 the victorious governor and Republican legislature passed measures that changed Dartmouth from a college to a university and brought it under state legislative control—in effect voiding its original charter. At that point two Dartmouths came into existence in the small town of Hanover—one was Wheelock's state university, the other the trustees' Dartmouth College. The Superior Court of New Hampshire decided against the trustees and declared the college subject to legislative control. But when the case reached the Supreme Court in Washington, the trustees were represented by Daniel Webster, who, before an attentive Chief Justice John Marshall, argued that the state must not be allowed to capriciously void a charter or contract.

This, sir, is my case. It is the case, not merely of that humble institution, it is the case of every college in the land. It is more. It is the case
of every eleemosynary institution throughout our country . . . the case
of everyman who has property of which he may be stripped—for the
question is simply this: Shall our state legislature be allowed to take
that which is not their own, to turn it from its original use, and apply it
to such ends or purposes as they, in their discretion shall see fit? Sir,
you may destroy this little institution . . . but if you do . . . you must extinguish, one after another, all those great lights of science, which for
more than a century, have thrown their radiance over the land! It is sir,
as I have said, a small college, and yet there are those who love it.

Often obscured by the fact that Marshall's decision in favor of the
trustees also sanctified the right of private contract and property in the
United States is the further significance that in this case Marshall defended
the local, sectarian prerogative against the state's public encroachments.
The historic 1819 decision allayed but never quite stilled the fears of private school trustees that state planners might someday extinguish the "radiance" of their institutional lights. As a result of the case, state legislatures
began to be more and more circumspect in granting charters to eleemosynary, or charitable, institutions, large or small, while even today city coun-
cils, ever mindful of shrinking urban tax bases, are tempted to control the
growth of such tax-free institutions and even private homes by the simple
device of refusing to grant building permits or tearing down existing homes
for local business (called "taking" to cover up "theft").

Another dramatic issue of early nineteenth-century education turned
on the question of religious instruction in the schools. When the Public
School Society of New York City—a private, Protestant organization—
was designated the sole recipient of grants made for elementary education
in New York City, the decision caused great consternation because it gave
the society a monopolistic control over education in the city. To the newly
arrived Irish Catholic immigrants, this was especially galling. Required to
pay taxes for school support, they found themselves supporting Protestant-
oriented schools. Soon they set up their own parallel school system supported by contributions to their church, requiring them to pay double for
their education. Not only was a religion involved, but also the issues of

monopolism, elitism, and special favoritism to one group, the Public School Society.

In 1840, at the instigation of Bishop Hughes, Catholics petitioned the New York City Council to distribute funds to the Catholic school system. They argued that the so-called Public School Society was also private and Protestant sectarian, and that it sponsored teachers, texts, and versions of the Bible offensive to Catholics. If the principle of separation of church and state were to stand, then the city could hardly support Protestant sectarianism. If the principle did not govern, then the Catholics wanted their share of the funding. A great debate ensued, bringing forth strong expressions from Protestant sects on behalf of the Public School Society. For example, the Methodists evoked the "Edict of Nantes; the massacre of Saint Bartholomew's day; the fires of Smithfield" and "the crusades against the Waldenses" in opposing the Catholic petition. "Your memorialists had hoped that the intolerance and exclusiveness which had characterized the Roman Catholic Church in Europe, had been greatly softened under the benign influences of our civil institutions," added the Methodists in a not-so-subtle evocation of nativist sentiments. The city council, of course, went on supporting the Public School Society on the grounds that "nonsectarian" Protestant education had redeeming social value, though they agreed that some textbooks might offend community standards and needed to be changed.

II

Despite the contentions and contradictions that marked educational progress in the early republic, the whole endeavor of education—the visible symbols of achievement, the blue-sky status potential, the satisfactions of a just and righteous cause, the money to be made, even the spirit of competition—stimulated college-building as a "booster" enterprise. As the decades passed in nineteenth-century America, it became clear that every new state—every county, city, or would-be town, for that matter—must have its colleges because the presence of a college signified the arrival of civilization. More than that, it spelled permanence for the booster community that missed the canal, resided outside the reach of the railroad, and was blessed with no steamboat river. The average American college was residential, unlike the European urban university, and it served to bring more people to a new community with some reliability if the college succeeded. Since it was residential it could be located in the country or a small town so that, like a frontier fort, mining camp, or state prison, it brought commerce along with it. The college made its own community and often left its indelible stamp on the town—as had those earlier colleges in Cambridge, Princeton, and New Haven.

Beyond the economic and social competition, religious competition also stimulated college-building. Denominational college-building permeated the Old Northwest between 1790 and 1860. In Ohio alone, forty-three such institutions were founded, including Kenyon (1824), Western Reserve (1826), Marietta (1835), Denison (1831), and Oberlin (1833). By 1881 Ohio had thirty-seven institutions of higher learning to minister to its three million souls, while England had only four universities for a population of twenty-three million; small wonder that Thorstein Veblen associated *The Higher Learning* in America with conspicuous consumption. But college-building was hardly free of hardships to attend its great ambitions. Professor Frederick Rudolph vividly described the odyssey of the Reverend John W. Browne, who in 1811, on behalf of the new Miami University in Oxford, Ohio, set out on a trip to raise funds.

> His visit to James Madison at the White House was unproductive, but he picked up a five-volume history of Ireland from a senator from Kentucky; in the state of Delaware he collected $22.00, the good president of Princeton gave him $5.00, and from old John Adams of Quincy there were kind words, two books and $10.00. All in all [he garnered] a wagonload of books and $700.00 for the new college in Ohio. A few weeks later the Reverend Browne ... slipped as he crossed the Little Miami River and was drowned.

The principal building at Ohio College in Athens was struck by lightning before it was even completed. In November 1832, five young Presbyterian ministers knelt in the snow near Crawfordsville, Indiana, to ask God's blessing at the founding of Wabash College. Six years later it was destroyed by fire. Many other colleges perished from bad management, poor financing, lack of students (most enrolled twenty-five or fewer), competition from other religious sects, or internal strife. That so many survived the educational marketplace is a monument to human endurance—if not student tolerance.

Generally a college was a one-structure community in which most of the courses were given by the president, perhaps assisted by one or two tutors, who received room and board and little else except abuse from the students. One college president in one year lectured fourteen times on political economy, twenty-seven on classical literature, twenty-seven each on chemistry and geology, thirty-four on natural philosophy, and six on astronomy, besides setting the moral tone of the college. At the University of South Carolina, the president purchased books, provided coat hooks for the classrooms, and took attendance at faculty prayer meetings. The president of the University of Vermont taught *all* the classes and chopped down trees for construction of the college building. Besides his varied duties, the president usually led a precarious and meagerly paid existence. He was directly responsible to a board of trustees (the title often varied) who were usually ministers and tradesmen with little knowledge of the educational process. Largely they were on the board to ensure the college's high moral rectitude, possibly because they contributed funds, and to scrutinize the president and his faculty. If he had a faculty the president appeared to them as the trustees' agent and the faculty as the hired help. Under such circumstances it is not difficult to see why most colleges in early America suffered from severely diluted educational standards and why the life of the mind was scarcely appealing to students as a career.

Indeed, for most early nineteenth-century students, college was perhaps the way to success, but given the routine drilling, the recitation system, the limited curriculum, the miniature libraries, the strict discipline, and the remoteness of the college from civilization, education must have seemed like Alexander Pope's "progress of dullness." Pranks and riots, usually at the expense of pathetic faculty members, seemed the only worthwhile diversion in a society deliberately kept from maturity. Russell Nye provided an inventory of this facet of college life in early America where liberty at least was not dead:

In 1807, 125 of Princeton's total enrollment of 200 were expelled for rioting. Harvard freshmen and sophomores in 1817 smashed all the college crockery; that same year Princeton students broke the dormitory windows and threw wine bottles and firewood at the faculty. At Hobart students rolled red-hot cannonballs down a dormitory corridor and seriously injured a faculty member. At North Carolina students shot out windows with guns, and at Virginia the high-spirited Southern boys horse-whipped several faculty members. In 1814 Princeton students constructed a giant firecracker with a hollow log and two pounds of gunpowder and nearly blew up Nassau Hall. The class of 1824, in preparation for graduation at Dartmouth, burnt one barn, stoned Professor Chamberlain, burnt him and Tudor Parley and hung the President in effigy.

And yet little by little the students began to construct their own learning environments. Yale students formed the Linonia and Brothers debating societies, which held forensic contests and built up large libraries of books that students actually wished to read. To be elected to either society was an honor. Similar groups were organized at Harvard and numerous other colleges, as students themselves sought out a life of the mind that bypassed the sermonizing of the college chaplain in favor of a more interesting and relevant education. In addition, in the 1820s at Union College, students organized social clubs that adopted Greek letters and came to be known as fraternities. Now much maligned, fraternities in early America derived somewhat from the Masonic rites students saw about them in the real world and, most important, they served as a device for organizing an otherwise dull social life. In part, fraternities were a protest against dormitory living and dormitory food (the cause of many riots). They were an assertion of the student's right to privacy, to the selection of his own company, and the creation of his own learning environment away from the baleful inspection of some wretched tutor. Surely elitist institutions that chose their own members who could afford them, in the age of Jacksonian democracy, fraternities in the context in which they arose were also blows for liberty and the right to express the idiosyncrasies of one's own personality and one's own group. They were a species of the American talent for community-building in the wilderness and perhaps they were, like government itself, "a badge of lost innocence."

III

Despite the gross and humiliating exploitation of college presidents and faculty on all levels of instruction by immature students, bigoted clergymen, and get-rich-quick "solid citizens" on boards of trustees, early American educational ideas and innovations somehow developed and advanced. Most of the ideas began as imports, adapted to American conditions. Lockean psychology and its Scottish Common Sense variants were fundamental to American theories of learning. The "faculty psychology," with its belief in the moral faculty or conscience, was generally espoused by the philosophizers, the Old Light evangelists, the universalists, and the Unitarians in America. However, it was also possible for a New Light evangelical to espouse the concept of the innate moral sense in one of two ways. Either God directly influenced or disposed the moral sense through supernatural grace or, if one inquired closely into the laws of God's natural world, the evidence he inevitably found would predispose him to make the right moral decision. The latter position was most characteristic of the Scottish educators but it was also explicit in the writings of the English Deacon William Paley, the most widely read natural philosopher of his day.

Paley, addicted to the glories of natural science, saw God everywhere in nature. In *Natural Theology or Evidences of the Existence and Attributes of the Deity, Collected from the Appearances of Nature* (1822), Paley articulated his famous analogy between the watch found on the garden path as evidence of a watchmaker and the beautiful order of nature as evidence of a "supreme artificer." His argument was for the existence of God from design. To follow the design in nature was to find God. For his book, Paley collected every piece of evidence or anecdote he could find that pointed to the intricate functionalism of God's world. This made him very often a victim of absurdly apocryphal stories. For example, he believed that God made boars with curved tusks so that they might hang from the branches of trees when they slept at night, rocking to and fro like babies in cradles. Nothing better illustrates his wonderfully naive dogmatism than his reaction to the introduction of organized sports in England. He scorned them and advised the young to plant gardens instead—perhaps in imitation of the "supreme artificer."

Building on the powerful logic of faculty psychology, it followed that the role of education was to perfect the use of the faculties—to develop the senses like muscles so that they might better perceive nature and nature's laws, to drill the reason through logic, and constantly to exercise the moral sense. All this meant continual discipline, a sense of the order of nature, and endless practice and training. The early American student body under the "faculty psychology" of Locke and his Scottish Common Sense successors was an Olympic team dedicated to intellectual and emotional endurance.

Another facet of early educational theory was also derived from the Scots and the English in the eighteenth century. This was the idea of Associationism, made popular by the aesthetic writings of Lord Kames, a friend of Benjamin Franklin's, and Hugh Blair, a retired professor at Edinburgh. In his popular *Lectures on Rhetoric* (1783), Blair noted the order in the world and formulated a system of appropriate tropes, or figures of speech, that would most perfectly suggest the general aspects of that order. For example, one would never use Jove-like metaphors to suggest the common man or colloquialisms to describe an epic hero. Certain words, constructions, allusions, syntax, metaphors, meters, rhymes, etc. must fit most perfectly the exact situation, figure, event, or argument laid before the reader or auditor. Associationism was thus a rhetorical variety of Paley's natural functionalism, of the parts of nature "intended for an use." Blair's study of rhetoric, of course, grew out of the Scottish school's preoccupation with common sense in both nature and the mind. What he and Kames had done in their works was articulate or set down a set of mental signals that, when read or heard, denoted kinds of experience originally derived from the senses but temporarily stored away in memory. Theirs was the science of evoking emotions, and as men better understood this science they could resort to synecdoche and let a part stand for a whole range of emotions. Later this approach would be called symbolism and became the core of romantic theories of knowledge and perception. In the meantime, like everything else that came from the Scottish school, associationism required drill—drill in logic, rhetoric, and literary copybook exercises that so characterized education on all levels in the early republic. The absorption of these principles of faculty psychology, Scottish moralism, and rhetorical associationism made for a standardization in education that in turn subtly made for a standardization in the educated American's life.

But though the Scottish school largely prevailed, other national influences impinged upon the development of American education. The whole idea of a public school system was based upon the Prussian educational system, deemed by many to be the finest in the world. The development of engineering education at West Point in 1802 and Rensselaer Polytechnical Institute in 1829 stemmed from the French example of the national *Ecole Polytechnique*, and most of the best teachers at West Point either had French backgrounds or learned from French textbooks. Denis Hart Mahan, who redesigned the West Point curriculum in 1837 and wrote most of the modern textbooks then in use, studied four years in France with French engineering masters at government expense.

From Switzerland came the ideas of Johann Pestalozzi, whose school at Yverdon opened in 1800. Pestalozzi was an incipient romantic, influenced by Rousseau's ideas. He believed the imposition of standardization and drill upon children was not the key to education. Rather, he advanced an early version of the "study the child" theory. A Pestalozzian teacher had to be sensitive to the way in which each child's mind worked at various stages in his growth. As early as 1809 a Pestalozzian school opened in Philadelphia, and after 1819, when American John Griscom published his book about Pestalozzi, *A Year in Europe*, a large number of American educators came under his influence and made the pilgrimage to Switzerland to study with the great man. Griscom himself became a pioneer in the study and correction of juvenile delinquency in America. Pestalozzi's work with the poor, his association with the German M. Phillip Fellenberg at Hofwyl, and his influence upon Joseph Vehrly, another European master teacher of "difficult" children, made him very influential in German educational thought, which, by about midcentury, came to absorb American intellectuals. Pestalozzi's fascination with the specific, concrete task for the child at each stage in his growth had clear implications for Friedrich Froebel's development of the kindergarten method, with its special blocks and idealized shapes, and later for Maria Montessori, who, working with the poor in Italy, followed closely along the lines of the Pestalozzian method.

And finally, due to the long excursions for study in Germany by such Cambridge scholars as George Ticknor, Edward Everett, George Bancroft, and Frederick Henry Hedge, the idea of a true university entered American educational thought. In Germany the visiting Americans discovered the seminar method of teaching, the value of real research in everything from philosophy to agricultural chemistry, and the importance of the great scholar as professor who was no lackey to an ignorant board of trustees. Significantly, when the first wave of Americans to study in Germany came home to America, they left the academic profession as it existed in the United States as soon as they could. In legislatures and publishing houses, on educational commissions and in their writings, they exerted an academic power that gradually brought real universities and real education to America.

Thus in the realm of educational theory, though Scottish philosophy and fundamentalist values largely set the tone, many other streams of thought flowed into America from the European continent, where they were soon absorbed and put to use in the "eclectic republic."

IV

In contrast to the increasing eclecticism of teaching philosophies, the primary device for instilling piety, patriotism, and standardized values in early America was the school textbook. Child psychologist Ruth Miller Elson has called them "guardians of the tradition," concluding:

> The world created in nineteenth-century schoolbooks is essentially a world of fantasy—a fantasy made up by adults as a guide for their children, but inhabited by no one outside the pages of schoolbooks. They were vehicles for a set of ideals and images that, taken together, represented what early American educators wished the new country to be, and thus constituted a future-oriented myth made out of the collective "wisdom" of the past to be handed on to the coming generations. The myths in the schoolbooks, especially since they were perforce learned by rote under the rod of the schoolmaster, were as powerful as any myths in the new land and should not be discounted in any analysis of American culture.

Elson perceptively has called the schoolbooks "the lowest common denominator of American intellectual history." School texts fell into a number of categories—primers, spellers, readers, geographies, histories, and arithmetic and science books of increasing specialization. Most of them were written by New Englanders and reflected the New England values that seem to have dominated the life of the mind in America, on one level at least, for nearly two centuries. The earliest significant American primer was *The New England Primer* (first edition in 1690), containing lessons on the alphabet, spelling words, reading, moral lessons from scripture, some geography, and a little history. The primer was intended to serve as the single book needed for study in any phase of school activity. The most popular of the early primers was the Reverend Samuel Willard's *Franklin Primer*, published in 1802. More than any other, the *Franklin Primer* established a new learning framework upon which subsequent books could build. It contained "tales, moral lessons, and sentences, a concise history and geography of the world, appropriate hymns, Bible readings, and the Assembly of Divines' catechism." In other words, it ranged over a relatively broad number of subjects except science, the whole content of which, in author Willard's opinion, could be found in the Bible. All subject matter, in the New England way, was colored by the Protestant point of view.

Soon schoolbooks, like schools and colleges, began to proliferate in both number and variety. *The Franklin Primer* was succeeded by Samuel Goodrich's *Peter Parley Primer*, and by 1830 there were many competing books, such as *Easy Road to Learning for Good Boys and Girls*, Matthew Carey's *American Primer*, and *Tom Thumb's Picture Alphabet*. Between 1804 and 1832, according to Professor Russell Nye, the number of different schoolbooks increased from 93 to 407.

The most heroic effort to standardize the American schoolchild's knowledge was probably that of Noah Webster. In 1783 he published the first of his famous "blue-backed spellers," which persisted as a standard educational tool until well into the twentieth century. Webster asserted that his speller was intended to "diffuse a uniformity and purity of language in America . . . and to promote the interests of literature and the harmony of the United States." Called *The American Spelling Book*, Webster's little "blue volume" clearly signaled its patriotic purpose by its coloring of Continental Army blue.

In 1785 Webster published another important school text, pompously titled *The Grammatical Institute of the English Language, Part 3*. Later the title was changed to *An American Selection of Lessons in Reading and Speaking, Being the Third Part of a Grammatical Institute*. This was the first of many readers published in America that came to serve as prime vehicles for nationalistic and religious propaganda. Webster's idea of a reader had been anticipated in the age of revolutionary nationalism by a German, Erich von Rachow, who in 1776 published *Der Kinderfreund*, or *Children's Friend*, in Germany, thus establishing a pattern. Although Prussian education was widely admired throughout the western world, there is no evidence that Webster derived his concept directly from the Germans.

Webster's *Grammatical Institute*, unlike his dictionary and spelling book, did not capture popular enthusiasm, and he soon turned away from this kind of work. The market at the time was dominated by the works of a Boston schoolmaster, Caleb Bingham, a New Yorker who became an expatriate in England in 1784. Bingham's most famous books were *Child's Companion, Columbian Orator*, and *American Preceptor*. None of these books contained any real system of pedagogy, leaving the teacher free to use them as he or she wished. Clearly, however, these readers, like almost all readers of the period, were designed to be read aloud so as to develop the child's pronunciation and future forensic skills, perhaps even to the level attained by the Romans, or Franklin, Washington, Jefferson, Patrick Henry, and other Founding Fathers for whom oratory was a crucial skill. Bingham's *American Preceptor* was a tremendous success. It went through sixty-eight editions and sold about 640,000 copies, which provides some index to the rapidly rising rate of education and, hopefully, literacy in early America.

If anything, Lindley Murray's books were more popular than Bingham's readers, though he rather cunningly hedged his bet by aiming his readers at both the English and American markets. One of the Murray family for whom Murray Hill neighborhood in New York is named, he seems to have been a true cosmopolitan. His book *The English Reader* featured writings from most of the best writers of England's Augustan Age. The large selections from the works of Hugh Blair and Samuel Johnson probably did more to fashion literary taste in America than anything else in print, especially since many early American writers were not college-educated and received little exposure to the more advanced treatises on literature then in existence. By the same token, Murray's texts served to subtly restore the cultural ties with Britain that had been severed in the Revolution. For Americans searching for a national literature, he held up British rhetorical principles and British authors as models. In one of his texts he included fifty biographical sketches of writers; forty-five were British, two were French, two were from the ancient world, and the only American worthy was Benjamin Franklin. The popularity of Murray's books, given their cosmopolitan emphasis that contrasted so strongly with the nationalism of Webster and Bingham, suggests something important about early American culture—even at the height of nationalistic fervor, Americans were still inclined to base their new culture on world culture. Mother Europe was never entirely or successfully rejected.

The same point can be made about the works of America's greatest writer of reading texts, William Holmes McGuffey. Born in western Pennsylvania in 1800, McGuffey was a teacher of ancient languages. In 1836 he was serving as president of Cincinnati College when he was approached by a local publishing house to put together a school reader. He received the proposition through the agency of Harriet Beecher Stowe's husband, Calvin, then teaching at the Cincinnati Theological Seminary as his wife gathered material in Ohio and Kentucky for *Uncle Tom's Cabin.* Stowe and McGuffey were good friends and at Stowe's urging, McGuffey signed what was probably the worst literary contract in American history. He received a 10 percent royalty on each copy sold, not to exceed the sum of $1,000 per year. Over the course of his lifetime, McGuffey's *Eclectic Readers* sold over 122 million copies, but he never renegotiated his original contract and instead lived out most of his life quietly as a professor at the University of Virginia, exemplifying the true Jeffersonian spirit.

The popularity of McGuffey's books often surprises modern readers. By and large they were simply collections of reading selections from famous and not-so-famous authors. But the books had several advantages. A long introduction provided, in effect, a teacher's manual showing how to use the book and prepare the child in all phases of reading and rhetorical instruction. Then each selection followed a lesson plan and included not only explanations and footnotes but also questions and exercises. In effect, McGuffey had packaged the teaching process so that even the most inexperienced teacher would know what to do. This has become standard practice today, but in

McGuffey's time it was relatively new, and certainly needed, given the quality of teacher education in nineteenth-century America. Most important
for students of American thought, however, was that McGuffey's readers
were eclectic. That is, in the words of Professor Henry Steele Commager,
they were "cosmopolitan rather than parochial." Commager went on to
add that readers "could not but have a lively sense of the past, and of the
rich cultural tradition of other nations. The Greeks were here, and the Romans, William Tell and Arnold Winkelreid, Hamlet and Shylock, and the
Highland clansmen. Irving described the Alhambra, and Southey celebrated the Battle of Blenheim, and Thomas Campbell provided a sample of
the Scots dialect." And as far as the *Fifth Eclectic Reader* was concerned, a
reader might have added that the "Generous Russian Peasant" and the
"Soldier of the Rhine" were also in the Ohioan's immortal volumes.
McGuffey's readers came before the public when romanticism was at high
tide and Americans and Europeans alike were curious, even sentimental,
about people, adventures, and local-color incidents everywhere in the
world, especially if an element of heroism, large or small, was implicit in
the story.

Growing out of the hundreds of texts of all sizes, formats, and varieties
in nineteenth-century America was, as Ruth Miller Elson has pointed out,
the emergent sense of an American myth. This sense of American myth can
be looked at in two ways. Elson sees it as basically pernicious. In matters of
religion, she traces a persistent theme of anti-intellectual fundamentalism
through the books. God's Bible is all the science one needs to know. In
good Scottish Common Sense fashion, nature and geography are to be
studied so as to learn the thoughts of the Creator. According to Elson:

> Perhaps the most fundamental assumption in nineteenth century
> schoolbooks is the moral character of the universe—an assumption at
> the base of American culture in the period. . . . To be well adjusted the
> nineteenth century child must be in harmony with the decrees of God
> and nature rather than his peers.
>
> This meant that the schoolbooks decreed that God, nature, nation-
> alism and the mission of Americans went hand-in-hand with the good
> moral life of the hardworking white, Anglo-Saxon Protestant rural
> citizen, who admired his citizen-soldier leaders, deemed it his duty to

labor harder without complaint if poor, believed that riches, abundance and success constituted an outward sign of God's favor, fervently believed that democracy meant opportunity not necessarily equality, that republicanism was the best form of government for all time because it preserved liberty, and that the place of women was in the home.

From Elson's analysis emerges the devastating portrait of a class-, sex-, and race-oriented, messianically driven culture. In the textbooks, at least to a latter-day observer, Americans, almost from the beginning, stepped down from Olympus and the unique high hopes of Tom Paine to join the rest of mankind in a "chosen people" quest for identity. On the other hand, quite clearly these emerging American values were nothing more than an amalgam of all the cultural values that had gone before them with the exception of liberty—freedom of the individual and the culture seemed to have the highest priority—except for women and blacks. American schoolbook myth-makers and educators were thus caught in a paradox. Their most cherished value was liberty, but they strove mightily to bring about order and standardization—even to entrench prejudices they thought right. But to a people weaned on John Locke and devoted to a Constitution that was a "compromise by combination," the contradiction did not then seem apparent. Without God there was no order. Without order there could be no liberty because barbaric might and mere man would make right. Without liberty there could be no freedom to choose the best of the world's lifestyles past and present—no freedom even to be educated as to what these might be. But within a Common Sense framework of order, individualism, and community, both were possible, as were innovation and eccentricities that respected the rights of others. The American people could be the "chosen people" because they alone could choose what they liked from the world and fuse it into a culture by combination. Everyone could be right in his own fashion. Nineteenth-century America, despite extreme moral aging, was the country of the everlasting "yes," which meant that out of all of our foreign influences, the natural language that defined the culture would be English.

CHAPTER EIGHT

The Writer and the Republic

Long before *The American Scholar* in 1837, when Ralph Waldo Emerson declared New World literary independence, American intellectuals had already become enthusiasts for national achievement in the arts and letters. As early as 1771, shortly after the Boston Massacre and five years before the Declaration of Independence, Connecticut poet John Trumbull declaimed before a Yale graduating class on the "Prospect of the Future Glory of America." He coupled American martial prospects with future cultural achievement, which he saw in sharp contrast to those of a declining Europe.

> *For pleasing Arts behold her matchless charms,*
> *The first in letters, as the first in arms.*
> *See bolder genius quit the narrow shore,*
> *And realms of science, yet untraced explore,*
> *Hiding in brightness of superior day,*
> *The fainting gleams of Europe's setting ray.*

During and after the Revolution, these sentiments were echoed ceaselessly by the Connecticut Wits, sometimes called the Rising Glory

School—John Trumbull, Joel Barlow, Timothy Dwight, and David Humphreys—by the lyrical Jeffersonian poet Philip Freneau; by such dramatists as William Dunlap; by such novelists as Suzanna Rowson, Charles Brockden Brown, James Kirke Paulding, and Robert Montgomery Bird; and by dozens of American literary critics, newspaper prophets, and Phi Beta Kappa orators from William Tudor to the mighty Emerson himself.

But the problem of establishing an American literary tradition and of raising it to a level of high achievement was a profound one. It reached directly into the heart of American national character and ultimately helped to define it, for if American people of letters were to be true to the ideals of the Revolution, the nature of American literature must above all be universal—a parallel to, or even an embellishment of, the boundless sentiments of Paine, Jefferson, Franklin, and the other Founding Fathers. Yet it must also be distinctly American and not a pale reflection of English or even European letters. It must somehow suggest an indigenous American "place where," but, alas, in a language inherited from Britain. Thus, from the beginning American writers were caught in a series of paradoxes. They must look outward over the globe and yet inward at American soil and American things. They must speak with their own voices in the language of a disowned mother country. They must eschew traditional forms yet win approval from world critics to whom such forms were the only hallmarks of good taste in an Augustan Age of literature and the arts. And on a practical level, they had to compete with vast importations of British literature that was both cheaper and better than the homemade works of busy writers for whom literature was only an avocation. Due to a lack of international copyright laws, the best English books could be and frequently were pirated by American printers who thus, in a reverse of Gresham's law, drove out inferior American books on the American market. In the early days of the republic it was virtually impossible to be a professional creative writer, much less a full-time spokesperson for the cause of literary nationalism. Though a cosmopolitan nation, Americans wrote in English.

Beyond this, American writers, however bold and strident the tone of their literary efforts, were often discouraged because they saw few subjects about which to write that compared with those of the older European world. As late as 1828 James Fenimore Cooper lamented the poverty of American literary material:

> There is scarcely an ore which contributes to the wealth of the author that is found here in veins as rich as in Europe. There are no annals for the historian; no follies (beyond the most vulgar and common-place) for the satirist; no manners for the dramatist; no obscure fictions for the writer of romance; no gross and hardy offences against decorum for the moralist; nor any of the rich artificial auxiliaries of poetry. The weakest hand can extract a spark from the flint, but it would baffle the strength of a giant to attempt kindling a flame with a pudding stone. . . . I have never seen a nation so much alike in my life as the people of the United States.

Nathaniel Hawthorne and, later in the century, Henry James would echo these sentiments. Moreover, offering an outsider's view, the French traveler Tocqueville, in his classic *Democracy in America* (1840), made a sweeping attribution of all patterns of American behavior to a democratic leveling. He seemed to add a carefully observed European point of view to the literary impressions of the American Cooper. Moreover, those who continually called for a national literature based upon the excellencies of mass democratic institutions played directly into the hands of such aristocratic critics of American culture.

The way out of the American literary dilemma proved not to be so difficult as at first it seemed, however. Within approximately sixty-five years, by 1855, the United States had produced not only a literary tradition of its own, but also a New World cultural hero in Cooper's Leatherstocking, and a very respectable body of writing that commanded world attention. At least three writers, Cooper, Edgar Allan Poe, and Washington Irving, had made a profound impact on the American literary tradition. And a sense of national character emerged, in large part defined by the writers in whose works could be seen their complex facets. The very rapidity of the American literary maturation process is a fact sometimes forgotten by students of American culture. If the mid-nineteenth century may be characterized as an American literary renaissance, it must also be seen as virtually an instant renaissance by any reasonable measurement of comparative cultural time.

Greece, Rome, France, Germany, Italy, Scotland, Ireland, Spain, even Britain itself took far longer to reach such maturity. America, of course, was able to take its great leap forward because, as in science and technology, it could launch itself from, or take advantage of, all the other traditions of Europe that had taken so long to establish.

Essentially, the road to renaissance, American-style, passed through three literary phases that were not unrelated to cultural and political concerns: Classical, Associationist, and Transcendental. All represented general emphases in American writing rather than sharply defined, mutually exclusive stylistic periods comparable to, for example, abrupt changes in Pueblo pottery styles. Rather, they tended to reinforce or flow into one another until, at the height of the literary flowering, elements of all three could be seen to fuse. Indeed the secret of real uniqueness in American literature, just as in American character, was its very syncretic nature. It absorbed, included, blended, and sometimes forced together elements of all literary traditions in an American literature that was nothing if not universal in its strivings. It accumulated, borrowed, proliferated, and progressed much like science into ever-larger generalizations, with America itself usually standing as a model or focus for cultural generalizations.

At first the most obvious way to define America through the medium of literature was, as Trumbull's early point implied, by means of heightening the contrasts between the New World and the Old. It indicated what America was not and never hoped to be. This strategy of contrast followed quite logically from the rhetoric of the Revolution itself in which the corruptions of Walpole's ministry and George III's court, the licentiousness of high living in London, and the wickedness of the established church were fertile sources of imagery for American revolutionary pamphleteers. Carrying on in this tradition, virtually all of the Connecticut Wits, when they attempted satiric verse or grandiose epics, relied heavily on the contrast theme. An example of their work is Timothy Dwight's "Columbia," written while he was a chaplain in the Revolutionary Army:

> *Columbia, Colombia, to glory arise,*
> *The queen of the world, and child of the skies!*
> *Thy genius commands thee; with rapture behold,*
> *While ages on ages thy splendors unfold.*

Thy reign is the last, and the noblest of time,
Most fruitful thy soil, most inviting that clime;
Let the crimes to the east ne'er encrimson thy name,
Be freedom and science and virtue thy fame.
To conquest and slaughter, let Europe aspire.

Dwight's poem not only contrasted free "Columbia" with bloody Europe, it also followed the logic of revolutionary leaders and saw the war as part of a worldwide movement for freedom—"a world is thy realm." In addition, like those of most of the other epic writings of the period, "Columbia's" point of view was visionary and utopian. Europe was predestined to destroy itself, and free America would prevail. A similar strategy was pursued by Joel Barlow in his ambitious epic, *The Vision of Columbus*, published in 1787 and issued in a revised edition titled *The Columbiad* in 1807. With Columbus, a Genoese, as his hero and central figure, Barlow found it difficult to introduce American characters and episodes into his poem. He solved this problem, however, by giving his Italian hero a vision of the utopian future of the New World before him. Barlow, an eclectic, wandering, adventurous man who served for a time as U.S. consul to the Barbary Pirates, not only included in his epic glorious scenes from North American history largely borrowed from the Scotsman William Robertson's *The History of America*, but he also drew heavily on the works of "El Inca," Garcilaso de la Vega, especially his *Royal Commentaries of the Inca*, which depicted the glories and myths of pre-Columbian New World civilization, contrasting them favorably with the fading splendors of Europe. This was to be a theme exploited by many American writers, among them historian William Hickling Prescott.

Perhaps the most famous use of the contrast theme in early American literature was in Royall Tyler's *The Contrast*, presented in 1787. It was the first American play on an American theme to be professionally produced in the United States. Tyler belligerently declared in his prologue:

On native themes his Muse displays her pow'rs;
If ours the faults, the virtues too are ours.
Why should our thoughts to distant countries roam,
When each refinement may be found at home?

In *The Contrast*, which was heavily based on the British playwright William Brinsley Sheridan's *The Rivals*, Tyler created some memorable caricatures to illustrate the contrast between decadent England and pure America. The American hero was Colonel Manly. His British rival was Dimple, an absurd fop suffering from over-refinement. The scene was set in New York, and, in counterpoint to the contest between Manly and Dimple, Tyler added a subplot pitting Jessamy, a sly, knowing product of the London Strand, against Jonathan, the colonel's servant who is a simple country bumpkin. Although Manly and Dimple proved to be somewhat heavy-handed characters, the witty dialogue between Jessamy and Jonathan helped to make indelible not only the image of contrast but also that of the comic Yankee, Brother Jonathan. Somehow, while he was totally ignorant and blundering at all times, Jonathan's good spirit prevailed, even when he mistook New York's notorious red-light district, the "Holy Ground," for a prayer meeting center, and a girl he met there for the deacon's daughter. When Jessamy, with a broad smirk to the audience, whispered loudly to poor Jonathan, "That girl you saw was a . . ." and Jonathan replied naively, "Mercy on my soul! Was that young woman a harlot?" a new American folk hero was born, whom Constance Rourke told us became not only the archetype of the comic Yankee, but also eventually the basis for Uncle Sam, one of the few comic characters to symbolize a nation.

In another vein, Noah Webster, in addition to being a schoolbook writer, was perhaps the most lucid literary thinker in early America. He concentrated his efforts on fashioning an American language. But as he began his labors he also saw the whole linguistic problem in terms of the contrast theme. In his *Dissertations on the English Language*, published in 1789, Webster argued that Britain's language had been determined by the whim or caprice of foppish court usage and hence constantly corrupted by fashionable foreign words brought to court by travelers. British English, due to the Island Kingdom's proximity to Europe, was rapidly being changed and corrupted, while America, so he thought erroneously, existed in relative isolation, dependent on the inherent conservatism of broad democratic usage, and therefore could remain a sanctuary for the purity of the English language. In his early efforts, Webster sought to safeguard the purity of American English by writing a dictionary and a speller that would standardize the American language over the whole country, not just to draw together the diverse land by means of linguistic nationalism, but also to rest the language on the broad basis of popular or democratic usage so it would change very slowly. Perhaps this is why Americans wrote in American English.

Webster admitted, however, that all languages were constantly changing "from age to age, in proportion to improvements in science." Still, he added, "when a language has arrived at a certain stage of improvement, it must be stationary or become retrograde." In England, language had been in retrogression since the days of Queen Anne, Webster declared, reintroducing the contrast theme by implication. "Few improvements have been made since that time, but innumerable corruptions in pronunciation have been introduced by Garrick and in style by Johnson, Gibbon and their imitators."

Still, despite the prevalence of the contrast theme, wherever one looked into American letters, poetry, drama, linguistics, the essay, the sermon, histories, literary magazines, which began to be published in great numbers after 1787, and even the early novel, virtually all American literature was, formalistically speaking, imitative, specifically of English or classical models. In almost every piece calling for American literary nationalism, this fact was decried over and over again. With the establishment in 1815 of the *North American Review* (modeled after the Scottish *Edinburgh Review)* the subject became an obsession. The case was tried and retried again and again in virtually every issue of the *Review*, which also deliberately introduced German and other continental literature as alternative models, down to the 1840s. Yet in their primary dependence upon classical and Augustan Age British models, early American writers were finding exactly the vehicles for the universalizing of American ideals that they so ardently desired. Classicism, whether derived directly from the ancient world or strained through British translators like Alexander Pope, was the very language and form of world generalization the cosmopolitan political vision of America demanded.

Aside from Aristotle's *Poetics* and the literary works of the ancients themselves, the chief philosophical inspiration for American classicism appears to have been the Scottish Common Sense writer Henry Home, Lord Kames. As mentioned previously, his *Elements of Criticism*, published in 1762, became, along with Hugh Blair's *Lectures on Rhetoric and Belles-Lettres*, the standard text used in American colleges, North and South. Kames's preference for classicism stemmed from his belief that it best reflected nature's fundamental order, balance, and harmony. As such, classicism provided models of universal and timeless appeal to all men everywhere who, by definition, shared a common nature. He declared:

> We are so constituted as to conceive this common nature to be not only invariable, but also *perfect* and *right*; and consequently that individuals ought to be made conformable to it. Every remarkable deviation from the standard makes accordingly an impression upon us of imperfection, irregularity, or disorder. This conviction of a common nature or standard and of its perfection accounts clearly for that remarkable conception we have of a right and a wrong sense or taste in morals. It accounts not less clearly for the conception we have of a right and a wrong sense or taste in the fine arts.

As a proponent of the Scottish Common Sense school of philosophy, Kames began with the assumption, like that of Jefferson, that there was a "common sense of mankind" that would set standards of morality and hence of taste, and that these standards would always tend toward the uniformities reflected in nature. In this philosophy one can see reflected not only the source for Jefferson's "decent respect for the opinions of mankind," but also Webster's faith in "common usage" as the true basis of language. Moreover, such early American writers as Benjamin Franklin, Thomas Jefferson, John Adams, James Madison, Timothy Dwight, John Trumbull, and Joel Barlow followed Kames almost unquestioningly in matters of taste and style. He set the tone for virtually all the literary taste of the American "heroic age," as indeed he did for a great many writers of Britain's Augustan Age.

Beyond laying down rules of taste, Kames also made obvious the models worthy of imitation. Much in the way T. S. Eliot would do later, Kames pointed to such obvious greats as Homer, Virgil, Horace, and the "newcomer" John Milton. Of course, the works of Alexander Pope and other Enlightenment writers reflected his taste admirably. In addition, Kames also had a conception of the sublime and of the importance of grandeur that was to become extremely important in American writing. Sublimity and grandeur were virtually interchangeable because the sublime was the emotion felt by the writer and presumably by the reader when, as he gained true insight into nature, he approached the thoughts of the Creator. Therefore, sublime emotion was also grand. It was also reasonable, but at the same time it went beyond reason to the uncharted perimeters of the imagination, the exploration of which would preoccupy the attention of the major philosophers in Europe and America for the next century. Because of his belief in the strict rules of philosophy and art, Kames made the quest for the sublime for the most part mechanical and wooden. In a poem, for example, the balanced line, the regular meter, and the undeviating rhyme scheme such as the heroic couplet were the proper goals to strive for—the molds into which experience had best be forced. The choice of words, characters, setting, and allusion, too, were rule-bound. Lofty words fit only lofty subjects, unless a burlesque was intended. Heroic characters must be people of high station who used lofty language. The setting should be concretely rendered but if possible convey the mind always upward from plain to mountain and thus toward heaven and the sublime. One is reminded of Jefferson's passage in *Notes on Virginia* describing the sublimity of the Shenandoah Valley as it led from rocky crags in the foreground to a sublimely peaceful (possibly heavenly) plain beyond. Indeed the whole orderly Chain of Being structure of *Notes on Virginia*, though grounded in science, also reflects Kames's principles of literary composition.

Guided by such a powerful weapon of literary logic, early American political writers easily reached the level of the universal and sometimes even the sublime. The poets had a much more difficult time. All of the Connecticut Wits—Dwight, Humphreys, Barlow, and Trumbull—stumbled through the composition of jerry-built epics that were intended to be American but whose form was bastard Kamesian. As Joseph Howard put it in describing Dwight's epic, *The Conquest of Canaan*, "In short Dwight's poem was full of eighteenth century Americans with Hebrew names who talked like Milton's angels and fought like prehistoric Greeks." He added, "All the machinery and many of the structural and expository devices were Miltonic," while the battle scenes were modeled on Pope's version of the *Iliad*. The same author's "Greenfield Hill" was a cosmopolitan pastiche of the work of such acceptable authors as Oliver Goldsmith, James Thompson, James Beattie, Alexander Pope, Horace, Virgil, John Milton, and John Calvin. Only the hill was Dwight's own, for the deserted village looked more like Fairfield, Connecticut, when Dwight's pen had finished with it.

Trumbull's mock epic, *M'Fingal*, parodying Samuel Butler's *Hudibras* and James MacPherson's *Ossian*, though more original than Dwight's hackneyed efforts, still suffered from the same lack of originality. Like all early writers, they strove for too much—grandeur before simplicity, sublimity before concreteness, status before real achievement. Mighty though their New World subject was, as far as literature was concerned the classical models that promised universal appeal actually impeded its full expression. And yet, given the American belief in the universality of their democratic revolution, what better place for the artist to turn in the eighteenth century than to the classical? It was a phase of literary experimentalism through which American writers inevitably had to pass, just as the early architects and builders of the republic dotted the landscape with endless and often inappropriate varieties of Georgian baroque architecture largely derived from English carpenter books by Batty Langley and Asher Benjamin. These works were the architects' equivalents of Kames's *Elements of Criticism*.

In many ways the most significant of the early American epics was Barlow's *Vision of Columbus*, published in 1787 and later revised as *The Columbiad*, which he published in 1807. He dedicated *The Columbiad* to his friend Robert Fulton, who seemed to symbolize the civilized progress through reason and science that Barlow so much admired. A congenial, optimistic, adventurous man, Barlow had graduated from Yale in 1778 during the American Revolution. A student of Dwight, and a would-be writer who was a friend and classmate of Noah Webster's, early on Barlow was steeped in Scottish principles of devotion to science, faculty psychology, environmentalism, and the aesthetic canons of Kames and Blair. He was an ardent patriot, participating in the Battle of Long Island and serving as chaplain of the 4th Massachusetts Brigade during the war. Like Tom Paine, however, whom he later befriended, Barlow saw the American Revolution as the opening skirmish of a world revolution on behalf of the rights of all humanity. All through the war, even while soldiering from 1779 to 1785, he worked on his great epic poem, *The Vision of Columbus*. When it was published (at the author's own expense) in 1787, to Barlow's surprise, it received great acclaim. He should not have been surprised, because, however clumsy and derivative it may have been, *The Vision of Columbus* gave form to the revolutionary American's quest for a world civilization. A sweeping, eclectic work of global scope, Barlow's *Vision of Columbus* drew upon Robertson's history of the Americas.

The basic structure of Barlow's poem was as old as the Bible. He employed the device of an angel presenting visions of the future to the imprisoned Columbus, who despaired over his failure to achieve "the last crusade" with his discovery of the New World. Shot through with sentimental concern for Columbus's emotional health, Barlow's work, of course, had a far more serious purpose. In nine books of rhymed couplets, he outlined the history of the New World, changes in the Old World, the glorious triumphs of America—the model civilization that was not yet perfect—and the inevitable future of all mankind united in one religion, one language, and one Newtonian harmonious whole. In Barlow's view, mankind's last great congregation would take place at the rebuilt temple of Jerusalem standing on the spot where the "first parents" had first emerged on the globe. Thus, in his poem, Barlow succeeded in granting the mystical Columbus his most ardent wish. He gave him a vision of a balanced, rational, harmonious world place.

Emotionally, Barlow's poem was a paean to what Professor Kenneth Silverman has called "the troubled progress of cosmopolitanism." Philosophically it took its cue from the Scottish thought that Barlow had imbibed at Yale, together with the latitudinarianism of Englishman Richard Price and the free-thinking eclecticism of continental nature philosophers. For Barlow, ever the optimist, science and republican progress, coupled with religion and the growing humanity of man, portended the millennium, which he believed would take place on earth before the second coming of God.

Stylistically, *The Vision of Columbus* was hardly a literary masterpiece. It was nonetheless important as evidence of a swing toward baroque classicism in American taste. Rich, eclectic, highly charged emotionally, full of ornament dedicated to the faculties of association so espoused by Kames and Blair, it was a poetic Palladian villa—almost a literary Monticello. Yet it was not quite refined into the Adamic subtleties derived from the discoveries of the antiquities at Herculaneum and Pompeii and Rome that so characterized later English classicism in the arts, architecture, and letters, and that so dazzled the eye of that other cosmopolite, Thomas Jefferson.

Like Jefferson, Paine, Franklin, and his friend Fulton, Barlow never ceased to be the cosmopolite. To him American civilization was world civilization, and he became so enthused about the cause of world republicanism that he stood for election to the French Assembly, accepted French citizenship, and, despite having dedicated *The Vision of Columbus* to Louis XVI, called out in the end for that monarch's beheading. As American counsel to Algiers, he spent ten years diplomatically fencing with the sultans and the Barbary Pirates. And fittingly enough, his life came to a melodramatic end at Zarnowiec, an obscure village in Poland, as he died on a diplomatic mission trying to catch up with Napoleon retreating from Russia. Barlow's many activities as well as his vision made him famous as a New World prophet. Not contrast and narrow nationalism, but world harmony and combination or consensus was his theme.

But while Barlow and the cosmopolitan prophets enjoyed fame, other early American writers, perhaps just as remarkable, met with failure.

Perhaps the most noteworthy of these was Philadelphia novelist Charles Brockden Brown. Though he lived only thirty-nine years, between 1771 and 1810, Brown, in an incredible burst of literary energy, managed to write seven novels between 1797 and 1799 followed by two more novels shortly after 1800, while part of the time editing an ill-fated literary magazine that was largely filled with his shorter pieces. A shy, retiring man who had only a few literary friends in Philadelphia and New York, Brown lived largely in the world of imagination. His best novels, *Wieland, Arthur Mervyn,* and *Edgar Huntly,* were based on newspaper stories and personal experiences as he attempted, somewhat as Henry Fielding had done for England, to present a broad picture of American life. Influenced also by the English gothic writers William Godwin and Mary Shelley (the creator of *Frankenstein*), Brown composed panoramas of American life that were anything but the comic masterpieces of Fielding. Rather, he seized upon lurid incidents and dark, demonic characters as vehicles for his stories. The central figure in *Wieland* is a mad ventriloquist who murders his family in perhaps the first American tragedy. *Arthur Mervyn* is dominated by the horrors of the plague that hung like "the masque of the red death" over Philadelphia in 1798 and a mysterious swindler who buries his victims in the cellar at midnight. *Edgar Huntly* focuses on the disastrous consequences of sleepwalking while attempting to portray life on the western frontier. Hastily written and absurdly contrived though they were, Brown's best novels were nevertheless fascinating. At a time when reason and classical balance held sway as literary criteria, Brown's works were decidedly unbalanced and served as guides to the world of the nonrational imagination. In them he attempted to explain or at least comprehend the experience of the irrational, drawing moral lessons from his exercises in literary scientific investigation.

In *Arthur Mervyn* he went even further; not only did he portray the dark terrors of plague-stricken Philadelphia with its charnel-house hospitals, corpse-strewn streets, and empty, elegant houses, but he also juxtaposed the city and the country in a unique way. In seemingly conventional fashion the country youth, Arthur Mervyn, comes to the city and learns of its evils, including among his experiences a bizarre adventure in a house of prostitution. And yet unlike the protagonists in so many American (and English) novels celebrating the glories of nature as opposed to the city, Mervyn finds life in the country equally nasty, brutish, and short. At the end, in most un-American and amoral fashion, Mervyn abandons his loving country lass, gives up his resolve to become a physician and helper of suffering humanity, and instead marries a rich, mysterious, Jewish divorcée considerably older than he, who promises to take him away from Philadelphia and maintain him in grand style in Europe. No Protestant ethic or Puritan conscience thus governs Brown's hero. Of course, in Dwight's America, Brown's books went unread. As late as 1835, in the second *Salmagundi Papers*, author James Kirke Paulding was still calling for the resurrection of Brown's works, which he termed "among the most vigorous and original efforts of our native literature."

The other important novelist of the period, Hugh Henry Brackenridge, fared considerably better than Brown, though he too was unable to support himself as a man of letters and became a Pennsylvania Supreme Court judge for the last fifteen years of his life. Brackenridge, born in 1748 in York County, Pennsylvania, wrote essentially one novel throughout his literary career, *Modern Chivalry*, which appeared in a series of volumes published between 1792 and 1815. Perhaps its greatest claim to fame was that it was the first important piece of literature to come out of the West. Brackenridge wrote his initial volume in the frontier town of Pittsburgh, where he was editor of the *Pittsburgh Gazette*, proprietor of the West's first bookstore, and founder of the Pittsburgh Academy.

Influenced primarily by Miguel Cervantes and perhaps also by Henry Fielding, John Butler, and Jonathan Swift, Brackenridge's *Modern Chivalry* is the picaresque story of a latter-day Don Quixote, Captain Farrago, and his Irish servant, Teague O'Reagan, who set out on a journey from Pittsburgh to Philadelphia. Loosely strung together in a series of comic episodes, the story is punctuated by poems and Brackenridge's didactic sermons, holdovers from his days as a failed Presbyterian minister. The book intends to be a satirical examination of American democratic society and its institutions and pretensions. Breckenridge himself was a believer in a strong national government, but he also upheld the cause of the backwoodsman, though with reservations and prejudices. These reservations and his nativist prejudices are strewn throughout the book. They are best exemplified by the antics of the Irish servant O'Reagan (referred to throughout as "the bog-trotter"), who, though ignorant, dishonest, and unqualified, is ready to accept any role, honor, or elective office that comes his way, including a senatorial seat. He has to continually be put down by his absurd better, Captain Farrago, Brackenridge's voice of prejudice against Irish immigrants.

Though in book after book Brackenridge's story grew tedious and sometimes testy, its great significance lies in its matchless portrait of the frontier's grassroots political, economic, and religious institutions at work. It was a landmark in the "literature of information" that has come to be so characteristic of American writing, from William Bradford to Herman Melville and Sinclair Lewis to Truman Capote and Tom Wolfe. Equally significant was the fact that Brackenridge by no means wholeheartedly espoused the American democratic faith. He had reason to doubt that the republic would survive. As a public official out west with the responsibility for maintaining government and order, and, moreover, caught in the middle of the Whiskey Rebellion, Brackenridge knew firsthand the experience of "mobocracy" the Constitution-makers so feared. His interminable novel is thus the first to reflect American ambivalence over the important choice between frontier and civilization, and popular government and rule by the elite. Profound though his instincts were, Brackenridge, like most other early American authors, never received the major recognition his cultural insights deserved. Belletristically, he was a failure. Indeed his very efforts to cast his view of America into clumsy, derivative fiction impeded his reaching the audience he desired, and denied him coveted praise from European critics who believed that travel books and the nonfiction literature of information, such as William Bartram's *Travels* and Franklin's autobiography, were invariably the most valuable of American literary contributions.

After the War of 1812, American literature began to command new attention. A new theory of literature moved to the fore, carried forward in the pages of the *North American Review*. As explained by Archibald Allison in his *Nature and Principles of Taste* (1790), when a person allows his imagination to range freely over the form of nature perceived through his senses, "various trains of correspondent imagery rise before his imagination." Nature's forms become interrelated with other ideas and images in men's minds through memory and analogy, and the richer and more extensive the memories and analogies, the more sublime the emotion. This was the principle of association or correspondence. This theory also built on the Scottish Common Sense philosophy, but it was less concerned with classical and rational models than it was with the work of Kames and Blair. Rather, it dwelt on the inherent value of nature itself and celebrated the nonrational imagination as a means not only of perceiving nature's sublimities but also of enhancing nature's power over man's emotions through the principle of association. It released the artist from the mere rational organization of forms to a wide-ranging series of emotional relationships that enriched perception.

I

No one depended on the principle of association more than Washington Irving, America's first successful professional author. Born in New York in 1783, Irving was not a product of Yale or any of the New England colleges where Kames's *Principles* were standard fare, and there is no direct evidence that he ever read Allison. Rather, he was largely self-educated. A voracious reader and central figure among the New York Knickerbocker literati, Irving preferred to wander the streets of that bustling city absorbing its sights and sounds and dreaming of far-off places. "How wistfully," he remembered, "would I wander about the pier-heads in fine weather, and watch the parting ships, bound to distant climes; with what longing eyes would I gaze after their lessening sails, and waft myself in imagination to the ends of the earth!" Much of his writing derived its delicate meaning from this propensity to dream about the faraway, remote in both space and time, the legendary, the marvelous, and the nostalgic, convincing his readers that they too shared in his voyages of the imagination. In these respects Irving was America's first important Romantic writer. Though in his early works he adopted an Addisonian style and adhered to principles of simplicity in all his prose, he eschewed the heavy-handed didacticism and rule-bound writing of the classicists. Rather, he represented his themes subtly, through the emotions and the technique of association, which added just enough mystery to the easy grace of his writing to allow his readers' imaginations to roam as freely as did his own.

A traveler and an antiquarian at heart, Irving was at once a cosmopolitan (an expatriate, he lived abroad for seventeen years, chiefly in Germany, England, and Spain) and was perhaps the first man to discover and write about the true nature of his country's history. For Irving, world history, legend, and myth were part of America's heritage. He wasted little time lamenting the "thinness" of American experience, in the style of Cooper and other writers of his day. Nor did he manifest a provincial nationalism. Instead, by appropriating the exotic in world experience for his own, he achieved a kind of universalism that brought him critical applause both at home and abroad, making him not only foremost among American writers, but also the symbol of a different and better kind of New World man representing a nation that had the potential to absorb or include everything.

Irving's first works were satirical, the *Salmagundi Papers* written with his friend James Kirke Paulding and published in 1807, and "Diedrich Knickerbocker's" *A History of New York*, published in 1809. The *Knickerbocker History of New York* gained him wide acclaim. It reconnected with the ancient Dutch heritage of old New Amsterdam and chronicled the trivial skirmishes between the Dutch and the English by means of a caricatured series of fictional leaders, such as William the Testy (Wilhemus Kieft); Jacobus Van Curlet, the warrior who was "seized by the nape of the neck, conducted to the gate and . . . dismissed with a kick in the crupper"; General Jacobus Van Poffenburg, his successor; and the enormous, redoubtable leader, Wouter van Twiller. Clearly this was a New World struggle in which British readers could take some satisfaction, and about which the American revolutionary generation could also laugh. From the beginning, the amiable Irving served as a bridge between American and European culture. He could also use the Dutch caricatures to lampoon some of his own pompous countrymen (e.g., Thomas Jefferson). And ever so subtly he put the Revolution in a perspective less exalted than strident nationalists assumed it to be.

The Sketch-Book of Geoffrey Crayon Esq., published in 1819–1820, while he was abroad in England, brought Irving lasting fame. Greatly influenced by Sir Walter Scott, who became his friend in 1817, Irving shared his mentor's fascination with border tales, medieval histories, ruined abbeys, castles, and the folklore and legends of Germany and the Continent. *The Sketch-Book* was deliberately unpretentious: "As it is the fashion for modern tourists to travel pencil in hand, and bring home their portfolios filled with sketches, I am disposed to get up a few for the entertainment of my friends." And yet it was not entirely what it purported to be. Instead *The Sketch-Book* interspersed the first-person European travel accounts of Geoffrey Crayon (Irving) with legends about America, some of which, relating to Indians, he had previously published in the *Analectic Magazine* as early as 1814–1815. Most of his legends, however, were largely borrowed from Germany and Spain and recast in Catskill Mountain settings. In its very structure *The Sketch-Book* suggested a synthesis of Old and New Worlds. By setting down well-known European legends in American dress, Irving underscored America's role as inheritor of an older universal folk culture. "Rip Van Winkle" and "The Legend of Sleepy Hollow" have long been considered as children's stories to be fundamental parts of the American heritage, but they are in reality universal tales and Irving, the collector, knew them as such. If one scans the whole of Irving's writings, one finds the same process continually at work. *Bracebridge Hall* (1822), a loving portrait of life in an English manor house, recalls similar estates on the Hudson and in upstate New York, such as Judge Cooper's Otsego Hall. *Tales of a Traveller* (1832) brings German and French folklore to America. *The Life and Voyages of Columbus* (1828) is less concerned with the stirring voyages than the folklore behind them. And the other Spanish works, *The Conquest of Grenada* (1829) and *The Alhambra* (1832), in countless subtle ways suggest the ancient basis of the Spanish heritage of America that lies behind the voyages of Columbus and the culture that followed him in the New World. Due to these latter works, Irving became a hero in Spain.

When Irving returned to the United States, he was determined to go west and visit that most American of American places, the frontier. Irving's unique travel book, *A Tour in the Prairies* (1835), and later his masterful histories *Astoria* (1836) and *The Adventures of Captain Bonneville* (1837), saw the West largely through European eyes. In *Astoria*, his sprawling chronicle describing magnate John Jacob Astor's global plan to span the continent overland to Oregon and supply it by sea from ships sailing around Cape Horn, Irving made as much as he could of the role of the French Canadians, and the Highland Scots of the Hudson's Bay Company, whose Bacchanalian feasts in Montreal had inspired the immigrant Astor in the first place. The rude American mountain men he saw as "romantic banditti" of the Rocky Mountains, not so far removed from those he had met in Italy's Apennines and in Spain's Andalusia region. Likewise, the dramatic story of Captain Bonneville's adventures as an explorer in the Far West, written to do justice to the gallant captain who had been unfairly court-martialed by the U.S. Army, was also the story of a remarkable instance of the European heritage of America. Bonneville's French father had been a friend and protégé of Lafayette and Franklin. Captain Benjamin-Louis-Eulalie de Bonneville thus represented a second dramatic generation of meaningful French influence in America. He stood for the host of French generals and engineers who not only had fought in the Revolution but also had brought mathematics and learning to America in the succeeding decades when they helped found West Point and the Coast and Geodetic Survey and explored the West. With French trappers, some sponsored by the St. Louis Choteau family, Bonneville was thus another of Irving's clever bridges between Europe and America.

As many critics have pointed out, Irving was interested in the phenomena of change, mutability, and time, and actually understood time as working in two ways. The old ages passed and faded into picturesque ruins, antique libraries with long-forgotten books, and dimly remembered folk tales or histories. Men grew old, as did his greatest character, Rip Van Winkle, by a process that was almost magical and certainly beyond common-sense understanding. But like Rip Van Winkle, the past always came back and helped shape the present and the future. Without the past, neither man nor culture had definition. For Irving, the remembrance of things past, however far back they went and broadly they proliferated geographically, the powers of association, correspondence, and analogy generated by pastness were as critical in making a rich literature and defining a profound national culture as that other great influence on the American mind, nature. Significantly, he joined the two basic experiences in the superb introduction to his *Sketch-Book:* "never need an American look beyond his own country for the sublime and beautiful of natural scenery," he wrote, "But Europe held forth the charms of storied and poetical association." Irving, as Crayon, needed both, so he escaped "from the commonplace realities of the present" to lose himself "among the shadowy grandeurs of the past."

For Irving, Allison's associations, bound up in the terms "sublime" and "grandeur," could be used to define the American experience only if one comprehended the grandeur of the European past as well as the sublimity of a sunrise over the faint green hills of the Catskills and the silent sweep of the blue Tappan Zee—where time itself stood still in the face of nature and even on occasion looked backward.

II

Another interesting poet to arrive on the scene was young Henry Wadsworth Longfellow of Portland, Maine. He would, in time, become the nation's "good grey poet." He attended Bowdoin College, where his classmates were Nathaniel Hawthorne and future president Franklin Pierce. After graduating, Longfellow was offered a position as language teacher on the condition that he make a pilgrimage to Europe. Longfellow gladly went to Europe and stayed for three years, 1826–1829, before returning to teach at Bowdoin. By this time he was as steeped in European languages and culture as Washington Irving. He had experienced England, Holland, France, Germany, Italy, and Spain. In 1834 he was offered a chair professorship at Harvard on the condition that he spend more time in Europe. His new bride, Mary Storer Potter, died of a miscarriage in Holland, so he soon came to know sorrow—a theme that permeates such poems as

Hiawatha and *Evangeline*. A few years later, his second wife died horribly in a fire, compounding his gloom.

Perhaps influenced by Nathaniel Hawthorne's early novel *Fanshawe*, Longfellow based his first major work, *Hyperion*, on a Norwegian ballad about a fictitious character, Harold the Fair, who wandered through Europe in search of wisdom and fair women. In Longfellow's work, Harold the Fair is renamed Paul Flemming and made far more masculine, like some twentieth-century comic book hero. Longfellow was especially fascinated by Scandinavia. He knew its languages and folk literature well. He based his most famous poem, *The Song of Hiawatha* (1855), on the Finnish national epic with factual help from Henry Rowe Schoolcraft's journal of his search for the source of the Mississippi in 1821 and his six-volume *Indian Tribes of the United States* (1851). It is said that Hiawatha and his tribe were not of Minnesota but were eastern Indians; however, Schoolcraft's works in Minnesota make it almost inevitable that *The Song of Hiawatha* be set in the North Country—certainly that is the way it is taught in Minnesota!

Except for Irving, few writers of the early nineteenth century embodied European folklore in their works as Longfellow, who was unique in his interest in Scandinavia, which other bards left alone, unaware of the Norse saga tradition.

Ironically, Longfellow was often labeled a Fireside Poet, which meant that his works such as *The Song of Hiawatha*, *Evangeline*, *The Wreck of the Hesperus*, and hundreds of his other poems, such as *The Midnight Ride of Paul Revere*, were fit only for unsophisticated family consumption. He has been regarded by critics ever since as a kind of Norman Rockwell of poetry, whose subtlety by the way is only recently being discovered. Like Rockwell's, Longfellow's popularity disguised his subtlety. To critics, he had had no metaphysics, no hidden symbols to unearth, no stream of consciousness to decode. And yet the flowing rhyme and meter of his poems *are* a stream of consciousness, just as the old ballads were. Moreover, Scottish Associationism and even meaningful symbolism ran throughout his poems without being obtrusive, as they later became in modern poetry.

In any case, his publishers, Harpers and Carey, Lea, and Blanchard, thought them worthy best sellers. So did newspapers and family magazines just at the point of economic takeoff where, even in the fast-opening trans-

Allegheny West, they were eagerly purchased and read in book form in the small towns along canals and railroad stops, on farms and even in huts and cabins, though money was still scarce. Longfellow's work, widely regarded as American homespun, was nonetheless a product of the ancient European imagination. Moreover, his works formed a transition in America between Scottish Associationism and the German Romanticism of Heidelberg and Goethe.

III

The most successful and most widely read of American professional authors was James Fenimore Cooper.

While Irving was introducing Americans to a Romantic cosmopolitanism, and the New York poet-editor William Cullen Bryant was discovering the Wordsworthian qualities of American nature in poems like "Thanatopsis," "To a Waterfowl," "Oh Fairest of the Rural Maids," "June," and "A Forest Hymn," all published between 1815 and 1825, the first synthesis of an American literary imagination suddenly began to appear with the works of Cooper. In some thirty-eight novels, travel books, and volumes of political essays published between 1821 and 1851, Cooper presented a matchless panorama of American society. Relying largely on the border tales and the Romantic narrative tradition made popular by Walter Scott, Cooper described, in a seemingly endless series of adventure stories, the richly varied textures of the American experience on the seas and great lakes, in the towns and villages, and out in the forests and prairies of the vast beckoning continent. The sheer volume and breadth of his work belied his own worries about the "thinness" of American life. He reached back into history—to the Puritans, the tales of the French and Indian War, and the American Revolution—and he wrote about Europe, with its ruined castles and Machiavellian political machinations, as a means of pointing up the comparative uniqueness of the American experience. He wrote the first American utopian novel, the first American sea novels, the first important novels of social class, and the first significant novels of Indian and frontier life, and he was the first American novelist to experiment with different forms of narrative point of view. In all his books, he used dramatic action

and movement to focus sharply and profoundly upon the basic moral problems of American and European life. Most important of all, in his Leatherstocking Tales, Cooper created the first great American nature myth. Out
of the vast, pristine forests stalked a New World hero, the buckskin-clad
hunter Natty Bumppo, who was not like anything spawned by the European imagination, and whose grand religious affinity with the moral character of nature symbolized the true source of American spiritual values. In
Natty Bumppo, Cooper dramatized America's national character.

Cooper grew up on his father's baronial estate at Otsego, New York, was
dismissed from Yale College, served almost six years at sea, part of the time
in the U.S. Navy, and finally settled down as a well-to-do family man in
Scarsdale, New York. He began his writing career characteristically on impulse. While reading a sentimental English novel to his wife, Cooper
vowed he could do better, so he wrote and published *Precaution* in 1820. A
Jane Austen–like story centering on the problem of marrying off one's
daughter properly, *Precaution* was barely literature. But with his next novel,
The Spy (1821), a story about the American Revolution, Cooper was an instant success both popularly and artistically.

In all, between 1820 and 1826 Cooper published six novels, five of them
very successful, and he rose to abrupt prominence as a leading figure in
American letters—the "American Walter Scott." During this period, he
took up many of the themes that would dominate his work for the rest of
his life. *The Spy: A Tale of the Neutral Ground* dealt not only with the Revolution but also with the theme of amorality on the neutral ground, that territory in Westchester County between the lines of the American and
British armies where spies operated unhindered and the deception and
masquerade of spies were commonplace. Cooper's novel raised the moral
questions of appearance versus reality, and the relationship of deception
and lack of true law and order to the values of the Revolution. Each of the
characters is not what he seems and most often is not even heroic. Even the
noble Washington assumes a disguise (if such is imaginable) and the "hero"
Harvey Birch, a spy who appears the most wretched and contemptible of
creatures, is in reality the noblest man because of his humility and resigna-
tion before God.

In 1823 Cooper began his great Leatherstocking series with *The Pioneers*, a tale set on the shores of Lake Otsego, his family home. *The Pioneers*

is really the first of an artfully structured three-part epic chronicling the life of Natty Bumppo, or Leatherstocking. In *The Pioneers* the reader meets Leatherstocking in middle age. He has just killed a deer out of season because he needs food. However, in so doing he has broken "the law of the clearings," which has been established to prevent the settlers from wantonly destroying what is left of the forest and the wildlife. As a consequence, Leatherstocking, who is otherwise consummately in tune with nature's laws, ironically is sentenced by his old friend Judge Marmaduke Temple to public humiliation in the stocks. Brokenhearted and disgusted with the ways of civilization, Leatherstocking heads west to the uncharted forests and prairies, where he can be free.

The second novel in the Leatherstocking series, *The Last of the Mohicans* (1826), takes Natty back to his youth and his adventures in the French and Indian War. It describes the death of the noble Uncas, son of Natty's friend Chingachacook, the last of the New England Mohican tribe. In 1827, while living in Paris, Cooper published the third, and in many ways the most profound, novel in the series, *The Prairie*. This story finds Leatherstocking, a man well over eighty, away out on the southwestern plains, which are desolate and redolent of death, a far cry from the rich green forests of his youth. Out on the prairie, Leatherstocking confronts Ishmael Bush, a crude Caliban who represents the lumbering exploiter who is destroying everything in his path, including nature. The story turns on the education of Bush, who, by virtue of Leatherstocking's tutoring and personal tragedy, learns the values of law and order and of nature. Meanwhile, as civilization's law and order come to the far western frontier, Natty, an allegorical nature god, fades back into the setting sun and dies.

Over all three of the early Leatherstocking novels is cast the Romantic spell of doom and death. First the noble savage Uncas dies, the last member of his tribe. Then the settlers with ax and gun begin the despoiling of nature. And finally the frontiersman himself passes from the scene and civilization triumphs over all. Thus in its simplest terms, the early Leatherstocking trilogy focuses attention on nature as the new nation's greatest moral resource and contrasts it with civilization, which could very well be the vehicle by which human greed is enabled to destroy the American dream. And yet, though he loved nature and the natural man, Cooper also recognized the inevitability of civilization's advance. The problem for

America thus became how to cope with and control it. In the character of Ishmael Bush, Cooper recognized the powerful potential of the greedy masses. In Judge Temple, with his rigid, inhuman legal code, and in Dr. Obed Bat, the abstraction-minded scientist, Cooper recognized the reasons for nature's corruption and downfall. But he also saw some cause for hope, if judges like Temple and Bush acquired wisdom, humanity, and a reverence for nature and administered their laws accordingly. Likewise, if Dr. Bat would shed his scientistic blindness and turn his attention to the Romantic and qualitative study of nature, then his knowledge might be of some use. Though, like the country itself, Cooper could never make up his mind which he admired most, nature or civilization, he thus attempted to resolve his dilemma by suggesting that civilized man learn from nature and conduct himself accordingly instead of succumbing to the greed and demagoguery of city men, like two of his characters, Steadfast Dodge, the shifty land speculator, and Aristabulus Bragg, the dishonest newspaper editor. Thus the pattern of Cooper's Leatherstocking Tales forms perhaps the first ecological sermon.

The result of these three tales was to draw the American reader's attention most powerfully to nature and to make Leatherstocking the symbol of something peculiarly and preciously American that was closely tied to nature and individualism as sources of moral values. Nature rather than imitative classicism, as early as 1823, thus began to be the prime organizing focus of the American literary imagination.

In *The Pilot* (1824) and *The Red Rover* (1827), Cooper used the sea as a neutral ground wherein the values of American civilization could be tested. These novels, as well, focus on the question of authority versus democracy or anarchy, and the truth is brought out by examining the role of authority on shipboard. He who best knows the ways of nature is best fitted to command, even though he himself may be, like the Red Rover, a man outside of "civilized" law. Only out in nature—in this case the wild and cruel sea—can the question really be put to the test and moral truth discovered.

In 1826, Cooper sailed for Europe, complaining that American experience was too "thin." He continued to write about America, but he remained abroad for seven years living in London, Paris, the Rhine Country, Switzerland, Austria, and Italy. During this period he published four novels dealing with the American scene: *The Prairie, The Red Rover, The Water*

Witch, and *The Wept of Wish-ton-Wish*. The latter was a story of Puritan days in New England, examining the early stages of civilization's assault on the Indian and the wilderness in which Puritanism, which the Episcopalian Cooper never liked, was the vehicle for evil and tragedy.

While abroad, Cooper wrote three novels about Europe that, in shrewdly examining the European power structure, offered a lesson not only to Europeans but also to Americans. The best of these novels, *The Bravo*, was set in Venice. The hero is a bravo, a bandit rebel, a man of honor who operates outside the labyrinthian and cynical ways of established Venetian law. Using the decaying and beautiful city of Venice as his prime symbol, and making maximum advantage out of descriptions of the dark, winding corridors and dungeons inside the impressive pink birthday-cake Doge's Palace, Cooper showed that the city's "republican" government was rotten within. It was not republican at all but an oligarchical conspiracy between the tradesmen, the politicians, and the Church. The people were ignored or deceived. Even love and honor were betrayed, and the bravo hero, Jocapo, is beheaded at the story's climax.

The Heidenmauer, set in the Rhine Country and using a castle, an abbey, and a bourgeois town as symbols of the power structure, continued Cooper's analysis of European society with conclusions similar to those in *The Bravo*. Greed, money, lust for power, and callous disregard of moral values also characterized traditional German society. *The Headsman*, the last of Cooper's European trilogy, shifted the scene to Bern, Switzerland, but the conclusions were essentially the same. This last novel is redeemed from a certain banality by the character of the Headsman, paradoxically a noble and tragic man who unwillingly follows his grisly trade, beheading the guilty and sometimes not guilty, because heredity, the code that dominates his society, demands it and will allow him no other occupation. So much, in Cooper's view, for a hereditary aristocracy as the basis for a moral society.

Predictably, Cooper's European novels were not well received in Europe, and they never proved to be interesting to Americans, who preferred to see their Europe through the sunnier lights of Walter Scott. Yet the three European novels, in a most interesting way, provided an ironic contrast to the Leatherstocking trilogy. Europe had no vast forests and prairies, and an outsider like Leatherstocking would inevitably be trapped

within the system. Lacking nature's moral magic, there was no way to re-
vive decency and honor in Europe. The grandeur of its ruins was symbolically hollow and decayed. The truly sublime was represented in *The
Headsman*, for example, by the mountain that stood at the far end of Lake
Constance—only a dimly visible reminder that in all of this, God was
watching.

It was the same set of images that dominated the work of Cooper's expatriate contemporary and sometime illustrator Thomas Cole. In his most famous series of paintings, *The Course of Empire*, Cole depicted the rise and
fall of a great civilization, like that of Rome, from Arcadian beginnings
through grossly luxurious grandeur to final destruction through war. In
each painting a mountain, not unlike that which looked down upon
Cooper's Lake Constance, seemed to represent the eternal God viewing
the transitory and inevitable follies of man's loss of innocence and quest for
imperial grandeur.

Clearly from the beginning, Cooper had fastened on a set of powerful
moral themes that went to the heart of trans-Atlantic civilization. He had
also completely understood the power of literary association and intuitive
correspondence, skillfully employing symbolic settings, legend, action, and
heroic mythical characters in tremendous variety and to profound effect as
a social commentator. Cooper's writing was a panorama of the Romantic as
sermon so vast as to make it difficult to comprehend for the average reader
and so diffuse and variegated as to lose the focused narrative enjoyed by the
border balladeer, Scott, or the symbolist poet Samuel Taylor Coleridge. In
a pique at his audience, Cooper retired as a novelist shortly after his return
to America in 1834, leaving *A Letter to His Countrymen* as his legacy. The
Letter warned Americans that if they did not control their headlong pursuit
of power and wealth, they too would end up like the decadent societies of
Europe.

But Cooper could not really stop writing. In 1835 he published a petu-
lant fantasy of life among the monkeys at the Antarctic titled *The Monikins*,
which perhaps depended too much on Jonathan Swift. From 1836 to 1838
he published five travel books candidly chronicling his European wander-
ings. In 1837 he became embroiled in a controversy with local squatters,
supported by the Whig Party, over the rights to a picnic ground on his ancestral estate. Perhaps as a relief from his days before courts, lawyers, and

judges, Cooper began to write fiction again. In 1838 he wrote two novels, *Homeward Bound* and *Home as Found*, plus *The American Democrat*, a classic credo of the Jeffersonian Democrat as conservative. In his advocacy of liberty and democracy yet controlled by men of education, intelligence, and sensitivity to moral law, Cooper must have sounded in his day of Jacksonian revolution like John Adams worrying about the consequences of 1776. *Homeward Bound* and *Home as Found* continued Cooper's story of the search for moral identity, and each novel featured an archetypal character of the booming Jacksonian era as Cooper found it after his long absence in Europe. Steadfast Dodge and Aristabulus Bragg symbolized the emerging crassness of a democratic society without moral restraint and easily led by demagogues. However, the two novels, with their tone of petulance, brought Cooper nothing but criticism from his American readers.

As if he could bear the contemporary scene and the criticism of his work no longer, Cooper turned in the next years to a further examination of the past. He wrote a history of the U.S. Navy; two more sea novels; *Mercedes of Castile*, a feeble romance of Columbus's voyage; and three more frontier novels. *Wyandotte* rather melodramatically chronicled the story of an Indian's revenge against a white man who abused him. But in the other two frontier novels Cooper returned once again to the forests and the glimmerglass lakes and to Leatherstocking's saga. In 1840 he published *The Pathfinder*, a story of the forest and the Great Lakes in which Leatherstocking and his young counterpart, the sailor Jasper Western, vie for the hand of Mabel Dunham. By this time Cooper had become more and more fascinated with social class, and his story of frontier versus civilization is obscured by his penchant for social pairing. Fortunately, Leatherstocking loses the lady because of his low social status and disappears into the forest, forever free. In *The Deerslayer* (1841), Cooper takes Natty Bumppo back to the days of his young manhood, where he is initiated into the love of the wilderness and kills his first Indian—in self-defense, of course, since Natty respects every living thing, including unspoiled nature, the true basis of his morality.

As he grew older, Cooper became ever more conservative. His final major work was the *Littlepage Trilogy*, which chronicled the lives of two American families, the Effinghams and the Littlepages, through three generations to establish their just claims to social leadership and natural aristocracy. The inspiration for the trilogy was the anti-rent war that began in 1844 in upstate New York, where the tenants of the great landed estates revolted against the patroon families and demanded ownership of the lands they worked. Cooper, of course, sided with the landed gentry and used the story of the Littlepages to demonstrate the true worth of the aristocracy while being realistic enough to acknowledge their weaknesses. The villains are landsharks, developers, demagogues, and sinister revolutionaries who don calico dresses to look like Indians in their raids on the estates of the gentry. *Satanstoe* (1845) and *The Chainbearer* (1845) are effective novels. *The Redskins* (1846), insofar as it brings real Indians from way out west to the defense of the gentry against the calicoed clansmen, degenerates into far-fetched melodrama and spoils the effect of what could have been Cooper's last masterpiece.

In his declining years, however, between 1847 and 1851, when he died, Cooper retained amazing vitality as a writer. Always a man of energetic temper, during the last four years of his life he wrote five novels. Included among these were *The Crater* (1847), the first American utopian novel, and *The Sea Lions*, which effectively used the exciting facts of the search for Antarctica, where the marooned and frozen heroes find morality on the edge of an ice-bound eternity. Cooper's last novel, *The Ways of the Hour* (1850), was an experiment with point of view in the narrative that foreshadows much better–known twentieth-century writing. The heroine, Mary Monson, accused of murder, narrates the proceedings of her own jury trial, never revealing anything the jury would not have heard. As he did in all his novels, Cooper was examining the nature of reality as a rabble-filled jury can know it. After the jury errs predictably and the heroine is condemned to death, the "real truth" comes out and she is saved. However, as part of the denouement the reader discovers that the heroine narrator has been mad all along. Hers is thus "a tale told by an idiot," suggesting that, after all, who can know true reality?

With Cooper, American writing was launched out in the full tide of the Romantic revolution in sensibility. Although each of his stories focused on a moral dilemma he examined with a sometimes too relentless logic, the main corpus of Cooper's writing pointed to the vastness, sublimity, and, most important, ultimate mystery of nature, both human and physical. Unlike the eighteenth-century classicist, Cooper was never certain of the true nature of reality, a question he pursued on a global scale and in infinite variations in time, space, and personages. He was the relentless metaphysical quester whose vision was ultimately religious and came through most clearly when his characters were isolated in the forest, on rafts at sea, alone on islands, or marooned in the frozen wastes of the Antarctic. There, Cooper saw that man must first establish his humble relationship with God and God's nature, and only then could he, like noble Leatherstocking, remain serene in the face of civilization's accidents and calamities. Thus Cooper pointed up the religious nature of the rising Romantic revolution in consciousness and sensibility and he caught as well as anyone the sense of mystery that Romantics believed lies just beyond the world's appearances.

And perhaps most important for students of American thought, Cooper's chase through ambiguities after the definitions and realities of American life provided a matchless insight into the complex of paradoxes, insecurities, and contradictions that made up the many-faceted American character in the early republic. Inadvertently, perhaps because he could never entirely make up his own mind, Cooper revealed the dilemmas and paradoxes of an emerging culture over a vast range and great variety of instances. This took him far beyond the realm of pure adventure, into the confused heart of America at its most insecure period, belying its outward display of supreme confidence. Nevertheless, as time wore on, Americans forgot or ignored Cooper's tortured bouts with paradox and reality. They remember only Leatherstocking, that immortal symbol of innocence and the mythical Adamic virtues for which he and America would presumably always stand.

BOOK III

INFORMATION CREATES THE ROMANTIC CONSCIOUSNESS

CHAPTER NINE

Americans Join the Second Great Age of Discovery

Since Americans continually saw themselves as a global civilization, they partook to the fullest of European ideas and enthusiasms, one of which was romanticism. For literary scholars its roots have traditionally been traced back to Walpole and Beckford in eighteenth-century England, to the Schlegels and Schiller in Germany, and to Goethe, who in *The Sorrows of Young Werther* discovered "the man of feeling." Still another source seems equally germane to the emergence of the romantic worldview: a second Great Age of Discovery that began with space—the scientific exploration of the whole earth—and concluded in a fascination with the romantic as the central organizing principle of natural development and human consciousness. Thus the explorations of the Second Great Age of Discovery that introduced the exotic wonders of the globe created a new intellectual paradigm.

I

The Second Great Age of Discovery represents a lost horizon of world cultural experience. Largely overshadowed by the initial expansion of Europe into the New World during the time of Columbus, the Second Age of Discovery took place almost unnoticed by historians from 1750 to the end of the nineteenth century. Such men as Captain James Cook, Sir George Vancouver, Captain Frederick Beechey, Louis Antoine de Bougainville, Vitus Bering, Edmund La Perousse, Edward Fanning, Lieutenant Charles Wilkes, Elisha Kent Kane, and Robert E. Peary charted the world's oceans, discovered two continents, penetrated the Arctic and Antarctic, and spread the exoticism of the South Seas before the eyes of western man. Meanwhile, others such as the Prussian Alexander von Humboldt, Peter Pallas, Mungo Park, Charles Marie de la Condamine, Samuel Hearne, Alexander Mackenzie, and Lewis and Clark opened up the interiors of the great continents, mapped their mountains and rivers, collected specimens of their natural history, and described their exotic and hitherto little-known peoples.

Humboldt virtually created the romance of exploration with his five years of travel in South America's mountains and jungles (1799–1805), which he published as *Personal Narrative of a Journey to the Equinoctial Regions of the New Continent*. A friend of Goethe and others of the Romantic school at Jena, Humboldt made exploration romantic, but also scientific on a grand scale. He made geography a new dramatic science as he climbed the highest mountain in South America, Mount Chimborazo. He was also the first to scientifically map Mexico. Humboldt stood for adventure on a grand scale, but his greatest scientific theory posited an "isothermic zodical belt" around the earth in temperate climes over which civilizations would inevitably migrate. He was a romantic giant of the early nineteenth century and influenced scientist-naturalists as well as explorers who sought to imitate him.

Like the explorers of the fifteenth and sixteenth centuries—immortalized in Hakluyt's *Voyages*—the men of the Second Age of Discovery caused significant changes in western thought. In the centuries that intervened since the time of Columbus, the Scientific Revolution had taken place. This event reoriented the aims of exploration and greatly increased western man's capacity for absorbing, interpreting, and organizing new knowledge. Thus explorers of the Second Age of Discovery differed significantly from the adventurers of the earlier age. They were most often men of science in search of knowledge rather than paradise, gold from the Indies, or the establishment of the New Jerusalem. In this role they assembled an extensive inventory of the earth's natural phenomena that shattered previous structures of ordered knowledge and generated profound series of cultural crises that were reflected in the consciousness of American intellectuals and in the creation of new institutions.

Sir James Edward Smith, the first president of the Linnaean Society, reporting on his research in Australia in 1793 suggested what was happening:

> When a botanist first enters on the investigation of so remote a country as New Holland, he finds himself as it were in a new world. He can scarcely meet with any fixed points from whence to draw his analogies and even those that appear most promising, are frequently in danger of misleading, instead of informing him. The whole tribes of plants which at first sight seem familiar to his acquaintance, as occupying links in nature's chain, on which he is accustomed to depend, prove, on nearer examination, total strangers, with other configurations, other economies, and other qualities; not only the species themselves are new, but most of the genera, and even natural orders.

The new explorer-scientists were dedicated believers in the Great Chain of Being, but at the same time devoted to Baconian or Lockean empiricism. After 1753, equipped with Linnaeus's natural history classification system, they found so much new data, so many anomalies in the Chain of Being, as to expand it to the breaking point. As early as 1800 they began looking for a new set of principles upon which to organize the natural history of the world. It was just at this point that American explorers and scientists entered the Second Great Age of Discovery.

II

Science in early America took place within the exciting global framework and the immense wilderness of North America, with its painted Indians, trackless forests, lush everglades, mountain ranges, stunning falls at Niagara, and mighty Mississippi, which flowed through its heart continually attracting European savants and gentleman sportsmen as well. Many who came to America's wilderness did so in the hope of hunting the grizzly bear (*ursus horribilus*) or riding the wild chase after the buffalo that roamed the endless prairies in herds of thousands. Jefferson himself attracted a number of Europeans, including Humboldt, who stopped by Monticello on his way home from Mexico to compare notes with the American polymath, who, next to Franklin, stood highest in the esteem of European savants.

The Sage of Monticello also encouraged the immigration of Joseph Priestly, codiscoverer of oxygen, to the United States, and he sponsored the expedition of French botanist André Michaux into the Ohio Country. Michaux turned out to be something of a spy, but that did not disillusion Jefferson, who had, after all, allowed the French general Collot to make a detailed survey of the Ohio and Mississippi rivers so that France might better guard the frontiers of Louisiana. It was Jefferson and his party who encouraged French engineers, such as Claudius Bernard and Claudius Crozet (two of Napoleon's staff), to stay on in America, where they helped found not only West Point but the science of engineering as well. Also in Jefferson's era came Ferdinand Hassler, a Swiss geophysicist who founded the U.S. Coast Survey, which gained the respect of the world's scientific community by 1830.

Other European explorer-scientist-adventurers emigrated of their own accord. William Maclure of Scotland, who made the first geologic map of the United States in 1809, was a valuable acquisition, as was his countryman Robert Dale Owen. In 1825 Maclure established a utopian scientific community at New Harmony, Indiana, that included a French zoologist who had sailed to the South Pacific with Nicolas Baudin and also a Dutch botanist. At Bethlehem, Pennsylvania, the German Moravian bishop, Henry Muhlenberg, became a world authority on botany, while the Englemann brothers, George and Henry, settled in the German community at St. Louis and became the primary source of information concerning the botany of the Trans-Mississippi West. Meanwhile, freelance explorers—such as the Swede Peter Kalm, the Scotsman Alexander Wilson, the Italian Giacomo Beltrami, and the French émigré John James Audubon—roamed all over pristine America searching out its wonders, and in the case of Audubon's *in situ* life-like bird drawings, producing some of the world's artistic masterpieces.

One of the more interesting of backwoods explorers was the eccentric Frenchman Constantine Rafinesque, who won, and then lost, a job (because of bizarre behavior) at Transylvania College in Kentucky, the first college west of the Appalachians. Rafinesque, like Jefferson, was a polymath. He was an authority on all forms of geology and natural history and was a map-maker as well, but his mind was too active to settle seriously into one pursuit, so he was frequently dismissed as a crank. Yet, long before Charles Darwin, Constantine, Rafinesque, the Edgar Allan Poe of science, proposed an evolutionary hypothesis that he believed made order out of all the multifarious data he saw around him. His proposal was, of course, ignored.

The eastern United States held rich charms for the explorer-scientist, but the Trans-Mississippi West had an even greater appeal. In 1822, his mind heated like the "knight of La Mancha" and by Alexander von Humboldt's example and encouragement, young Paul, Duke of Wurtumburg, made the first of seven expeditions into the heart of the continent. By the time he had finished exploring North America in the 1850s, the duke had assembled perhaps the largest collection of natural history and ethnological specimens from western America then extant in Europe. During the course of his travels and adventures, he had also seen more of the West than nearly any American. Möllhausen, his assistant, stayed on in the United States accompanying U.S. government expeditions and publishing spectacularly illustrated scientific travel books. When he returned to Germany, Heinrich Balduin Möllhausen had absorbed so much of the adventurous lore of the frontier that he turned to writing dozens of novels and became known as the "German Fenimore Cooper."

Not to be outdone, in 1833, Maximillian, Prince of Wied Neuwied, left his comfortable castle at Coblentz to journey far up the Missouri River into the heart of the hostile Blackfeet country, taking *his* artist with him as well. The prince was a serious scientist inspired by Humboldt and exotic America. His carefully written scientific notebooks, less familiar than his travel book, attest to this. And the work of his artist, Karl Bodmer, was perhaps unmatched as an ethnological record of the fast-vanishing American Indian. Certainly Bodmer's watercolors and oil paintings of western America and its native inhabitants are the most vivid and beautiful ever done of western America and its indigenous inhabitants. His paintings of the Mandans of North Dakota remain among the few significant pictorial records of that once-powerful tribe, which was nearly destroyed by an epidemic in 1837.

Bodmer's rival as a western painter was the American Alfred Jacob Miller of Baltimore, who accompanied the Scottish baronet, Sir William

Drummond Stewart, on an expedition to the Rocky Mountains in 1837. While Stewart, ever the sportsman, was busy chasing buffalo and trapping beaver with the wild mountain men, Miller recorded the whole untamed landscape of mountains, prairies, Indians, and fur trappers with an astonishing romantic verve that yet preserved an authenticity that few, if any, Europeans ever matched in any part of the world. Although many Europeans visited the American west, none except Bodmer matched the romantic achievements of the American George Catlin, who painted all of the western tribes, many of those in South America and the whole West Coast of North America.

III

A combination of national pride, a sense of the utility of science in subduing a vast continent, and a Humboldtean sense of grandeur and sublimity inspired the scientists and the masses alike in the romantic Second Great Age of Discovery. This was most clearly expressed in the projects undertaken by early American scientists—projects that inevitably led them into the world community of science.

The most pressing need, as early as the American Revolution, was a simple geographic knowledge of the thirteen colonies that would become the United States. Virtually all maps of North America were made in Europe by professional cartographers, such as Aaron Arrowsmith in London and A. H. Brué in Paris. Even the map of Virginia and Maryland made by Jefferson's father in 1751 was published only in England. Largely because of the long struggle with France, the English Board of Trade and Plantations began commissioning New World land surveys. William DeBrahm, a German, was appointed Surveyor General for the Southern District of North America. Between 1764 and 1770, he and a crew of surveyors mapped South Carolina, Georgia, and Florida. In 1760, an official position of Geographer to the King had been established, and Thomas Jeffreys, a specialist in North American and West Indian cartography, received the appointment.

Both Britain and France in the eighteenth century were rapidly accumulating cartographical knowledge, not only about North America, but about the globe as well. The worldwide cooperative efforts in 1761 and 1769 to observe the transits of Venus, which took Captain James Cook to Tahiti and John Winthrop Jr. to Newfoundland, were part of an effort to determine the shape of the globe.

In all of this, the United States started at a disadvantage but developed very rapidly until geophysical, geographical, and geological exploration became the strength of American scientific endeavor. The realization that America needed its own mapmakers first occurred to George Washington, himself a former surveyor. During the Revolution, he appointed Scottish engineer Robert Erskine as Surveyor General of the Continental Army. Erskine gradually assembled a staff of twenty "young gentlemen of Mathematical genius, who are acquainted with the principles of Geometry and who have a taste for drawing." Erskine's chief assistant was a young Rutgers graduate, Simeon De Witt, who at the age of twenty-four assumed Erskine's position as surveyor general when Erskine died in 1780.

Meanwhile, to the south, Thomas Hutchins, a veteran of the British army, who laid out Fort Pitt and traveled through Louisiana and west Florida, was appointed geographer to the Southern Continental Army in 1781. In 1778 he published in London *A Topographical Description of Virginia, Maryland and North Carolina*. He knew Ben Franklin, and it was through his offices that Hutchins secured his commission in the Continental Army. Hutchins gained everlasting fame in the history of American cartography because in 1785 he was appointed surveyor of the Seven Ranges of Ohio, which laid down the basic land division system of the United States. Starting with a baseline, Hutchins laid out a grid pattern of 160 one-acre sections that eventually was carried across the United States. This enabled the federal government to locate land parcels for sale or distribution to the settlers moving west. In the words of Daniel Boorstin, Hutchins "packaged a continent."

IV

Republican American science took other forms, however, even more consonant with the Humboldtean spatial vision. Early in his administration, Jefferson sent expeditions out into the wilderness frontier. Dr. George

Featherstonehaugh was dispatched to the Ozark Plateau Country of present-day Arkansas. Drs. William Dunbar and George Hunter explored the Red River Country of Louisiana, and Zebulon Pike took a skiff up the Mississippi River.

But Jefferson's most important venture was the dispatching of Meriwether Lewis and William Clark to the Pacific. To the Spanish ambassador, Jefferson represented their mission as a literary or scientific endeavor, taking advantage of the vogue for such operations. To Congress, Jefferson advanced the expedition as a commercial venture. In fact, it was both, and it had political implications as well. Jefferson hoped to secure the allegiance of Indian tribes in that region, so tenuously claimed by Spain. Nonetheless, the scientific aspect of Lewis and Clark's expedition was paramount. Lewis was specially trained by the leading savants of Philadelphia in all phases of science, from the geophysical skills of the mapmaker to the recognizing talents of the naturalist.

The explorers were to be not specialists but generalists, charged with presenting an integrated picture of the whole continent they traversed. Jefferson's instructions make this clear. They were first of all to locate "the most direct and practicable water communication across this continent for the purposes of commerce." In the process they were to construct a map, carefully based on astronomical observations, placing upon it the location of all natural and human features—such as mountains, rivers, and Indian villages—they encountered. They were to pay particular attention to the "soil and face of the country," its plants, animals, minerals, fossils, and evidences of volcanic action in addition to keeping a daily log of the weather. Finally, they were to take particular note of the Indian inhabitants—"their language, dress, and monuments, their numbers, their relations with other tribes, their houses, diseases, remedies, laws, and customs." In short, Lewis and Clark were to do on a continental scale what Jefferson had done for his native state in *Notes on Virginia*, except that they were also to incorporate this data on a map.

Lewis and Clark set the tone for the most characteristic American scientific activity of the early nineteenth century—extensive geographical expeditions, comprehensive in nature, that spanned immense stretches of the country and brought back, in addition to increasingly exact maps, a torrent of natural history. These undertakings tied up the talents of America's best natural scientists for most of the pre–Civil War period. But in terms of basic, background science, it was ultimately worthwhile: American data eventually became crucial to forming a new paradigm of knowledge not only in science but in intellectual history as well.

After Lewis and Clark's continental crossing, the most important of the early American expeditions sent out into the interior of the continent were those of Lieutenant Zebulon Pike and Major Stephen H. Long. In 1805, Pike, who had explored the Mississippi the previous year, set off across the prairie from St. Louis. He conducted a general reconnaissance of the High Plains and entered into the Rocky Mountains. Though he failed in an attempt to climb what is now Pike's Peak, he and his men did succeed in climbing Cheyenne Peak fifteen miles away, which afforded them a panoramic view of the southern Rockies. This view governed his conceptualization of the whole West. Then he took his expedition into a winter encampment in the Sangre de Christo Mountains, where he was captured by the Spaniards and imprisoned. Most of his equipment and notebooks were confiscated before he was escorted across Texas back to the United States. Pike, however, did manage to secrete some notes on what he had observed—sufficient to construct a map of the Rocky Mountain region as he had seen it. This map was based primarily, however, on one made by Humboldt and included in the great explorer's atlas to the *Political Essay on the Kingdom of New Spain*. Pike repeated Humboldt's error in linking the southern Rockies directly to the northern Rockies, which had been carefully mapped by Lewis and Clark, thus leaving out the central Rockies or much of present-day Colorado, which he had reason to know well. Likewise, both men believed that somewhere in the heart of the Rockies lay "a grand reservoir of snows and fountains" from which flowed all the rivers of the West, both eastward and westward.

Major Stephen H. Long's expedition of 1819–1820 was better organized. Originally it was part of the Yellowstone Expedition sent to chastise the hostile Indians of the Upper Missouri. But once that expedition disbanded, Long was ordered south across the High Plains, once again to search for the sources of the Red River. Long's party was much better equipped scientifically, including the accomplished Philadelphia naturalists

Thomas Say and Titian Peale, the son of Charles Wilson Peale, Edwin James, another naturalist, and the artist Samuel Seymour, plus two West Point topographers.

Long's march took him along the front range of the Rocky Mountains, where they were represented for the first time in Seymour's drawings. Long and his men climbed Pike's Peak and measured its altitude above the plain, and they made collections and notes sufficient to add greatly to Peale's museum, where the materials eventually came to rest, causing the complete reorganization of the museum according to professional scientific standards. Among the products of the Long expedition were Titian Peale's expert drawings of western fauna. But most important was Long's map, published in 1821, in which he, following Pike's lead, labeled the Central Plains of the United States a "Great Desert," unfit for civilized inhabitation. For years afterward, travelers, would-be settlers, and government policy-makers considered it as such. It became a place to get across on the way West to California and Oregon rather than a place to settle, and most of it was considered so undesirable that part of it was set aside as "Indian Territory" to which Andrew Jackson removed the Cherokee.

The 1820s saw the opening of the Rocky Mountains by fur trappers and the discovery of routes to California and Oregon. The latter was made into a kind of "international road" by a government expedition that gave only a passing glance to anything scientific. But in 1842, Lieutenant John C. Frémont entered the scene as perhaps the most popular of all western explorers. In that year he journeyed over the Oregon Trail and climbed the Wind River Mountains in the Rockies, unfurling an eagle flag as the symbol of Manifest Destiny. An arch romantic, Frémont was a correspondent of Humboldt, who came to greatly admire the Pathfinder's works. Of Frémont's many expeditions, the most significant was undertaken in 1843–1844 when he followed the Oregon Trail to the Pacific, then turned and marched south along the eastern wall of the Sierra Nevada, pausing to name the Humboldt River after his hero before entering California. He then turned east and crossed eastward over the Rocky Mountains. Frémont, as it were, had circumnavigated the entire American West.

The myth of the Rio Buenaventura, the idea that a navigable river flowed west to the Pacific across the Rockies and the Great Basin, was now finally laid to rest. Frémont had also determined the true geographical character of the Great Basin and had constructed the first overall map of the West based on geophysical principles. His report included data on geology, zoology, and Indians. Moreover, his Prussian cartographer-assistant, Charles Preuss, made a detailed emigrant map in seven sections, which was to prove particularly useful to westering parties.

Frémont, like the other American explorer-scientists of his day, felt himself very much a part of the Humboldtean tradition. His reports, edited by his wife, Jessie, are full of poetic descriptions of nature's wonders, and yet the primary drift of his comprehensive report on the West was as an environment for settlement. His glowing descriptions of California caused many settlers to emigrate to the pastoral Pacific shores, and his description of the Salt Lake Valley as "a bucolic place" influenced Mormon leader Brigham Young to establish the Mormon Kingdom of the Desert on the shores of the great inland sea.

In 1838, the U.S. Army had created the Corps of Topographical Engineers, of which Frémont was one, and the Topographical Bureau, whose specific duty was to explore the heart of the continent, map it, and complete its scientific description. Between 1838 and the Civil War, officers of the Corps of Topographical Engineers, who considered themselves scientists in their own right, spread out all over the interior of the continent and brought back scientific data to the growing scientific community in torrential quantities. Asa Gray at Harvard and John Torrey in New York worked almost full-time analyzing plant specimens brought back by army explorers. In the course of their work in botany they introduced the natural system of classification into the United States. This system compared plant specimens on the basis of similarity in overall appearances instead of one characteristic. Such a method made botany much more difficult and helped bring about an increased professionalization of the field.

I have elsewhere described the entire work of the army explorers during this period, but many important results arose from their expeditions. Geologists working in the Southwest became convinced that massive igneous intrusions had shaped the country. They also clearly saw the effects of erosion on a grand scale, evidence of Sir Charles Lyell's theory of uniformitarianism put forth in his *Principles of Geology* (1831–1833). Beyond water erosion, the geologists with army expeditions also noted other forces at work on the earth—the grinding effects of glaciation, the abrasion of rocks by wind and sand, and the cracking and faulting of the earth's crust they believed to cause earthquakes.

In 1857, Ohio geologist John Strong Newberry descended to the floor of the Grand Canyon and constructed a geologic column that reached farther back into time than perhaps any other such examination of the earth up to his day. This had its counterpart in the work of Ferdinand V. Hayden and Fielding B. Meek with Captain William Raynolds in the Dakota Badlands, where they located the entire cretaceous horizon and discovered ancient dinosaur fossils. These they sent to Dr. Joseph Leidy in Philadelphia, whose published report *The Ancient Fauna of Nebraska* was supplemented with the first description of an animal's evolutionary development. He traced the growth of the horse from protohippus, the miniature "dawn horse" of the Pleistocene era, to the modern hooved variety just when Darwin was writing his *On the Origin of Species.* Leidy's work was much obscured and eventually forgotten until, in 1867, Othniel Charles Marsh of Yale revived the concept, wrote the definitive work on it, and provided, in Darwin's view, the best support for his theory of evolution through natural selection.

Most important of the army scientific undertakings in pre–Civil War America were the great surveys for a railroad to the Pacific. These were authorized and took place in 1853. Expeditions crossed the American West along four separate parallels, while a fifth expedition coursed up and down the Pacific slope looking for passes to link possible transcontinental lines. A massive undertaking for its day, the Pacific Railroad Survey included 160 scientists and hundreds of auxiliaries and assistants. One party leader, Captain John W. Gunnison, and his scouting group were massacred by hostile Indians; unshaken, Captain Andrew Atkinson Humphreys supervised the completion of all the surveys within one year. The scientific results were supposed to prove objectively which was the best route for a railroad to the Pacific. Instead, each expedition leader proclaimed his the most feasible route, and hence science proved to be no help at all in making what ultimately became a political decision.

The result of these studies was instead a Humboldtean scientific inventory of the entire trans-Mississippi West. It was as if the entirety of Europe or Australia had been completely studied within one year. Not even Humboldt could match this feat, but the characteristically American effort was conducted by team or group efforts that foreshadowed most modern scientific approaches to problems.

Two sets of reports were published by Congress. The first, a short series issued in 1855, was a preliminary report. This was followed by a lavishly illustrated thirteen-volume report. Each expedition leader published a narrative of his line of march, which made interesting reading for the layman. Then there were extensive geological reports, separate volumes on botany, mammals, reptiles, birds, and fish; monographs on paleontology, Indian ethnology, and archaeology; plus tables of astronomical positions and a whole volume of large map sheets. Included were three geological maps, one by Jules Marcou, a Swiss; one by W. P. Blake of Columbia; and one by James Hall of Albany, who had never seen the West at all but who was the doyen of geologists in America. There were also pages of barometric profiles, geological cross-sections, and even an ingenious diagram that, in hundreds of tiny drawings, related tree growth to altitude. All of this data was synthesized by Lieutenant Governor Kemble Warren on a master map of the West published in 1857. It was the most accurate and comprehensive western map of its day and certainly one of the greatest of American maps.

The Pacific Railroad Surveys were the apogee of the Humboldtean tradition in American science. An encyclopedia of the western environment, they combined geophysics with natural history to present a picture of the West that related directly to transportation, settlement, capitalistic exploitation, and public policy. At the same time, they were a contribution to world science, and copies were distributed to all the European centers of learning with great national pride.

V

But from the beginning, American men of the sea had been very much a part of the Second Great Age of Discovery. In 1802, Nathaniel Bowditch of Salem produced an indispensable work for sea captains, *The New American Practical Navigator.* His work on this aid to navigation also led him to substantially revise Pierre-Simon Laplace's *Celestial Mechanics*, which gained Bowditch great acclaim in Europe. Later, Lieutenant Matthew Fontaine Maury, who had charge of the Naval Observatory in Washington, began the systematic study of the sea and hence founded the science of oceanography. Under his direction, the observatory issued wind and current charts on the world's oceans, enabling packet boats, clipper ships, and whalers to set speed records for ocean travel between distant ports. Maury also compiled charts on whale migrations, which compared—in fact, were superior to—the plant and animal distribution maps made by naturalists on land, because they accurately traced the mobility of the great leviathans instead of picturing them in static colonies. Maury's charts and his mapping for the first time the floor of the Atlantic Ocean were his crowning achievements. History remembers him, however, for his somewhat garbled but first comprehensive oceanography treatise, *The Physical Geography of the Sea* (1855).

But while federal oceanographers were at work in Washington, American sailors were also performing spectacular feats at sea. Very early in the nineteenth century, American explorers solved the problem of *Terra Australis Incognita*, or the location of a continent south of Cape Horn, which Magellan had suggested in the sixteenth century. In 1819 seal hunters from Stonington, Connecticut, working in the fog and sleet off the South Shetlands sighted the Antarctic Coast. In that year, James P. Sheffield in the *Hersillia* was the first to see the southern continent. He was followed in early 1820 by Edward Bransfield in the *Williams* and in November 1820 by Nathaniel Palmer in the *Hero*. John Davis of New Haven made the first landing on the southern continent when he rowed ashore from the *Cecelia* in 1831. The dramatic achievements of these intrepid men were obscured by later international quarrels over priority of the scientific discovery of the Antarctic as a continent.

In 1838, Lieutenant Charles Wilkes left Hampton Roads, Virginia, in command of a flotilla of six ships staffed with scientists, mapmakers, and artists in imitation of the great Captain James Cook. His mission was to definitively establish the existence of the Antarctic continent, to cruise the South Pacific, and to explore the Oregon coast looking for possible ports on the Pacific and perhaps the outlet of a Northwest Passage.

Wilkes and his men were gone for four years in one of the great voyages in Pacific history. Not only did he find Antarctica and land on it, but he mapped its hazardous coasts for 1500 leagues. Then he sailed through the Pacific Islands, establishing America as a Pacific power and gathering rich data on the exotic islands and coral atolls. Wilkes's charts of the Pacific were the most accurate made of the whole area before the end of the nine-teenth century, and the scientific work of James Dwight Dana and the corps of scientists proved extremely important. Dana eventually incorporated his experiences with Wilkes into his lectures at Yale, promoting scientific exploration as the most exciting occupation in the world.

From the South Pacific, Wilkes sailed on to Hawaii and then to the mouth of the Columbia River, where one of his ships went down, smashed on the bar while trying to enter the river. Because of this experience, Wilkes urged negotiators of the Northwest Boundary with Canada to hold out for a parallel north of the Columbia where safer harbors might be found. As such, he had a basic influence not only on American foreign policy but literally on the shape of the country as well. Despite his contributions to national policy and world science, Captain Wilkes returned to the United States not in triumph but in disgrace. His officers preferred charges against him for favoritism and cruelty, foreign ambassadors questioned his Antarctic data, and Congress thought so little of his great discoveries that it ordered only one hundred copies of his multivolume report printed.

However, American naval exploration continued. Captain Cadwalader Ringgold commanded an expedition to explore the North Pacific, and when he went mad in Singapore, Commander John Rogers took over. When the voyage was finished it had extended as far as Japan and brought back natural-history specimens that became crucial to the history of world science. The Rogers-Ringgold expedition followed in the wake of Commodore Matthew Calbraith Perry's dramatic voyage to Japan in 1852–1854, intended to open Japan and all of east Asia to American trade and locate islands and ports where coaling stations might be established to service the new steam warships then coming into use. Perry's experience in Japan as well as the Rogers-Ringgold North Pacific Expedition brought Japan's long-hidden exotic culture to the attention of an astonished world. Henceforth, things Japanese would have a significant impact on American thought, from James A. McNeill Whistler in art to Lafcadio Hearn in literature and Ernest Fenollosa in art, and the establishment of American museums, such as the Freer Museum in Washington, dedicated to traditional Japanese art.

During the same period, other American explorer-scientists were deploying into South America, Africa, and the Arctic. In 1850, Navy Lieutenant

Edwin DeHaven, sponsored by philanthropist Henry Grinnell, set out on an expedition to rescue Sir John Franklin, a British explorer lost in the Arctic. In 1853 Lieutenant Elisha Kent Kane commanded a second expedition that reached the highest known point of north latitude, 80° 10' at Cape Constitution on the Kennedy Channel between Greenland and Ellesmere Island. He did not ultimately find Franklin, but his vivid accounts of the voyage set in motion a whole series of American Arctic explorations by A. W. Greeley, Charles F. Hall, Isaac Hayes, and later Robert E. Peary.

In the mid-nineteenth century, visions of the Arctic and its adventurous, often tragic explorers had a profound effect on the American imagination in the works of such artists as Frederick Church and William Bradford and writers such as James Fenimore Cooper and Edgar Allan Poe. Elisha Kent Kane made his own sketches on his perilous voyage, but his trip was dramatized by Canadian artist James Hamilton, whose works pictured the perilous Arctic as no other artist had.

To the south, Lieutenant Melville Gilliss, following in the footsteps of Charles Marie La Condamine and Humboldt, explored the Chilean Andes and attempted to measure the transit of Venus across the sun from the Southern Hemisphere at the same time that Maury was to make observations in Washington. While Gilliss was in Chile, Lieutenants Lardner Gibbon and William Herndon led an expedition into the valley of the Amazon looking for a suitable place to colonize American slaves. Ironically, a bit later, in 1858–1859, Dr. Martin Delany, who became the first black officer in the U.S. Army, explored Africa's west coast and signed a treaty with the Abbeokuta chiefs of the Niger in the region of Timbuktu for the same purpose. The first half of the nineteenth century was indeed a Second Great Age of Discovery in many dimensions, in which Americans took part in the worldwide spirit of the age with zest, imagination, and skill.

VI

In large measure, explorer-scientists of the Second Great Age of Discovery discovered not only open space but also nature's plenitude. As explorers, naturalists, and scientific artists fanned out over the globe, they opened up immense new territories—even continents—for examination. The discovery of these new territories in turn greatly increased the data flowing into centers of scientific learning and created a demand for greater discoveries, more advanced interpretations, and new structures for ordering information in meaningful ways. In Jacksonian America, outside of the military, a few governmental agencies such as the Coast Survey, and widely scattered private learned societies and emerging colleges, there was no real mechanism or institution for coordinating research and the dissemination of knowledge so vital to the new republic. Almost providentially, a foreigner who had never set foot in America came to the rescue.

James Smithson, heir to the Duke of Northumberland, chemist, and Fellow of the Royal Society, died at Genoa on June 27, 1829, leaving a will that eventually bequeathed his entire fortune to the United States for "the increase and diffusion of knowledge among men." Smithson, though he had never come to America, was a well-traveled cosmopolitan gentleman who resided most of his life in Paris, where he was a friend of Francois Arago, the French physicist. In close touch with the expansive labors of the Second Great Age of Discovery as reflected by activity in England, France, Italy, Germany, and Sweden, Smithson clearly saw the need for some focus or center for American activity, though his will was eloquently unspecific as to what form this might take. He concentrated only on the essentials, which, in fact, constituted a primary problem for American scientists and politicians alike.

Smithson's legacy at first raised more problems than it solved in republican America. When President Andrew Jackson announced the gift in his annual Message to Congress on December 17, 1835, many solons, including John C. Calhoun, advocated refusing it on the grounds that Congress was not empowered to accept gifts and, furthermore, that such gifts, especially from foreigners, were beneath the dignity of a free people. Humbler and wiser opinions prevailed, fortunately. John Quincy Adams, as chairman of the joint legislative committee to investigate the problem, brought in a favorable report in January 1836, and by July, Congress had passed a bill accepting the gift. Richard Rush, a Philadelphia lawyer, was sent to England to claim the legacy before the British Courts in Chancery, and he returned two years later, in the summer of 1838, literally bearing dozens of bags of gold coins to the value of $508,318.46. Later the bequest was increased to $550,000 and invested in Arkansas state bonds.

At this point serious debate began over the proper institutional mechanism for "the increase and diffusion of knowledge among men." Ex-president John Quincy Adams returned once again in his old advocacy of a national observatory—an idea for "lighthouses in the sky," once so venomously ridiculed by Congress as to virtually drive him from the presidency. Rufus Choate, of Connecticut, argued for a national library. Others favored a national university or a national agricultural experiment station. The ongoing debate between practical and theoretical science dominated virtually every discussion. For nearly eight years, matters stood at an impasse, during which time expeditions continued to collect more data, scientists began to create their own informal network for the exchange of information, and Arkansas defaulted on its bond interest payments, causing the federal government to make up the loss on Smithson's legacy.

Finally the model for a meaningful institution began to emerge. In 1840 at the home of Navy Secretary Joel Poinsett, leading members of Congress, the federal departments, the military, and a number of important savants organized the National Institution, whose deliberately vague object was "to increase and diffuse knowledge among men." The National Institute, as it came to be called, was primarily the creation of Poinsett, himself a world traveler and lover of science. It was conceived of as not only a national clearinghouse for scientific information but also as a kind of holding company for the Smithson bequest. Poinsett, who was also a diplomat, had found a way out of the impasse of conflicting ideologies that for eight years had impeded action on Smithson's legacy through combining most of the interests in his all-encompassing goal of the Smithsonian. The National Institute, granted a charter of incorporation by Congress in 1842, was actually a caucus of the country's leading savants and interested politicians designed to generate consensus about what to do with Smithson's money. Like the Constitutional Convention, the National Institute represented a "compromise by combination." Every branch of learning and educational interest was represented and given national prestige at its first formal annual meeting in April 1844.

Instead, by 1846, as a result of Poinsett's maneuverings, Historian George Brown Goode declared, "The country was prepared to expect it to be a general agency for the advancement of scientific interests of all kinds—as catholic, as unselfish, as universal as the National Institute had been prepared to be." Basically the Smithsonian represented a last institutionalized attempt to encompass all knowledge as rapidly as it expanded. Its first secretary, Joseph Henry, was in a sense a polymath who wielded great influence in the Association of American Scientists.

The Smithsonian itself had an even larger significance than its first secretary. It symbolized, indeed dramatized, American scientists attempting to come to grips with the information explosion in the Second Great Age of Discovery. It was the outward, visible sign of encouragement for science, the importance of collections as background research and the value of knowledge as culture. Even more important, it was an attempt to structure knowledge through a massive cooperative indexing operation that had become institutionalized as an ongoing social process.

But the Smithsonian was not the most important outcome of the Second Great Age of Discovery. Due to his voyage to South America, Charles Darwin eventually discovered the chance universe that lay behind the theory of evolution. He published his theory in 1859 in *On the Origin of Species*. It took some time for the theory to catch on after many religious battles following the American Civil War, but when it did, the world of nature and man would never be the same again.

CHAPTER TEN

I Am "Part or Parcel of God": The Romantic Search for the Self

The apogee of Romantic revolution in America was reached appropriately enough on the earliest battlefields of the first American Revolution—Boston and Concord. The struggle was led by Ralph Waldo Emerson, the genial poet whose "Concord Hymn" celebrated "the shot heard round the world." His legions consisted of a motley group of contentious scholars, ministers, poets, and philosophers who styled themselves "Transcendentalists."

Though for a time the scene of their struggle was very local, the Transcendentalists were in reality citizens of the world. Indeed, in their own parlance they were citizens of the "cosmos." Their true aim was to redefine man, God, and nature. They were out to change reality itself and in so doing to change the patterns of human behavior that depended upon these more basic relationships. Though the course of their thought generally paralleled, and in many ways duplicated, that of the revivalists, especially in their emphasis on emotion and intuition as the source of true knowledge and their rejection of predestination in favor of a gospel of hope, the Transcendentalists had other, more sophisticated sources of inspiration than the

Bible and personal revelation. They were the American avant garde of the Romantic Movement. In the name of nationalism, self-reliance, and a newly minted morality that stood as a rebuke to the onrushing tides of materialism, Transcendentalists borrowed the latest ideas and even their name from Europe, and from them they fashioned a new, American metaphysics.

Since much of the Romantic Movement was philosophically and behaviorally bound up in role-playing—exploring the infinite possibilities of the self and other selves—one cannot help but be struck by the parallels between the Boston and Concord Transcendentalists and the Romantic circle at Weimar and Jena, now Germany. For the Americans, Boston, like Weimar, was their metropolis; Concord was their Jena. At these two New World seats, a motley group of intellectuals gathered to dream the same dreams and act out the same roles as the Romantic avant-gardists in Germany.

They were for the most part sensitive, intelligent, questing people who had been born into a world dominated by Enlightenment or Common Sense materialistic ideas against which they felt obliged to revolt. They formed a community out of their individualisms that Johann Fichte would have admired, and that led to the flowering of New England thought. The most prominent among them were: Emerson, the poet and philosopher; Theodore Parker, a fiery preacher; William H. Channing, a less fiery preacher; Henry Thoreau, a naturalist and mystic; Bronson Alcott, a seer who believed himself an oracle; George Ripley, a formidable scholar and student of European thought; Margaret Fuller, master of German erudition and arts critic for the *New York Tribune*; Elizabeth Peabody, proprietress of the West Street bookstore, the Boston center of Transcendental activity; Orestes Brownson, social critic, true believer, and restless spirit; and two minor poets, Christopher Perse Cranch and Jones Very, the latter, perfectly in keeping with the Romantic spirit, quite mad. On the fringes of the group, observers but no less distinguished, were novelist Nathaniel Hawthorne and his wife, Sophia Peabody.

Though history has called them the Transcendentalists, and they met in Boston and Concord in what was later called the Transcendentalist Club— they even published a short-lived journal called the *Dial*—like the free spirits of Weimar they were never precisely of one mind. Rather, they formed a loose confederation of minds dedicated to absolute individualism and the personal independence of the soul. In this sense they represented the final fractionalization of New England Protestantism. Though each insisted upon his own eccentricities, whether it was Thoreau engaged in solitary play-pioneering at Walden Pond, or Parker being Jehovah thundering down from an alien pulpit at a smug congregation, or Bronson Alcott struggling hopelessly to establish Utopia in a Boston suburb, they nonetheless reacted to the same sense of cultural crisis. They all shared at base a common vision of the new reality that was dawning over the western world—the new rays of light emanating from Weimar and Jena. According to Emerson, "Germany had created criticism for us in vain until 1820 when Edward Everett returned from his five years in Europe, and brought to Cambridge his rich results. . . . There was an influence on the young people from the genius of Everett which was almost comparable to that of Pericles in Athens."

German thought, the Sturm und Drang of the new metaphysics, struck the spark, but the tinder for the New England conflagration was supplied from a more traditional source—religion. By 1820 the rise of liberal Unitarianism had come to dominate the best pulpits in Boston and the chairs of divinity at Harvard College, where Emerson somewhat mistakenly believed dwelled the intellectuals, the young men "with knives in their brains." Lyman Beecher and the old-time evangelicals from New Haven continually assaulted that fortress of new rationalism, but to outward appearances it did no good.

Unitarianism or liberal Congregationalism had its beginnings as far back as the Great Awakening of 1740, when established figures such as Jonathan Mayhew and especially Charles Chauncy gradually abandoned the old Calvinist piety in favor of a rational and ethical approach to the civilized congregations of cosmopolitan Boston. They were called New Lights. Chauncy, for example, after smiting the Antinomians hip and thigh, went through a succession of religious phases wherein he espoused Arminianism, a new belief in God's mercy bordering on Perfectionism, and finally by the end of his life had become a Universalist who believed that all men would be saved. According to some authorities, the old man was an incipient Unitarian.

Critical studies of the historical origins of the Bible, mounted first by Enlightenment skeptics and later by such German rationalists as David

Friedrich Strauss, had a profound effect upon the liberal clergy in Boston. Many of them came to believe that there was no Trinity since it had never been explicitly mentioned in the New Testament. Other thinkers were convinced that Christ was not God, but an extremely perfect man to whom God had given miraculous powers, signaling that he was His prophet and the symbol of the infinite perfectibility of man. The doctrines of original sin and atonement were nonsense. Instead, liberal religion consisted of adopting as a model Christ, the infinitely good man, and striving in a reasonable way for the kind of perfect holy conduct that guaranteed salvation. This was in sharp contrast to the backwoods ecstasies and fundamentalism of Cane Ridge Kentucky revivalism, not to mention the new fire issuing from Timothy Dwight's New Haven.

As early as 1785, the Reverend James Freeman adopted the new rational religion and purged King's Chapel in New York of all references to the Trinity. The first Episcopal church in America was transformed into the first Unitarian church. In 1803, William Ellery Channing became minister of the Federal Street Church in Boston, and more than anyone else, he unleashed the new liberal religion upon Boston's faithful. By 1815, conservative Calvinist ministers had become alarmed and attempted to purge Unitarianism from their pulpits. Channing soon became the leader of the liberal faction of Congregationalism. In 1819 at Baltimore he preached a ringing sermon, "Unitarian Christianity," which defended the liberal faith and, in effect, gave form to the new rational religion. The next year the Berry Street Conference of liberal ministers organized, and by 1821 they were publishing an important official journal, the *Christian Examiner*. In 1825, coincidental with the election of the Unitarian Henry Ware to the presidency of Harvard and the selection of another Unitarian to the chair of divinity, the American Unitarianism Association came into being. By 1825, after a relatively short but bitter struggle, Unitarianism had become the established religion of Boston. It was rational, intelligent, worldly, and perfectly in tune with the mercantile values of Boston's sophisticates, whose worldly success had caused them to have increasing impatience with hell's fire and damnation, and certainly with predestination, and a degrading anxiety over the fate of one's soul. Unitarianism was the ultimate in Lockean common sense, a reasonable religion for the intelligent and unsuperstitious. "The corpse cold religion of Brattle Street," Emerson called it.

For the Transcendentalist, Unitarianism was highly unsatisfactory. It did not carry higher criticism of the Bible far enough, and by the same token it had no heart and hence no soul. In the 1830s the Transcendentalists declared war on the Unitarians via the pages of the *Christian Examiner* and Ralph Waldo Emerson's actions, writings, and sermons. Essentially what the Transcendentalists objected to in Unitarianism was its adherence to a belief in the authenticity of the miracles as recounted in the New Testament. If one took the rational criticism of the Bible seriously, then it was sheer hypocrisy to believe in miracles. The only real miracle was God's whole universe and man in it. Channing, himself a genuinely liberal person, as were most Unitarians, was in a quandary. Believing themselves to be the avant garde in Christianity, the liberal ministers suddenly found themselves superseded in this respect and attacked as conservatives, reactionaries, and hypocrites. Though they opened the pages of the *Christian Examiner* to the full flow of debate and invective in good liberal fashion, they soon became alarmed. Christianity was at stake. If one did not believe in the New Testament miracles, one could hardly believe in Christ as God's representative because Christ himself offered the miracles as evidences of his divine mission. If one followed the Transcendentalist logic, Christ was a hypocrite and a liar. Leading the Unitarian reaction was Andrews Norton, Professor of Sacred Literature at Harvard. In a series of communications in Boston newspapers he vigorously attacked Transcendentalism as "the latest form of infidelity." It was for Norton, dubbed the "Unitarian Pope," an anti-Christian pantheism that submerged God in nature.

But the war was more than a pamphlet war. In the summer of 1832, Emerson, who had been minister to the prestigious Second Church of Boston since 1829, announced that he no longer believed in the Lord's Supper and therefore could not participate in communion. By the fall of that year he resigned, disillusioned with all formal church rites, though still on friendly terms with many of his church colleagues. In December he sailed for Europe, where he met the men he considered the three greatest thinkers of his day: Walter Savage Landor, Samuel Taylor Coleridge, and Thomas Carlyle. From Coleridge he eventually borrowed German philosophy and from Carlyle he gained advice, encouragement, lifelong friendship, and confirmation of the correctness of his tilt toward German Idealism. From Landor he acquired literary Romanticism. Equally important, Emerson visited the vast Jardin des Plantes in Paris—by that time one of the most systematically organized botanical gardens in the world. From this experience he gained a profound sense of the Humboldtean interrelatedness of all nature. At the same time, he was reading the work of Jean-Baptiste Lamarck and developing a sense of an evolving, changing nature that coincided with the *naturphilosophie* of the Germans and, in a curious way, with the theories of nature's spiraling symbolic development espoused by Emanuel Swedenborg, a Swedish scientist-theologian who believed that nature's facts corresponded with God's spiritual facts. On the voyage back from Europe, as his journals indicate, Emerson had already begun work on his literary and philosophical masterpiece, *Nature*, which was published in 1836. *Nature*, though published in an original edition of only five hundred copies, became the supreme manifesto of Transcendentalism and a basic document in the whole Romantic revolution.

The following year, in 1837, Emerson delivered an oration to the Phi Beta Kappa Society at Harvard, an organization to which he had not been elected as an undergraduate. Titling his address "The American Scholar," Emerson surprisingly, in view of his own devotion to European savants, took the occasion to declare American literary independence from Europe. "We will listen no longer to the courtly muses of Europe," he said. "We will walk with our own feet; we will work with our own hands. We will speak our own minds. . . . A nation of men will for the first time exist, because each believes himself to be inspired by the Divine Soul which inspires all men." In short, he advised the Harvard scholars to throw off their borrowed scholarly apparatus, to avoid the pedantic and the derivative, and to be intellectually self-reliant. For Emerson, the scholar was "man thinking" and nothing more; hence, all men had the potential to be scholars. His address was revered not because it attacked the artificial apparatus of scholarship in the same sense in which he had attacked the artificial rituals of the church, but because it seemed to sound the arrival of a native American intellectual tradition, even though it was covertly based on European thought.

In 1838 Emerson's subversive meaning became clearer. Addressing the Harvard Divinity School over the faculty's protests, he asserted that man's own moral imagination applied to Nature (by now capitalized) was the best of all religions. "Historical Christianity," according to Emerson, had

"fallen into the error that corrupts all attempts to communicate religion
... it is not the doctrine of the soul, but an exaggeration of the personal,
the positive, the ritual. It has dwelt with noxious exaggeration about the
person of Jesus. The soul knows no person. It invites every man to expand to
the full circle of the universe, and will have no preferences but those of
spontaneous love." Elsewhere in his address Emerson even more explicitly
attacked the heart of the Unitarian controversy, "But the word Miracle, as
pronounced by Christian churches gives a false impression; it is Monster. It
is not one with the blowing clover and the falling rain."

After his Divinity School Address, Emerson was not asked back to Harvard for thirty years. But some ministers took his message to heart. The
greatest of these was Theodore Parker, who espoused Emerson's scorn for
organized Christianity and overly sophisticated Biblical fundamentalism almost verbatim. The Transcendentalist revolt against Unitarianism,
pedantry, and materialism reached a kind of crescendo in Parker's vigorous
sermons, which attacked all these things, as well as the complacent Boston
upper classes. Parker was a sensitive Romantic who wept frequently in and
out of the pulpit, and invited persecution for his blunt views, but he kept
on until only eight churches in all of Boston would allow him to speak. In
1841 at the South Boston Church, Parker brought the whole debate over
Christianity to a thunderous climax with his great sermon on "The Transient and the Permanent in Christianity." Its message was simply and eloquently put. The "permanent" was the word of God, unadorned by
particular institutionalized interpretation. It was "true like the axioms of
geometry because it is true, and is to be tried by the oracle God places in
every breast." The "transient" was all the particular dogma and ritual of
Bible, miracle, church, institution, and theology in general at any particular
time and place. Unitarianism, like all organized religion, was irrelevant and
transient. Only man, God, nature, and the great law of love mattered.

Emerson and Parker, though perhaps ultimately in a losing cause, had
managed to shatter the theological basis of Unitarianism. They had shown
its rituals to be as false and artificial as any other establishment religion, its
leaders, such as Andrews Norton and all those who refused pulpits to
Parker, to be mean-spirited and defensive. In this sense they had acted out
the same drama as Jonathan Edwards and the evangelicals of the Great
Awakening. Beyond this, Emerson and Parker, assisted by George Ripley,

had mastered Locke's rational sensationalism and turned it against the Unitarians. Locke's philosophy carried to its logical extremes certainly precluded the miracles and the mythologizing of Jesus, though it did not vitiate his fundamental message, which Emerson and his cohorts found to be congruent with that of all the other moral philosophies they had been investigating. Nonetheless, for the Transcendentalists even reason did not go far enough or encompass enough human, or for that matter divine, experience. So for them, in the course of the Unitarian debates Locke and the "common sense" had been tried and found wanting as a guide both to right moral conduct and to the true spiritual nature of reality itself.

I

The American Transcendentalists, in the midst of their dispute over Boston Unitarianism, had fashioned a philosophy that transcended rational empiricism. They were able to do this by borrowing Europe's avant garde Romanticism. To them the struggle with Boston's churches was not trivial. As one wag would have it, "the age of Reason in a patty-pan." Rather, it was symbolic of the larger struggle for cultural redefinition engrossing the western world. For their part of the struggle, Boston and its environs proved—for the time being, at least—to be the most immediate and available revolutionary battleground. Later, Emerson and Bronson Alcott spread their ideas across the country, traveling annually as lecturers as far west as Chicago and St. Louis. Although he was largely despised at Harvard, to the nation the "good, grey" Emerson became "the Sage of Concord."

But if the Transcendentalists had transcended Common Sense Realism in the name of European Romanticism, the question remains: in what fashion, to what end? They were not explorer-travelers like Humboldt, whom they greatly admired, yet Emerson's first important work, *Nature* (1836), clearly sought the widest possible scope. It was a slim volume, but for Emerson it was *Cosmos* with a different conclusion. Likewise, Henry Thoreau, though he scoffed at the American Academy of Arts and Sciences' attempts at Baconian empiricism and professional attention to specialization, also wrote, "Let us not underrate 'the value of a fact; it will one day flower in a truth.'" And in his journal he noted, "The fact is I am a mystic, a Transcendentalist and a natural philosopher to boot." Just as Emerson had gained, all at once in the Jardin des Plantes, some idea of the whole comprehensive interrelatedness of the parts of the natural world, so too did Thoreau grasp this idea at Walden Pond, his universe, or on solitary walks through the countryside around Concord where sunrise, moving clouds, cocks crowing, dogs barking in the early morning, colors, sounds, motions, and creatures large and small, perfectly adapted to their habitat, provided him with evidence that all nature moved in accordance with some higher law the patient and sensitive man could discover.

Still, the problem for the Transcendentalist, as indeed it had been for the mighty Humboldt, was how to comprehend nature in all its parts and yet as a whole. How could infinitely variegated nature, of which men of the Second Great Age of Discovery were acutely aware, be made to yield up its secret order so that the chaos of recognition might be stilled and man could once more enjoy a "satisfying relationship with the universe"? The Transcendentalists resorted to synecdoche. They accepted the part for the whole because to them the whole universe was symbolic. This in turn gave them a new gospel, accessible to all men: learn about God, truth, and morality from close observation of the parts of nature. Read, as Emerson said, "the emblems of the universe," which are available to any man who takes up the mantle of the poet. Each man, imbued with the poetic spirit, could then find his way to truth—universal truth—in his own way without the aid of organized clergy. Thus, as they themselves saw it, the American Transcendentalists, by espousing a new philosophy of perception, were out to individualize and at the same time democratize religion, which was the key to all meaningful knowledge. If one discovered the "self" as poet and utilized the powers of symbolic perception that related one's "self" to the "other," which was nature, then one discovered God. It was this message Emerson embodied in his Transcendentalist manifesto and greatest work, *Nature*.

Nature derived from at least four sources in addition to his experience at the Jardin des Plantes: the ideas of Immanuel Kant, Samuel Taylor Coleridge, Friedrich Schelling, and Emanuel Swedenborg. Following the poet Coleridge, who in turn acknowledged his debt to Kant and Schelling, Emerson accepted the dual world of phenomena and noumena. Like Coleridge he used different terms to denote epistemological qualities. The world of the noumena became the world of "reason" or "imagination." The phenomena became what was subject to the powers of "understanding" or "fancy"—the mind's play over sensual forms in nature. Thus Emerson, like Coleridge, subtly transformed the "is" of Kant's description of reality to the "how" of perception. Epistemology eclipsed ontology for these two poets as seekers after knowledge. The imagination (or reason) was the self-generating power of the spirit, a God-like quality. The fancy (or understanding) was the equivalent of empirical ordering of forms observable in the phenomenal world.

After making this fundamental distinction among powers and realms of existence, Emerson and Coleridge both followed Schelling's two-way version of Kant's two worlds. One could proceed from the imagination, the world of pure mind, to order the external world, or one could reverse the process and proceed from the facts of the external world to a knowledge of mind and God's supreme order. The point at which one fused these two worlds was through the symbol that had the quality Coleridge had called "esemplastic." Emerson mercifully avoided this word but followed Coleridge and Schelling in the poetic philosophy of symbolic perception. Not really familiar with the intricacies of German metaphysics, which provided analysis of the noumenal world of mind, however, Emerson focused primarily on nature as a guide to spirit. That is, he chose to start with the phenomenal world and, via symbolic perception, work his way through the veil of nature to a knowledge of spirit that, like Schelling, he defined as broadly and richly as possible. If one successfully "mounted the upward spirals of form," a Swedenborgian concept, and crossed over into the world of spirit he would find himself on the Elysian fields of God's unbounded imagination. Thus, in the process of symbolic perception, the richer and more varied the associations one could make, the more profoundly he partook of God's imagination. Nothing better illustrates the point than a close analysis of *Nature*.

In *Nature*, Emerson called at the outset for man to abandon old dogmas and take "an original relation to the universe." Sounding a bit like Schelling, he saw all nature as a shimmering projection of the mind of God and bade men "interrogate the great apparition that shines so peacefully around us. Let us inquire, to what end is Nature." And if nature was the mind of God, man was a part of that mind, unique only as a perceiver. He was the only creature endowed with the ability, through his own intuition (imagination, Emerson called it) of penetrating to the mystery of the universe, of perfecting himself to the point where he could assume the qualities of God himself: "Standing on the bare ground," Emerson declared in a famous passage, "my head bathed by blithe air and uplifted into infinite space—all mean egotism vanishes. I become a transparent eyeball; I am nothing, I see all; the currents of the Universal Being circulate through me; I am part or parcel of God."

Therefore, to become God, a possibility inherent in every man, one must read the emblems of the universe much as did the old Puritan Platonists or the new German *naturphilosophers*. One must pay close and sensitive attention to nature and the poetic or symbolic representation of nature, for, declared Emerson,

1. Words are signs of natural facts.
2. Particular natural facts are symbols of particular spiritual facts.
3. Nature is the symbol of spirit.

For Emerson each particle of nature, each fragment of the "great apparition" was emblematic—a microcosm of the whole truth as projected by the mind of God. Thus the way to total truth was through the sensitive symbolic perception of the poet whose concrete words stood for spiritual truths. The idea that "Nature is the symbol of spirit" derived from Swedenborg as well as Schelling.

In *Nature*, Emerson carefully contrived not only a modern metaphysic but also a method of proceeding to the overarching truth of God. There are eight parts to his essay: "Nature," "Commodity," "Beauty," "Language," "Discipline," "Idealism," "Spirit," and "Prospects." The first invites the reader to examine nature and defines it as the "great apparition." The second, "Commodity," meanders through the practical uses of nature. The third, "Beauty," points up the inherent pleasure to be derived from the forms of nature as perceived by the senses only. These three parts define the role of "fancy" ("understanding," or the Kantian "phenomena").

But then one suddenly and dramatically finds the means to go on beyond the phenomena—to penetrate the veil of nature. It is in the section on

"Language" that Emerson enunciates his formula for symbolic perception: "Words are signs of natural facts," etc. At this dramatic turning point in the essay, the reader passes from the world of "fancy" to the world of "imagination." The world of imagination includes a Kantian "Discipline" of mental categories. It also includes the solipsistic possibility, always implicit in Kant, that the whole dualistic world exists only in the mind of the individual—that is, in the "post-structuralist" sense it was self-referential. Emerson called this section "Idealism." But in any case, the world of imagination is the world of "Spirit," free spirit for the creation of one's own morality, and one's own civilization. These are the "Prospects" that lay before "man thinking." If he enters into the true poetic spirit of Emerson's *Nature*, the world is all before him. He can thus become a God.

Emerson had unveiled a new reality for Americans—the universe of mind and spirit that lay beyond the appearances of nature. More than this, he had replaced the minister or priest with a new cultural holy man—the poet-seer, who through his intuition and artistic perception of symbols afforded mankind a breakthrough in knowledge. Moreover, it was a democratic breakthrough in that every man, not just clergymen and the smug "elect" of the Christian churches, could, if he followed Emerson's dictum, became "part or parcel of God." Every man in his own way could be the poet or holy man. And conversely, Emerson implied that those who failed to develop this awareness were not holy men, much as did another poet, E. E. Cummings, nearly one hundred years later, when he wrote in his World War I classic "The Enormous Room":

Q. What do you think happens to people who aren't artists?
  What do you think people who aren't artists become?
A. I feel they don't become; I feel nothing happens to them;
  I feel negation becomes of them.

II

But if the world was a world of spirit and the way to ultimate truth was through aesthetics, then which aesthetics? What was the "new church" epistemology, and how could one judge true poetic success? Emerson formulated the answer most clearly in a lecture titled "Beauty" that he presented over and over on a tour out West in the Ohio Country in 1850 and then later published in *The Conduct of Life* (1860). In this essay, his devotion to Goethe's scientific aesthetic principle of metamorphosis, Swedenborg's theory of the spiral-like progress of nature, the aesthetic theories of his friend the sculptor Horatio Greenough, and the high moralism of such poets as William Wordsworth and John Keats and the architectural critic John Ruskin were all fused into a systematic plan whereby the poetic pilgrim could judge his progress on the meandering path to truth and the sublime consciousness of the oversoul.

As did that of most of Emerson's writings, the structure of "Beauty" roughly parallels that of *Nature*. He first disposed of Lockean empiricism in favor of the "science of the human heart," quoting Goethe, who wrote, "The beautiful is a manifestation of secret laws of Nature which but for this appearance had been forever concealed from us." The problem was to examine closely the forms of nature with their higher meaning constantly in mind. If one looked at nature carefully, one noted that nature was simple and had no superfluous parts. Emerson declared, "It is a rule of largest application, true in a plant, true in a loaf of bread, that in the construction of any fabric or organism any real increase of fitness to its end is an increase of beauty." He added emphatically, "All beauty must be organic . . . outside embellishment is deformity."

Thus he enunciated a fundamental principle of American art—*form follows function*—a dictum that has provided the basis for much of modern American aesthetic achievement, from Walt Whitman's free-verse "barbaric yawps" in *Leaves of Grass*, through the architectural works of Louis Sullivan and Frank Lloyd Wright, the naturalism of Mark Twain and Ernest Hemingway, and the modernism of such symbolist writers as T. S. Eliot and William Faulkner, to the more contemporary mixed-media art of Alexander Calder and Tom Wolfe. In proclaiming this principle, Emerson was following the lead of Horatio Greenough, who lived many years in Italy and perpetrated the nude seated statue of the Zeus-like Washington in a toga that now sits in the Smithsonian Institution. Greenough's essay "American Architecture" was first published in the *United States Magazine and Democratic Review* in 1843. It was a sermon on the gospel that form should follow function in art just as it does in nature.

> Observe a ship at sea! Mark the majestic form of her hull as she rushes through the water, observe the graceful bend of her body, the gentle transition from round to flat, the grasp of her keel, the leap of her bows, the symmetry and rich tracery of her spars and rigging, and those grand wind muscles, her sails. Behold an organization second only to that of an animal, obedient as the horse, swift as the stag, and bearing the burden of a thousand camels from pole to pole! What academy of design, what research of connoisseurship, what imitation of the Greeks produced this marvel of construction? Here is the result of the study of man upon the great deep, where Nature spake of the laws of building, not in the feather and in the flower, but in the winds and waves, and he bent all his mind to hear and to obey.

For Emerson and others of the functionalist faith, this meant that all derivative schools of art, architecture, and literature, especially classicism, were as inappropriate to America as Unitarianism. Balance, symmetry, proportion, rhyme, heroic couplet, column and pilaster, the Aristotelian dramatic unities—all the canons of classicism were irrelevant, as absurd as the toga that cloaked Greenough's seated Washington. They were, in Greenough's terms, the transient. Only symbolic functionalism in art—which was life—was permanent.

The ideal source for the study of functional form, as Greenough implied, was nature, which was perfect in this respect. However, in studying nature's forms, the biological and organic rather than the mathematical and the physical of the post-Newton Enlightenment occupied the Romantic's attention. Emerson linked this organicism to Goethe:

> The German poet Goethe revolted against the science of the day, against French and English science, declared war against the great name of Newton, proposed his own new and simple optics; in Botany, his simple theory of metamorphosis—the eye of a leaf is all; every part of the plant from root to fruit is only a modified leaf, the branch of a tree is nothing but a leaf whose serratures have become twigs. He extended this into anatomy and animal life, and his views were accepted. The revolt became a revolution. Schelling and Oken introduced their

ideal natural philosophy. Hegel his metaphysics, and extended it to
Civil History.

Emerson recognized that the central, dominating image of the philosophical and poetic imagination in the western world was no longer Newton's clocklike world machine. It was organic. It was an exfoliating seed, a
tree, the "motion of the brindled tiger," or as Emerson put it, "the charm
of running water, seawaves, the flight of birds and the locomotion of animals." When he undertook to launch his friend Henry Thoreau on a career
as a poet, Emerson procured a set of official scientific reports on the plants,
animals, and insects of the commonwealth of Massachusetts and "set
Henry Thoreau on the good track of giving an account of them in *The
Dial*." Thoreau's first article was a poetical "Natural History of Massachusetts," a forerunner of his mini-Humboldtean classics, *Walden* and *A Week
on the Concord and Merrimack Rivers*. Examples such as this could be multiplied many times in the writings of the American Romantics. A new organic image based on symbolic perception had come to dominate the life of
the mind in America. Poets such as Whitman arose to tell "the tale of the
tribe" in endlessly exfoliating verse celebrating nature in *Leaves of Grass*, a
continually revised, ever-growing epic of America that was never really
finished—just as man's knowledge of himself, nature, and God could never
really be complete.

"The age of miracles is each moment thus returned," wrote Thoreau in
his journal. "Now it is wild apples, now river reflections, now a flock of lesser
redpolls. In winter, too, resides immortal youth and perennial summer."

Beyond the organic, Emerson also saw beauty and hence reality as consisting of change and flux, the flow of one form into another—a constant
metamorphosis. "Beauty is the moment of transition, as if the form were
just ready to flow into other forms," he declared. Evolution and change and
metamorphosis for Emerson moved in ever-widening circles and spiraled
inevitably upward toward cosmic consciousness and perfection. Even
Spencerism and Darwinism seemed to fit into this philosophy as Emerson
understood it.

But the cosmic and the spiritual could really be derived only through
symbolic perception. Each concrete fact of nature was a trope—a part that

stood for the whole. "There is a joy in perceiving the representative or symbolic character of a fact which no bare fact or event can give," he wrote. Symbolic perception was the new form of knowledge. In effect it was knowledge by analogy with the fact or the symbol being an analogue of a whole range of intuitive understandings and correspondences that could be gained in no other way—according to Emerson, "particular natural facts are symbols of particular spiritual facts, nature is the symbol of spirit." Belief in the fundamental significance of symbolic perception made possible the most profound American literary statements of modern times, from Herman Melville's white whale and Mark Twain's mystical river to Ernest Hemingway's leopard on Mount Kilimanjaro. They were profound because of their analogical vagueness, which allowed each individual perceiver access to his own vast world of spiritual significance. Ambiguity and resonance that reflected the basic paradoxes of man become a literary value as a result of the Romantic Movement.

And finally, for Emerson, "All high beauty has a moral element in it." This made the poet or artist an everyman who followed in his footsteps a secular saint, or rather a member of a community of saints who, by first insisting on the value of their own fresh, individual perceptions of nature, had inevitably found unity in the bewildering diversity of nature and the modern world. And because they understood the transcendent beauty of nature they could thus function as moral commentators on life in competitive Jacksonian America.

In effect, Emerson's philosophical chronicle told the story of what had happened to western civilization, of which America was a part. As we have seen, the rapid expansion of knowledge through critical reason and the collection of data expanded man's intellectual horizon infinitely, beyond the bounds of the Enlightenment's rationalistic system. It had also thrust sense data before him in bewildering and kaleidoscopic fashion. The counterforce to such an explosion was implosion. For Emerson and like-minded Romantics, retreat into the self, individual awareness, and symbolic perception of the part for the whole was the way to salvation. It became their primary grasp on reality, which in turn gave strength to their belief that there was after all a Platonic unity comprehensible somewhere beyond the infinite appearances of nature. Some Romantics, notably Melville, Carlyle, and Goethe, never quite settled for synecdoche, and they characteristically were caught in a Faustian tension. Could they be gods and comprehend the world in all its detail as a whole despite the expansion of knowledge? Could the artist-philosopher be a truly cosmic hero? Or must he inevitably and tragically be overwhelmed by the world? Must he be content to settle for a part of the truth? Emerson and most of the Concord Transcendentalists thought they had found a middle, and more democratic way.

III

With Emerson as the leader, the Transcendentalists, borrowing from Europe, had formulated a new metaphysic for democracy and a religion of art, but all this was on a lofty plane and to some seemed to relate to American society only subtly and indirectly. The Emersonian revolution was to take place within the heart of every individual. The Sage of Concord personally eschewed conventional politics and organized activism as much as he could, though he became an ardent advocate of the antislavery movement, encouraging its leaders and making speeches on behalf of the cause. On the whole, however, Emerson's Concord serenity pointed up a great division in Transcendentalism. He believed that society could be changed only by reforming each separate individual, whose heart would eventually vibrate to "that iron string," the moral oversoul. Most of the other Transcendentalists took a more active stance with regard to the issues of the day.

Henry Thoreau went to jail for refusing to pay his taxes as a protest against the Mexican War and slavery. His essay *Civil Disobedience*, published in 1849, has become a world classic in the literature of nonviolent social protest. Orestes Brownson, a disciple of the French Saint-Simonians, tried mightily to weld Transcendentalism to the class struggle. His sermons as a Universalist and later freelance Transcendentalist minister attacked Unitarianism primarily on the grounds that it was the religion of Boston's smug, upper-class, mercantile society. He turned to socialism and then to trade unionism, where he helped organize the Workingman's Party. From 1838 to 1842, in the pages of his journal the *Boston Quarterly Review*, he mounted some of the period's most potent attacks on organized Christianity in the name of the laboring classes. A tough, irascible fighter, he gave no quarter and was not afraid to take an active part in any political arena.

Then suddenly in 1844, Brownson, who had been a seeker of religious truth, moving in and out of churches all his life, converted to Roman Catholicism. This shocked and alienated the whole Transcendentalist community, whose "infinite" toleration had limits after all. Brownson's political allies were further shocked when he became a supporter of John C. Calhoun in the 1844 election. After years of defending the laboring classes, Brownson abruptly decided that democracy was a failure. It could not stop the grinding march of materialism, and so in later life, he cast his lot with the cause of elitism and Calhoun, "the Marx of the Master Class," as Richard Hofstadter aptly termed the Southern leader. Brownson's story was one of Transcendentalism's deeply felt tragedies.

Another was the death of Margaret Fuller in a shipwreck off Fire Island in 1850. Fuller, who called Emerson's attention to Goethe's genius, was perhaps the first truly intellectual female revolutionary in America. A staunch advocate of women's rights, Fuller, nonetheless in the spirit of Romantic Transcendentalism, otherwise followed a course of supreme individualism. Tremendously erudite due to an extensive, serious education at her father's hands, Fuller, like Goethe and Humboldt, had attempted to encompass all knowledge—to make of herself not only the American Corinne or Madame de Stöel, but a female Faust or Prometheus. In so doing she came to regard herself as an ideal to which all intellectual women could and should aspire. Tall, dark-haired, severe, ill-favored with an unnaturally long neck, Fuller nonetheless possessed not only intellect but also a peculiar sexual magnetism that brought out the enthusiasm of those with whom she came in contact. In her time she was a mystery, an excitement, an anomaly. According to Edgar Allan Poe, whom she admired, there were, "men, women and Margaret Fuller."

In many ways the story of the Romantic revolt in America can best be told through Fuller's brief but incandescent career. While in her twenties living in Cambridge, Massachusetts, she discovered the German Romantics, mastering that difficult language and the ideas of Johann Wolfgang von Goethe, Friedrich von Schiller, Ludwig Tieck, Novalis (Georg von Hardenberg), Jean Paul Richter, and eventually Johann Fichte and Friedrich von Schelling. Even in the formative years of her life, in company with a small group of the Cambridge avant garde, which included James Freeman Clarke and her dear friend Lydia Maria Francis (soon to be Lydia

Child), she fully comprehended Weimar and Jena, and all that they stood for in the human development of either sex.

In 1835 she became a teacher at Bronson Alcott's famous Temple Street School, where the development of the individual child was paramount. When Alcott's venture collapsed she moved on to the Green Street School in Providence, Rhode Island, where she proved to be a warm, inspiring, and humane teacher, her ideas "flowing clear and bright as amber." However, for a citizen of the cosmos, Providence was too restricting, and in 1839 she moved back to Boston and earned her living tutoring the educated ladies of that city in a series of inspiring weekly "conversations." In her charismatic way, she pursued what she called "the beauties of a stricter method" in spreading the gospel of Romanticism and its potential for the development of all humanity regardless of sex. "Love and creativeness" were dynamic forces infused into each individual by God so they might go forth "bearing his image." Women could "add constantly to the total sum of existence" by "becoming more ourselves." They could "attain to absolute freedom" and absolute consciousness of the holy self. "In short," she once declared, "we become gods." Thus was the message of Goethe, Fichte, and Emerson broadcast in the less conventional educational circles of Boston.

In the meantime, she remained in contact, partly through their wives, with the leading men of the Transcendental persuasion. She became fast friends with Emerson, Ripley, and William Ellery Channing. By 1840, when the Transcendentalists decided to publish a journal interrogating life and its symbolic expression, literature, Fuller was the logical choice for its first editor. The aims of the *Dial*, first expressed in a joint statement by Emerson and Fuller, were much like those of *Nature*. Taking as their symbol a sundial, which catches celestial radiance in the middle of a garden rather than the "dead face of a clock," they proposed to proclaim "what state of life and growth is now arrived and arriving," with a view toward "raising man to the level of nature" and reconciling "the practical with the speculative powers."

The *Dial* lasted four years. During the first two, Margaret Fuller served as editor. Many of its issues were largely devoted to her own strong-minded opinions. Perhaps her most famous piece was her essay on Goethe, which shocked the bourgeoisie because she appeared to be defending his immoral behavior, though her translation of the correspondence between Bettina Brentano von Arnim, Goethe's mistress, and the pious German intellectual nun Gunderode more profoundly focused on the true direction of Fuller's thought. Dichotomies and antinomies, the two worlds of Kant, continually challenged her and framed her intellectual responses. The basic task for man and woman was to transcend in a Schellingean way the division between the worlds of nature and spirit, which von Arnim did as a result of her correspondence with Gunderode. This was what intellectual women must do in a struggle to realize themselves in a society dominated by men. Fuller further projected her personal sense of life's dichotomies in an article that appeared in the *Dial* in 1843, "The Great Lawsuit. Man versus Men. Woman versus Women," which formed the basis for her greatest book, *Woman in the Nineteenth Century* (1844). The first attempt at a systematic analysis of the roles of men and women in the modern world, this book has been called by Professor Susan P. Conrad "a *Moby Dick* of feminine love."

Written just before she accepted a position as critic of the arts on Horace Greeley's *New York Tribune, Woman in the Nineteenth Century* is not so much systematic as inspirational. Characteristically, as a Romantic she resorted to history, searching out models of heroic womanhood from the past, including Madame de Stael, Xenophon's Panthea, and the Countess Emilie Plater of Poland who became general of that country's armies without compromising the "gentility of her sex." In addition, Fuller created a fictional composite of womanly ideals, *Miranda*, whose heroine embodied the stages of female roles as they moved upward from the mundane world of domestic "fancy" to the true spiritual world of the ideal creator. It was a powerful book that set the stage for her entrance into the New York literary scene.

As a critic for the *Tribune*, Fuller covered all phases of literature, art, and entertainment, reflecting the eclectic tastes of the day. And in her reviews, she stood somewhat above the literary wars of New York—wars between the cosmopolitan realists and the cosmopolitan Romantics who paradoxically labeled themselves "Young America." Most closely allied with Poe, she viewed literature or any art as sui generis—the Coleridgian way to attaining, through concrete expression, an insight into the world of spirit. And that world, for New York City, or for the young republic, was a boundlessly cosmopolitan world. Americans should learn from the English giants, Coleridge, Carlyle, and Wordsworth, they could learn from the sociological French writers, Eugene Sue, George Sand, and Honoré de Balzac, and above all they must imbibe the spirit of Germany. As a critic, Fuller saw the cosmopolitan possibilities of America:

> As men of all countries come hither to find a home and become parts of a new life, so do the books of all countries gravitate towards the new center. Copious infusions from all quarters mingle daily with the new thought which is to grow into [the] American mind and develop American literature.

But New York, the emerging vital center of American artistic life, proved too small a theater for Fuller. After a foolish affair with ersatz bohemian deceiver James Nathan, she sailed for Europe as a correspondent for the *Tribune* in 1845. In the Italian struggle for independence from Austria she found a Byronic cause that seemed to fuse her sense of the real and the ideal. She also found the Marquis Giovanni Angelo Ossoli, who fathered her child. In the midst of tending the wounded and dying, of fleeing through the Italian countryside or hiding out in bandit caves in the mountains, Fuller and Ossoli carried on their love affair in true Romantic style. In effect, she was Goethe, Byron, Emilie Plater, and Schiller's *Die Räuber* all rolled into one radiant persona. And when the Italian cause collapsed she could carry this image—this inner strength—back to America with her along with her illegitimate son and Count Ossoli, who had at last become her husband.

Public opinion would not matter to Margaret Fuller—never could matter, in fact, as her ship smashed on the rocks off Fire Island and she and Ossoli, hand in hand, stood on the deck of the ship as it went down while attempts to bring their son ashore tragically failed. Her death became an existential moment to the American Transcendentalists because she so completely symbolized their own visions in both ideals and the role-playing behavior of "reality." And, dramatically in the end, she had been claimed only by nature itself in all its wildness and turbulence.

Theodore Parker, too, was in his own life a far cry from Emersonian tranquility. Ostracized from most Boston churches, Parker continued to preach wherever he could find a pulpit, espousing all the reform causes of the day—temperance, women's rights, vegetarianism, workingman's rights, and most of all abolitionism. By 1845 he was established in his own church, the Twenty-Eighth Congregational Church, converted from a Boston music hall. There he held forth on the wickedness of the Mexican War and deplored the spread of slavery. In 1848 he published *A Letter to the People of the United States Touching the Matter of Slavery*, a fiery Christian blast at the "peculiar institution." And in 1850, he, along with a number of Boston's citizens, took on the mighty Daniel Webster for his part in the Compromise of 1850, which included a fugitive slave law. From that point on, Parker actively assisted runaway slaves whenever he could, even leading an assault on the Boston jail in a vain attempt to free the runaway Anthony Burns. For this he stood trial but was saved from conviction by legal technicalities. Beyond his Boston activities, Parker was also a staunch supporter of John Brown, revering him almost as a saint. He helped supply Brown with guns for his Kansas campaign and he was privy to Brown's plans for a raid on Harper's Ferry. By 1859 Parker, worn out from his strenuous life, sailed for Italy, where he died in Florence in 1860, never to see the Civil War, which he had helped to bring about. For Parker Transcendentalism had been far more than mere tranquil cognition of the universe. It opened the door to the moral imperative of freedom and made him see that Emerson's millennium could never be achieved unless all men's hearts, black and white, could vibrate to the same "iron string." The holy community must include everyone, or it was not holy at all.

Though Parker's violent activism was the most radical of Transcendentalist activities, the utopian communities established by George Ripley at Brook Farm and Bronson Alcott at Fruitlands received the most attention. Alcott's venture began and ended in 1841–1842, a testament to the monumental impracticality of Transcendentalism's most unworldly and hence most revered holy man. Neglecting to include anyone with real experience as a farmer, the colony was largely sustained through the winter of 1841–1842 by the heroic labors of his wife and daughters, while Alcott, like some Hindu guru, took to the surrounding highways and byways to preach his gentle gospel. After nearly starving, the Alcotts moved back to Concord and the protection of Emerson's largess.

Ripley's venture at Brook Farm was another matter. A tremendous Germanic scholar, of fearsome intellect, and cofounder of the Transcendentalist Club, Ripley was far more practical than Alcott. In 1841 Ripley, his wife and twenty other people, including Nathaniel Hawthorne and the son of Orestes Brownson, set up the Brook Farm community at West Roxbury, nine miles south of Boston. Like the early Puritan venture in Massachusetts Bay, Brook Farm was a joint stock venture. Goods and manual labor were shared, but to vote in the community one had to be a stockholder. Hawthorne, for example, hardly wealthy, invested $1,500. Government was by committees and most decisions were reached in democratic discussions. The overall purpose of the society was a radical one—to provide a model community that would demonstrate an alternative lifestyle to the existing capitalistic and overly rationalized mass society in America. It was to be another "city on a hill" whose successful example the rest of society presumably would eventually follow. According to Ripley, Brook Farm's objectives were:

> to insure a more natural union between intellectual and manual labor than now exists; to combine the thinker and the worker, as far as possible in the same individual; to guarantee the highest mental freedom, by providing all with labor adopted to their tastes and talents, and securing to them the fruits of their industry; to do away with the necessity of menial services by opening the benefits of education and the profits of labor to all; and thus to prepare a society of liberal, intelligent, and cultivated persons, whose relations with each other would permit a more wholesome and simple life than can be led amidst the pressure of our competitive institutions.

From 1841 to 1845 Brook Farm was reasonably successful, principally because it conducted an excellent school employing every new pedagogical technique, including a Froebelian kindergarten and its variant, a cram course for entry into Harvard. Life was pleasant as well, and to some degree resembled a greenbelt suburban community as the members, living in cottages picturesquely named the Hive, the Eyrie, the Nest, the Cottage, and the Pilgrim House, shared both mental and physical labors. Only

Hawthorne suffered violent disillusion due to his dislike of manual labor and certain kinds of animal refuse.

In 1844, however, Ripley succumbed to the blandishments of the New York socialist reformer Albert Brisbane and converted Brook Farm into a Fourier community that was regimented into phalanxes of 1,750 people. An expensive dormitory, or phalanstery, was built and proved to be the undoing of Brook Farm. In the winter of 1846 the phalanstery burned, leaving the community bankrupt. The whole venture dissolved and Ripley spent years personally repaying its debts. In the context of its time, Brook Farm seemed more idyllically Romantic—an experiment in "radical chic," perhaps—than anything particularly revolutionary. At least this was the way Hawthorne saw it in *The Blithedale Romance*, his devastating fictional account of the unfortunate adventure.

Taken as a whole, however, Transcendentalism stood for a profound revolution in American thought. Borrowing their metaphysic largely from Germany, France, and England, the Transcendentalists nevertheless made a direct assault on the rationalistic, matter-of-fact world of John Locke and his Common Sense American followers. They also attacked the materialism and commercialism of the economic takeoff of the day. The Transcendentalists—along with the revivalists and cultists, such as the phrenologists and the followers of Mesmer and hypnotism—reintroduced mystery into American life. They also reintroduced, or more accurately, broadened, the idea of freedom to include the spiritual and the intuitive as part of the life of the mind. They dramatized nature as the prime source of spiritual values and made it a national symbol that seemed to distinguish America from Europe. Theirs was indeed a metaphysic for democracy and democratic experimentation that freed every man or woman from class and institutional constrictions and made him or her at least potentially relevant to the universe. Above all, by their actions, sermons, and writings they gave a tone of confidence to American culture. And by their sophisticated development of the concept of symbolic perception, they made possible a renaissance in American literature and the arts.

CHAPTER ELEVEN

The Romantic Writer as Cosmopolitan Seer

The Romantic Renaissance in American literature did not spring full-blown from the heads of German or Transcendental metaphysicians; instead it arose in two centers, New York and New England, as part of a bitter partisan struggle between so-called cosmopolitan realists and nationalistic Romantics.

The cosmopolitanism of the realists was primarily linked to a literature of traditional English writing, which meant a traditional form and a subject matter composed of one part sentiment and one part Common Sense Realism perfectly epitomized by, for example, James Russell Lowell's *Fable for Critics*. The nationalists, on the other hand, looked to Coleridgian and German Transcendentalism for their philosophical orientation. Theirs was an equally international literature—a literature of metaphysics that was to make a series of profound comments upon midcentury America. Paradoxically, the nationalists were thus aligned with German Transcendentalists, and their opponents, the cosmopolitans, with English traditional writing.

The struggle of the Concord Transcendentalists against the Unitarian, State Street–Harvard establishment reveals something of the split in New England's literary world. Though they were superficially friendly, social light years separated Ralph Waldo Emerson, Henry Thoreau, and Nathaniel Hawthorne from the Boston literary establishment as exemplified by Henry Wadsworth Longfellow, James Russell Lowell, and Oliver Wendell Holmes, America's most widely read poets. The latter three were polished, erudite, civilized—the pillars of the *North American Review*—and distinctly Whiggish in their political sentiments. The Transcendentalists often seemed crude and passionate in their search for truth. They clearly belonged in another social class, as befitted supporters of the Democratic Party. By 1840, however, New England had already begun to seem somewhat on the periphery of the literary and political marketplace. During this decade and the succeeding one, while Emerson and Thoreau were camping out in Concord, literary New York seethed with controversy as it struggled to become the capital of national culture—a move that strikingly paralleled the rise of New York Port to commercial ascendancy during the same period.

I

The drive for literary glory was central to the bitter feud between the cosmopolitans, led by Lewis Gaylord Clark and his *Knickerbocker Magazine*, and the nationalists, headed by Evert Duyckinck, editor of several literary magazines and the *Cyclopedia of American Literature*. Duyckinck's brief moment of glory came in 1847 when he brought together all his forces for a homegrown literature in a collection called *The Literary World*, published by Wiley and Putnam. Though the battle cry of the nationalists—Young America, as they styled themselves—was the creation of an international copyright law that would protect American writers from pirated British editions, actually both sides agreed on this issue. In fact, the cosmopolitans were unqualified admirers of Charles Dickens and wished to see him paid royalties for his books published in America. Most of all, they resented the rejection of the copyright issue by Cornelius Matthews, Duyckinck's pompous friend.

The real points at issue between the two groups as they attempted to define the future of American literature through the standards of literary taste were: (1) The question of whether, to be American, a writer had to write exclusively about the American scene, (2) the question of quality, i.e., is an inferior American scene book to be preferred over a better work with another setting and frankly imitative of European style? (3) the question of the validity of German Transcendental metaphysics as the basis for an American literary philosophy, (4) the political persuasion underlying the different literary groups, and (5) the individual egos and personalities involved.

Given these concerns, the lines of polarization are relatively easy to perceive. Clark and the *Knickerbocker* set, which included no writer of note in New York but did count as allies Washington Irving, Longfellow, and Lowell, were dedicated Whigs who detested Duyckinck, Matthews, and their sometime allies Edgar Allan Poe, Herman Melville, and John L. O'Sullivan. O'Sullivan was himself publisher of the *United States Magazine and Democratic Review*, the primary organ of the Democratic Party that stood for capitalism, military expansionism, squatter sovereignty, and alliance with the South. On a loftier level, however, Clark and his friends also deplored "Germanism" and New England Transcendentalism as being too vague, foreign (meaning not British), and essentially nonliterary. Instead, they lionized Dickens, praising even his sentimentality, and employed a new critical term to denote good literature, *vraisemblance*, which in effect meant realism or concrete truthfulness to the details of everyday life as opposed to allegory and symbolism. On the other hand, Young America, though it included a number of hardheaded journalists as well as Southerners like William Gilmore Simms, dubbed the "American Walter Scott" whose works Southerners read with unbounded admiration, tended to ally itself with Transcendentalism and to ally with the Democratic Party and mystical interpreters of America as if they were the essential ties that bound the country together.

The question of quality revolved around the silly works of Washington Matthews and innumerable failures by other writers who wrote about the American scene, under the banner of "Young Americans."

And if, as Young America demanded, one focused exclusively on the American scene, one necessarily threw out the cosmopolitan dream in favor of the narrowest kind of nationalism. To do so insulted the existing "giants" of American literature: Irving, Cooper, and Longfellow, all of whom had written on foreign themes. Even Poe was forced to agree with this argument, not out of reverence for the "giants," but out of a commitment to the cause of good writing wherever it appeared and whatever metaphors it employed. In fact, though he was an ally of Young America, in retrospect most of Poe's work places him in the cosmopolitan camp. His commitment to quality over narrow provincialism made his reputation abroad, just as had been the case with Irving. As a result, he received the earliest and most enduring accolades of any American writer of the period.

Thus the campaign of Young America, actually the third round of a continuing debate over literary nationalism and American self-definition, ended in a defeat that paralleled that of the Democratic Party. The chieftains of the movement were all dispersed and plunged into obscurity. A surprising number of them, such as Herman Melville, were saved by positions in the New York Custom House, where they continued to write but received little attention and few rewards. It would be hard to say, however, that they "left not a rack behind," because they left literary productions that form the basis of the Romantic Renaissance in America—the works of Melville, Hawthorne, Poe, and Walt Whitman, who had observed the struggle from his post as editor of the Brooklyn *Eagle*.

II

This unlucky group of writers of the Young America school, composed of New Englanders, New Yorkers, and even Southerners, such as William Gilmore Simms, managed to generate in American literature an aesthetic, borrowed from the Germans and Samuel Taylor Coleridge, that was profoundly American. Yet at the same time, that aesthetic was deeply, rather than superficially, cosmopolitan. Once again in characteristic fashion, a revolution in European thought became new knowledge to be absorbed by Americans and put to work for their own purposes, and American literature moved syncretically forward to new heights of attainment. Emerson had been the boldest borrower, taking Coleridge's distinction between fancy and imagination as the basis for his symbolic view of nature—*all* nature, not just American nature, in spite of his Phi Beta Kappa address. The implications of Emerson's work and that of the German and English Romantics from which it was derived were that the appearances of nature, concrete and interesting though they were, betokened a vastly more important universe of spirit and moral principle beyond. Thus the American writer, set down in a pristine world, had as his duty to inquire into nature. He was obliged to read and interpret the emblems of the natural universe to arrive at the moral truth that should define the American character.

All of the major writers of the American renaissance in one way or another wrote from this premise. They all saw America as a transcendent country, for better or for worse. Their adherence to the Transcendental principle had at least two significant social implications. The most obvious was that it made the writer or the poet the moral arbiter of the whole culture. Walt Whitman made this clear in *Leaves of Grass:*

> *After the seas are all cross'd (as they seem already cross'd),*
> *After the great captains and engineers have accomplish'd their work,*
> *After the noble inventors, after the scientists, the chemist,*
> *the geologist, ethnologist,*
> *Finally shall come the poet worth that name,*
> *The true son of God shall come singing his songs.*

Beyond this, to be Transcendental was to be individualistic, the seer in control of his context and his universe—an interpreter of the future. More important, on a social level, to be Transcendental was to be critical of materialism, crassness, and the overly rationalized society that America threatened to become. The Romantic Renaissance was thus a blow for poetic individualism and at the same time a profound commentary on the midcentury society of Steadfast Dodge and Aristabulus Bragg. They thus continued where Cooper had left off, only at a higher pitch and with greater intensity, largely free from the conventions of the Romantic novel or the classical poem. They were poets in process, creating their own literary context and hence their own moral and social matrix as they went along exploring the mysteries of nature and the cosmos.

This common focus, however, produced profound philosophical disagreements among the principals of the Romantic Renaissance. Some, like Poe, Hawthorne, and Melville, caught the basic insecurities of the period, and their work was dominated by a darker vision. Thoreau and Whitman, on the other hand, appeared in the end optimistic in the spirit of Emerson. And in thus opposing one another they revealed en masse the inner contradiction of life in Jacksonian America.

III

The scattered works of Edgar Allan Poe reveal a remarkably consistent pattern of "dark side" Transcendentalism. Deriving his literary principles almost completely from Coleridge, Poe lived largely in a grotesque and gothic world of the imagination, exaggerating, distorting, bending, and twisting the concrete details of the world of fancy to his own haunted intuitive purposes. As a result, his writing bore little overt relation to the American scene, but its power and inimitable uniqueness won him applause on both sides of the Atlantic as the first truly original American author. Charles Baudelaire and Stephane Mallarmé in France admired especially the decadent tone and symbolism of Poe's work, which inspired their own pioneer efforts in the European symbolist movement. Poe thus became the first American writer to influence European styles in a significant way.

The true sources of Poe's literary genius have never been completely and satisfactorily explained. As Leslie Fiedler astutely observed, Poe was a self-made eccentric, an admirer of Byron, and his life was in a sense his work. He made it a kind of continuous tragic "happening" from which he abstracted his haunting themes of lost love, incest, horror, feverish ratiocination, lunacy, and death. He was also apparently an assiduous reader of the vast eclectic literature that fascinated the Romantic Era. His range of interests included everything occult, from works on necromancy, alchemy, spiritualism, and mesmerism to treatises on cryptography, European and Oriental folklore, and the countless great travel books of the day. Though few of his biographers have noted it, Poe was a frequent visitor to Bartlett and Welford's Bookstore in New York's Astor Hotel. There the great travelers, explorers, and connoisseurs of the exotic gathered in a kind of informal literary club. There, for example, Poe met Jeremiah N. Reynolds, promoter of the U.S. Exploring Expedition to the Antarctic, who explained to him the theory of Symmes' Hole, which envisioned all the earth's oceans racing rapidly and inevitably into polar whirlpools. This powerful theory with its attendant images remained with Poe all his life. It formed the motif for such stories as "A MS Found in a Bottle," "The Descent into the Maelstrom," and the novelette *The Narrative of Arthur Gordon Pym of Nantucket*. It rose before him as a specter of whiteness even as he lay dying of delirium tremens in a Baltimore hospital in 1849.

A dapper, erect, handsome man with a wide forehead and a dark toothbrush mustache who invariably dressed in black broadcloth suits, Poe seemed hardly real even to his contemporaries. When sober he resembled a figure in a waxworks moved by wires. When intoxicated he was wild. When in love he was beguiling and sinister and usually merciless. When trapped in the snare of poverty he became a wretch who would do anything for money. And always there was the drink, the irresponsibility, the calculated decadence. Even his marriage to his thirteen-year-old cousin, Virginia Clemm, the one woman to whom he remained relatively loyal, and his simultaneous cohabitation with her mother, his aunt, would have made Humbert Humbert blush. Poe had already started on this sexual "Owl Hoot Trail" long before, when as a very young man, he managed to seduce his best friend's mother in a Richmond graveyard. When the lady died, Poe became fascinated with funeral customs and frequently spread himself upon her grave at midnight in vain if unorthodox attempts to reach sexually beyond the pale of mortality. This experience and this theme— necrophilia—likewise became central to his work in such classics as "Ligeia," "The Assignation," and "The Fall of the House of Usher."

As he moved through life, Poe conducted a dedicated campaign of failure, and from it emerged a lifestyle of decadence that by implication mocked bourgeois, bustling, expectant Jacksonian America. He was an individualist and cared little for morality, custom, or the Protestant work ethic. Thrown out of the University of Virginia for dissipation; dismissed from West Point for dereliction of duty; fired from half a dozen magazine editorships, in some of which, such as *Graham's* and the *Southern Literary Messenger*, he performed brilliantly; jilted and humiliated by numerous ladies—widows and young girls, upon whom he preyed; ostracized by the best families from Boston to Charleston, Poe was a true dramatic persona on the American scene.

Even his heightened fascination with puzzles, detective stories, codes, and the process of ratiocination mocked the mind, mocked the very process of reason that lay behind the "common sense" of American life. His love of the hoax and his brilliant successes in this vein are clues to his deep contempt for all of society. And in the end, by implication, he mocked even the hallowed Benjamin Franklin. The noble Ben had left a success story, his *Autobiography*. Everything the flamboyant Poe did mocked Franklin's success story and false modesty. Poe made his worst enemy, the scoundrel Rufus Griswold, his literary executor, knowing full well that Griswold would enhance, embellish, and exaggerate to the fullest extent the legend of Poe's decadence and contempt for society. In his obituary for Poe, the hateful Griswold wrote the ultimate in antisuccess stories. His lies, his forgeries, his suppression of evidence so effectively distorted Poe's life that scholars were thrown off the track for a hundred years. But clearly that was precisely the way "the mystery man" would have wanted it.

Behind Poe's sinister image, however, lies his transcendentally dark view of the world. In most of Poe's stories, appearances are scrupulously concrete but invariably either deceiving or, as in his most famous poem, "The Raven," inscrutable. In such stories as "Ligeia," "The Oval Portrait," "The Assignation," "The Masque of the Red Death," and "The Fall of the House of Usher," Poe paid elaborate attention to the details of furnishings, costumes, and even reading matter. But the mystery lies behind all these details. One had to open a tomb, tear down a wall, or descend into a maelstrom to find true reality—the reality of Poe's haunted imagination. One had to penetrate somehow the veil of nature, the mocking claustrophobic cardboard sets of life to understand the dark world of spirit.

From the beginning, the meaning of this spiritual world was clear. As early as 1833, when he first gained fame by winning a prize with "A MS Found in a Bottle," published in the *Baltimore Sunday Visitor*, Poe revealed his view of reality. The first-person hero, cast adrift somewhere in the South Pacific, suddenly finds himself propelled along through a "supernatural sea" on a ghostly ship peopled with a spectral crew who "will not see." The ship, porous and worm-eaten, as though resurrected from the deep, scuds along. "The crew glide to and fro, like the ghosts of buried centuries." Approaching the ice-bound Antarctic, the ship strikes a whirlpool, "and amid a roaring, and bellowing, and thundering of ocean and tempest, the ship is quivering—oh God! And—going down." The narrator, whose only legacy, significantly enough, is the message in the bottle, has learned of true transcendent reality, the horror of a life that all along had foretold death itself.

At the end of *The Narrative of Arthur Gordon Pym of Nantucket*, the same situation is reproduced more vividly as the climax to a voyage on oceans and treks across mysterious islands and through caves covered with indecipherable hieroglyphics (some have suggested they spell "Oedipus"), all of which result in misleading clues to the nature of existence. He reproduced a typical page from an explorer's journal:

> March 22d.—The darkness had materially increased, relieved only by the glare of the water thrown back from the white curtain before us. Many gigantic and palucidly white birds flew continuously now from beyond the veil, and their scream was the eternal Tekeli-li! as they retreated from our vision. Hereupon Nu-Nu stirred in the bottom of the boat; but upon touching him, we found his spirit departed. And now we rushed into the embraces of the cataract, where a chasm threw itself open to receive us. But there arose in our pathway a shrouded human figure, very far larger in its proportions than any dweller among men. And the hue of the skin of the figure was of the perfect whiteness of the snow.

Beyond the inscrutable veil of nature, so assiduously investigated by the naturalists of the day, lies only the true reality of death—a horrible death—by drowning in an ice-cold Antarctic whirlpool.

But death itself, invariably and repeatedly taking the form of suffocation by drowning, premature burial, or being walled up alive, did not exhaust Poe's total vision of nihilism and horror as the basis of reality. Madness ran a race with death. The two elements are combined in Poe's greatest story, "The Fall of the House of Usher," which was published in his first important book, *Tales of the Grotesque and the Arabesque* (1839). In this story the narrator is summoned to the castle of his friend Roderick Usher, who, along with his sister, Madeline, is suffering from a heightened intensity of the senses, which he can hardly bear. Madeline appears to die. Roderick continues in his anguish until Madeline comes crashing and banging out of her tomb to gain revenge on him, and they both die. The hero departs and, looking back, sees the ghostly house of Usher crack in two and sink into the tarn. Around this relatively standard gothic story, however, Poe has focused his symbols on the meaning of horror. Of the house, for example, he wrote:

> I looked upon the scene before me—upon the sere house and the simple landscape features of the domain—upon the bleak walls—upon the vacant eye-like windows—upon a few rank sedges—and upon a few white trunks of decayed trees—with an utter depression of soul which I can compare to no earthly sensation more properly than to the after-dream of a reveler upon opium—the bitter lapse into every-day life—the hideous dropping off of the veil.

The hero reflects, "What was it—I paused to think—what was it that so unnerved me in the contemplation of the House of Usher?" Then he glances into the tarn and the tarn mirrors the house, producing "inverted images of the grey sedge, and the ghastly tree stems and the vacant eye-like windows." As he approaches the house, the hero notices a zigzag crack running across its face. Inside, the story spins out its claustrophobic and fevered way toward its ghastly climax.

Within the house, Roderick entertains the hero by singing a song, accompanying himself feverishly on the guitar. "I fancied that I perceive," the hero relates, "and for the first time, a full consciousness of the part of Usher, of the tottering of his lofty reason upon her throne." The song, titled "The Haunted Palace," tells of a palace through whose "two luminous windows" travelers saw "spirits moving musically to a lute's well tuned law." Sparkling sounds issued from the "pearl and ruby glowing" palace door. Roderick's castle song ended, however, on a contrasting note:

> *And travelers now within that valley,*
> *Through the red-litten windows see*
> *Vast forms that move fantastically*
> *To a discordant melody*
> *While like a rapid ghastly river,*
> *Through the pale door;*
> *A hideous throng rush out forever,*
> *And laugh—but smile no more.*

The hero confronts a vision of madness in the image of a castle that was also the image of a face (perhaps Poe's), now with two "red-litten windows" like eyes and a pale door where ruby lips and pearly teeth once were. But this in turn reminds the reader of Roderick's cracked house itself, with its vacant, eyelike windows, its rank sedge (mustache?), and its withered trees (teeth?). The house resembles a face, and Poe has recognized his own castle of a mind in the process of becoming unbalanced and agonizingly racing with death itself.

The noble Roderick, experiencing the anguish of madness, tries to bury his sister to spare her, but she will not stay buried and returns to compound his horror and his anguish, and madness and death rule over all. But the ghastly house, a seat of madness, is reflected in the tarn as in a mirror, and the mirror image in its detail reflects a countenance, perhaps of Poe himself. In a motif, like that of an earlier doppelganger story, "William Wilson," the hero (Poe) sees, in the house and the tarn, mirror images or reflections of his own destruction. In the Germanic or Hegelian sense he has learned about the "self" from the "other." Through a complex of symbols within symbols, Poe conveyed his own perception of himself and his own grim existential condition. Even at the exotic ends of the earth, the Romantic artist hero confronts only himself.

IV

If Poe's cracked and fragmented vision of Jacksonian America was the product of his own nihilistic experience of life, Nathaniel Hawthorne brought to "dark-side" Transcendentalism the awesome Romantic weight of history, especially the Puritan past. Born in Salem, Massachusetts, in 1804, his father was a sea captain who went down off Surinam in 1808, leaving him in the care of a recluse widowed mother, two spinster sisters, and an eccentric aunt who dressed in black all her life. Hawthorne was descended from one of the oldest Puritan families—one ancestor had come over from England with John Winthrop in 1630, and another had presided as a judge at the Salem witch trials in 1691–1692. Hawthorne, in Salem and in genteel poverty, grew up in an atmosphere of genealogy, which was the only thing that defined his family's status in Salem life during the world-spanning, mercantile-shipping days of the Crowninshield and Derby families. An avid reader, especially after he was confined to the house for two years with a foot injury, Hawthorne devoured the works of Walter Scott and Charles Brockden Brown, and the gothic romances of his day coming in from Europe, such as those of Victor Hugo and Eugène Sue. A bit later, he steeped himself in New England history, the archives and publications of the Essex Institute in Salem being his main sources of information.

In 1821 he entered Bowdoin, a new college in Maine, where his friends were Henry Wadsworth Longfellow, Franklin Pierce, and Horatio Bridge, who formed Bowdoin's literary club. Almost from the outset of his young manhood, Hawthorne determined to be a writer—at a time when perhaps only Washington Irving was able to make his living from writing alone. In 1828 he published at his own expense *Fanshawe*, a chivalric romance in the Walter Scott mode that was such a dismal failure that he promptly attempted to destroy all existing copies.

The key event in Hawthorne's life, however, was his return to Salem from Bowdoin in 1825. In that year he came back to his native village, shut himself up in the attic of his house, and remained largely in seclusion for twelve years. While others, such as Melville, went to sea or traveled in Europe, Hawthorne gestated in Salem, writing constantly and largely for his own pleasure, walking about the town's gloomy streets every evening at dusk, talking to a very few friends and the intimate circle of his family. Every summer he took a solitary vacation, even on one occasion going as far west as Niagara Falls and Detroit. Generally the keys to his life in those days were solitude and contemplation—a narcissistic, even, as some biographers would have it, autoerotic detachment from life. On Sundays he liked to stand by his attic window and furtively peer down at the people going to church.

He thought the most desirable mode of existence "might be that of a spiritualized Paul Pry, hovering invisible round man and woman, witnessing their deeds, searching into their hearts, borrowing brightness from their felicity and shade from their sorrow and retaining no emotion peculiar to himself." During this time he developed a deep sense of loneliness and detachment from the world; a genealogical and historical perspective on his own situation; a sure sense of literature through trial and error in writing; and a strong sense of guilt and evil, growing perhaps out of his own puritanical narcissism and constant self-examination. Hawthorne's secluded twelve years were perhaps the longest "identity crisis" in America before graduate schools came into fashion.

Then, in 1836, he emerged from seclusion, went to Boston, and, through friends, secured the editorship of the *American Magazine of Useful and Entertaining Knowledge*. The next year, with a self-deprecating preface, he published his first book, *Twice Told Tales*, whose very title, suggesting warmed-over material, doomed its popularity. Included in this work, however, were such classic stories as "The Minister's Black Veil," "Wakefield," "The Prophetic Pictures," "The Grey Champion," "The Gentle Boy," and "The May-Pole of Merry Mount." The latter two stories delved directly into Puritan history, one vividly re-creating the Puritan persecution of Quakers, the other making use of the contemporary accounts of Thomas Morton's scandalous pagan orgies at Merry Mount and their suppression by the Pilgrims under Miles Standish, or "Captain Shrimp," as Morton called him in his own colorful narrative.

In 1836 Hawthorne became engaged to Sophia Peabody, one of two sisters, enamored of Transcendentalism, who ran a bookstore in Boston. The next year, he took a job in the Boston Custom House, quitting it in 1841 to invest his savings in Brook Farm. For nine months he lived at the Transcendentalist utopian colony at West Roxbury, Massachusetts, hoping to leave behind "the weary tread-mill of the established system and to give up whatever we had heretofore attained, for the sake of showing mankind the example of a life governed by other than the false and cruel principles on which human society has all along been based." He left Brook Farm in the autumn of 1841, disenchanted with the experiment and concluding "that a man's soul may be buried and perish under a dung-heap or in the furrow of a field, just as well as under a pile of money."

In 1842 he married Sophia Peabody and went to live in the Old Manse at Concord, where Emerson had finished writing *Nature*. In the tight Concord society, Emerson was his neighbor, living just down the road. Thoreau was his friend and Ellery Channing his fishing companion. The air was redolent of Transcendentalism, and Hawthorne perforce became a slightly bemused spectator of the dreamlike pageantry of Transcendental individualism that unfolded before him as he was frequently a silent guest on the fringes of Emersonian convocations. In the course of time, his admiration for Thoreau's sturdy independence increased even as he grew to loathe the Germanic erudition worn so pretentiously by Margaret Fuller. Hawthorne alone of the group was not sorry to see Margaret perish along with what he termed her "clownish husband," Giovanni Ossoli, in the shipwreck off Fire Island.

Soon Hawthorne became supervisor of the Salem Custom House and published *Mosses from an Old Manse*, perhaps his most impressive group of stories. The collection included his finest story, "Young Goodman Brown," a moral allegory in which the young hero penetrates to the heart of sin and darkness to discover the nature and universality of evil as a determinant of reality in the world about him.

In 1849, due to the Whig victory in electing President Zachary Taylor, Hawthorne, a Democrat, lost his job in the Custom House. Thrown desperately upon his own resources, he commenced to write as a serious professional. His first great success, *The Scarlet Letter*, published in 1850, he knew to be a profound work. In later years he remembered, "I read the last scene of the *Scarlet Letter* to my wife, just after writing it—tried to read it, rather, for my voice swelled and heaved, as if I were tossed up and down on an ocean, as it subsided after a storm. But I was in a very nervous state, then, having gone through a great diversity and severity of emotion, for many months past. I think I have never overcome my own adamant in any other instance." Yet he gave the publisher, George Ticknor, the first part of the manuscript almost as an afterthought in despair at being able to earn a living at anything else.

The years 1849 to 1852 were Hawthorne's most productive. Living in the Red House at Lenox, Massachusetts, and later in West Newton, he published two other novels, *The House of the Seven Gables* and *The Blithedale Romance;* two collections of stories, *The Snow Image* and *Tanglewood Tales;* a campaign biography of Franklin Pierce; plus a children's book, *A Wonder-Book for Boys and Girls*. He was never again to be so productive, since in 1852 his friend President Pierce secured for him the lucrative post as U.S. consul in Liverpool, England. From 1852 to 1860 Hawthorne lived abroad, filling his notebooks with traveler's observations rather than ideas for stories, and thus dissipating his writing talent in the trivial details of diplomacy and expatriate social life. In 1859, however, he wrote his last novel in Italy and revised it in Redcar, on England's Yorkshire coast. This was *The*

Marble Faun, a tale of Italy published in 1860. After he returned to the United States in 1860, Hawthorne lived in Concord and tried to regain his powers as a writer, but his creative life was finished. His health soon declined and he died in a hotel in Plymouth, New Hampshire, while on a walking trip through New England in 1864.

In all his serious writing, Hawthorne was a true Romantic. He was the metaphysical quester in search of an ultimate reality behind the appearances of the natural surroundings in which he was forced to live. Though he was generally disdainful of the Transcendentalist Movement as such, his writing betrayed the deep impression Transcendentalism and Coleridgian thinking had made on his mind. He was fond of allegories. John Bunyan's *Pilgrim's Progress* was his favorite book, and in his stories, such as "Young Goodman Brown" and "The Celestial Railroad," he probed the range of allegory's possibilities as a vehicle for modern fiction. More important, however, Hawthorne was a masterful symbolist who took that magic Coleridgian path into a world of profound metaphysical reality. Houses, mirrors, birthmarks, flowers, wells and pools, costumes, veils, the sun and the moon, the woods, fire, railroads, gold teeth, serpents, footprints in the snow, and the scarlet letter "A" were all examples of the variety of symbols he used to spin out a delicate tissue of super-reality that gave profounder meaning to his stories' characters and events.

In general, Hawthorne's work, using Transcendental techniques, offers a resounding negative to the sunny optimism of Emerson and his friends. When he inquired deeply into life, he found himself a Puritan interested primarily in the moral state of man, which he called the human heart, and in the all-pervasiveness of sin that spanned centuries and proliferated so widely that it virtually defined human existence. In "Young Goodman Brown," the hero takes leave of his innocent young bride to keep an appointment with Satan deep in the woods. Along the way he continually wishes to turn back but at every turn he sees his fellow townsmen, including his father, heading for the dreaded rendezvous with the knowledge of evil. Even his wife, he finds, has preceded him on the dreary path. And after the terrifying climax of the story wherein he is inducted into the evil fraternity of men and returns to the town, his innocence lost in the knowledge that virtually all of his fellow men and loved ones live in sin, he finds it impossible ever to really communicate with anyone again.

In another story, "Ethan Brand," after searching for twenty years for the "unpardonable sin," the hero discovers it in his own heart, in the intellectual egotism that led him on the quest in the first place. And so he hurls himself into a lime kiln, which turns his heart into the marble it really always was. Parson Hooper, in "The Minister's Black Veil," while wearing his black veil discovers that all his parishioners really wear the same sinister cloth to cover their multifarious secret sins. The world was thus defined by evil, sadness, and sin. But it also had rare instances of nobility and redemption. Hester Prynne in *The Scarlet Letter*, after sinning with Parson Dimmesdale, accepts the stigma of the scarlet letter, publicly raises her unnatural child, Pearl, refrains from exposing Dimmesdale, and spends her life in humility and charity, which promises her redemption. Dimmesdale's own ultimate public confession of guilt promises a similar redemption for him. Thus over the whole of *The Scarlet Letter* is cast a tone of profound sadness, of nobility gone astray. It was, as Hawthorne termed it, "a tale of human frailty and sorrow."

In *The House of the Seven Gables*, Hawthorne was concerned with the persistence of sin through time, symbolized by the old house itself. Long ago the family of Matthew Maule, a sturdy farmer, was dispossessed of his land by the lawyer Pyncheon, who built on it a fine pretentious house with seven gables that stood out prominently like the seven deadly sins. Maule cursed him and all his descendents. The story Hawthorne tells is that of Maule's ultimate revenge upon the Pyncheons, and the redemption of the family through the goodness of Phoebe, who, in marrying Holgrave, a descendent of Maule, restores the property to its rightful owner.

The death scene of Judge Pyncheon in the parlor of the old house, narrated by the voice of unseen mockery, encapsulates the whole book, and it is perhaps Hawthorne's greatest tour de force. Time pervades the event. The ticking of the judge's watch as his life runs out, the portrait of his thieving ancestor on the wall that hides the original deed to the property, the influx of afternoon sunbeams, then moonbeams as the day and the night pass by, and finally the reincarnation of past generations of Pyncheons who trace out the course of family sin through time, while the ghost of old Matthew Maule laughs scornfully in the corner—all tell a powerful tale of original sin. At the same time the mocking voice calls attention to the judge's now useless earthly possessions, pretensions, and pleasures; his properties; his gargantuan public feasts untasted; his business deals left unfinished; his political future left now and forever in abeyance. In thus playing these themes against one another, Hawthorne offers his comment on the society of midcentury America. The outward pretension, the materialism, the power, the wealth, the mechanical improvements, the pleasures, are as nothing before the ongoing guilt or nobility of the human heart—which in the judge's case has stopped beating. Through Pyncheon, Hawthorne scorned the materialism of the age in which he lived. More than that, being a Democrat of the Jacksonian (and Franklin Pierce) persuasion, in *The House of the Seven Gables* he implicitly called for a rejection of the wealth and power generated by "artificial property," such as that of bankers, lawyers, and speculators, in favor of a return to the honest agrarian toil of the Matthew Maules. His novel thus made vivid the pastoral argument of John Taylor of Caroline and the rhetoric of the Jacksonians who had fought for over a decade against "the monster bank." Though he could not abide the artificial pastoralism of Brook Farm, Hawthorne always staunchly supported the agrarian party of Andrew Jackson even when it meant offending his Whig abolitionist friends by his outspoken support of Franklin Pierce in 1852.

Perhaps Hawthorne's cleverest social commentary is expressed in his novel of Brook Farm, *The Blithedale Romance* (1852). Using the farm as "a theater, a little removed from the highway of ordinary travel," Hawthorne wrote a dreamlike detective story in an exotic setting that, through the first-person narrative of its antihero, Miles Coverdale, traced out the labyrinthian turns of reality and its ultimately tragic nature.

Coverdale is a poet who is also a blasé observer of society rather than a real participant. He is Hawthorne's "Paul Pry," a voyeur of life who can never quite communicate with his fellow men and so spends his time observing them, probing into their secrets. What he discovers through his observations amounts to a scathing indictment of midcentury American society. *The Blithedale Romance* presents a comprehensive series of comments on the major developments of the period and suggests how they all dehumanize the individual. Hawthorne also underscores the futility of reform in view of the ultimate sinful nature of man. Boston is seen as crowded, suffused with "an atmosphere of city smoke," "dingy," dedicated to mere money-grubbing and evil. The country at least has "air that had not been

breathed once and again! Air that had not been spoken into words of false-
hood, formality and error, like all the air of the dusky city!" But life in the
country also could be nasty and brutish, especially when the Blithedalers
found themselves forced to operate as true farmers in competition with
other more commercial farmers, forced to get "the advantage over the outside barbarians in their own field of labor," thrust even as socialists back
into the world of competition. In *Blithedale*, Hawthorne also offers a critical analysis of humanitarianism in general, the women's rights movement,
temperance reform, mesmerism and clairvoyance, the role of the author
and artist in American society, and nature itself as a deceiving source of
moral values.

The book opens with Coverdale musing over the mystery of a veiled
lady he has seen in a mesmeric show on the eve of his departure for
Blithedale. Somehow intuitively he connects an understanding of
Blithedale and its occupants with a solution to the mystery of the veiled
lady. In a skillful manner, part Henry James and part Alfred Hitchcock,
Hawthorne moves Coverdale toward a solution of one mystery by means of
his observation of the details of another. Blithedale itself is seen as a pastoral masquerade, peopled with impractical characters with secrets to hide.
The imagery used to describe Blithedale is drawn from chivalric romance.
Nothing seems quite real, including the principal characters. Zenobia is a
dark queen who always wears a fresh hothouse flower in her hair, even
when the snow swirls about and there is no greenhouse for miles around.
Priscilla is the snow-maiden, princesslike and innocent, but capable of un-
conscious cruelty to Coverdale. Hollingsworth, the leader of the group, has
no belief in the experiment at all; rather, he hopes to turn the whole farm
into a reform school for juveniles. In short, he is a heartless fanatic who
cares for no one but himself and his egotistical schemes. He is forever
gulling the rest of the young idealists and tyrannizing over their dreams.

In a series of tableaux, Coverdale penetrates the mystery of the veiled
lady and the secrets of the actors at Blithedale. The book reads like a movie
scenario. After the opening with the veiled lady, Coverdale goes to
Blithedale. In a scene before the hearthside, he is introduced to the main
characters. He observes them more closely from his sickbed both within his
room and through the window. He has another view from his perch in a
tree where his eyes zoom in, cameralike, on a clandestine meeting between

Zenobia and Westervelt, the gold-toothed proprietor of the mesmeric show. Then, back in the city in a scene reminiscent of Hitchcock's movie *Rear Window*, Coverdale glances across the alley from his chamber and sees Westervelt, Zenobia, and the veiled dancer, Priscilla, together. The lens moves into the interior carried through the eyes of Coverdale. The solution to the mystery becomes clearer: Zenobia has sold her sister to Westervelt. Cut to the mesmeric show, and the sordid relationship between Westervelt, Zenobia, and the near nude Pricilla becomes obvious. Then back to Blithedale and the masquerade, where Hollingsworth and Zenobia have rescued Priscilla from Westervelt's Svengali-like clutches. Then an interior shot in a dark cavernous bar where Old Moody, the girl's father, who appears at the opening of the story, tells how he deserted his family. And finally the dramatic denouement where Zenobia is dragged from the river, her heart bruised by the grappling hook used to pull her in, and where Hollingsworth and Priscilla stand by, sad and chastened, while Coverdale, who has learned all the secrets, is still unable to communicate with Priscilla, whom he loves after all.

The secret Coverdale has learned is that of selfishness, which ironically prevailed among the idealistic socialists. Old Moody, once the proud aristocrat Fauntleroy, has dissipated his fortune on rum and has sold Zenobia in marriage to Westervelt. Westervelt has forced Zenobia to place Priscilla, her sister, in his power as the veiled lady. Hollingsworth, no better than Westervelt, has taken advantage of both ladies' desire for escape and placed them in his own power as parties to his visionary scheme. Zenobia and Priscilla selfishly compete for the love of Hollingsworth. Thus, because of Old Moody's original sin, and then because of all their sins, all the characters are doomed. Despite their utopian dreams of progress they cannot change reality. The stain of the past is upon them as surely as ever it was on the Puritan Pyncheons. Hawthorne is thus saying, apparently facetiously but actually in deadly earnest, that brotherhood, reform, progress, even democracy—all those ideals based on the assumed goodness of man—are only noble but false dreams. Like an insubstantial pageant they fade away as quickly as Blithedale at the end of a summer, or Zenobia's flower at the end of a day. Man is not good at heart.

In Hawthorne's voice, one civilization, the Puritan, comments on another, the midcentury age of the common man when the democratic faith ran at high tide in the apparent sunshine of optimism. As interpreted by an obscure and "detached" writer in West Newton, Massachusetts, the inevitable corruption of the human heart cast a shadow over the noontide of America. This was Hawthorne's view of America's progress, which paralleled the lurid tales of much lesser erotic writers. No writer of the American renaissance offered a profounder or more subtle insight into the secret, underlying insecurities of the day, which the lurid penny papers and ten-cent novels emphasized in their works distributed by the thousands. Indeed, in many ways Hawthorne's "highbrow" resembles George Thompson's salacious pop-culture work, *Venus in Boston*.

V

A reader in midcentury America who was interested primarily in its important literature could, from the writings of Cooper, Poe, and Hawthorne, readily discern a disturbing pattern of life emerging in what was supposed to be a model republic. Cooper had lamented the loss of innocence implied in the invasion of unspoiled nature by hordes of careless and greedy settlers, and he fell into despair at the decline of the great families who could be expected to provide moral leadership, especially those patroons of upstate New York who had not the fiber to stand before the self-serving democracy of the marketplace. Poe, coming out of Richmond, reflected in his wild, exotic metaphors the decadence of the South—a decadence that was permeating the whole country and threatened to split it in two like Roderick Usher's madhouse. Hawthorne's cool New England eye gazed steadily into the darkness and gloom he saw all around him and that he felt composed the texture of reality, from Adam's first sin to the turbulent course of current events. Each writer found the rapidly changing, expanding, boundless, bustling world of republican America difficult to come to terms with—difficult to understand in a moral sense. And so each directed his attention to the immoral nature of humanity itself.

While Longfellow, Lowell, and Holmes in New England and the great majority of New York literati who admired Walter Scott and Charles Dickens were content to skate on the surfaces of life, the major American writers of the period, in their gloomy questioning of reality itself, signified an awareness of the fact that, in a basic sense, the whole paradigm of American thought had changed. The eighteenth-century-inspired utopian adventure was in truth already over, even as writers such as Alexis de Tocqueville and Whitman were celebrating its climax. Of all the writers who investigated the state of the American soul underlying the state of the American Union, none delved deeper than Herman Melville of New York—a man who had lived among the cannibals and hence could recognize such a culture when he saw it.

Like most of the other important writers of the period, for much of his life Melville was a dispossessed and even alienated person. Poe was disinherited and banished by his wealthy foster father, Hawthorne lived in genteel Salem poverty, sustaining himself on genealogical memories of a once-proud family, and Cooper returned to Otsego Hall to find the family prestige greatly diminished in the tin horn and calico revolt of the commoners. Similarly, Melville could only distantly remember the vanished Gansevoort fortunes of his famous ancestors and his own father's financial collapse when young Herman was only twelve years old. Instead of the patrimony and the formal education his early aristocratic upbringing would have led him to expect, Melville went only a few years to the Albany Academy and then at seventeen was sent out to work. Proudly, but with more than a tinge of bitterness, he recalled, "a whaling ship was my Yale College and my Harvard." This early deprivation, however, not only led to his experiences on whalers and in the South Seas upon which he built his literary career, but it also made him value books and the miscellaneous learning of all kinds that he absorbed as he "swam through libraries" and that, as he incorporated it into his own books, gave them their matchless resonance and power.

The romantic story of Melville's early life as a sailor is well known. In 1836, at age seventeen, to escape the monotony of clerking in his brother's store and teaching in a local school, Melville shipped as a cabin boy on a vessel bound for Liverpool. Then in 1841 he sailed aboard the whaler *Acushnet*, bound for the South Seas. After eighteen grueling months aboard this vessel, he and his friend Toby jumped ship in the Marquesas Islands. Later he was picked up by another ship, was dropped off in Tahiti, and made his way back to the United States by enlisting in the navy and serving on the frigate USS *United States*. When he returned to Boston, one phase of his life was over and another commenced. He began to write of his experiences in the South Seas with the hope of becoming a professional writer. The idea was exhilarating, and as he put it, "from my twenty-fifth year, I date my life."

Melville's first book was *Typee: A Peep at Polynesian Life* (1846). This was an exciting travel narrative of the exotic South Seas that chronicled his adventures with a companion, Toby, among the cannibal Typees. The book achieved great success both in England and America because of the Romantic vogue for travel accounts of exotic places, and because it was written not by a slick professional travel-book writer but by a rude sailor who had actually experienced the adventures. Much of Melville's reputation and that of Evert Duyckinck's Young America literary group, which had hitched its wagon to his star, depended strangely enough on the book's veracity—as if to say that if the book was false, the Young Americans and all they stood for was false as well. When hardest pressed by critics both in England and America on this score, the real Toby—Richard Tobias Greene—miraculously appeared and, in a letter in the Buffalo *Commercial Advertiser*, confirmed the truth of Melville's incredible tale.

Life in the cannibal paradise was real, as were their friends Kory-Kory and the lovely Fayaway, Melville's Polynesian Venus, forever silhouetted in the sailor's imagination standing in the prow of a canoe holding her only garment aloft as a sail, her tresses flying in the soft South Sea winds. *Typee* was thus a kind of hymn to the exotic on the other side of the world as Melville, Toby, Kory-Kory, Fayaway, and all the others in the cannibal valley lived the easy natural life becoming, as one beautiful day followed another, almost a part of the landscape, like figures in a Gauguin painting. But long before Gauguin, the South Seas had entered the European and American imagination. The corrupting Whiggish missionaries and grasping men of commerce who invaded the harbor at Nuku Hiva with "civilization" were almost forgotten except as objects of scorn. But Toby grew restless and made his escape. Then Melville, at least in his novel, discovered that at the heart of this lovely island culture was a ghastly evil secret—the black cannibal rites complete with shrunken heads, perhaps of poor sailors like himself. And so he, too, began the journey back into civilization and contemporary time. Most of his readers who admired nature extravagantly missed Melville's real meaning. Not only was commercial civilization and all its attendant trappings, such as missionaries, consuls, ship captains, and traders, evil, but, so, too, at base were nature and natural man himself. From the outset, Melville was prepared to see darkness at noon.

Capitalizing on the success of his first story, Melville quickly wrote and published *Omoo* (1847), a continuation of his South Seas adventures that included a blunt castigation of the missionaries and their artificially imposed Protestant work ethic. In 1849 he published *Redburn*, the story of his voyage to Liverpool, and in 1850 *White Jacket*, a fictionalized account of his life on the man-of-war USS *United States*. In the meantime, he had become acquainted with Evert Duyckinck's library, where he found a number of works on the South Seas in which he did research to bolster the details of his eyewitness accounts. More important, in Duyckinck's library Melville found culture. He read Shakespeare with amazement, and Rabelais, Cervantes, Burton, and Sir Thomas Browne. He discovered metaphysics and the "deep questions" of reality. The exuberance of these literary discoveries was reflected in *Mardi*, an interminable allegorical story studded with references to current political events, of a voyage through the South Seas undertaken in search of happiness and the meaning of life. The narrator seeks Yillah, the symbol of happiness, and, accompanied by Babbalanja, a philosopher, Moky, a chronicler, and Yoomy, a minstrel, he sails about like Odysseus, never quite attaining the object of his quest. In its day, *Mardi* was a literary disaster. Most of its readers considered it a pretentious, ill-conceived, confused shaggy-dog story and demanded that Melville abandon the romance and the allegory and return to the "unvarnished" truth of his earlier novels.

Melville, of course, was disappointed, though he did quickly publish *Redburn* and *White Jacket* to mend his reputation. He was disappointed because in *Mardi* he had put everything he had all in one book—symbols, images, allegories, all his bookish learning, his most profound speculations on the great questions, and even his thoughts on the many political issues of the day, of which he was always sharply aware. But, chastened, he resolved to write no more metaphysical books, like his clumsy version of *The Odyssey*.

Then in 1850, sprawled on a haystack on his Pittsfield, Massachusetts, farm, Melville read Hawthorne's *Mosses from an Old Manse*. He had found his kindred spirit—another dark metaphysician who wrote with extraordinary skill and could, as Melville so eloquently put it, "say no! in thunder." At that point, Melville's newest romance, *Moby Dick*, based on J. N. Reynolds's story of Mocha Dick, a whale that had rammed and sunk a whaler off the coast of South America, was almost finished. By all existing evidence it was destined to be another of Melville's adventure yarns, perhaps the best, fusing the story of Mocha Dick with the stories of Bulkington, Steelkilt, and the evil Radney and featuring a mutiny somewhat similar in outcome to his later story "Billy Budd." After reading Hawthorne, and after a historic summer meeting in Pittsfield with Hawthorne and Oliver Wendell Holmes, whose scoffing at metaphysical writing infuriated him, Melville began in November 1850 to rewrite *Moby Dick* into the classic it became.

Moby Dick is the Faustian story of man's attempt to strike through "the pasteboard masks" of external appearances to an understanding of transcendent reality. It is a collective voyage composed of men from all nations, mostly nonwhites—"an Anacarsus Cloots convention," as Melville significantly put it—aboard the *Pequod*, a whaling ship bound from Nantucket in search of "that grand hooded phantom," the white whale, Moby Dick. The ship's commercial objective is doomed, as are all merely commercial enterprises, by a metaphysician, the monomaniacal Captain Ahab, who has lost a leg to the white whale and whose face is scarred with a zigzag crack, like the House of Usher. Ahab cannot help himself. He is predestined by the fates operating through his hatred and his metaphysical anxiety to find and come to grips with the white whale. "He tasks me; he heaps me," declares Ahab. "I see in him outrageous strength, with an inscrutable malice sinewing it. That inscrutable thing is chiefly what I hate." Essentially Ahab's objective is blasphemous—"I'd strike the sun if it insulted me"—and the reader is warned of his blasphemy by the eloquent Father Mapple in his sermon on the eve of the vessel's departure. After recounting the story of the prideful Jonah, who repented and was cast up from the deep, Father Mapple concludes with a stricture against presuming Faustlike to know God, "for what is man," Father Mapple asserted, "that he should live out the lifetime of his God?"

Admonished by Father Mapple, warned by a crazy shoreside prophet named Elijah, Ishmael sets off on the *Pequod*, commanded by Ahab and freighted with a black satanic boat crew led by the sinister Fedallah, on a mad blasphemous mission in search of ultimate knowledge. The events of the voyage are narrated in part by Ishmael, the alienated observer who ironically goes to sea to be rid of the "damp and drizzly November" in his soul. Ishmael as narrator is the man who learns from the *Pequod*'s tragic experience. He learns tolerance and kindness from his exotic bedmate, Queequeg, the tattooed South Sea cannibal king, and this eventually saves him, as it is Queequeg's coffin that keeps him afloat after the *Pequod* goes down with all hands. He also learns of evil and grandeur and the tragic nature of the search for reality as he witnesses Ahab's mad but wonderful quest. And most of all he learns a kind of existential acceptance of man's fate in the face of the inscrutable mask of God in nature. The white whale is beautiful, powerful, untamable, ferocious—but above all unknowable, the symbol of nature and nature's God. And man, like Ishmael, is a cork tossed upon the boundless sea, only by chance rescued when all others—some better, such as Queequeg, some worse, such as Ahab—have perished.

"I have written a wicked book," Melville wrote gleefully to Hawthorne, "yet I feel as innocent as a lamb." Indeed he had. Ahab, like Satan in *Paradise Lost*, is easily the most powerful and attractive character in the book, and the reader cannot help but applaud his quest and feel the tragic grandeur of his defeat. For as the metaphysical quester of the age of Romanticism, Ahab, like Faust, is a towering climactic figure. Metaphysically he, and Melville himself, stand as gigantic heroes in the eye of the maelstrom of human experience, actual and symbolic. They attempt to bring under control all the multifarious and boundless aspects of human consciousness, from the details of cetology to the "thousand Patagonian sights and sounds" of life. For them the centrifugal force of metaphysical reality is tremendous—and ultimately beyond the power of a mad sea captain, but perhaps not a metaphysically driven author who does not care about his literary reputation or if he "strikes the sun." In *Moby Dick* it is the author who is the real hero. By means of his incredible technical virtuosity, the amazingly orchestrated variety of experiences, the fantastic use of symbols— whale, dubloon, etc.—Melville delivered a profound message to midcentury America. Progress and commerce, even the Manifest Destiny of expansion is an illusion. Man's fate is determined by an inscrutable and not always magnanimous Creator. Americans were still "sinners in the hands of an angry God."

The book was, of course, a failure in its time and remained so until it was rediscovered in 1920 and came to be regarded as one of the two or three great masterpieces in American literature. Still in a metaphysical frenzy after *Moby Dick*, Melville wrote *Pierre, or the Ambiguities* (1852), a strange autobiographical novel about an author struggling to write a masterpiece while at the same time living ambiguously with his half-sister and in a platonic "marriage" with his fiancée. Ultimately the story ends in the tragic death of all three principals, but not before Pierre realizes from reading Plotinus Plinlimmon that earthly morality and heavenly morality are two different things.

In 1855 Melville published *The Confidence Man*, perhaps his strangest book. The setting is a Mississippi river steamboat on which a confidence man is said to be operating. He appears in at least eight guises, such as a black beggar, a stock speculator, a philanthropist, a medical quack, and a self-proclaimed "cosmopolitan" who says he loves all mankind. In the end no one, including the reader, who is also duped, knows who he is, or even if he had really been there at all. Studded with some of Melville's richest and most brilliant metaphorical writing, *The Confidence Man* is an almost totally nihilistic analysis of American society.

After its publication his family sent Melville, who was close to a physical and mental breakdown, on a trip to Europe and the Holy Land. On his way through England he stopped off to see Hawthorne at Liverpool. Pacing up and down on the sand dunes along the gloomy seashore, Melville confessed that he "had just about decided to be annihilated." Upon his return Melville tried public lecturing, sought a naval appointment at the outset of the Civil War, and finally in 1866 surrendered to trade and spent most of the rest of his life working in the New York Custom House. He did not fade completely from the literary scene, however. During this time he published a number of short stories, including the strong tale of a clerk not unlike himself named Bartleby who rejects the counting house and refuses to work any longer; a volume of Civil War poems, *Battle Pieces* (1866); and a long metaphysical poem about his trip to the Holy Land, *Clarel* (1876). Three months before his death, in 1891, Melville finished another masterpiece, *Billy Budd*. Taking up the long-forgotten Steelkilt mutiny (subordinated in the final version of *Moby Dick*), *Billy Budd* makes it into a moral tale of earthly and celestial justice in which the good must be punished according to earthly laws, but with faith they will be rewarded in heaven. Melville had at last achieved a reconciliation with his God.

It is impossible to do justice to either Melville's poetic language or the grand power and resonance of his symbolic view of the world. With all the furious energy and magnificence of the towering Romantic hero, Melville himself, in his virtuosity, overshadowed even his own mighty characters. On midcentury optimistic America he cast a dark, demonic shadow. To shallow materialism and the age of Dodge and Bragg he, too, said "no! in thunder." To the world at large, which demanded untaxing adventure books, just like his Bartleby the Scrivener, he said, "I would prefer not to." He became an existential hero unto himself. As far as Melville was concerned, the shimmering mirage of Emerson's nature and all its hues and forms had proved to be inscrutable after all, and the self—what Hawthorne would have called the human heart—was the only reality. In America and perhaps everywhere, according to Melville, the noble dream of community had failed. It was predestined to fail despite the rhetoric and heroism of the Founding Fathers. True union, true community, was an impossible dream when man could not even begin to comprehend social reality and himself.

VI

Perhaps the best antidote to the despair of the "dark-side" Romantic writers was discovered by Walt Whitman, sometime editor of the Brooklyn *Eagle* who in the bustling days of Manifest Destiny became a dropout, carefully cultivating the image of the tramp as seer and prophet (shaman). Conforming more than he liked to admit to the canons of Concord Transcendentalism—as preached and practiced especially by Emerson, Thoreau, and Bronson Alcott—Whitman was a self-made Hindu holy man set down in "Manahatto." He preached a gospel of universal love growing out of the concrete savoring of life everywhere as the salvation of man in general and Americans in particular.

Born in Huntington, Long Island, in 1819, the son of a carpenter, Whitman had had an astonishingly varied experience before he rose suddenly to fame. He had worked the farms and eel fisheries of Long Island. He had labored as a carpenter, helping his father build houses; as an office boy for a doctor; as a teacher at countless local schools; and as a printer's devil and printer. He had tried his hand at writing popular novels and poems, he had been a Democratic Party Tammany Hall hack, and he had worked in various capacities on at least ten newspapers. In 1848, accompanied by his brother, he tramped across Virginia and Pennsylvania and descended the Ohio and the Mississippi to New Orleans, where he worked for a time on the New Orleans *Crescent.* Some biographers have made this trip the central point in the transformation of Whitman's life, and in a sense it was, for it took him out of the regular habits of New York newspaper life, to which he never really returned. Whitman had discovered vastness and humanity and the open road of the universal prophet. From 1848 to 1855 he worked away steadily, in remote Camden, New Jersey, on his didactic masterpiece, *Leaves of Grass.*

When *Leaves of Grass* appeared in 1855, it went virtually unnoticed amidst the literary wars of New York. Not only had Whitman written it, but he also had designed it, printed it, and published it himself. The latter proved to be a distinct disadvantage in calling public attention to it. However, *Leaves of Grass* received most favorable notice, as might be expected, in New England, where its Transcendental message and didactic tone appealed not only to the reviewer in the *North American Review* but also to the mighty Emerson himself, who wrote Whitman a personal letter of congratulations, which Whitman immediately incorporated as a sort of dust-jacket blurb for the 1856 edition of his poem.

Most literary New Yorkers, addicted to Dickensian realism, and most clergymen, offended by his frankly sexual approach to life, either dismissed or condemned the book. In so doing they were perhaps shrewder than they knew because Whitman's underground collection of poems and indeed his own lifestyle were revolutionary gestures that ran counter to the whole commercial Protestant-ethic competitive, rationalized American way of life. And yet he did so, not in an overtly negative, gloomy way, but in resoundingly positive, all-embracing terms, full of gusto, full of life, full of America and its cosmopolitan, universalist future. Sin and selfishness were banished from the center of his large concerns. In Whitman the human heart, which had been growing ever smaller among literary men, expanded— "I am large, I contain multitudes." He killed bourgeois America with kindness. Whitman was perhaps the foremost of the nineteenth-century cosmotopians.

Though others from the Connecticut Wits and the would-be national novelists onward had struggled to create an American epic worthy to be placed beside the great European "tales of the tribe," in 1855 with *Leaves of Grass* Whitman had at last achieved that goal. The first edition of *Leaves of Grass* was essentially "The Song of Myself," and as such, though a climactic event, was only a beginning, as all through his life Whitman revised and expanded his great poem to include additional experiences and restate his propositions from different points of view, so that the changing poem itself became an example of organic growth and the poet's own behavior, a protean, teeming work of cosmopolitan art itself.

The intent of Whitman's work, however, was clear from the outset. In his remarkable preface to the 1855 edition, he set out to establish two points: the poet is the true hero and seer of the culture, and the United States, because it is a nation made up of all nations—"Here is not merely a nation but a teeming nation of nations"—is the truest subject for a universal epic embracing all time, all space, all cultures, and all peoples. "Here is the hospitality," he wrote, "which forever indicates heroes." He added, "The Americans of all nations at any time upon the earth have probably the fullest poetical nature. The United States themselves are essentially the greatest poem." But "the genius of the United States is not best or most in its executives or legislatures, nor in its ambassadors or authors or colleges or churches or parlors, nor even in its newspapers or inventors . . . but always most in the common people." And so Whitman, the poet-seer, bard of the concrete present and the future, identifying himself as the existential "objective correlative" of the common man everywhere and the United States as the "objective correlative" of all people, places, and things, wrote his cosmotopian epic that celebrated in the perilous times of midcentury America those high ideals that Tom Paine had broadcast in *Common Sense* generations previously during the Revolution. Thus Whitman once again restored the Revolution and gave that lasting definition to the American character that the philosophers, statesmen, orators, and literati had been so earnestly searching for since the War of 1812.

Leaves of Grass is a deceptively complex poem. In the opening lines, Whitman establishes his fundamental principle:

> *I celebrate myself,*
> *And what I assume you shall assume,*
> *For every atom belongs to me as good belongs to you.*

In a later version of the poem, he added a new beginning that elaborated his meaning.

> *One's-Self I sing, a simple separate person,*
> *Yet utter the word Democratic, the word En-Masse.*

So Whitman sang of an individual—himself. But he also identified with every other individual in a nation supposed to be made up of individuals. As the bard he empathized with everyone and everything—"I am the man . . . I suffered . . . I was there"—past, present, and future. Thus in an Emersonian and Transcendental way he resolved the problem of the one and the many. By implication, however—the very necessity of writing the poem indicated this—not all Americans understood this simple solution, and so Whitman's poem was also didactic, a sermon on a mount of his own making.

A detailed analysis of the structure and language of his endless poem is beyond the scope of this book, but as critic James Miller has shown—behind the free verse, the seemingly loose arrangement, and the "barbaric yawp" of his artificially contrived American language—is a subtle but discernable structure. Essentially, after establishing himself as an individual and spokesman for the masses, the poet projects himself over the surfaces of American culture "joining the crowd" in catalogs of experience from every walk of life. He appears in the past—at the Alamo and Goliad and with John Paul Jones. He appears in the future and probes into the nature of time. He surveys all nations and the cultural traditions that have contributed to America. He identifies with both male and female, sinner and saint, and examines, in Dantean fashion, hell as well as heaven. He is one with the driven slave and the suicide and the "city fireman with the mashed breastbone." He is also one with nature itself at times, imitating the beautiful musical forms such as the aria that he loved so well, to dramatize this fact:

> *I am he that walks with the tender and growing night;*
> *I call to the earth and sea half-held by the night.*
> *Press close barebosomed night! Press close magnetic nourishing night!*
> *Night of south winds! Night of the large few stars!*
> *Still nodding light! Mad, naked summer night!*

Smile O voluptuous coolbreathed earth!
Earth of the slumbering and liquid trees!
Earth of the departed sunset! Earth of the mountains misty-topt!
Earth of the vitreous pour of the full moon just tinged with blue!
Earth of shine and dark mottling the tide of the river!
Earth of the limpid gray of clouds brighter and clearer for my sake!
Far-swooping elbowed earth! Rich apple-blossomed earth!
Smile, for your lover comes!

At other times Whitman employs litanies, chants, lyrical stanzas, near-prose narratives, word pictures, and rhythmical imitations of nature. He coins new colloquial words and strikes off authentic Americanisms at times. In Transcendentalist fashion he speaks in symbols, but in a technique closer to Thoreau than to Emerson in that the stress is placed much more strongly on the concrete than the ethereal. His natural facts do not spiral upward but instead swirl all around him, engulfing him, immersing him in the center of experience, since the poet as simple, solitary individual is the measure of the universe. And in his own words, "Camerado who touches this touches no book, he touches a man,—the most important thing in the universe."

Moreover, though the poem teems with life, and with love both spiritual and sensual, Whitman also is continually fascinated with death. Unlike Poe, however, he does not regard it with horror, but rather in Hindu fashion as another form of life. All men eventually become leaves of grass and both are holy and demand reverence. The poet's apparent egotism dissolves into a reverence for the humblest things of creation, from the common man to common clay. And he concludes "The Song of Myself" by saying:

I bequeath myself to the dirt to grow from the grass I love,
If you want me again look for me under your bootsoles.

The true strength of America was thus plain enough if one took Whitman's epic as literally as possible. The heritage of the United States was not the predestined darkness and sin of the Protestant past, nor did it require, as the evangelicals insisted, direct visions of God and Satan and abject howling repentance. The holiness was all around waiting only to be noticed—to be touched into life by the spirit of love and community and yet with a tolerance that allowed every man to be himself, to adopt that peculiar lifestyle that made him a man or a woman in every aspect. Only in America, as Whitman asserted, was this yet possible and indeed, as he saw it, probable.

The Civil War, with its attendant horrors and the sudden cruel death of the sainted Lincoln, failed to entirely dampen Whitman's faith in his universalist gospel. But the results of the war, the onrushing tide of mechanization, competitiveness, callous industrialization, and antisocial greed did cause him alarm. In 1871, he felt the need to exhort the American people again. In his long essay "Democratic Vistas," he noted that something had gone wrong with American life, and he held out the old promise of cosmotopia if only the values of *Leaves of Grass* could once again be embraced. But at the height of the Gilded Age this was not to be, and Whitman remained a prophet unheard somewhere in Camden, New Jersey. As many have noted, his popularity and literary influence are, paradoxically enough, greater abroad even today than in his own country. Such is the lot of seers and prophets.

VII

What role had American literature thus played in American thought in the eighty years since the birth of the republic? And what were its outstanding characteristics? Primarily it was one of the most significant channels through which new ideas and new knowledge from Europe and elsewhere funneled into the mainstream of American thought, and helped form a national character that changed with startling swiftness. If the kaleidoscopic, shifting structure of American thought and institutions owed much to the impact of scientific and technological ideas that struck America at the height of a European scientific industrial revolution, literary and philosophical concepts were also forms of a new consciousness that reinforced and accelerated the incredible process of change in North America. The shift from classicism to a full-blown Romanticism that had taken well over one hundred years of conflict among European artists and intellectuals to bring about hit the United States in a virtually simultaneous barrage, and the drama of conflicting styles and ideologies was enacted in the New World over the span of a few decades, which accounts for the furious literary wars in New York and New England.

Moreover, the intense drive for an American literature that it was hoped would symbolize the real achievement of a distinctively American culture accentuated the continual sense of intellectual crisis and carried American men and women of letters deep into an analysis of the culture itself. The writings of the early American authors reflected the weaknesses and strengths of the culture, the factors making for cohesiveness and disparity, its evident shortcomings, and its unique resources, its prospects, and the perils that lay before it. Nearly all of the writers, for example, lamented the lack of an ancient tradition in North America, a thinness of historical background. They extolled the importance of unspoiled nature as a source of literary and cultural creativity but failed to take notice (except for Whitman) of America's cosmopolitan, worldwide heritage. Clearly, few of the major American writers spoke directly for the masses. They conducted no opinion polls and their works, especially those critical of the country, were rarely embraced by the people as were, for example, the works of Scott and Dickens in England and Honoré de Balzac and Victor Hugo in France. Rather, the American writers functioned as cultural analysts—an early warning system for a nation that was still in the process of forming as late as 1861. This role put them distinctly in tension with the organizing and rationalizing tendencies of most materialistically oriented American institutions that derived from the Common Sense tradition of the scientific and industrial revolutions. The early American writer, if he was serious, was thus in some sense from the beginning a critic of American culture at the same time he sought to bring it into being. Like Thoreau, most major American writers put their primary faith in a "majority of one." In so doing, however, they were only implicitly underscoring the individualistic philosophy that dominated the early republic.

In ideological terms they did more than this, however. As individualistic critics and cultural analysts who insisted upon the importance of the new in lifestyles, they exposed the endless possibilities inherent in a pluralistic society. Melville's *Pequod*, as it set out to sea with its "deputations from all nations," was more than symbolic; it was a "first congregation," a cosmopolitan congregation, which stood for America.

In their borrowings from Europe and elsewhere in the name of American nationalism, the writers of the early republic underscored not only the eclectic but also the syncretic quality of American civilization. Quite literally they continually emphasized that American culture was a culture built up out of all cultures and all historical traditions. Though they were not always conscious of doing so, they demonstrated that America was indeed a hospitable, cosmopolitan culture—in Whitman's words, "a teeming nation of nations." The "new man," the American, if he only knew it, could select whatever lifestyle he chose from the world's supply of options that presented themselves insistently to the nation in the pre–Civil War period. It was a story of infinite possibilities.

BOOK IV

THE SYMBOLIC UNION: CONSCIOUSNESS OUTRUNS NATIONALITY

CHAPTER TWELVE

The Wild Jacksonian Age

Politically speaking, it is sometimes overlooked that, as often as not, Americans of the early republic turned to military heroes as rallying symbols of nationalism, and then somewhat incongruously read into these heroes a whole series of republican values. George Washington was a military hero. Yet to the myth-makers he was "Cincinnatus with the Plow"—a citizen soldier who longed to return to his Mount Vernon farm. John Paul Jones was a professional "sailor of fortune" who, after his success in the American Revolution, sold his services to the empress of Russia. Stephen Decatur, a hero of 1812, was the product of a naval family whose fondness for dueling unfortunately outran his skill at it and the country early lost one of its heroes. After Washington, however, the greatest American military and political hero was General Andrew Jackson.

Much has been written by American historians about Jackson and the Jacksonians. Despite this, no one yet knows just who the Jacksonians were, or whether their leader really stood for democracy, an egalitarian revolution, or any political ideology at all. The one fact about which most historians can agree is that Jackson was a military hero who dominated the American imagination from at least 1824 until his death in 1845. Even the barest outline of his life is ambiguous. Born in a backwoods Waxhaw settlement of South

Carolina and orphaned at an early age, Jackson nonetheless began his life very much connected with war and revolution. Two of his brothers died fighting the British. His mother succumbed to disease while nursing American prisoners of war aboard a prison ship in Charleston Harbor. And, according to legend, at only nine years old Jackson himself was abused and slashed by an arrogant British officer. That this "child of the Revolution" would grow up to be a confirmed Anglophobe was thus understandable. That he would become in this role a military hero was less certain.

Orphaned at fourteen, he found himself in Charleston and soon came into an inheritance from a distant relative. He studied law for a time and learned the ways of the Charleston aristocrats, including dueling skills. Then he moved west, to the frontier of North Carolina and on to Nashville. There as a backwoods attorney he collected debts for absentee landowners, speculated in vast tracts of land himself, served as prosecuting attorney in Nashville, delegate to the Tennessee Constitutional Convention, and U.S. senator. Most important, in 1802 he became commanding general of the state militia.

During all this time, as his modern biographers have pointed out, Jackson, like many others in the West, suffered great ups and downs of personal fortune growing out of the frontier's speculative boom-and-bust cycle. In the panic of 1819, for example, he almost lost the Hermitage, his home near Nashville, and its surrounding plantation lands, which he and his slaves had hacked out of the wilderness at great labor. Such vicissitudes of personal fortune could not but have made him suspicious of bankers and speculators, whose operations were beyond his control.

He also suffered for the cause of honor. In 1806 he fought a duel with Charles Dickinson, a crack shot who could cut a string with a pistol ball. Though severely wounded by a shot close to the heart, Jackson calmly took dead aim at Dickinson and killed him with a painful shot through the groin. As Jackson lay grievously wounded on his bed after the affair, he was quoted as declaring, "I should have killed him sir even had he put a shot through my brain." A noisier affair was his "OK Corral" shootout at the City Hotel in Nashville in 1813 with Thomas Hart Benton and Benton's brother Jesse, in which Jackson nearly lost his arm and lay bleeding and prostrate on his bed in the hotel while outside Benton shouted epithets and broke the general's sword across his knee. Benton went on to other duels, as did Jackson, who had killed nine men by the time he sought the presidency in 1824. In spite of their early differences, Benton and Jackson eventually became military comrades-in-arms and staunch political allies.

The beginning of Jackson's national ascendancy came with his campaign as major general of the Tennessee militia. He led his frontier fighters against the Creek Indians, which culminated in the Battle of Horseshoe Bend. During the 1814 battle, he and his men annihilated the Red Stick Creeks and thus avenged the massacre of Americans by these Indians under British leadership at Fort Mims in Alabama in 1812. On his grueling march back to Tennessee from that campaign, Jackson received the nickname "Old Hickory." He also received a commission as major general in the U.S. Army, relieving General Edmund Pendleton Gaines as commander of the Southwest Military District. It was thus that he was in command on those fateful days of January 1815 at New Orleans when the country's honor and, for all he knew, survival hung on his great battle with Wellington's veteran redcoats under General Richard Packenham. Jackson and his army of backwoodsmen, U.S. regulars, New Orleans townspeople, and Jean Laffite's pirates emerged victorious over the conquerors of Napoleon, and General Jackson became the best-known American military hero since Washington. Despite the fact that the war technically was over before the battle was fought, Jackson's victory was a powerful symbol of the innate strength of a republican government and gained for the people at least a second emotional sense of independence.

Further, when General Jackson marched an army into Florida in defiance of international law to hang British provocateurs Robert Armbrister and Alexander Arbuthnot, the people applauded while the government, under James Monroe, grudgingly went along. The aristocratic Virginia dynasty could not stand against the popular appeal of the military hero of the West. In 1824, Old Hickory, nominated for the presidency by Tennessee, received a plurality of popular votes for that office, only to lose to John Quincy Adams of Massachusetts. When the electoral college became deadlocked, the decision was thrown into the House of Representatives, where Adams received enough support from Kentucky's Henry Clay to win. Four years later, it was no real contest. Smarting from his "unfair" defeat at the hands of the "Judas of the West," as Clay was called, Jackson forged a national political machine composed of Southern planters, western farmers, the New York bankers of the Albany Regency, allied merchant interests, and urban immigrants, which carried him to victory in 1828. His election campaign was messianic and possibly the first internal political war in American history. Throughout his two terms as president, Jackson continued to wage war on what he considered to be the evils of American society, thus coining a political approach that has persisted among Democrats even into the twenty-first century.

He was a militant evangelical in government out to cleanse it of artificiality, immorality, and undemocratic practices that had grown up during the tie-wig dynasty of aristocratic Virginia presidents. As historian Marvin Meyers has remarked, his was a "revolution of restoration." With fiery zeal and a great gift for timing and self-dramatization, Jackson as leader of the people directly attacked the "rationalizations" and complexities of an emerging industrial society, hoping to "restore the ways of the plain republican order."

Virtually everything Jackson did and every role he played was redolent of a military and purifying evangelical drama. At his inauguration ball, he turned his political army loose on the White House and made much of a "spoils system" ("to the victors belong the spoils") that his predecessors long had practiced on the quiet. Like a conquering general, he felt himself answerable only to his army—that is, the people who voted for him. He ruthlessly "removed" the Cherokee and Creek Indians from their homelands, and he advocated militant expansion to the Pacific, including the annexation of Texas one way or another. In the Nullification Crisis of 1832 he ordered South Carolina to be blockaded. And in his finest hours he made what he and his followers described as "war" on the "monster bank," which was the Second Bank of the United States.

Impatient with fiscal complexity, he stood for purified currency—hard coin—and so issued the disastrous Specie Circular, which demanded payment for federal lands in cash. He opposed tariffs and surplus cash for the federal government; an elite federal army in favor of a people's militia; and exclusive corporate charters granted by national or federal legislatures. And in general he believed in the slogan of his party journal, the *United States Magazine and Democratic Review*, that "the World is Too Much Governed"—except by evangelical generals whose followers believed that Providence was on their side. As if to prove this point, Jackson was the first president to survive an assassination attempt. In 1835 Richard Lawrence, who believed himself to be the heir to the British Crown, fired two pistols at him from six feet away. Both pistols misfired. The general survived—miraculously, since the odds against *two* pistols misfiring were approximately 125,000 to 1. Jackson's enemies, however, believed the episode to be just one further contrived occasion for the general to demonstrate his flair for self-dramatization.

Nevertheless, the fact remains that for something more than a fleeting moment in history, Andrew Jackson brought together and symbolized a number of contradictory aspirations of the American people. He stood for something new and something old at the same time. Thanks to his incredible energy and his warlike stance on all issues, he embodied a newfound confidence in popular democratic power. As an expansionist, he appeared to cut through the niceties of diplomacy as he supported Anthony Butler's reckless attempt to bribe Mexican officials into selling Texas and the entire Southwest. He appeared also to have a true continental vision when he instructed William S. Parrott to purchase San Diego and Monterey, California, the two major ports on the Pacific. And he gave these maneuvers the gloss of morality when, as in the case of his outspoken support for annexing Texas, he declared himself to be merely "extending the area of freedom." Jackson's views on expansionism continued to dominate the party long after he left the presidency. They reached a culmination with the election of his protégé, "Young Hickory," James K. Polk, whose Oregon and Mexican War diplomacy were hallowed by a ringing phrase, "Manifest Destiny." Little did Jackson, the staunch Unionist, realize that his expansionist policies, launched in the name of nationalism, would eventually be a prime cause for dismembering the Union, as North and South began to focus their differences in a clash over control of the West.

Jackson's antimonopolist policies—his advocacy of charters of incorporation for everyone—also had far-reaching consequences. It unleashed the full energies of speculative capitalism by liberating business from government under an essentially laissez-faire philosophy. In his message vetoing the recharter of the Second Bank of the United States, Jackson delivered a classic statement of his philosophy of government. The government, "if it would confine itself to equal protection, and as Heaven does its rains, shower its favors alike on the high and the low, the rich and the poor . . . would be an unqualified blessing." The government's true strength "consists in leaving individuals and States as much as possible to themselves, in making itself felt not in its power, but in its beneficence; not in its control, but in its protection; not in binding the States more closely to the center, but leaving each to move unobstructed in its proper orbit." Liberal historian Arthur Schlesinger Jr. saw this policy as part "of that enduring struggle between the business community and the rest of society which is the guarantee of freedom in a liberal capitalist state." To most other historians it meant pet banks, floods of wildcat paper money, and unregulated corporations, which led first to a panic in 1837 that spawned depression until 1844, then to another panic in 1857 and to the overripeness of Gilded Age capitalism during and after the Civil War.

Jackson, however, upheld the rights of the common laborer and had what might be described as a primitive labor theory of value. He also saw his antimonopoly position as something of a class struggle, "part of that enduring struggle between the house of have and the house of want," as his friend George Bancroft put it, "that is as old as social union." In line with these sentiments, Jackson staunchly preferred hard money so that a laborer would not have his wages depleted by a sudden inflationary softening of currency by bankers. He also favored labor union movements, though as the work of historian Lee Benson on New York state indicates, they did not always favor him. And whenever he could, Jackson placed himself at the head of the movements for broadened suffrage that were changing state voting laws in states up and down the country. In all of this he demanded that the courts be more responsive to the electorate, which the president alone represented. As we have seen, under Jackson's chief justice, Roger B. Taney, the Supreme Court became so, while Jackson himself was the first president to use the veto to nullify legislation, not because it was unconstitutional but because he considered it politically immoral. Taney lived on to bungle the Dred Scott case, keeping Scott a slave in a free territory.

Then there was the significance of his war on the Second Bank of the United States. In his view the bank represented special privilege not unlike the hated Bank of England, which concentrated too much power in private hands. This was immoral no matter how the bank conducted itself under Nicholas Biddle. Thus the bank was a "monster" and unnatural, and had to go, in the interests of purifying, simplifying, and redemocratizing the

Union. And if the Specie Circular of 1836 worked a hardship on his friends in the West and caused a panic the following year, this was again only part of the purification process necessary to bring the country back to a true state of Jeffersonian yeoman democracy.

Basically, Jackson did not regard himself as an innovator, but rather as a traditionalist. Moreover, his followers represented a whole spectrum of economic and political thought. John L. O'Sullivan, in the first issue of the *United States Magazine and Democratic Review* (1837), related the mighty Newton to Jackson's policies as he saw the proper administration of justice among men operating entirely according to unfettered natural law, which he called the "voluntary principle." "Under the sure operation of this principle," he declared, "the floating atoms will distribute and combine themselves, as we see in the beautiful natural process of crystallization, into a far more perfect and harmonious result than if government, with its 'fostering hand,' undertake to disturb, under the plea of directing, the process." William Gouge, Jackson's chief financial authority, had been guided by similar assumptions in such treatises as *A Short History of Money and Banking*, which he published in 1833. Gouge very conservatively favored hard money, an independent treasury, and no special connection between the government and the banks.

Other Jacksonians, such as Theodore Sedgwick, son of an old Federalist family, were distinctly antimonopoly but not anticorporation. Sedgwick, closely following the doctrines of Adam Smith, went so far as to draw up a table of good and evil corporations. Corporations for public improvement were good. Banks were evil. Somewhere in between came ferry or water companies, insurance companies, private manufacturing companies, and town incorporations ranging on a scale from evil to good. His opinion closely paralleled that of Supreme Court Justice Roger Taney's in the *Charles River Bridge Case* (1837), which upset the Charles River Bridge Company's monopoly charter for transportation between Boston and Cambridge in favor of a second bridge, which would be competitive in the public's interest.

Still other Jacksonians were western pet-bank men, such as Francis Preston Blair, Amos Kendall, and W. T. Berry of Kentucky, who thought Jackson's laissez-faire policy would benefit western growth and, incidentally, banks such as the Commonwealth Bank of Kentucky, owned by Blair. Out in St. Louis, Jackson's staunchest ally in the fight against the Second Bank for hard money was his Senate floor leader, Thomas Hart Benton, Jackson's former dueling opponent, better known by this time as "Old Bullion." Benton was for expansionism, free land, a transcontinental railroad, hard money, the Union, and strict construction of the Constitution. He was against the Bank, the Mexican War, and slavery. In short, Benton was the most consistent man of principle among all the Jacksonians. His firm stands did not always make him popular in St. Louis. In fact, his antislavery position cost him his political career in 1852.

George Bancroft, a historian from Massachusetts, took time out from writing his ten-volume history of the United States to bring Transcendentalism to the support of General Jackson. In addition to his belief in the class struggle derived from his studies in Germany, Bancroft also believed in a transcendental basis for Jacksonian democracy. "There is a spirit in man," he declared, "not in the privileged few; not in those of us only who by the favor of Providence have been nursed in public schools. It is in man; it is the attribute of the race. The spirit, which in the guide to truth, is the gracious gift to each member of the human family." This was reasoning not derived from Lockean sense data but "that higher faculty which from the infinite treasures of its own consciousness originates truth and assents to it by the force of intuitive evidence; that faculty which raises us beyond the control of time and space, and gives us faith in things eternal and invisible." For Bancroft, Jackson possessed this faculty in the highest degree. He was a romantic hero, a "representative man" who belonged in any pantheon of heroes, whether created by Emerson or his Scottish friend Thomas Carlyle, or even the mighty Johann von Goethe himself, with whom Bancroft had studied.

In an age of New England historical writing, in which the indefatigable Francis Parkman was fashioning an epic around the exploits of the giants Montcalm and Wolfe in nature's vast forests, and the almost blind William Hickling Prescott was limning out Cortez as an Iberian "puritan" man of iron fated to overthrow the sybaritic Montezuma, Bancroft had just two real heroes: the people and General Jackson. For his loyalty he became Polk's navy secretary and consequently a chief architect of the Mexican War. Afterward, he was appointed minister to England and, much later, ambassador to Berlin, where he became fast friends with another military leader, Otto von Bismarck, the "Iron Chancellor" of Prussia.

Another Jackson supporter from Massachusetts was the radical Transcendentalist, Orestes Brownson. Warmly applauding the war on the Bank and everything that smacked of the class struggle, Brownson even had his doubts about republican government. "The only way to get rid of evils," he wrote, "is to change the system not its managers." He saw a benevolent socialism as the outcome of a class struggle in America. In 1840, preceding economist Thorstein Veblen by nearly sixty years, he foreshadowed the struggle in historical terms:

> The old war between the King and the Barons is well nigh ended, and so is that between the Barons and Merchants and Manufacturers, landed capital and commercial capital. The businessman has become the peer of the land. And now commences the struggle between the operative and his employer, between wealth and labor.

Whether he knew it or not, Jackson was head of a movement that looked forward toward a radical revolution, as well as backward to an "old republican idyll." He represented capitalism in full swing, passionate socialists, land speculators and slave holders, farmers, mechanics, intellectuals, expansionists, filibusters, lovers of martial glory, poets, Anglophobes, evangelical preachers, and violent backwoodsmen. In Jackson the culture as well as the politics of the early republic achieved a kind of cohesion, helped along by the general's willingness to be all things to all men and by the beautiful timing and public drama of his war on the Bank. The latter became a symbol of what was wrong with "other people," the "vested interests" in American society. Upon the Bank, all of the boomers and malcontents of early America could symbolically project their own guilt. It was a primitive sacrificial victim slain by a noble primitive warrior straight from the West and nature.

Once the Bank was slain and the guilt purged, people of the day went on repeating its sins unfettered, multiplying them ad infinitum into the excesses of the Gilded Age. Meanwhile, Jackson, the people's general, had made symbolic and irrational thinking so common in American politics that his successor, Martin Van Buren, was easily dispatched by another "people's general," William Henry Harrison, the hero of Tippecanoe, whose own set of campaign symbols, the log cabin and the jug of hard

· cider, became more famous than the old general himself. Only by means of large political symbols could American political culture be held together. They served to obscure the deep divisions within society as it headed toward April 1861 and the hellfire on Fort Sumter in Charleston Harbor.

I

Between 1820 and 1860, the population in the United States rose from ten million to thirty-two million, six times faster than the world average. Most of these people came from Ireland as a result of the potato famine, but a great many others came from Germany, France, and England. Of these immigrants, 20 percent settled in rapidly growing seaports or in cities on the Ohio and Mississippi rivers. Thus America became an urban nation with Boston, New York, and Philadelphia as its leading metropolises, though New Orleans, St. Louis, and Cincinnati were not far behind. In the process, America most definitely became a multicultural country—especially after 1846, when San Francisco became American, and even more so after the Gold Rush of 1849 added people from as far away as Australia (the "Sydney Ducks"), China, and Russia, not to mention Hispanics already settled in California and the Southwest.

Living in these urban environments placed people in close proximity to one another while at the same time dividing them by national origin and class. A good example of this is when Nathaniel Hawthorne's hero in *The Blithedale Romance* happens to look out of his hotel window and sees the villain Westervelt, Zenobia, and the ingenue Priscilla engaged in "secret" commerce, revealing their sordid story of white, even sisterly, slavery. The sordid was all around and not very private in the cities. This was enhanced when young women left farms and the supervised spinning mills for the excitement of the cities and the possibility of finding a husband who would provide a safe family haven. The duping and deceiving of these young women became almost an everyday happening, swelling the number of prostitutes and houses of assignation. A fear of these "happenings" became almost a national myth and spawned a whole best-selling literature that shaped the political values of the masses.

managed by the fiend-murderer Devil Bug and two black assistants, plus two women, whose role was to seduce young women into prostitution. Monk's Hall itself had various strange aspects, including a trap door that sent victims to the "Dead Room" in the basement. Indeed, so complex and mysterious was Monk's Hall that it is difficult to see it as a regular meeting place for the affluent. The environment was one of horror that only someone like Poe could imagine. The story itself, one of violence and deception, as Reynolds has pointed out, was like a television series with many different aspects and stories within stories.

Three loosely related plots dominate the book. The first is a seduction and revenge murder. The second is an attempt by a woman born poor, but who now is wealthy, to climb socially by deserting her husband for a fake English lord, who is poisoned by her lover, then she dies in a fire at his estate. The third plot revolves around Mabel (who is described explicitly in dishabille), the daughter of the pimp, Devil Bug, who tries to present her to the world as the daughter of a rich man. A man posing as a preacher, F. A. T. Pyne, drugs and tries to rape her, but she is saved by Devil Bug. She becomes the priestess of a mad sorcerer whom Devil Bug kills, and she finally ends up a married, rich woman. Incidental to all this, Devil Bug murders a man and a wealthy widow, and dies for his crimes.

There are a number of other subplots, but as is clear from the above, the main themes of *The Quaker City* are social climbing and evil life among the wealthy, who prey upon the helpless and avaricious. In *The Quaker City*, Lippard rips aside the veil of wealth to reveal the evil within. Later he formed the Brotherhood of the Union, a very left-wing labor union that was partially successful, and then he died at age thirty-two in 1854, just as *Uncle Tom's Cabin* was about to replace his *Quaker City* as the best selling American novel.

Lippard also exposed the preachers and their churches in such works as *Memoirs of a Preacher: A Revelation of Church and Home* (1849) and the legal system in *The Killers: A Narrative of Real Life in Philadelphia by a Member of the Philadelphia Bar* (1850) and *The Bank Director's Son* (1851). He wrote about New York and its inequities in *The Empire City: Or New York by Night* (1853), *The Midnight Queen: Or Leaves from New York Life* (1853), and his last book, *New York: Its Upper Ten and Lower Million* (1854), in which he was still fighting the class struggle.

About the same time as *Monks of Monk's Hall*, a virtual avalanche of inferior city horror novels appeared. Books by George Thompson, such as *Venus in Boston* (1849), the story of a butler who murders his imagined paramour's husband, cuts off his head, then puts his bleeding corpse in a wine barrel and serves his "paramour" and her new lover wine from the barrel, were typical. Yet in his introduction, Thompson declared that his books were realistic and drawn from his own experiences! Indeed influenced by the cannibalism of the California Donner Party, Thompson could not resist writing *Road to Ruin* (1849), about a starving man who eats the corpses of his dead comrades and then starts upon his own arms.

Other works, reeking of sex, were published daily. Henri Foster's *Ellen Grafton, the Den of Crime* (1850), James Rees's *Mysteries of City Life* (1849), and Harrison Gray Buchanan's *Asmodeus* (1848), *The Life and Confession of Mary Jane Gordon* (1847), and *The Female Land Pirate* (1847) were just a few of the titles involving women and sex. These of course were not moral treatises or arguments against squalor and poverty like the work of Lippard—a genuine crusader.

Perhaps the most colorful of the writers of "trash literature" was E. Z. C. Judson, most often known as Ned Buntline. Born in Stamford/Harper's Field, New York, in 1823, Buntline became a cabin boy on a ship by pluck and luck. Thereafter, he sailed the seas for several years, then fought in the Seminole War in Florida and the War with Mexico. He had several wives, and he started the antichurch and anti-immigrant Know-Nothing Party. He instigated the Astor Place riot in New York in May 1849 because William McCready, an Irishman, was playing the lead in *Macbeth* instead of an Englishman in James Hackett and Fred Niblo's theater, the Astor Place Opera House, while the polished English actor Edmund Forrest was playing the same role at another theater. Buntline's Bowery Boys hailed McCready as one of their own and attacked Forrest. The theaters rang with jeers and shots. Police were called and serious casualties ensued. Meanwhile, Buntline stood on the sidelines cheering on the mayhem and touting his Know-Nothing Party. The new nation was shocked, but the potential for riots existed in every big city. Multicultural Americans had not learned to live together. *This* was an important aspect of their "mentalité" and a critical dimension of American intellectual history.

Buntline stirred the pot with such masterful works as *The B'hoys of New York: A Sequel to the Mysteries and Miseries of New York* (1850), *The G'hals of New York* (1850), *The Death Mystery: A Crimson Tale of Life in New York* (1861), *Love's Desperation; Or the President's Only Daughter: A Romance of Reality* (1847), and even *The Mysteries and Miseries of New Orleans* (1884). He also wrote many sea tales and later wild westerns, such as *Buckskin Sam, the Scalp Taker* (1891). In all, Buntline published an impressive 152 books. In his later life he attached himself to Buffalo Bill and even became a featured player in Bill's absurd melodrama, *Scouts on the Prairie*. A great number of Buntline's later books were paeans of praise for Buffalo Bill, whom he regarded as a true American and guardian of its traditions.

Given the Panic of 1837, produced by Jackson, it clearly was possible that gruesome city mysteries, such as *Monks of Monk's Hall,* were in fact products of mass panic at the instability of life just when urban living was a relatively new experience for most city dwellers, uncertain of their safety and of just how to live. In addition, the city mysteries had as a main theme, besides rape and murder, the awful difference between the poor and the rich. Thus, just when the elements of the cities were able to take advantage of the transportation revolution and economic take-off, class envy was trumpeted by city mystery writers who, unlike the newspapers, did not have to be "boosters" catering to commercial interests who placed ads in their papers, and bankers who owned the notes to their enterprises. Printers thrived. Turning out ten-cent books was almost too easy to resist, and for a curious public eager to revel in scandal—real or imagined. Dozens of real magazines also sprang up, such as *Graham's,* for which Poe wrote, and *The Spirit of the Times,* where Buntline worked. *The Police Gazette,* which lasted the longest of all, became a national paper with western subjects. All of these media had to have something to write about. One has to ask, are the city mysteries and Flash papers of the Jackson era a real index to the thought of the common city people? Clearly they were.

In contrast to the city mystery media, one could look at the views in the mass-distributed Currier and Ives prints that showed clean, well-swept views of city streets with fire as the only calamity. They portrayed harbors full of ships, steamboats, new railroads, lovers, and happy families. One series portrayed "The Four Seasons of Life," with middle age as the "Season of Strength" and youth the "Season of Love." This was a vision of the bourgeois life, though happy farm and town scenes abounded, as well as scenes of sport. The Currier and Ives pictures were also patriotic, with prominent pictures of the president and Statue of Liberty as well as those of military heroes, victorious armies, and people on the way west to California. Of course, these cheap prints were fantasies, but so were city mysteries.

The more affluent preferred the works of the Hudson River School, peaceful paintings like Asher B. Durand's *Kindred Spirits*, which showed the poet William Cullen Bryant and artist Thomas Cole engaged in a conversation in a woody glen in the Catskills. *Kindred Spirits* was first exhibited at the National Academy of Design in May 1848, suggesting that peace and friendship were the habits of the time. Dozens, perhaps even hundreds of artists of this period, few of them rich, painted wilderness scenes of great beauty. Among them were Thomas Cole, Samuel Coleman, Frederic Church, Asher B. Durand, Martin Johnson Heade, and John F. Kensett. None of these artists painted the city. Rather, on most occasions, they fantasized nature in all its glory, or a pastoral past with ruins or picturesque Indian encampments as if going west was just a visit to the neighbors. No artist pictured violence, except for Cole. He painted four large panels called *The Course of Empire*, which showed the various stages of a civilization from the pastoral to the height of the empire to its violent destruction and its return to gloomy nature. Did he mean this as an allegory for America? In one other painting, he also hinted at a kind of disaster. This was his painting of the *Oxbow of the Connecticut* (1836) where, on the right side of the picture, the sun is shining down on fields and mountains along the river, but coming in from the left with lightning-blasted trees in the foreground is a tremendous and threatening storm. Is that America's ominous future? In the same vein, Heade painted the blackness of an approaching storm, called *The Coming Storm* (1859). Was this foretelling the Civil War? Perhaps not, because he also painted several other storm scenes in the late 1860s and 1870s, the best of which is *Newburyport Meadows*, which features a meadow with haystacks over which a storm has just passed. Church, however, painted a roaring Niagara Falls from a precarious point over the falls. He also painted the *Iceberg*, a lonely scene of a wrecked ship where sailors obviously clung to life before succumbing to the cold northern waters Church himself had cruised.

Many of these artists were cosmopolitans who had either traveled or studied in Europe at such places as Paris, Rome, and Dusseldorf, Germany. From the very beginning, young American artists had been pupils of England's court painter, Benjamin West (himself an American). Then, too, almost all the important painters of the 1820s to 1860s had been to Italy. In 1832 Cole made a magnificent painting of the interior of the ruined Roman Coliseum. Durand painted *Head of a Roman* (1840–1841), and Jasper Cropsey worked on his painting *The Roman Forum* from 1849 to 1895. George Innes, standing just uphill from a ruined wall, painted a distant view of St. Peter's Basilica in a glowing Italian light, for it was the soft light that brought painters to Italy. Others studied at the Beaux Arts Academy in Paris while Albert Bierstadt, soon to be the master painter of the Rocky Mountains, studied in both Italy and Dusseldorf. Church and Heade also made masterful paintings of South America. Fine art, which was aristocratic, derived from Europe just as much as Currier and Ives bourgeois art derived from the lithographic process, and lithographic stones imported from Germany.

Clearly, cosmopolitan culture in the Jacksonian era down to the Civil War ranged over many thinkers and creators, from the low-life to the aristocratic, and, as pioneers and gold seekers rolled west across the plains and the Rockies, they carried much of this culture with them, except that most argonauts, like those who sailed around Cape Horn or came from Russia or China, believed that due to the 1849 Gold Rush, they were headed for the land of opportunity, not the misery of the city they had left. As Buntline's western novels made clear, the West was the land of adventure. In 1849 some 300,000 argonauts made it to California, the land of sunshine, Spaniards, the wide blue Pacific, and gold.

CHAPTER THIRTEEN

The Imperial Mind:
The West and the
Future as Reality

Paradoxically, the free American republic was born the child of imperialism. Andrew Jackson and James K. Polk, as recent historians have averred, did not invent it. The French and Indian War—that great struggle over forests and lakes between the two imperialist powers, Britain and France—first alerted the colonists to the possibility of an empire of their own in the backcountry of America. The proclamation line of 1763, closing the West to American settlers, was an important factor in precipitating the Revolution. And during the War for Independence, the insurgents by no means ignored the West, as George Rogers Clark's heroics at Vincennes and Kaskaskia clearly indicate.

From the beginning, the new United States intended to exert its control over the vast wilderness that lay beyond the Appalachians and stretched, they knew not how far, to the Pacific. In 1787, still under the old Confederation government, America's political leaders passed a far-reaching piece of legislation that seemed to answer the problems raised by the heavy-handed British imperial system and at the same time advanced the cause of republicanism—the Northwest Ordinance. This provided for the admission of new states in the West to the original Confederation on an equal footing with the original thirteen. Thus the pioneer colonist, unlike his earlier counterpart under the British system, could be represented in the highest deliberating bodies of the new government. It provided for the continuous replication of new states under a system of republican representative and democratic rule. Though Fisher Ames and other New England Federalists bewailed the potential dispersion of the American people across the continent, others such as Ben Franklin and Hector St. John de Crèvecoeur saw the West and the vast frontier as the new nation's future. In time the belief that the frontier was the future became a national article of faith so strong as to become an intellectual reality. So powerful was this faith in the West as the future of the republic that even as a hypothetical—a still-unsettled land—it became the prize for which not only the North and South contended, but interests all up and down the Mississippi Valley as well. In one sense the West in the early nineteenth century was the cement of the Union of States. But in another sense, particularly after the Mexican War and the Kansas-Nebraska Act, the West as the future threatened to tear apart the nation and with it all dreams of a model continental republic.

I

The architects of westward expansion were Thomas Jefferson and John Quincy Adams. Jefferson, a product of Virginia's frontier, was intensely interested in the West. He knew George Rogers Clark and the importance of his western campaigns. He also knew of Alexander Mackenzie's march across Canada from Montreal to the Pacific in the interest of the British fur trade and what that portended as a hedge against America's own possible objectives in the West. Jefferson also lived through the Burr-Wilkinson conspiracy, which threatened to detach the trans-Appalachian country and the Mississippi Valley from the new United States. Consequently, he was always sending expeditions into the West such as those by André Michaux, Zebulon Pike, and especially the great continental expedition of Lewis and Clark through Spanish territory to the Pacific. Jefferson's was a continental vision, but his most important feat was, of course, the acquisition of Louisiana and with it control of the Mississippi, key to the West.

When he looked to the West, however, Jefferson did not see one vast imperial state. Rather, he saw a string of "sister republics" scattered across the North American continent. He encouraged John Jacob Astor to establish his fur trading post in the Oregon Country as the nucleus of one such future "sister republic." So strong was Jefferson's faith in the power of republican government and the virtuous yeoman culture that made it possible, that he believed republican nations would spring up all over both North and South America and the Caribbean. It became American policy to encourage such new republics. The line of succession in this belief passed down from Jefferson to Albert Gallatin, James Monroe, Andrew Jackson, and Senator Thomas Hart Benton of Missouri, who became a chief spokesman for western expansion. Jackson repeatedly declared that the American investment in the continent was a means of "extending the area of freedom."

In the meantime, Jackson's bitter rival, John Quincy Adams of Massachusetts, in his early years subscribed to the same philosophy. He quietly supported Jackson's invasion of Spanish Florida. He was the architect of the Monroe Doctrine, which forbade all foreign autocracies from recolonizing the Western Hemisphere. He urged the instant recognition of the newly independent republics of Latin America and skillfully negotiated the Transcontinental Boundary Treaty of 1819 with Spain, which gave the United States eastern and western Florida and a strong claim to all the land north of the 42nd parallel to the Pacific, thus assuring the United States a window on the western ocean. Jackson continued this strategy when he tried to purchase all the land north of the 37th parallel and took a particular interest in acquiring ports on the Pacific in California. For both Adams and Jackson the maritime interests were as important as the agrarian interests, and attention to both, as well as the rising tide of inland commerce—especially that flowing down the trail to Santa Fe, which was opened with the Mexican Revolution in 1821—were intended to appeal to all factions in support of the republic.

In addition, as I have argued in other books, all the early architects of westward expansion down to the Civil War—including those who dreamed of a Caribbean empire—were motivated by the desire to maintain American security. In the early days, Spain as well as Napoleonic France were distinct threats, with Florida deemed "a pistol pointed at the heart of the United States," and the control of the port at New Orleans by the French emperor a menace to any republican future in the Mississippi Valley. As these obstacles were gradually removed, Britain, the world's most powerful nation, remained as the chief threat to America. Fear of Britain caused the War of 1812, the annexation of Texas, the Mexican War, and the acquisition of California. These confrontations led to the Oregon Boundary Treaty and to America's quixotic adventures in the Caribbean, designed to secure Cuba and Santo Domingo and to gain control of the Isthmian transit routes. The Clayton-Bulwer Treaty of 1850, guaranteeing freedom of passage across the isthmus connecting North and South America, was the culmination of these efforts. This treaty bore directly upon American efforts to secure gold-rich California from a possible invasion by foreign powers. To see these early American diplomatic maneuvers and even the Mexican War as evidence of an American desire for security against the most powerful nations on earth is to suggest the complexity of motives for westward expansion.

II

The visions that propelled Americans west are many. Some were wildly mystical. Some were narrowly practical. From the beginning, the West, as Crèvecoeur's story of Andrew the Hebridean suggests, was seen by Americans as the land of republican yeoman opportunity. Henry Nash Smith, in his classic *Virgin Land: The American West as Symbol and Myth* (1950), has dramatized the existence of this powerful theme as it appeared in political speeches, the epic poems of Walt Whitman, frontier newspapers, early novels—including Caroline Kirkland's *A New Home, Who'll Follow?* (1839)—and the penny dreadfuls and dime novels so popular in the mid-nineteenth century. The primary myth of the West, as Smith describes it, is really not a myth at all. It is a tableau—a Currier and Ives print peopled with symbolic images, the most important of which is the yeoman with his "sacred plow." What the plantation was to the South, the cabin in the clearing and the yeoman with his plow, wagon, ax, and oxen, not to mention his sturdy family, all set down in nature's abundance of America, was to the American West. There is no contesting the power of this agrarian dream. It carried the western pioneers through the awesome forests of Kentucky, Ohio, and Indiana out onto the "Great American Desert," or Great Plains, where farming at the time was hardly feasible. It also carried them across the Rockies and the South Pass to Oregon and California, where farming *was* feasible. And along with them the yeoman invariably brought republican ideas and institutions. As early as 1833, the mountain man Zenas Leonard, as he crossed over into California, speculated in this vein on America's future in the West:

> Much of this vast waste of territory belongs to the Republic of the United States. What a theme to contemplate its settlement and civilization. Will the jurisdiction of the federal government ever succeed in civilizing the thousands of savages now roaming over these plains and her hardy freeborn population here plant their homes, build their towns and cities and say here shall the arts and sciences of civilization take root and flourish?

An epitaph for another mountain man put it even more succinctly:

> Here lies the bones of old Black Harris
> Who often traveled beyond the far west
> And for the freedom of Equal rights
> He crossed the snowy mountain Heights.

Yeomanism, republicanism, and democratic visions of liberty were powerful propellants to the pioneer, but he was also swayed by a variety of other motives. Commerce was one. Josiah Gregg's classic *Commerce of the Prairies* (1844) described in graphic detail the rich trade of the Santa Fe Trail, opened by William Becknell in 1821. So rich was this traffic that merchants with wagonloads of goods actually preceded the American army into hostile towns during the Mexican War. William Magoffin, for one, languished in Chihuahua and Durango prisons for his rashness in pursuit of commerce. The trade on the Santa Fe Trail helped make Missouri rich, as such towns as Independence, Franklin, and St. Louis sold vast quantities of goods and received equally vast quantities of silver and gold from Mexico. This made it easy for Benton to stand solidly behind Jackson in his hard-money policy. But something more came with the Santa Fe trade. The Anglo traders mixed with and sometimes married into Mexican families. Spanish words such as *vacquero* and *fandango* mingled with English, and Spanish customs and even religion made inroads upon the traders— not enough to change the stern contours of Protestant republicanism, but inroads on American lifestyles, nonetheless.

Still another form of commerce was the fur trade. Largely organized and under the control of John Jacob Astor's American Fur Company, the fur trade brought first forts and trading posts, then towns and cities, up the Missouri River, out on the Columbia River, and even into the heart of the Rocky Mountains. Whether independent trapper, a member of William Ashley's Rocky Mountain Fur Company, or Astor's colossal combine, the fur trapper and trader was a man of commerce. Like the Santa Fe trader, he was part of the Jacksonian world of expectant capitalism. The mountains and their beaver-laden streams were his immediate future, and he usually relished the opportunity they represented. At the same time, the mountain man, too, absorbed traits from other cultures, particularly those of the Indians, with whom he was most closely associated, and the French down from Canada, or up from New Orleans for whom the Missouri and Green rivers and the fur trade were a way of life. At the height of the fur trade era (1820–1835), St. Louis was one of the great polyglot cities of America, peopled by French first families, Spaniards, Anglos, Indians, blacks, and even a few Germans.

Clearly, along with the republican yeoman, the freely competing capitalist fur trapper of Jacksonian America existed on the far western frontier and contributed his dreams and visions to its settlement.

But the most dramatic configuration of capitalists of all were the gold-seekers of '49 who poured across the plains and the Rockies to California, or made the trip around Cape Horn or across the mosquito-infested Isthmus of Panama. They completely changed the pastoral character of California with their dreams of Golconda. They made San Francisco still another of the great cosmopolitan American cities, from the heights of Russian Hill to the shores of Yerba Buena. Besides the Americans of all nationalities who poured into San Francisco, there were hordes of "Sydney

Ducks" from Australia, Chinese laborers, Russian noblemen, and Europeans of every national origin, from the enterprising Jewish inventor of blue jeans, Levi Strauss, to the great Heinrich Schliemann, the German who would one day discover Troy.

After the Gold Rush in California and other mineral rushes in Nevada, Arizona, Colorado, and elsewhere, the West could hardly be considered pastoral. It was increasingly populated with men of commerce, miners, real estate promoters, and high-flying boomers of all kinds. Many of them were itinerant—a professional corps—who moved about the West seeking ever-newer opportunities and setting a pattern of mobility there that has persisted to the present. In every new town, mining camp, or wagon train community, there could be found the itinerant lawyer, preacher, and even the scholar, who helped the frontiersmen reconstitute the societies they'd left behind in the republican Protestant American pattern—with the emigrants at the top instead of at the bottom of the social and economic ladder. No wonder they all believed so fervently in Manifest Destiny. The frontier, a great stage of opportunity, had indeed become their future and they had to believe that this future, this opportunity, was real. American institutions—law, representative government, sober Protestantism—were needed to protect this future, to guarantee this reality, and therefore necessity dictated the need for an American inland empire to the West. But from the beginning the inland empire was also a colony. It was derived from and ultimately dependent upon the older culture of the eastern states. It also overwhelmed the even older cultures and empires of the Native American tribes who had once roamed the whole continent. With the rise of anthropology in the late nineteenth century, Native American ideas and beliefs began to be taken more seriously. They were always there, fierce, fighting tribes who, in the eyes of the settlers, massacred innocent families and hence were declared a species of barbarous pagans that had to be stamped out in favor of a moral, Christianized, capitalist nation.

III

One of the great prophets and representative men of the "rising American empire" was William Gilpin of Brandywine and Philadelphia, Pennsylvania.

Born into the household of an important early Pennsylvania industrialist, Gilpin in his youth had seen visits to his house by the Du Ponts, Benjamin Latrobe, Thomas Dickinson, Thomas Jefferson, Andrew Jackson, and those important French travelers Count Alexis de Tocqueville and Gustave Beaumont. In every way the product of a cosmopolitan family, Gilpin remembered all his life his early association with Tocqueville. "He taught me," Gilpin declared, "the importance and value of statistics and how to look into the future with a good deal of reliability from the data the present affords."

Educated at the University of Pennsylvania and West Point, to which he received a personal appointment from Andrew Jackson, Gilpin found it difficult to settle down in Philadelphia. Instead he took part as an officer in the Seminole War, then moved to frontier Missouri, where he became an ardent disciple of Thomas Hart Benton and publisher of the *Missouri Argus*, the only Democratic Party paper in St. Louis. A fierce partisan of Jackson and Benton, Gilpin lauded Jacksonian democracy and became a militant expansionist. After his colleague Senator Lewis F. Linn introduced a series of bills in Congress calling for the organization of Oregon, Benton promptly followed his lead. In a series of editorials for the *St. Louis Enquirer*, he began to see the West as a passage to India. Basing his ideas on Zebulon Pike's map, which saw the rivers of the West all interlocking and then flowing west from the Continental Divide to the Pacific, Benton thought these rivers would become "what the Euphrates, the Oxus, the Phasis and the Cyrus were to the ancient Romans, lines of communication with eastern Asia, and channels for that rich commerce which for forty centuries has created so much wealth and power wherever it has flowed." He saw mankind returning full circle to its ancestors via the North American continent. Grandiloquently he arose in Congress and, pointing west, declared, "There lies the East. There lies India." In 1849 he called for a central national road across the continent that would allow "the rich commerce of Asia" to flow "through our centre." "The American road to India," he declared, "will also become the European track to that region." Along the way, in the West, would grow up American equivalents of Tyre, Sidon, Balbec, Palmyra, and Alexandria, cosmopolitan world centers of incredible richness and cultural enlightenment. It was no wonder that by the mid-nineteenth century Missourians were calling St. Louis the "Future Great City of the World."

Gilpin followed Benton's rhetoric with perfect comprehension and even more enthusiasm. In 1843 he had traveled with John C. Frémont to Oregon, where he took part in the Champoeg Convention, calling for American sovereignty over the new land. On his return trip, virtually alone, he had traveled the Rockies extensively, making maps and observations. By the time he returned he was calling for the occupation of Oregon and the construction of a central road to the Pacific via the South Pass of the Rocky Mountains. In a letter to Senator David Rice Atchison of Missouri, he asserted, "Oregon is the maritime wing of the Mississippi Valley upon the Pacific as New England is on the Atlantic." By opening an American port on the Pacific, American merchants would have access to a market of 651,014,100 Pacific peoples. He had learned well his Tocquevillian lesson in statistics, as he called for "the opening of the Chinese empire; the independence and civilization of the Sandwich islands, the occupation of the north Pacific by the American whaling fleet," and the "completion of a wagon road across the continent."

These were grandiose, Romantic ideas and Gilpin later used them to support a railroad to the Pacific. By 1846 he had become a full-fledged seer. He grandly proclaimed:

> The *untransacted* destiny of the American people is to subdue the continent—to rush over this vast field to the Pacific Ocean—to animate the many hundred millions of its people, and to cheer them upward . . . to agitate these Herculean masses—to establish a new order in human affairs—to regenerate superannuated nations . . . to stir up the sleep of a hundred centuries—to teach all nations a new civilization— to confirm the destiny of the human race—to carry the career of mankind to its culminating point—to cause stagnant people to be reborn—to perfect science—to emblazon history with the conquest of peace—to shed a new and resplendent glory upon mankind—to unite the world in one social family.

Gilpin's jeremiad in favor of the world civilization did not spring full-blown from the banks of the Missouri. He was a close student of Prussian geographer Alexander von Humboldt, and hence he thought in global terms and in the characteristically German or Hegelian fashion of great stages of civilization, one succeeding the other. He was a student of the social laws of time and space. As such he could argue for the cumulative advance of civilizations through time to a globe-encircling point of perfection. He could also believe, as he told young Julius Froebel, an educator from Germany, that American culture must attain its regeneration from Chinese civilization, which was "still found in its pure state." Moreover, following Humboldt, he believed that the march of world civilization and progress must proceed along an "Isothermal Zodiacal" belt in the temperate zone—roughly a swath along the 40th parallel, hence the necessity for a central road or railroad to the Pacific.

Gilpin forever made maps and geographical calculations in the manner of the great Humboldt. He also calculated that North America, unlike any of the other great continents, was concave. The Mississippi rather than the Alps or the Himalayas ran through its heartlands. Hence by geographical determinism people would flow into the great central valley of America in immense numbers. And since he had land interests in Independence, Missouri, he calculated that it stood in the center of America exactly equidistant from the Atlantic, the Pacific, and the Gulf of Mexico; therefore, it should become a kind of hub of North America, if not the world.

As a serious geographer, Gilpin overlooked almost nothing. He noted the vast mineral deposits in the Rocky Mountains, labeling them the "Central Gold Region," and helped start the Colorado Gold Rush. He was also one of the first to point out the value of the Great Plains as rich grassland areas for the grazing of flocks and herds, thus predicting (as anyone who had seen the buffalo should have) the rise of the High Plains cattle industry. As Professor Thomas Karnes has pointed out, Gilpin's was a shrewd observation but he has been blamed unfairly by western writer Wallace Stegner for promoting Dust Bowl farming and the "rain follows the plow" theory. In point of fact, the latter was the brainchild of archaeologist-climatologist Dr. Cyrus Thomas on Ferdinand B. Hayden's survey of Nebraska in 1867.

Whether Gilpin was a particularly astute prophet of westward expansion or the progress of civilization is of no particular concern here. The fact is, he touched upon many of the dreams of the westering American in his letters and in his books: *The Central Gold Region* (1860), *The Mission of the North American People* (1873), *Notes on Colorado* (1870), and *The Cosmopoli-*

tan Railway (1890). These books were largely made up of earlier letters, reports to Congress, and articles published and unpublished. The staying power of his ideas—until nearly the turn of the century—is some indication of the interest he generated, and of how he reflected the multifaceted ideas that Americans held about the West. A member of the eastern educated elite, though vastly experienced in the West, and governor of the Colorado Territory, he crystallized a vision of the future for the West and the westerner. Gilpin's Manifest Destiny was a many-splendored thing.

IV

"Manifest destiny" thus took on many connotations, which to enthusiastic expansionists were all to the good. Jane McManus Storm, a female expansionist who coined the term "Manifest Destiny" in the *United States Magazine and Democratic Review*, argued that the American claim to Oregon "is by the right of our manifest destiny to overspread and to possess the whole of the continent which Providence has given us for the development of the great experiment of liberty and federative self government entrusted to us." In addition to invoking God, the principle of liberty, and states' rights, Storm also reverted to nature and the Romantic organicism of the day. The American claim to Oregon was "a right such as that of a tree to the space of air and earth suitable for the full expansion of its principle and destiny of growth."

Other spokespeople evoked the contrast theme, as did George H. Evans in the *Workingman's Advocate*, in which he saw aristocratic England excluding its citizens from landholding while American expansion promoted it. An Alabama congressman speaking of Texan annexation embellished on this theme in a way that was to grow more familiar in the late nineteenth-century years of mass immigration:

> Long may our country prove itself the asylum of the oppressed. Let
> its institutions and its people be extended far and wide, and when the
> waters of despotism shall have inundated other portions of the globe,
> and the votery of liberty be compelled to betake himself to his ark, let
> this government be the Ararat on which it shall rest.

According to other spokespeople, expansion would also be a safety valve for the depressed classes of immigrants pouring into our American cities. It would be a refuge from financial panics such as that of 1837. It would be a Christianizing force and would regenerate the "backward" peoples of the continent. For most ardent expansionists, investment of the continent would, in its larger terms, be a great cultural reform movement.

But who was to be reformed? Principally Native Americans and Mexicans. Prejudice against the latter, as Professor Raymund Paredes has pointed out, goes back to the generation of the "Black Legend" by Protestants in the Reformation. Drawing upon sixteenth-century Catholic reformer Father Bartolomé de Las Casas's indictment of the Spanish Catholic conquistadors in the sixteenth century, militant Puritans eventually drew little distinction between the conquerors and the conquered in Mexico. Their descendents followed suit. John Adams wrote:

> The people of South America are the most ignorant, the most bigoted, the most superstitious of all the Roman Catholics in Christendom . . . Was it probable, was it possible, that . . . a free government . . . should be introduced and established among such a people . . . ? It appeared to me more extravagant than . . . similar plans would be to establish democracies among the birds, beasts, and fishes.

But for New Englanders, who largely controlled the dissemination of information in the new republic, the prime authority on the Latin world was Scotsman William Robertson's *History of America*, which continued the legend of the profligate native at a lower stage of civilization, the cruel but abler conquistador and the rapacious Catholic Church. The poet-seer Joel Barlow drew heavily on his work, though Barlow also had the more accurate work of Garcilaso de La Vega to temper Robertson's generalizations. William Hickling Prescott, too, reflected something of Robertson's viewpoint—especially his view of the natives as sybaritic and barbaric. By the early nineteenth century, a composite negative portrait of the Mexican had also been drawn. His religion, Roman Catholic, was wrong and idolatrous. His Indian background rendered him a bloodthirsty barbarian. He was as impervious to Enlightenment ideas of progress as he was to the virtues of Scottish moralism. In short, the Latino was a self-doomed civilization. As

Americans in the era of Manifest Destiny came into contact with the Mexicans, the picture changed little. Traveling the Santa Fe Trail, Lewis H. Garrard declared:

> The New Mexicans, when weakest, are the most contemptible servile objects to be seen; and with their whining voices, shrugs of the shoulder, and dastardly expression of their villainous countenances, they commend themselves unreservedly to one's contempt. But, when *they* have the mastery, the worst qualities of a craven's character are displayed in revenge, hatred and unbridled rage. Depraved in morals, they stop at nothing to accomplish their purpose.

According to Texan novelist Mary Austin Holley, "The Mexicans are commonly very indolent, of loose morals, and, if not infidels of which there are many, involved in the grossest superstition." John T. Hughes, a Baptist evangelical who rode with Colonel Alexander Doniphan's expedition in the Mexican War, was even more emphatic in his condemnation, though in some ways he seemed to be describing Yankees more than Mexicans:

> Gold is emphatically the god of the Mexicans. They have no motives but those of profit; no springs of action but those of self-love; no desires but those of gain; no restraints but those of force. The eternal jingle of cash is music to their ears.

Still another theme traced the inferiority of the Mexican to his mixed blood in overt racism. Writing of California in 1844, Thomas Jefferson Farnham asserted that "the law of Nature, which curses the mulatto here with a constitution less robust than that of either race from which he sprang, lays a similar penalty upon the mingling of the Indian and white races in California and Mexico. They must fade away." On the other hand, the mixture of Caucasians in the United States "will continue to produce a race of men, who will enlarge from period to period the field of their industry and civil dominion." This was repeated by United States–Mexican Boundary Commissioner John Russell Bartlett, New York's most prominent bookseller: "A vast gulf," he asserted in italics, "*intervenes between these Castilians and the masses, who are a mixed breed, possessing none of the virtues of their European ancestors, but all their vices, with those of the aborigines superadded.*" Major William H. Emory of the Boundary Commission reported to Congress that miscegenation, or interracial marriage—legally or adulterously—was the chief cause of the "decline and retrograde march of the population" in Latin America. According to Emory, "the process of absorption can never work any beneficial change."

Where did all of this leave Young America's reformers, not to mention those on the quest for a free and open world civilization along the lines Tom Paine had described? It certainly counterbalanced the theories of such visionaries as Gilpin, who thought the infusion of Chinese civilization would perfect American civilization, and Walt Whitman, who espoused expansion to realize the high ideals of the "teeming nation of nations." Moreover, there was little the Mexican could do about his mixed blood, leaving him incapable of reform, so Young America's slogans took on a hollow ring. On the other hand, for every racist there were many others like female expansionist Cora Storm Montgomery, who knew Mexico, had a great fondness for its people, and saw hope in establishing republican and democratic institutions that would replace the autocratic control of the Church, the army, and the opportunistic succession of dictators such as Santa Anna. Critical of Polk's war and Santa Anna's opportunism, she wrote in 1847:

> If they had patriotic and trustworthy leaders, the Mexicans would show the brave mettle of their fathers. It is the corruption and unfaithfulness of their leaders that unnerves and defeats them. In all times, as in the days of Cortez, in the colonial struggles, in the fiery trials of their revolution, when they marched in steady phalanx to the cannon's mouth and rivaled the Spartans of old in heroic self-sacrifice, always whenever they trusted their chief and believed in their cause, the Mexicans have gallantly proved their constancy and courage.

She called upon Polk to stop bribing dictators such as Santa Anna and "allow those states which are prepared for freedom, to escape the intolerable thraldom of their military despotism." Most immediately she called for the independence of the North Mexican states and the formation of a "Republic of the Rio Grande," nurtured by the United States. It was Jefferson's "sister republic" idea that she proposed as the outcome of Polk's war of 1846.

And what did a "cosmotopia," westwardly extended, hold out for Indians? Few settlers who were directly involved with westward expansion were so naive as to believe that they were entering "a great empty continent." Certainly the federal government and those out west who daily confronted Native Americans labored under no such delusion. Not everyone considered the Indian a problem, however. Jefferson was fascinated by the Indians. He considered them nature's noblemen, throwbacks to the ancient Saxon or Roman warriors, and he lamented that their civilization appeared to be fast dying out. In a famous letter to the Chevalier de Chastellux in 1785, he described with sentimental admiration the oration of the dying Mingo chief, Logan, comparing him to Demosthenes and Cicero. "They [Indian orators] astonish you with strokes of the most sublime oratory, such as to prove their reason and sentiment strong, their imagination glowing and elevated." He flatly asserted to Chastellux, "I believe the Indian, then, to be, in body and mind equal to the white man."

To Jefferson, educated on the principles of Scottish Common Sense philosophy, the Indian was part of the general family of mankind that was descended from Adam and Eve, crossed over the land bridge from Asia to America, and developed in isolation from European civilization. His comparative primitiveness was due to no innate quality but to his lack of proximity, in the vastness of North America, to large numbers of people with whom he could exchange ideas and customs. Never a pluralist, Jefferson believed now that the white man had arrived in North America, the Indian could be assimilated into the general culture. In the meantime, fascinated with the Indian's origin, nature, and history, Jefferson helped excavate mounds near Charlottesville, Virginia, set up a special "committee on Antiquities" to collect information on the aborigines during his presidency of the American Philosophical Society, made it a point to talk to every chief who came to Washington, and collected Indian vocabularies for over thirty years. He believed the vocabularies would yield the key to a comparative study of Indian cultures and, more important, to the diffusion question or where they came from.

One of the most important students of the Indian in the early nineteenth century was Albert Gallatin, Jefferson's friend and Secretary of the Treasury. Gallatin, a Swiss, had imbibed Enlightenment principles in central Europe and was a particular devotee of Alexander von Humboldt. As such he had a penchant for statistical geography as it related to the Indian. An armchair ethnologist himself, he sent out questionnaires about the Indians to missionaries, soldiers, frontiersmen, and so on. He was most interested in how the Indians adapted to the New World environment as measured by their population and their adoption of agriculture as opposed to hunting. A Malthusian, he believed that while the Indian was a man like all other men and infinitely capable of improvement, he could not improve if he remained a hunter. The population would always be limited by the number of animals in their hunting grounds, which, if encroached upon, would cause an automatic decrease in population or a decimating war. He also felt that the hunters, when not on the chase, sank "into a mental apathy and physical indolence, from which strong stimulants alone can rouse them." Thus they had a built-in weakness for "ardent spirits," which caused the tribe to degenerate. In Gallatin's view, the Indian needed careful civilizing and the civilizers had to learn as much as possible about the Indian to see to his improvement. Here Humboldtean geography and statistics came into play.

In 1836 Gallatin published his "A Synopsis of the Indian Tribes" in the American Antiquarian Society's *Transactions*, classifying the tribes by linguistic affinities and locating them for the first time on a map. It was in three sections; the first was a linguistic classification, the second dealt with the climate, means of subsistence, economic structure, questions of origin, and possibilities for civilizing them; the third section was a close analysis and comparison of various Indian grammars. The most important contribution was his map, for the first time incorporating much of this data graphically for North America. Gallatin's was a thoroughly scientific approach to the Indian question and since he lived a very long time—into the era of Manifest Destiny, when he founded the American Ethnological Society in 1841—he had great influence on American thinking about the Indian and his proper destiny. Always a man of the Enlightenment, Gallatin was optimistic and believed, given the proper social environment, that the Indian could be successfully amalgamated into Anglo culture. Of course, then the Indian's own culture would cease to exist.

Henry Rowe Schoolcraft was a much more ambivalent student of the Indian. Born near Albany, New York, in 1793, Schoolcraft first became a mineralogist and an accomplished geologist. This took him west to the Ozarks in 1817–1818. Two years later he accompanied Senator Lewis Cass, who was always his mentor, to Lake Superior on an expedition in search of copper deposits. In 1832 he helped discover the source of the Mississippi at Lake Itasca in Minnesota. As early as 1822, Cass had gained him an appointment as Indian Agent for the Lake Superior Region. Shortly thereafter he married a woman who was one-quarter Chippewa, Jane Johnson, and began a career as an ethnologist that was to culminate in some fifty-six books and pamphlets, fifty-nine articles, and seven definitive government documents.

Like Cass, Schoolcraft believed in fieldwork and made the Lake Superior tribes, particularly the Chippewa, his specialty. In this his wife and her family served him very well as informants, especially insofar as he never took the trouble to learn the Chippewa language. In the years 1821 to 1831, according to Professor Robert Bieder, he was a sympathetic student of the Indian, "especially interested in his myths and oral literature which he hoped to capitalize on as a professional writer." In 1831 Schoolcraft was converted to a strong brand of Presbyterian fundamentalism, and from this point on his observations were colored markedly by his religious convictions. He remained sympathetic to the Indian and studied him prodigiously, but predicted his doom unless he converted to Christianity. During this time, however, he wrote perhaps his most interesting work, *Algic Researches* (1839), where, in collecting myths and tales, he was able to offer a penetrating analysis of the Indian mind.

In 1841 he lost his job as Indian agent and he also lost his wife. This was a devastating period for Schoolcraft until later he remarried, this time to the daughter of a rich plantation owner in South Carolina. At this point he began to be extremely inconsistent. He opposed the polygenesis theories of S. G. Morton, George Glidden, and Josiah Nott that argued for the separate creation of five races, of which Indians were one and blacks another, in favor of monogenesis. Yet at the same time he became a proslavery advocate, believing blacks were innately inferior while Indians were capable of improvement. The longer he lived, however, the more confused he got, until he came to think that Indians were all Semites who had come from the Old World and degenerated in the New World—except for the meso-American cultures, which had received a cultural transfusion from the Old World sometime back in prehistory—possibly a visitation from the "Chariot of the Gods." He also believed that the Indians out beyond the Rockies were "robbers, thieves and bandits," and as always, following the lead of General Cass, he was a staunch advocate of removal.

With these "credentials" Schoolcraft was hardly the best man to head up a great federal survey of the Indian tribes, which he did between 1851 and 1857. By 1857 Schoolcraft had completed a lavishly illustrated six-volume government report, *Historical and Statistical Information Respecting the History, Condition and Prospects of the Indian Tribes of the United States*. It was a compilation of the articles by soldiers, missionaries, ethnographers, and virtually anyone he could get to write an article, all edited by him. As a result of this labor, he was touted as the ultimate authority on the American Indian. He had produced the capstone of field and statistical research. Thrown together, Schoolcraft's six-volume work was, nonetheless, a kind of culmination of the Humboldtean tradition as it related to Indians. It was geographical, comparative, and statistical and yet it also paid some attention to history and the Indian's place in it. To the end of his life, Schoolcraft was ambivalent about the Indian. He saw him as a degenerate race but one capable of great "subtlety" in his modes of "thought and belief" and in his possession of "spiritual and creative power." He advocated removal and yet at the same time he urged his readers to understand the Indian and to treat him with "greater kindness: and a more enlarged spirit of justice."

V

It was abundantly clear that Schoolcraft's rival, the artist George Catlin, believed the Indians were destined to be a doomed people, so he painted all the tribes in the West and South America. Catlin's was an exercise in salvage anthropology. As he put it, he had gone west "to extend a helping hand to a dying race." But why was this assumption, which, as Professor Brian Dippie has pointed out, all but universal among those who thought about the Indian in the early republic? Why didn't the Native American fit into America's "cosmotopian possibilities"? After all, the nation began on the optimistic note that all men were created equal, and much of the philosophy of the early republic was grounded on the assumption that no man or woman was predestined but rather that the improved environment in the New World would result in an improved species—the new man, the American. With the Revolution had come the belief in human perfectibility through improved institutions and an adherence to republican virtue. Yet such a belief in perfectibility did not seem to extend to the Indian and his mixed-blood cousin, the Mexican.

In a certain sense this attitude toward the Indian was an acknowledgment of the American's "badge of lost innocence." As Dippie has said, "At bottom the noble savage's primary virtue was his innocence of civilized vice." At the same time it came to be apparent that "upon contact with civilization, he [the Indian] surrendered what was good in his character and absorbed what was bad in that of the white man." White contact, now called "acculturation," inevitably destroyed Indian culture, suggesting to many that Indian culture was inferior and basically weak, and had to be protected by good white men. The evidence for this was the Indian's fondness for whiskey and his almost instant corruption by it; his childlike delight in the merest trifles of white manufacture; his proneness to smallpox and other diseases; his constant internecine warfare with other tribes; and his inability to adapt to the orderly ways of yeoman agriculture and urban commerce. Even blacks seemed more resilient and adaptable.

The Indian seemed to be rigid in his ways as a hunter, migrant, and warrior despite the obvious fact that many tribes were agricultural. Indeed, one of the early Shawnee chiefs was named Cornplanter. In certain ways the American admired Indian intransigence, his warrior qualities and his relative closeness to nature. But these very virtues doomed him. It became clear to Americans, after the War of 1812, that the Indians could not live with the "civilized" white man. Thus, though it had been accomplished by war and treaty-making before, the original policy of removal had its origins around 1819 and continued down to the Civil War. It was not invented by Jackson, but he was the most conspicuous implementer of the policy with his forced removal of the Cherokee and the Creeks to Oklahoma (Indian Territory) after the passage of the Removal Law of 1830.

Jackson himself appeared to regard removal as a benign policy despite the fact that of all the Indians, the Cherokee and the Creeks had proved themselves to already be sedentary and, therefore, "civilized" peoples. In 1829 he addressed the Creeks:

> Friends and brothers, listen; where you now are, you and my white
> children are too near to each other to live in harmony and peace. . . .
> Beyond the great river Mississippi, where a part of your nation has
> gone, your father has provided a country large enough for all of you,
> and he advises you to remove to it. There your white brothers will not
> trouble you; they will have no claim to the land, and you can live on it,
> you and all your children, as long as the grass grows or the water runs,
> in peace and plenty. It will be yours forever.

Kindness, however, as history has shown, hardly motivated Jackson. Rather, the desires of his Southern Democratic Party constituents for more land and the possible gold deposits in Georgia moved him much more deeply as a leader of his people.

But other, more intellectual attitudes toward the Indian also developed in the nineteenth century. Special creationism was one of these. Those who followed French biologist Georges Cuvier and Harvard paleontologist Louis Agassiz, for example, could see that God had made each creature specially adapted to his special environment at those times between catastrophes. Strangely enough, this point of view coincided almost exactly with the basic Indian outlook on reality and seems embodied not only in most Indian creation myths but also in their reverence for every aspect of their natural surroundings and their anthropomorphizing of birds, animals, fish, and insects. But for the white philosopher, the rise of complex civilization itself represented a world event—a social catastrophe that was somehow good but rendered primitive Indian culture unadaptable and hence doomed.

Beyond this, as German thought began to come into America, and with it ideas of cultural evolutionism, the Hegelian idea of succeeding civilizations arose. Edward Everett of Harvard, for example, began to argue in Hegelian fashion that one civilization inevitably succeeded another. As the barbaric Greeks fell before the more civilized Romans, so too must the Indian fall before the more civilized Anglo-Saxon. And between barbarism and civilization there are no degrees; Everett declared, "There appears to be an essential difference between them, which makes the highest point of barbarism a very different thing from a low degree of civilization." It was only a short step from this to Lewis Henry Morgan's Darwinian anthropology with its world-spanning stages of savagery, barbarism, and civilization. In a sense, the rediscovery of time and history contributed to the vision of doom for the Indian. Poor, simple people of the past, they were in the way, as Catlin put it, of the "juggernaut" of civilization that prophets, especially those of Manifest Destiny, believed had been gestating through all the ages and was heading toward some globe-encircling climax in the nineteenth century. There can be no blinking at the fact that Manifest Destiny, despite its grandiosity, represented a crisis for the world's model society.

VI

In fact, by 1850, for many Americans the Imperial Mind had come to substitute for "cosmotopian" ideals, and many scarcely realized the exchange. While pioneers and entrepreneurs were looking west, the South was looking to the Caribbean. The annexation of Texas had nearly split the Union, especially as it was dramatized by the Wilmot Proviso, and Southerners became alarmed lest they be left out of the expansionist-imperial future. Calhoun's speech on the Compromise of 1850 made this abundantly clear. Thus in the 1850s the South allied with New York shipping interests, especially Commodore Cornelius Vanderbilt, and the British Aspinwalls turned to the Caribbean. There arose what Professor Robert May has called the "Southern Dream of a Caribbean Empire." The rationales for southward expansion in many ways resembled those for westward expansion. The tropic isles, especially Cuba and Santo Domingo, were lush virgin lands, "tropical fruit," as the metaphor went, "ripe for the plucking." They could be settled and civilized by yeoman planters, and the backward Catholic mestizos, or those of mixed European and Indian ancestry, who inhabited the islands could be brought within the ken of civilization. Moreover, if they were not quickly seized they would fall prey to Britain, which already had control of prostrate Mexico, Honduras, and the Mosquito Coast in Central America, and designs on control of all Isthmian canal routes despite the Clayton-Bulwer Treaty of 1850 guaranteeing neutrality for the Isthmus Canal.

In 1851, aided by New York and New Orleans backers, Narciso Lopez and a ragtag army of American filibusters invaded Cuba intent upon liberating it for the United States. Mississippi Senator General John Quitman intended to join him but was detained at the docks by federal authorities. This was fortunate for him because Lopez did not meet with a groundswell of democratic enthusiasm in Cuba. Instead, he was soundly defeated and most of his army put to the firing squad.

In 1855, however, William Walker, the "Grey-eyed Man of Destiny," was much more successful. At the head of a band of fifty "immortals" he landed on the Pacific coast of Nicaragua and succeeded in capturing the whole country. His reign lasted two bloody years, and then he was defeated only because Commodore Vanderbilt, insulted by Walker, refused to send any more supply ships out of New York. Walker, like Lopez and other bands of Caribbean filibusters, was not really interested in "extending the area of freedom." They appealed mainly to the South and planned to extend the area of slavery—an important reason why they were rejected by the local inhabitants and denied even covert support by the American government.

All of this makes it obvious that expansionism—Manifest Destiny and the generation of the "imperial mind"—had grave consequences for the nation as Union and for the Union as the strength of a shared culture. The political steps in the sundering of the Union are mostly clear. The West itself became so great a prize, especially after the Gold Rush in 1849, that sectional rivalries rose to fever pitch. The Wilmot Proviso of 1848 raised the point concerning the westward expansion of slavery and caused the men of destiny to take a hard look at the future. And it was the future—the "imaginary Negro in an impossible place," to use Daniel Webster's phrase—that split the nation, hardening attitudes in both the North and South.

The Compromise of 1850, as Calhoun predicted, was only a temporary palliative, and the Fugitive Slave Law did more harm than good, as did the future-oriented railroad promoters who engineered the Kansas-Nebraska Act through Congress in the name of progress, states' rights, and squatter sovereignty. These political events, stemming from the overambition of western and southern expansionists, are all well known, save one: Senator George Bibb Crittenden's 1861 attempt to redraw the Missouri Compromise line to allow the South to continuously expand into the Caribbean. As recited in the textbooks and surveys of the Civil War period, the various compromises take on an inevitability all their own—a sequence of the tragic, political rituals of what some have called "the blundering genera-tion." But rather than a "blundering generation" it might better be called an "ambitious generation," because it attempted to invest the continent, seize the Caribbean and Central America, civilize all "backward" peoples, encircle the globe, reach out to the celestial empires of China and India, while at the same time digesting the world's information and trying out every new idea under the sun in a continuing attempt at self-definition. It may well have been the result of unrestrained competition in ideas and vi-sions that shattered the new republic.

But the dream of expansion had larger consequences even than cultural breakdown and Civil War. It obscured the generative dream of a free soci-ety for many, sectionalized the life of the mind and its relation to the mis-sion of America, and finally resulted in a vast inland empire that was and has remained even into the twenty-first century, still a colony dotted with Indian reservations funded by the U.S. government. The successful expan-sion to the Pacific meant primarily that not only the established institutions and values of the older states would be duplicated and predominate in the West—despite the quaint environmental theories of some historians—but also that the monied eastern establishment would largely control and even interpret the western experience.

The same was true when as a result of the Civil War, the eastern estab-lishment came to dominate the Southern experience. The consequences of these events, so large as to be difficult to see without a twenty-first-century perspective, have been the prolonged colonization and hence provincialization of inland America. Only recently have the interests and burgeoning power of this immense inland colony risen to prominence un-der such vapid journalistic labels as the "Southern Rim Conspiracy," the "Sun Belt," and the "Sagebrush Rebellion." But signs of anticolonialism have been visible all along in America: in the Civil War; in the Indian upris-ings in the West of the 1870s and 1880s; in the Populist revolts, which for a time joined West and South, black and white; in the violent western miners' strikes; in the recent resurgence of "Red Power" so celebrated by Indian Vine Deloria's *Custer Died for Your Sins* and Leslie Fiedler's *The Return of the Vanishing American;* and in the dynamic California counterculture move-ments and cults of the late twentieth century that seemed to have escalated inland anticolonialism into a national neurosis. The decolonization of

America—to a Hegelian, the inevitable consequence of the mid-nineteenth century's adventure in expansionism and expectant capitalism—is perhaps something for modern intellectuals and students of cultural growth to ponder and fit into the world scene. But even in the years before the Civil War, when expansion seemed a glorious adventure, the fundamental problem for intellectuals was achieving and maintaining cultural cohesion.

The struggle for cohesion continues into the present, as seen by the steady increase of Mexican immigrants in the West and the assertion of nationalistic and indigenous groups who desire recognition and independence. Some Chicano activists, in particular, have expressed a desire to reclaim portions of the American Southwest, which they call "Aztlan," under the belief that they hold ancestral rights to the lands that were annexed by the United States after the Mexican-American war.

CHAPTER FOURTEEN

The South and the Past as Reality

While most Americans, when they thought about the ideal nation-state, looked to the future, the people and leadership of the antebellum South believed they already lived in a near-perfect society and sought to resist change. By 1830, the cosmopolitanism and fervor of a revolutionary generation that included George Washington, Thomas Jefferson, James Madison, Charles Pinckney, Patrick Henry, Nathanael Greene, and Francis Marion, Southerners all, had waned. Grand Enlightenment generalizations about world revolution and the rights and opinions of mankind had given way to a species of Aristotelian thought that reordered the priorities of Southern loyalties. Love of the familiar predominated. First the home and family, then the plantation, county, or parish, next the state, region, or section, and perhaps lastly the nation governed Southern loyalties, which grew dimmer as they moved away from the local and the concrete. They took as their model classical Greek democracy, which was, after all, based on the city-state and therefore limited in geographical area and somewhat exclusive in terms of its relationship with the barbarians of the outside world.

The Southerner came to look upon the North, with its rapid industrialization, sudden growth of cities, influx of immigrants, and absorption of
new ideas from Europe, as virtually another country, and the feeling was
reciprocated by Northerners, who increasingly viewed the South as an exotic and backward colony where tempers flared and the dark hand of immoral violence predominated. Even though elements from both North and
South—the banker and the mechanic, besides the planter and the woods-
man—rallied behind Andrew Jackson and his party to bring about political
cohesion for a time, it was never a true cohesion. Down to the Civil War,
the United States was thus never really united.

This may seem tragic. Certainly antebellum history suggests that principles and ideals of one kind or another (however wrongheaded) took precedence over nationalism as the focus of loyalties in all sections of the
country, sometimes even in the face of a threat from abroad by England,
France, or the continental Holy Alliance. Despite the efforts of constitution-makers, legal thinkers, transportation promoters, would-be national
party leaders, Whig system builders, national bankers and financiers, public heroes, and epic poets, the early republic was held together largely by a
series of precarious compromises and the artful postponement of decision-
making on important and potentially divisive national questions.

It was thus no accident that Jefferson viewed the debates over the Missouri Compromise in 1820 as "a fire bell in the night"—a profound threat
to the delicate fabric of the new nation. Even after the political compromise limiting slavery to the area of the country below the geographical line
of 36° 30' except for the new state of Missouri, Jefferson wisely foresaw that
"the question sleeps for the present, but is not dead." The central theme
and prime generator of cultural anxiety in the early republic was the rapid
growth of feelings of nationalism and sectionalism at the same time. On the
one hand was the accelerating, kaleidoscopic, complex civilization of the
North, characterized by an emergent pattern of urban life and ably promoted by intellectuals and burgeoning mass media over which they had
some control. On the other hand was the South, complacent, largely satisfied with itself except for the cotton and sugar trade. For the most part
southern thinkers and cotton moguls were scornful of new ideas except as
they were imported from English country gentlemen's libraries, content to
rest on the "mudsill" foundation of black slavery, but at the same time

obliged always to defend themselves against the rest of the nation. Into this defensive battle the South threw whatever intellectuals it might have had, precluding, as Southern journalist W. J. Cash has pointed out, "that capacity . . . for detachment, without which no thinker, no artist, and no scholar can do his work." The genuine artist or intellectual in the South thus had considerably less chance than the helpless men of General George Pickett's brigade as they charged up Cemetery Ridge at Gettysburg in the decisive battle of the Civil War. Thus the first victim of Southern sectionalism was the freedom of intellectual inquiry.

To look at the intellectual and emotional history of the antebellum South is to study the "manly" art of self-defense, for as in most emergent, primitive planter countries attempting to escape colonial status, the idea of machismo usually lies behind the defensive rodomontade of the intellectual and the orator. All attempts at art for art's sake, intellectual detachment, are not, and were not then, as Southern apologist George Fitzhugh put it succinctly, "virile." Certainly, given the immediate situation, they were not useful in the pragmatic sense. But as the best Southern minds were perforce polarized into defense of the section, the "peculiar institution," and eventually the promotion of a separate Southern nationalism, this does not mean the South produced no formidable thinkers and made no original contributions to the general world of ideas. It is misleading to generalize, as did W. J. Cash, from the limited data provided by Henry Adams's narrow view of one feeble-minded Southern boy lost at Harvard and conclude, "Strictly, the Southerner had no mind; he had temperament. He was not a scholar; he had no intellectual training; he could not analyze an idea, and he could not even conceive of admitting two."

Unlike the citizens of the rest of the nation, the Southerner from the beginning had to live in a complex series of dual worlds and conflicting loyalties and principles. For example, he believed himself to be a citizen of the United States but he was also loyal to the South and to his state. Both allegiances bulked large in his thinking. In addition, the Southerner believed strongly in liberty and democracy, and the contradictory fact of slavery preoccupied him perhaps more than it did residents of slave-populated New York and other slave-holding Northerners who had nothing to lose by a simplistic resolution of the problem, "let the erring sisters depart in peace," except the huge banking and shipping commitments to their agents or factors in the South. It was their business to keep the indebted planters down on the farm and working their slaves in the most rationalistic, profit-yielding, efficient way possible.

Far from being a culturally simple position, the role of the Southern writer and intellectual was exceedingly complex, faced as he was with impossible dilemmas and freighted down with cross-currents of guilt and conflicting moral positions. Overwhelmed by the presence of blacks in great numbers, fearful of slave insurrections such as those in Haiti, Santo Domingo, and Southampton, Virginia, his economic activities frozen in place by the fact of indebtedness to Northern and English bankers such as the Browns and the Barings, the average Southerner was hardly hospitable to free and radical innovation. And so the Southern intellectual lived a life of "quiet desperation" that made that of Henry Thoreau seem almost euphoric and the intellectualized solutions of the abolitionists wildly simplistic.

I

The giant of antebellum Southern thought, and one who certainly made an original and timeless contribution to political thought in general, was John C. Calhoun. English busybody Harriet Martineau stamped his public image forever when she described him as "the cast iron man who looks as if he had never been born and could never be extinguished." He was a figure of history in his own lifetime, even from his early college days at Yale—Olympian, detached, Jove-like in his seeming abstractness, and yet, like that of many lesser Southern thinkers, the real genius of his thought stemmed from his direct engagement with the defense of the minority Southern position within the Union.

Calhoun came by his affinity for politics quite naturally. His father, Patrick Calhoun, a slaveholder of moderate means, was a leader of the Scotch-Irish up-country South Carolina planters who were continually at political odds over representation in the state legislature with the Tidewater aristocrats. Followers of the independent-minded Jefferson and the extreme decentralist John Randolph, Patrick Calhoun and his faction favored rejection of the new federal constitution in 1787 and anything else that resembled governmental centralization. To them, the state was sovereign over the nation. The local interests of the Piedmont took precedence even over the state. After a hard fight, the strong-willed Patrick Calhoun and his followers secured a fair reapportionment in the South Carolina legislature.

In addition to his affinity for Jeffersonian politics, the young John C. Calhoun also acquired the stern puritanical outlook of the "old side" Presbyterian. Never a Romantic, or even a revivalist, Calhoun began by believing in predestination, a concept that later underlay his whole philosophy of politics even after he had long abandoned belief in formal religion.

His Puritanism and devotion to hard work carried Calhoun through the demanding routine of Moses Waddel's Academy, where it was not uncommon for a boy to commit to memory two hundred lines of Latin and Greek per day. Waddel's Academy in turn enabled Calhoun to skip the first two years at Yale and enroll as a junior in 1802, which says something, however small, about the comparative qualities of Southern and Northern education at the turn of the century. At Yale, Calhoun began his role as a larger-than-life figure. He mixed little with his classmates, though he was an acknowledged leader, being elected to Phi Beta Kappa. Instead he related most closely to Yale's neopuritan president, Timothy Dwight, whose stern style simply reinforced his own religious preconceptions. He was also in great sympathy with Dwight's arguments for the right of New England's secession during Jefferson's difficult relations with France, which eventually culminated in the ruinous embargo.

After leaving Yale, Calhoun attended the Litchfield Law School, run by judges Tapping Reeve and James Gould, two staunch Federalists who also believed in the right of secession. As historian Margaret Coit so eloquently overstated it, "Not the South, not slavery, but Yale College and the Litchfield Law School made Calhoun a nullifier." These experiences certainly reinforced what he had already learned from his father. The memory of the Virginia and Kentucky resolutions, written by the great Southerners Jefferson and Madison, were fresh in his mind as well. Calhoun's New England experience suggested that the concept of local loyalty was not confined to the South. It was a generally believed concept in the early republic and hence a standard legal reading of the new Constitution. At this time, slavery, or its defense, did not bulk as large in his mind as it later did.

From the law school, Calhoun went on to his public career in the state and federal Houses of Representatives, the cabinet, the vice presidency, and finally the Senate, where he was a towering, formidable figure for nearly eighteen years. As a young member of the U.S. House of Representatives, Calhoun served as chairman of the Committee on Foreign Relations and was a leading nationalistic War Hawk in the War of 1812. In 1816, still a nationalist because he saw no conflict between national and sectional or local interests, Calhoun favored the protective tariff and made an impassioned speech for federally sponsored internal improvements. As secretary of war, he favored federal sponsorship of western exploration, such as the expedition of Major Stephen H. Long, launched in 1819, and federal aid to the American fur trade in the Rocky Mountains.

Eventually, despite the fact that he served as vice president under both John Quincy Adams and Andrew Jackson, Calhoun began to see that since the Missouri Compromise, the interests of his section and those of the nation had begun to diverge markedly. The tariff of 1828 raised the issue most vividly because in Calhoun's view it taxed the South over $16 million annually for the benefit of Northern manufacturers. In 1828, anonymously, since he was vice president, Calhoun published the *South Carolina Exposition and Protest*, which rejected the tariff and proclaimed the doctrine of nullification on behalf of South Carolina. Just as had Dwight, Gould, Reeve, Madison, and Jefferson, Calhoun believed the Union was a compact of states and thus a single sovereign state had the right to reject a law repugnant to its interests. President Jackson responded with the Force Bill, proclaiming federal sovereignty, and blockaded Carolina. But the Tariff of Abominations was repealed in 1833 in another of those compromises that held the fragile union together.

From this point on, Calhoun saw his role as the protector of Southern rights within the Union. He was never a secessionist, but rather, he thought defensively about the South and how it could maintain its rights within the Union. A crucial problem was the vast western territory acquired as a result of the Mexican War. In his speech opposing the Compromise of 1850, Calhoun argued that Southerners and slavery could not constitutionally be prohibited from the new territories, which after all belonged to the nation as a whole and hence to each sovereign state equally. He feared that if slaveholding states were denied equal access to the West, enough new free states would be formed as to enable the abolitionists to push through an amendment abolishing slavery throughout the whole

United States. By this time, too, Calhoun was declaring slavery "a good, a positive good."

Perhaps it was part of the South's general emotional posture before the irrational assaults of the abolitionists, perhaps it was his very close connection with the Bank of South Carolina, which owned mortgages on many of the slaves in his native state, perhaps it was his own status as a slaveholder that made Calhoun so vigorous in his defense of the sordid institution. Perhaps, however, Calhoun's defense of slavery also stemmed from his long-held view of predestination and the dependent role of man in the world. Uncompromising Calvinism can be seen implicit in his basic philosophical approach to the world, and thus paradoxically a religion born of revolution and the desire for freedom could be used as the basis for a defense of slavery in a much more subtle way than the recitation of endless passages from the Bible, as was the usual Southern custom.

In his *Disquisition on Government*, published posthumously in 1851, Calhoun argued that man is a social being who derives his identity and status from the group. He was never, as Locke had falsely proclaimed, an individual in a state of nature. Rather, man had individual feelings (perhaps a tendency to sin?) that clashed with the aims of the society into which he was born, and these tendencies must be either resolved in discussion with the group or repressed. For the solution of these problems there was government, which Calhoun termed "a gift from God." This meant there was no state of nature, no social contract, and that the state was more important than the individual. There were no natural rights, such as the rights to life, liberty, equality, or the pursuit of happiness. Instead society, operating through divine government, assigned people's places in the social and economic structure. It was clear by his defense of the status quo what place Calhoun was prepared to assign the black folk.

But how should divine government thus work? Not by democracy, which is a tyranny of the majority based on the false premise of inherent individual rights. Rather, it should work on the basis of a "concurrent majority." That is, each major sectional or economic interest should have the power to veto any measure that appears contrary to its interest. This is similar to the way in which the United Nations Security Council works today. If the government worked by a concurrent majority, Calhoun argued, a spirit of real compromise would prevail, because to maintain government at all, each interest would have to give a bit. Thus genuine compromise measures approved by all would be the law of the land and minority rights would prevail. It was never clear whether in this early theory of counter-vailing power Calhoun ever considered blacks, a minority whose rights might also be protected. It is doubtful if he even considered blacks as men since, for Calhoun, democracy meant Greek democracy, which rested on a "natural" custom (in Aristotelian terms) that allowed slavery.

At first Calhoun's theory of government appears to be absurd. Given the state of his own nation, nothing would have passed on a national level and government would have come to a standstill. Everything then would have had to be administered locally. Thus states' rights, county rights, etc., would prevail. Clearly, his was a governmental plan that desired that nothing at all be done on a national level. It was a defense of a states' rights–dominated status quo. But at least it prevented abolitionist economic and social aggression from the North by legal means.

With respect to the Union, Calhoun preferred a waiting game, some-times what he described as "masterful inactivity." If the status quo was maintained, he believed, capital and labor in the North would inevitably clash. Capital would have to join the cotton aristocracy to maintain its su-premacy. Greek democracy or rule by the master class over white wage slaves and black plantation slaves alike would result. Society would thus be stabilized, which was the ultimately desirable condition, and civil war would be prevented. Historian Richard Hofstadter has aptly termed Cal-houn "the Marx of the Master Class."

Since his concurrent-majority scheme was never adopted, one has no way of knowing how it would have worked. In any case, it was as creative and subtle a piece of political theory as the country had produced subse-quent to the Constitution. Yet it was sincerely designed to preserve the Union and to serve as an alternative to the Civil War, which, in 1850, Cal-houn believed was certain to come. Clearly, even while on the defensive and confined chiefly to preserving the Southern way of life—W. J. Cash to the contrary notwithstanding—at least one Southerner was capable of thinking powerfully and creatively. Calhoun was not the ignorant South-erner Rooney Lee at Henry Adams's Harvard. Instead, ironically, after his death he became something worse, the great hero of a cause he did not be-lieve in—secession and Civil War.

II

When he made his analysis of classes in the North and South, Calhoun sounded very modern, possibly because he drew upon the same kinds of data concerning the industrial revolution in England and Europe as various socialist critics in those countries were also drawing upon—especially Karl Marx, whose *Communist Manifesto* appeared in 1848, in Calhoun's own lifetime.

But modern as he was, Calhoun was only the most politically prominent of a number of Southerners who approached the study of society from several quasisocial scientific points of view, including anthropology, demography, sociology, and economics. For example, when Calhoun made his speeches concerning black inferiority and the blessings of slavery, he was fortified by anthropological data furnished him by Dr. Josiah C. Nott of South Carolina and the University of Louisiana and by George R. Gliddon of Mobile, Alabama, who together later published *Types of Mankind* (1854). Their work purported to prove "scientifically" blacks' inferiority by means of a comparison of their cranial capacity with that of other races.

Influenced by British anthropologists, notably Dr. Charles White and Sir William Lawrence, Gliddon and Nott were polygenists who believed that mankind consisted of specially created separate species. The research and speculations of Nott, who had studied in Europe, and Gliddon, an Englishman who had lived for a long time in Egypt, were part of a general debate among western intellectuals over the nature of man. Their book, *Types of Mankind*, though based on only about two hundred skull specimens, reflected another dimension of the enthusiasms of the Second Great Age of Discovery. Discovering and exploring all the exotic environments of the globe suggested to many that each species had been created especially appropriate to its environment.

Gliddon and Nott engaged in heated debate, which they called "parson skinning," with another Southerner, the Reverend John Bachman of Charleston, South Carolina. Bachman, a renowned naturalist as well as a clergyman, had collaborated with John James Audubon on *The Quadrupeds of North America*. He believed that mankind was a single species. Following Linnaeus's dictum, Bachman asserted that this was clear because blacks and even people of mixed race could and frequently did mate with whites to produce fertile offspring and thus met Linneaus's test for common species. Gradually, however, Bachman began to rely more and more on biblical arguments because the idea of separate races contradicted the Adam and Eve story. He, like many Southern apologists for slavery, preferred to believe that blacks were the descendents of Noah's accursed son, Ham. Thus, as debate developed over black men's status and hence the appropriateness of slavery, science and religion came into conflict, with science—current information—appearing to have the better argument.

Bachman's position was opposed by not only Gliddon and Nott, but also their mentor, Dr. Samuel George Morton of the Philadelphia Academy of Natural Sciences, the foremost ethnologist of his day. Morton had developed a technique for classifying skulls by cranial capacity. Plugging up all its orifices, he inverted the skull and carefully packed it with small white pepper seeds or shotgun pellets (later known as BBs). His research, though wildly fluctuating in results, even as to repeated measurements of the same skull, generally indicated that the black man had a smaller skull cavity and hence a smaller intellectual capacity. His smaller brain capacity definitely relegated the black man to a lower level of innate intelligence and probably denoted an entirely separate species. Morton also participated in a famous experiment at the Philadelphia academy in which a rather nervous naked Hottentot boy submitted to measurement of his lips, hair "wooling" capacity, skull shape, and the slope of his buttocks by a gathering of savants in "the friendly city."

All of this "research" greatly impressed Louis Agassiz, who visited the South and publicly declared that science had proved the validity of his own simultaneous special-creation hypothesis. He allied himself with what was sometimes called the American school of anthropology and lent it his formidable scientific reputation. This meant that the most advanced science and scientists of the day seemed to support the idea of black inferiority and hence the appropriateness of slavery. Agassiz's bold statements, however, only inspired bitterness among his New England colleagues who were much more concerned with religious values than science, however often Agassiz made reference to the Creator's responsibility for separate creation. They believed in the commonality of mankind and immorality of slavery. Agassiz's apparent defense of the "peculiar institution" marked the beginning of his downfall as a leader in American science. Meanwhile, though his theory actually reenforced biblical special creation, the vast majority of Southerners also rejected a "scientific" defense of slavery. They ignorantly believed it tended to undermine the authority of the Bible, which they as fundamentalists accepted absolutely and literally. In 1854 the *Richmond Enquirer*'s proslavery editor declared the doctrine of separate creation an "infidel" position and asserted that true Southerners could not afford to accept it if the Bible were "the price it must pay" for its use in defending the Southern cause. Needless to say, in the fundamentalist South, only the loftiest of intellectuals, such as Calhoun, made much use of Morton's and Gliddon and Nott's scientific weapons. And in the North, where science so evidently clashed with religious and moral values, science, in this case, was abandoned.

Additional social scientific information was also forthcoming from the 1850 national census, conducted by J. D. B. DeBow, a South Carolinian, who was the editor of the New Orleans–based *DeBow's Review*, one of the country's leading economic journals. The census of 1850 was a great event in American history because it was the most comprehensive conducted up to that time. From the census, however, Southern sociologists were able to construct a kind of "happiness quotient" for blacks, North and South. For example, they discovered that an overwhelming percentage of free blacks in the North suffered from insanity as compared with a very small number in the South. In certain cases in this strange census, more Northern blacks were reported as insane than the total number of blacks who existed in their given communities.

The same kind of "happiness quotient" was derived in terms of indigence, income, and employment. Not surprisingly, the Southern analysts found that there was practically no unemployment among blacks in the South and, consequently, relatively little indigence, and since they were totally provided for by plantation owners, there was a relatively higher income among black workers. Clearly the 1850 demographic study indicated that blacks were "better adjusted" and "more content" in the South than in the North. It was regarded as a great vindication of the Southern way of life.

No Southerner made more effective use of social science in defending the "peculiar institution" than did the editor of the *Richmond Enquirer*, George Fitzhugh, despite his attacks on the "infidelity" of Gliddon and Nott. Fitzhugh was the author of two devastatingly critical comparisons of

Northern and Southern society, *Sociology for the South* (1854) and *Cannibals All!* (1857). In these books, Fitzhugh's outlook was firmly Aristotelian, locally oriented, and contemptuous of Enlightenment ideas. The Declaration of Independence was wrong. No one had a *right* to life, liberty, or anything. History clearly indicated this. Rights and privileges had to be earned or wrested out of society and often with sad consequences. Slavery, he contended, was historically the normal state of man. Freedom was an exception and often disastrous. It led to competition between the strong and the weak in which the weak were certain to lose. Moreover, the idea of freedom led to deception and hypocrisy because workers assumed they were free when actually they were wage slaves of capitalist exploiters. The capitalist, unlike the slaveholder, assumed no responsibility for his workers. Instead, capitalistic efficiency dictated that the worker was to be exploited to the utmost and then turned out when he was old and inefficient, or when the profit-motive market so dictated. Slavery, on the other hand, was beneficial since it assumed responsibility for the worker from the cradle to the grave, which made him secure and, hence, happy. Exploitation and the artificial economic devices of rents and interest were the ways in which capitalists preyed on so-called "free" workers. It was, in Fitzhugh's view, a system that made the capitalists "Cannibals All."

To buttress these attacks, Fitzhugh made use of the lengthy and detailed studies of English workers and working conditions made by Parliament, partially as a response to the writings of Charles Dickens. These reports were full of horror stories—of tubercular children crawling through coal mines from dawn till dusk, of penniless women thrust out of their jobs into the streets, of men used as dray horses, broken in body and spirit and then discarded by ruthless exploiters. Calhoun used the same material, some of it called to his attention by Fitzhugh. Evidence that Fitzhugh was taken seriously by Northern reformers, who were likewise concerned with the exploitation of workers, is that he continuously enjoyed good relations with the reformers, and on his visit to New Haven in 1855 they took special pains to show him the bucolic cottages of the Whitney gun factory workers. No "dark satanic mills" there.

This, of course, left Fitzhugh unimpressed. He pointed out that these Northern workers could live better because they were living off the labor of the South as supplier of materials while the North was protected by tariffs. In addition, he pointed to clear signs of discontent with "wage slavery" and the factory capitalist system, which were signified by the frequency of agrarian handicraft–oriented utopian experiments such as John Humphrey Noyes's Oneida Community, Robert Dale Owen's New Harmony, Fruitlands, the numerous Fourier Communes, and Brook Farm. This was meant to strike home at least to Transcendentalists, but apparently it did not.

Beyond this, Fitzhugh declared that discontent in the North with "free" capitalism was further signified by the great migration out of the crowded cities and mill towns into the West. This was the first real formulation of the frontier safety-valve theory in American history, nearly fifty years before it was restated so memorably by historian Frederick Jackson Turner.

In summary, Fitzhugh's work resulted less in a justification of slavery than in a brilliant searching critique of the evils of emerging Northern industrialism. In a sense he stood outside the mainstream of the American capitalist myth and pointed out in unmistakable terms just how commonplace forms of slavery—subtle and not so subtle, as in wage slavery—were in America and the western world.

Fitzhugh could do this because he regarded himself as an Aristotelian, one who preferred the concrete to the abstract, and history to philosophy. Unlike most major American thinkers, he detested Locke and the whole Lockean liberal tradition. He once wrote of Enlightenment thinkers: "They confounded the moral with the physical world, and this was not strange, because they had begun to doubt whether there was any other than a physical world." To Fitzhugh, man was not a particle destined to collide forever with other particles in the universe, nor was he an interchangeable part. He was a member of a prescriptive society, a close-knit human family that reflected the benevolent patriarchy of God. Were his social insights less keen and his points less profound, one would be tempted to say that for Fitzhugh, the Creator was nothing more than "that great planter in the sky." However, for all his seeming parochialism and Southern apologetics, Fitzhugh deserves serious attention from students of culture. His was a penetrating if devastating view of the whole industrial process taking place in the western world. Few sought out its weaknesses better than he.

III

At least one other Southerner looked at the facts of Southern life with the eyes of a social scientist, but he came up with conclusions quite different from those of Fitzhugh. This was Hinton Rowan Helper, of the Yadkin River Country of North Carolina, a mountainous up-country region where non-slaveholding German yeomen predominated. Helper concluded in his important book *The Impending Crisis of the South* (1857) that slavery was the root of all evil and cultural backwardness in the South.

Helper's own life was a bizarre and colorful one. He grew up on his father's plantation, where with his brothers he worked hard in the fields beside some fifty slaves. He was self-educated and from the beginning seems to have had a marked sympathy for the non-slaveholding Southern yeoman. As soon as he could, he left the farm and became part owner in a bookstore. After a very short time he was turned out by his partner for embezzling $300, whereupon in 1850 he sailed by clipper ship to California, an eager member of the Gold Rush. Three years later he returned unsuccessful and bitter. In 1855 he published *The Land of Gold*, an exposé of the futility of California gold-seeking, one of the few pessimistic books written about California in the entire decade.

In 1854, working from DeBow's 1850 census records, he began writing another exposé, *The Impending Crisis of the South*. In 1856 he went North to help the Republicans in the Frémont campaign and to publish his book safe from reprisals by Southerners, who he knew, or at least hoped, would be angry. When his book was published, it became a bombshell almost comparable to *Uncle Tom's Cabin*, and it was banned in the South. The first year it sold 14,000 copies and when reprinted in a cheap edition sold 142,000 copies. As a reward for his services to the Union and the Republican Party, Helper was made U.S. consul in Buenos Aires, Argentina, in 1861. Five years later, he resigned under a cloud of suspicion when his accounts turned up short some $6,000.

Back home, Helper turned desperately once again to writing and produced a series of the strangest books in American literature. They were *Nojoque: A Question for a Continent* (1867) and *Negroes in Negroland* (1868), in both of which he advocated removing all blacks from North America forever. In 1871 he published *Noonday Exigencies in America,* which advocated a racist party that would overthrow radical Republican rule and make America a white Protestant country. Apparently in all of his strictures against slavery, Helper really was concerned only for the welfare of the white man. He regarded blacks with contempt and wished to remove them at all costs from the land. He seems to have felt no guilt over Southern slavery, only anger and indignation at both blacks and slaveholders alike.

Helper's last book was a piece of propaganda called *Oddments of Andean Diplomacy* (1879), intended to promote the building of a railroad from Cape Horn to Alaska and at the same time promote a scheme for removing Catholics as well as blacks from the New World. In 1899 his wife deserted him, and ten years later, tired of life, he committed suicide in a shabby rooming house on Pennsylvania Avenue in Washington, D.C.

In all the eighty checkered years of his life, Helper had only one great moment. That was the writing of his scorching tract, *The Impending Crisis of the South.* With a fine gift for invective, Helper took on the whole planter class, continually referring to them as "lords of the lash," "knights of the bludgeons," "chevaliers of bowie knives and pistols," and "haughty cavaliers of the shackles and handcuffs." The message of his book was the evil of slavery and the damage it had done to the South. His argument was primarily economic and sociological. The North and South, he asserted, had started off approximately even in 1789, but the 1850 census showed the North ahead in every way. The South had fallen behind solely because of slavery. Slavery kept industry from coming to the South. Slavery made the white man lazy and kept him uneducated. Slavery kept the common man down and exalted the few at the expense of the many. Because of this, Helper called for a class struggle. The poor whites should abandon their misplaced identification with the planters and organize to overthrow them. Much more realistic than Fitzhugh, Helper also saw the planter as part of the oppressive capitalist class. He advocated an eleven-point plan of attack against the slaveholders, including a total economic boycott, leading to abolition, if possible, and if not, a $60 tax on each slave and additional heavy taxes to be levied annually. He was for a direct frontal assault on the whole slaveholding class along any line that seemed expedient and promised success.

Perhaps the most startling essay in *Impending Crisis* was Helper's
analysis of Northern and Southern American literature, in which he concluded that, comparatively speaking, the South had no literature at all.
This was because there were no readers. Due to the astonishing illiteracy
rate—one in seven white people in North Carolina was illiterate, as contrasted with one in 250 white people in Connecticut in 1850—there was
no mental freedom in the South, and consequently there was little in-
centive to mental activity. Most would-be Southern writers were
scorned, forced to sell their books in the North, as was William Gilmore
Simms, or else they had to move there to survive. Helper concluded by
pointing out that almost all Southern books were printed and bound in
the North—even *DeBow's Review* and the *Journal* of the fire-eating Mississippi legislature.

As in most of his assertions, Helper overstated his case, but he was writing deliberate propaganda designed to awaken the Southern people to a
larger truth. He succeeded in awakening them but not, alas, in reforming
them. The classes to which he appealed in his book were either helpless,
such as the scattered impoverished writers who sympathized with him, or
else the vast illiterate masses who could not read his book in any case
should they happen to find one that had slipped past the Southern post office censors. Rhetoric and slashing invective appealed greatly to the average Southerner—however, only from the pulpit and the platform or stump,
not through the printed word.

But the work of all these men, from Calhoun to Helper, indicates that
the sectional division did at least produce some imaginative if not searching
cultural analysis in the South. Crude as they were in the use of the social sciences, these antebellum cultural analysts signified a brief period of extreme
originality in American thought. They formed a kind of Southern Renaissance of angry and sometimes defensive local philosophes who, because
Southern society was so different from the rest of society in the United
States, could view the country from both within and without the mainstream of American values. Their critiques further serve to illustrate not
only something of the quality of Southern thought but also, more important, the deep divisions in what had once promised to be a unified nation—
the "United States" of America.

IV

As Southerners became more conscious of a common way of life—of common interests and values that extended from Texas to South Carolina, from Virginia to Louisiana—so too did the South as a whole move rapidly in the direction of secession and outright Southern nationalism. This was not an easy road. There were many and close ties between North and South. The Mississippi River trade in some ways bound the western South, consisting of the upland Piedmont, the Appalachians, and beyond, more closely to the North than to the older Tidewater (eastern) Southern states. Then, throughout the South, the complex relationship between the planter, the factory, and the Northern money market, as well as the Northern textile market and Northern shipping and insurance industries, was a very tightly woven and interdependent network. Political parties, too, Whig and Democrat alike, after Jackson were national parties with staunch adherents North and South. And finally, too, the emergence of Southern nationalism meant the sundering of most of the major churches into Northern and Southern sects, though the division may not have been as traumatic as it at first seems because, as earlier chapters have indicated, Protestantism in America was forever dividing. Beyond all these factors, however, was the fact of incredible regional and cultural diversity within the South itself, which was split by the Appalachians and divided into "Old Dominion" Tidewater states, the Gulf Coast crescent, the upper or border South, the Mississippi and Red River Delta country, and the Texan Southwest. Many of these regions had little in common except an adherence to the slave system and a general feeling of being threatened by forces in the rest of the country.

Slavery, the cotton economy, and the common feeling of a threat from without clearly were important factors in predisposing Southerners toward united sectional action. The critical years of 1831 to 1832—when the Tariff of Abominations was in force, nullification was in the air, and Carolina was blockaded—were made even more dramatic by Nat Turner's slave rebellion, which killed fifty-six men, women, and children in Southampton, Virginia; the founding of the *Liberator*, a focal point for militant abolitionism, by the outspoken and uncompromising William Lloyd Garrison; and the

bitter debates in the Virginia legislature over the feasibility of abolition. In
the latter, so strong was the sentiment that in 1832, Professor Thomas Dew
of William and Mary published his *Review of the Debate in the Virginia Legislature of 1831–1832*, purporting to be an account of these debates but actually serving as a prime defense of the "peculiar institution" that he hoped
would silence Southern liberals forever. In 1852 it was reprinted as part of a
compendium under a more revealing title, *The Pro-Slavery Argument.* Thus,
as most historians have pointed out, 1831–1832 marked a crucial turning
point in Southern thought. The South began very definitely to feel itself on
the defensive vis-à-vis the North, and it likewise reached near panic over the
problem of internal order, with visions of Haitian massacres offering something less than the consolation of recent history.

But more than fear and negativism were needed to provide Southerners
with a cohesive emotional pattern of values that would form the matrix of a
culture that made Southern nationalism possible. This cultural cohesiveness was provided paradoxically in part by Northerners who, viewing the
South from without, tended to create stereotypes with which Southerners
could identify in a positive way. For example, the more the Northerner
portrayed the South as a land of slaveholders and careless cavaliers, the
more the average Southerner, whether he held slaves, rode fine horses, and
fought duels, tended to accept such figures as the leaders of his society and
to identify with them. It was this casual identification, of course, that so
outraged Helper. By accepting these stereotypes as the good and inevitable
leaders of Southern society, the average white and sometimes even black
Southerners gave unwarranted cultural status and unreal power to a class of
rather ignorant men who were conspicuous consumers, bad businessmen,
and largely the creatures of their factors (middlemen) and their bankers.
This acceptance of the planter and the cavalier as societal leaders in turn
forced these "leaders" ever deeper into their impractical roles and made
them consume even more, made them less and less provident and more and
more careless of anything but their other-directed status-roles. Joseph
Glover Baldwin in *Flush Times in Alabama and Mississippi* (1853) has perhaps the best portrait of such a "hero," the Honorable Sergeant S. Prentiss
of Mississippi. According to Baldwin, Prentiss was "a type of his times, a
representative of the qualities of the people, or rather of the better qualities
of the wilder and more impetuous part of them." Prentiss had:

all those qualities which made us charitable to the character of Prince Hal, as it is painted by Shakespeare, even when our approval is not fully bestowed. Generous as a prince of the royal blood, brave and chivalrous as a knight templar, of a spirit that scorned everything mean, underhand or servile, he was prodigal to improvidence, instant in resentment, and bitter in his animosities, yet magnanimous to forgive when reparation had been made or misconstruction explained away. There was no littleness about him.

Baldwin added:

Even in the vices of Prentiss, there were magnificence and brilliancy imposing in a high degree. When he treated it was a mass entertainment. On one occasion he chartered the theater for the special gratification of his friends—the public generally. He bet thousands on the turn of a card, and witnessed the success or failure of the wager with the nonchalance of a Mexican monte-player, or, as was most usual, with the light humor of a Spanish muleteer. He broke a faro bank by the nerve with which he laid his large bets, by exciting the passion of the veteran dealer, or awed him into honesty by the glance of his strong and steady eye.

Attachment to his friends was a passion. It was a part of the loyalty to the honorable and chivalric, which formed the subsoil of his strange and wayward nature. . . . He would put his name on the back of their paper, without looking at the face of it and give his carte blanche, if needed by the quire. . . .

He never seemed to despond or droop for a moment: the cares and anxieties of life were mere bagatelles to him. Sent to jail for fighting in the court-house, he made the walls of the prison resound with unaccustomed shouts of merriment and revelry. Starting to fight a duel, he laid down his hand at poker, to resume it with a smile when he returned, and went on the field laughing with his friends as to a picnic.

Such idealized models were and still are common in the South. And if Northern observers helped create them, Southern Romantics cherished, nurtured, and embellished them, elevating these "chivalric" heroes to gigantic proportions as the national leaders of society. As Baldwin observed, there was no "littleness" about them. Thus the differences between North and South, between the Yankees and the Cavalier, as Professor William Taylor has observed, were exaggerated in literature, the popular print, oratory, and folklore.

In the South this took the form of a great and simple myth—a tableau, as it were, which resulted in a pattern of images that all Southerners strove to identify with. It was a pastoral tableau, appropriate to a semi-frontier, with the plantation, the planter man-of-action careless of material possessions and even his life, the virtuous white plantation mistress, and a legion of dependent kinsmen, or admiring friends, forming the central motif, set down in the midst of the lushest nature imaginable. For nature, the endless provider, was of course the moral key to the Southerner's feudal dream. More than any other man, the Southerner believed himself to be closest and most in tune with nature and hence more moral than any person on earth. This closeness to nature as frontier, in a sense, accounted for the Southerner's parochialism, but on an intellectual level he had also his Aristotelian philosophy of loyalties to reinforce his prejudices. Moreover, intellectually inclined Southerners identified with English squires as depicted in the novels of Henry Fielding and Walter Scott, except for Edgar Allan Poe, who wrote of mystery, necromancy, and the horrid and was thus widely read in both North and South. At the same time they were also aware of the vast currents of the European Romantic Movement. Thus, as in the rest of the United States, contact with European currents of thought helped reinforce a myth that in turn generated a revolution that culminated in a civil war the Southerners compared to the wars between the Scots and the English, the Saxons and the Normans, or the Cavaliers and the Roundheads.

Southern Romantic thinkers drew upon many sources of inspiration. They worshipped Walter Scott, especially his traditionalist novels of embittered minorities, *Ivanhoe* and *Rob Roy*, which seemed to root contemporary Southern experience in the ancient past among a set of beloved ancestors. They also admired Lord Byron, as Baldwin's sketch of Prentiss clearly indicates. Byron's heroic devotion to the cause of Greek independence, which they identified with the resurgence of "Greek democracy," provided Southern poets with unbounded inspiration. The poet Henry Timrod wrote without a trace of irony:

The mountains look on Marathon,
And Marathon looks on the sea,
And musing there an hour alone,
I dreamed that Greece might still be free.

Southerners admired Burke for his delineation of the prescriptive society, and Carlyle, the squire-sage of Craigenputtock, for his conservatism and devotion to the power of the hero as opposed to the doltish masses. For the same reason they admired Alexandre Dumas with his musketeers, Victor Hugo, and above all Jules Michelet, the great French Romantic historian who vividly re-created the Middle Ages and Joan of Arc as the shining maiden heroine.

Surprisingly, Southern Romantic thought derived from the Germans as well, especially such writers as Ludwig Tieck, Friedrich Novalis, and the brothers Grimm who celebrated the earthy culture of the folk—of a people rooted in their homeland far back into time, rising in protest against the technologies and nationalistic dominance of the Enlightenment and Napoleon. Johann Gottfried von Herder, of course, with his dissertations on the folk culture, was a key philosophical figure to justify their mythology and emerging Southern nationalism.

V

All of this had its impact on Southern literature, which in a sense was schizophrenic. It was a cosmopolitan folk literature, based closely on a defense of localized Southern folk culture and its values but derived from and imitative of the European Romantic models briefly discussed above. Beginning in 1832, that fateful turning point, Southern writers began to produce a spate of novels that might generally be called plantation novels, designed to explore if not defend that best of all possible worlds, the "Southern way of life." In 1832 John Pendleton Kennedy published *Swallow Barn*, a loosely connected set of sketches and tales about an idyllic plantation on the James River in Virginia. In 1834 William Alexander Caruthers published *The Cavaliers of Virginia* and in 1845 *The Knights of the Horseshoe*, obvious contributions to the central Southern myth.

The best of the Southern novelists, however, was William Gilmore Simms, of Charleston. Deserted by his father, who went west to be a frontiersman in Mississippi shortly after William's mother died in 1808, Simms was raised by his grandmother in Charleston, South Carolina, on the Tidewater. There, despite his good marriage, the acquisition of Woodlands, a model plantation, and the company of a large and powerful circle of friends, Simms never felt quite accepted. As if he often regretted declining his father's invitation to join him in the wilds of Mississippi, in much of his work Simms focused on the frontier, comparing and contrasting it with the more familiar local plantation culture. He reflected in a way similar to that of James Fenimore Cooper ambivalence in terms of values between the frontier and what he regarded as civilization. Though he began his literary career writing Romantic poetry and a gothic novel, *Martin Faber*, which he composed in New Haven, Connecticut, Simms's earliest serious work was, as he put it, "meant to illustrate the border and domestic history of the South."

In *Guy Rivers* (1834) he explicitly examined Southern frontier life in a manner he believed to be "true and natural." The following year he published *The Yemassee*, a tale of the vanishing Indian in early Carolina reminiscent of Cooper's *Last of the Mohicans*. In the same year, 1835, he published *The Partisan*, which was the first of his seven novels dealing with the Revolutionary War in North and South Carolina. *The Partisan* described the dark days of the Revolution when the Continental Army's activities were largely restricted to guerrilla warfare and so it, too, focused perforce on the frontier and the swamp-fighters of Francis Marion, as did its sequels, *Mellichampe*, which came out in 1836, and *The Kinsman, or the Black Riders of the Congaree* (later entitled *The Scout*), published in 1841. Simms's Revolutionary War novels illustrated that the South under General Nathanael Greene played the preponderant part in driving British General Cornwallis out of North Carolina into Virginia, where the British army was trapped on the Yorktown peninsula between Greene's and Washington's armies and the French fleet offshore. As he developed his Revolutionary War series, Simms continued to write other books about the frontier. *Richard Hurdis* (1838) was set in Alabama, and *Border Beagles* (1840) and the collection of short stories titled *The Wigwam and the Cabin* (1845) focused on the gothic terrors of Mississippi backwoods existence. One true-life frontier story, the famous "Kentucky Tragedy," a murder involving wife, lover, and husband, haunted Simms so much that he wrote about it twice—in *Beauchampe* (1842) and *Charlemont* (1856). As late as 1950, the "Kentucky Tragedy" was still going strong as Robert Penn Warren used it as the basis for his novel *World Enough and Time*. So wide a reputation did Simms have for the accuracy of his Revolutionary War and frontier scenes and characters that in 1846 he complained to critic Rufus Griswold that "whole pages of *Guy Rivers* have been stolen by [the German novelist Charles] Sealsfield, and have been quoted abroad as superior to what could have been done by an American, even describing his own country."

In addition to his interest in history and the frontier, Simms was also very much interested in civilization, especially the aristocratic, socially stratified culture of the plantation South. Though William Taylor in *Cavalier and Yankee* has portrayed Simms's intense interest in things Southern and especially the Revolutionary War role of the South as stemming largely from political disillusionment in the 1840s, particularly over the anti-Southern conduct of the planter-president Zachary Taylor, it seems clear that Simms had always been a partisan of plantation culture and an enthusiastic student of the South's role in the War for Independence. His earliest works demonstrate that the Revolution had actually been won by Southern men, from Washington to Francis Marion and Nathaniel Greene. After all, the war ended in Virginia. From *The Partisan* onward through *Mellichampe*, *The Kinsman*, his history of early South Carolina (1840), and his *Life of Francis Marion* (1844) and *Views and Reviews* (1845), which was published by Evert Duyckinck as a volume in his "Young America" series, Simms kept busy defending the South. *Views and Reviews*, though a prime document in the New York movement for literary nationalism, also contained the long essay "Is Southern Civilization Worth Preserving?" Simms's most outspoken defense of plantation culture. During the late 1840s Simms also published a life of Chevalier Bayard (1847), the beau-ideal of all Southern cavaliers, and a biography of the outstanding Southern Revolutionary War general Nathanael Greene (1849).

All along in his writing Simms stressed the South's role in winning American independence as an implicit defense against the common notion, promulgated by George Bancroft and other New England historians, that the "cradle of liberty" swung somewhere north of Connecticut. Most of this time Simms saw himself as a nationalist and a Unionist. He opposed the nullifiers and their ideas. He stood with the liberal Barnburners against all of the Knickerbocker school of literary writings, attracted the Hunkers in the Democratic Party, and as suggested, he was a staunch ally of the New York literary Young Americans. In fact, his pro-Southern writings attracted the Young Americans because they, too, were opposed to the provincialism and sectionalism of the Whiggish New England writers. In a sense it was to save the Union against New England's dominance that Southern civilization was, as Simms put it, "worth preserving." He and the Young Americans stood for a national literature and a national culture made up out of the vastness of America and its diverse regionalism rather than the apparent dominance of New England's puritanical ways. In a sense, this literary and artistic war has never ceased. It continues through Mark Twain to William Faulkner and onward to the comparatively recent preoccupation with the novel of ethnic and cultural pluralism that dominated the 1960s.

It was also clear, however, that though Simms saw the noble Southern revolutionary leaders fighting for liberty, he did not see them fighting for equality. As a Unionist, Simms held views something akin to Senator Stephen Douglas, the political leader of the Young America Movement. He believed in a version of "squatter sovereignty" in which liberty meant that the people of a region should be free to follow their own customs protected in this right by the united nation-state to which they had agreed to become members. In the South this meant the plantation system, governed by the aristocracy and buttressed by slavery, which Simms, like Calhoun, whom he personally detested, always believed was a "positive good." There is no real evidence that Simms ever changed his mind on this point in a dramatic way. He simply became more strident in the 1850s. His role as editor of the *Southern Quarterly Review* from 1849 to 1853 required him to be somewhat more direct, as his contribution to the *Pro-Slavery Argument* (1852) indicates. And during the 1850s he had more time to write so that in the accumulation of his books his views became plainer while, as regional thought polarized, they came to seem more eccentric and more prominent.

During the 1850s especially, he returned to his Revolutionary War novels. In 1851 he published *Katherine Walton*, in 1853 *The Sword and the Distaff* (later titled *Woodcraft*), in 1855 *The Forayers*, and in 1856 *Eutaw*. These books covered the period of General Greene's successful campaign

against the British and the ending of the war. They are accordingly somewhat less concerned with the frontier and more concerned with chivalry
and the innate quality and strengths of Southern civilization as Simms saw
them. They also made clear that Simms believed that Southerners had won
the American Revolution, which is more than plausible.

After the success of Augustus Baldwin Longstreet's 1835 *Georgia Scenes*,
satirizing the pretensions of a rising Southern village middle class, there
were dozens of imitators, including George Washington Harris, whose *Sut
Lovingood* yarns, as they appeared in the New York humor paper the *Spirit
of the Times*, not only reflected the low intelligence and extraordinary lack
of gentility of the Southern yeoman, but also did so in the language of regional dialects that made for difficult reading but high humor. Other writers
of note in this vein were the Alabama census taker, James Johnson Hooper,
whose *Some Adventures of Captain Simon Suggs, Late of the Tallapoosa Volunteers* came out in 1845, and Thomas Bangs Thorpe, a Massachusetts-born
resident of Baton Rouge, Louisiana, whose "Big Bear of Arkansas," which
appeared in *The Big Bear of Arkansas and Other Stories* in 1845, was clearly
the prototype for William Faulkner's "The Bear." There were dozens of
similar authors—William Tappan Thompson, Joseph B. Cobb, Henry Clay
Lewis, John B. Robb—and, taken together, their writings provide a fascinating insight into the realities of life in the South among those classes
somehow excluded from the plantation dream. The significant thing about
the literary treatment of these classes in Southern life is that they were almost universally the object of satire and ridicule.

Borrowing from Professor Stanley Elkins's terminology in connection
with slavery, it would be only a slight exaggeration to say that it was the
poor and even middle-class white yeomen who were "Sambo-ized" along
with blacks. Both blacks and frontier poor whites, the descendents of the
descendents of a long line of hopelessly indentured workers, undoubtedly
suffered traumas sufficient to cause disorientation at various periods in
their difficult, pellagra-ridden lives, but the Southern poor white's trauma
appears to have been more subtle, if not more lasting. The vast majority
never ceased believing in the illusion of planter superiority and the justice
of a Southern way of life built on slavery, racism, and the whole complex of
Aristotelian clanlike local loyalties. It was because they believed so fervently, if hopelessly, in all aspects of this illusion rather than simply in the

cult of Southern womanhood ("gyneolatry"), as W. J. Cash amusingly suggests, that they were prepared to sacrifice themselves and follow their imperious captains and betters into bloody civil war. In a sense, even before the doughty Virginia farmer-fanatic Edmund Ruffin, full of "high good spirits and noble sentiments," pulled the lanyard on a cannon pointed at Fort Sumter in Charleston Harbor on that fateful day in 1861, for most of the rank and file in the South, the cause was already lost. They had for years, more docilely than they ever imagined, been chasing a dream that was impossible to attain.

CHAPTER FIFTEEN

The Black Man as Intellectual

If, on the one hand, the majority of Southern poor whites unquestioningly subscribed to the "Southern dream," though they were never really a part of it, on the other hand, the downtrodden black slave community in the Old South produced a surprising number of thinkers who were not docile. They by no means accepted the reality of the "Southern dream" and produced trenchant and profound thoughts about America.

Like their white Southern brethren, black thinkers had to operate within a subtle framework of divided loyalties. They were Americans, for the most part born on this soil and seemingly far removed from any African heritage, but they were also black—people of color—and by this token they belonged to a world community. Closely paralleling the ideas of Tom Paine, black intellectuals believed that the Americas, and particularly the United States, should be the focal point for a genuinely free, unprejudiced, pluralistic world civilization—one that took full advantage of the varied talents and ministered to the hopes and dreams of all people. As the mid-nineteenth-century black explorer Dr. Martin R. Delany put it, "That the continent of America seems to have been designed by providence as an asylum for all the various nations of the earth, is very apparent." And though most black intellectuals believed very strongly that America was their homeland, by virtue of their affinity to colored peoples everywhere and the encouragement they found in England, Ireland, and continental Europe, their personal experiences and ideas were extremely cosmopolitan. They were thus often able to avoid the pitfalls and backwashes of provincialism and sectionalism, and to focus very clearly upon what had been the prime ideals of the American nation and American culture as it emerged out of the cosmopolitan atmosphere of the late eighteenth century.

Black intellectual history in the antebellum period has been largely ignored because the traditional historical approach has focused on the sociological fact of slavery in the South in an attempt to build up a composite picture of the everyday life of common black folk. The very titles of key works in the field indicate this, beginning with Ulrich B. Phillips's pioneering *Life and Labor in the Old South* (1929) and extending into comparatively recent times with Kenneth Stampp's *The Peculiar Institution* (1956), Eugene Genovese's *Roll, Jordan, Roll* (1974), Robert Fogel and Stanley Engerman's *Time on the Cross* (1974), and Herbert Gutman's *The Black Family in Slavery and Freedom, 1750–1925* (1976). And though the title of Stanley Elkins's provocative *Slavery: A Problem in American Institutional and Intellectual Life* (1959) promised to change this focus, the main point of the book is to demonstrate, describe, and explain just how all antebellum blacks were turned into "Sambo." It is again a sociological work that dominates U.S. history today. Considerations of intellectual life are restricted to the ideas of white men in the period as if there was not and never could be, because of the experience of Elkins's "Sambo-ization," a formidable body of effective black thought.

The source of this bias is readily apparent. Since the Progressive Era, a major interest of American historians had been the study of the life of the common man—the masses. Implicit in this interest has been the desire to use history pragmatically to promote reform. And since the lot of the common black man continuously and notoriously has been one in need of reform, a natural tendency has been to study his common life and his common problems from an institutional point of view. Moreover, when one looks at the South for data on the black mind, what one finds is essentially "folk data"—Works Progress Administration interviews with aged former slaves, such as those appearing in Benjamin Botkin's *Lay My Burden Down*, plantation records, guarded Southern newspaper accounts of slave revolts such as those of Denmark Vesey and Nat Turner, and narratives of escaped slaves. Here and there a "successful" free barber or bootblack living in the South also published his Horatio Alger story. Black folk music also provided insight into blacks' covert culture, as did an outside view of black churches and their musical traditions as well as superstitions sometimes connected with voodoo ceremonies brought from the Caribbean, where they had lived. And so historians have not focused on the antebellum black thinkers. This is perhaps one of the dangers of the drive for sociological "relevance."

The primary oversight, of course, has been the almost exclusive focus on the South itself. Obviously the free expression of black ideas took place in the North and in Europe. But these expressions—despite that they very often were uttered by blacks who had escaped from slavery in the South or by blacks who felt that all forms of slavery did not end at 36°30' north latitude, and hence considered themselves intimate members of the whole black or colored community—have not traditionally been counted as a component of the Southern mind. This is like saying that because John C. Calhoun studied the right of secession at Yale and the Litchfield Law School, his ideas were not Southern, when in fact they have their most direct relevance in the Southern context. Antislavery societies, northern free schools, northern black and abolitionist churches, northern newspaper offices, and their European counterparts across the whole spectrum of activity were, for the black who came out of the South and his formerly enslaved northern cohorts, the equivalent of Herman Melville's famous whaling ship. They were the black intellectual's Yale College and his Harvard. It is not necessary, therefore, to resift endlessly the meager evidence for Southern slave revolts to see bolder Southern black minds in action. It is necessary only to take seriously the substantial body of ideas they managed to produce and distribute all over the western world in the mid-nineteenth century.

I

The media of black communication were as varied as those of their counterparts among the white intelligentsia. Public speeches, church sermons and hymns, resolutions of antislavery societies, appeals to state and national governments, and pamphlet literature were perhaps the strongest forms of expression. This is characteristic of any reform or revolutionary movement where time is important and there is a mass audience to be reached. In addition, literally thousands of letters appeared in such black newspapers and magazines as the *North Star* and the *Anglo-American* and in the white press, ranging from the American Colonization Society's *African Repository* to William Lloyd Garrison's *Liberator*. These letters, very self-consciously written, presented a whole range of black speculation concerning their own and America's role in the world. At their best they represented an ironic and slashing wit comparable to the better British productions of the eighteenth century. Frederick Douglass's series of annual letters to his former master, Thomas Auld, are masterpieces, and J. W. Loguen's reply to his whining hillbilly former mistress in Tennessee on the eve of the Civil War is a model of bitter invective:

> You say you have offers to buy me, and that you shall sell me if I do not send you $1,000, and in the same breath and almost in the same sentence, you say, "You know we raised you as we did our own children." Woman did you raise your *own children* for the market?

Such letters were commonly published in the *Liberator*, that most famous of all abolitionist tracts, where they formed a kind of long-range artillery duel of debate across the Mason-Dixon Line. Their basic oratorical content was their outstanding feature.

Black thinkers also expressed themselves in poems, ranging from Phillis Wheatley's gentle couplets to George B. Vashon's imitations of Byron and Scott. They also made use of the novel and the drama. William Wells Brown, a former slave, published a novel titled *Clotel, or the President's Daughter* (1853), and Martin R. Delany published *Blake, or the Huts of America* (1859–1862), based on his experiences in Louisiana and Texas in 1839. Brown also wrote a play, *Escape: Or, a Leap for Freedom*, in 1858, the first play published by an American black. In addition, Brown, Delany, and others turned to history and broad-gauged inquiries into the origin, nature, development, and contributions of men of color in world and American civilization. The list of such books is long, but the following are important and characteristic: William Wells Brown, *The Black Man: His Antecedents,*

His Genius, and His Achievements; Martin R. Delany, *The Condition, Elevation, Emigration, and Destiny of the Colored Peoples of the U.S. Politically Considered* (1852); Hosea Eaton, *A Treatise on the Intellectual Character . . . of the Colored People of the United States* (1837); George W. Williams, *A History of the Negro Race in America from 1619 to 1880,* two volumes (1883); A. Mott, *Biographical Sketches and Interesting Anecdotes of Persons of Color* (1826); and William C. Nell's two works, *Services of Colored Americans in the Wars of 1776 and 1812* (1851) and *Colored Patriots of the Age of Revolution, with Sketches of Several Distinguished Colored Persons: To Which Is Added a Brief Survey of the Conditions and Prospects of Colored Americans* (1855).

Nell's two books form, in a sense, the black counterpart to William Gilmore Simms's attempt to reassess the South's relationship to the War for Independence. They are an early version of the historiographical concept of the "usable past." Just as Simms was concluding in the 1850s that perhaps the South had not really gained the independence it sought from the war, so too was Nell asserting one of the main themes of black thought in the period: the black who fought in that great struggle for liberty also had not gained the independence he so richly deserved. It is certainly one of the fine ironies of black thought throughout the period that it mirrored and emphasized some of the loftiest generalizations of the Founding Fathers while chronicling the sad story of black people in America.

The most spectacular and unique form of expression was the escaped-slave narrative. These were inherently moral adventure stories that recounted in more or less lurid and factual detail the horrors of slavery and, after a thrilling narrative of the escape, concluded happily for the hero and with a glimmer of hope for his still-enslaved people. The inference was unmistakable. If one of the wretched of the earth could escape from bondage, all could, if they tried. Naturally such books were disliked in the South, but they were read everywhere in great numbers with printings of up to ten thousand copies for each edition. In England they rivaled or at least paralleled the works of Charles Dickens in popularity if not in authenticity. Frederick Douglass's *Narrative of the Life of Frederick Douglass* (1845) was the finest and most powerful of such accounts, essentially because of its unpretentiousness. There were many others, however, including William Craft's *Running a Thousand Miles for Freedom: Or the Escape of William and Ellen Craft from Slavery* (1860); Henry Box Brown, *Narrative of Henry Box*

Brown, Who Escaped from Slavery, Enclosed in a Box Three Feet Long and Two Feet Wide, Written from a Statement of Facts Made by Himself (1849); Josiah Henson, *"Uncle Tom's Story of His Life," An Autobiography of Josiah Henson (Mrs. Harriet Beecher Stowe's "Uncle Tom") from 1789–1876: with a Preface by Mrs. H. B. Stowe* (1876); Kate E. R. Pickard, *The Kidnapped and the Ransomed, Being Personal Recollections of Peter Still and His Wife "Vina," after 40 Years of Slavery* (1856); and *"Zamba," the Life and Adventures of Zamba, an African Negro King; and His Experiences of Slavery in South Carolina. Written by Himself. Corrected and Arranged by Peter Neilson* (1847).

Some of the escape narratives were obvious fictions written by white abolitionists, but by far the vast majority were actually written by the participants and had the ring of sincerity and authenticity. In the 1840s and 1850s, certainly on the level of mass appeal, the escaped slave took his place alongside Leatherstocking as an American hero in the North. Just as did Leatherstocking, he sought freedom. In his desperate search for freedom, the black escapee offered an unforgettable comment on American society. Though most of the world knows of these black Leatherstockings by way of Harriet Beecher Stowe's *Uncle Tom's Cabin*, the black writers themselves had long anticipated her, just as they did two other famous white ghostwriters of such tales, Lydia Maria Child and John Greenleaf Whittier, the Quaker poet.

II

Although certain overarching themes such as belief in evangelical Christianity, the unity of all mankind based on scripture, black cosmopolitanism, and continual reference to the universal Enlightenment values of the Founding Fathers dominated virtually all black thought in the antebellum period, the emphasis on one concept or another took place in more or less distinct stages. These stages were reflected at different times by the distinctive antislavery institutions that afforded blacks a chance for expression.

Since the days of preacher John Woolman, the Quakers had never ceased to espouse the emancipation cause. Beginning in 1815, one of their number, Benjamin Lundy, commenced the widespread formation of antislavery societies. He also began contributing to Charles Osborn's early antislavery newspaper, the *Philanthropist*, and as a result of the Missouri

Compromise he founded *The Genius of Universal Emancipation*, the most important of the early abolitionist newspapers. For fourteen years, Lundy wandered about the country, his press virtually carried on his back, publishing his antislavery sentiments. In the course of time he enlisted the aid of William Lloyd Garrison, who served as his assistant editor until in 1831 he began publishing his own paper, the *Liberator.*

During the early days, however, blacks' chief hope and interest was the American Colonization Society, founded in 1817. The object of the society, whose first president was Bushrod Washington, was to purchase the freedom of slaves and send the ex-slaves and as many black freemen as possible back to Africa, where a colony named Liberia was being established. The leaders of the American Colonization Society believed the American blacks would act as missionaries in darkest Africa and take the twin gospels of Christianity and republican government to their benighted brethren across the sea in a kind of reverse Manifest Destiny. At the outset, white and black cosmopolitan aspirations appeared to be theoretically in tune. One is struck, for example, by the series of pathetically earnest letters from would-be black emigrants to the society's journal, the *African Repository*. As early as 1818 one Abraham Camp of Lamont, Illinois (free) Territory, wrote:

> We love this country and its liberties, if we could share an equal right in them; but our freedom is partial, and we have no hope that it will ever be otherwise here; therefore we had rather be gone, though we should suffer hunger and nakedness for years. Your honor may be assured that nothing shall be lacking on our part in complying with whatever provision shall be made by the United States, whether it be to go to Africa or some other place; we shall hold ourselves in readiness, praying that God (who made man free in the beginning and who by his kind providence has broken the yoke from every white American) would inspire the heart of every true son of liberty with zeal and pity to open the door of freedom for us also.

And in 1847 Peter Butler of Virginia wrote:

> I wish to Go to Liberia So as I may teach Sinners the way of Salvation and also Educate my children and injoy [*sic*] the Right of a man.

Burrell W. Mann, a slave from the same state, deluged the Society with letters for years begging it to purchase his freedom so that he might be a missionary to Africa. When the Society finally raised the purchase price, the owner doubled it and Mann never was able to implement the "mission of America."

The Society, however, had its powerful and articulate black exponents. John B. Russwurm, a mixed-race man of Jamaican descent, became the first black to acquire an American college degree when he gradated from Bowdoin in 1826. Though at the outset an abolitionist and editor of the black newspaper *Freedom's Journal*, Russwurm eventually gave up and went to Liberia, where he became the first superintendent of public schools. Alexander Crummell, a clergyman and graduate of Oneida Institute in New York and the first American black to take a degree from Cambridge University in England, spent twenty years in Liberia promoting its cause in such tracts as *The Duty of a Rising Christian State to Contribute to the World's Well Being and Civilization* (1855). James T. Holly, the first American black Episcopal bishop, was a staunch advocate of emigration to Haiti, where he had spent most of his life. Martin R. Delany, in *The Condition, Elevation, Emigration and Destiny of the Colored People of the United States "Politically Considered"* (1852), argued for a mass black movement to New Granada (Colombia) and Nicaragua. Later, as a doctor in the U.S. Army, he wrote and published his *Official Report of the Niger Valley Exploring Party*, an account of his expedition to West Africa in which he was so struck by its possibilities that he purchased tracts of land along the Niger River and enthusiastically joined the back-to-Africa movement. The black man's advantage over the white man, Delany felt, was "that they can bear *more different* climates than the white race." West Africa offered exciting possibilities not for missionaries but for commerce and cotton production that would provide unbearable competition to the slaveholding South and make a great black civilization arise again. In the spirit of the age of Manifest Destiny, Delany exhorted his countrymen:

We must MAKE AN ISSUE, CREATE AN EVENT, and ESTAB-LISH A NATIONAL POSITION FOR OURSELVES; and never may expect to be respected as men and women, until we have undertaken,

some fearless, bold and adventurous deeds of daring—contending
against every odds—regardless of every consequence.

This black Frémont, one of the most famous men of his day, never realized his dream, but near the end of the Civil War he became a major in the
medical corps of the U.S. Army—the first high-ranking black officer.

Most partisans of emigration, including the radical ex-slave clergyman
Henry Highland Garnet, who converted to the Africa movement as a result
of his association with Delany, echoed the sentiments of those humbler
correspondents to the Colonization Society quoted previously. To a man,
they believed America was their country. American ideals were their ideals.
But since they could not fully share in these ideals and in the promise of
American life, they preferred to move. They had confidence in the black
man's ability to create or re-create his own great civilization with ethnic
roots deep in the past, and yet with all the modern advantages of technology and fairly administered republican political economy. Many of them,
such as James T. Holly and Robert B. Lewis, well-read men, were struck by
what they considered to be the great success of the Haitian Revolution.
Toussaint L'Ouverture and his successors proved to them that a black state
arising out of its own radical French Revolution could endure and flourish.
To the white Southerner, the revolution in Haiti was a nightmare, but to
black Southerners, even comparative nonintellectuals, such as tragic
Charleston revolutionary Denmark Vesey, it was a dream—a powerful
symbol of hope and dignity.

By the same token, almost from the outset, the American Colonization
Society and its aims were staunchly opposed by the majority of black intellectuals. As early as 1817, the very year of the society's formation, a delegation of blacks, led by their ministers in Philadelphia, publicly declared:

> We have no wish to separate from our present homes for any purpose
> whatever. Contented with our present situation and condition, we
> are not desirous of increasing their [the slaves'] prosperity but by
> honest efforts, and by use of those opportunities for their improve-
> ment, which the Constitution and laws allow to all. It is therefore and
> with painful solicitude and sorrowing regret, we have seen a plan for

colonizing the free people of color of the United States on the coast
of Africa.

What aroused black suspicion was, of course, that the first who were
slated to go to Liberia were the freemen. They regarded this as a plot to rid
the country of those able elements of the black community who were encouraging their enslaved brothers to escape to freedom. They felt that the
colonization scheme was a deliberate attempt to purge black intellectuals
and activist leaders who were demanding their rights as men under the
Declaration of Independence and the Constitution.

As time wore on, a sharp ideological division developed between blacks
who favored emigration and those who believed that the best course was to
stand and fight for their rights in America. The latter were much in the majority; consequently, the former came to be very often regarded as traitors to
the black man's cause. Significantly, most leading colonizationists left the
country and stayed away rather than actively proselytizing in the United
States. Perhaps the most disliked of these black emigrationists was John B.
Russwurm because he had so abruptly deserted the cause of abolition and
emancipation in America after having been one of its staunchest allies.

III

As far as black intellectuals were concerned, a dramatic turning point came
in 1829 with the publication and mass distribution of David Walker's *Appeal to the Colored Citizens of the World.* Walker was born in Wilmington,
North Carolina, in 1785, technically a free man, because though his father
was a slave, his mother was free and the status of the children of slaves was
determined by the maternal line. As a young man, Walker traveled extensively in the South, where at every hand he observed the wretched condition of the slaves and indignation built up within him. Sometime shortly
before 1827 he settled in Boston, where he became a tailor and dealer in
used clothing. By 1829 he had acquired enough money and leisure to write
his famous *Appeal.* In all he published three editions of the work, the first in
1829, the second and third in 1830. Each edition was more incendiary and
outspoken than the last. John Jay Chapman referred to it as "an outcrop of

subterranean fire," while black historian J. Saunders Redding has termed it "scurrilous, ranting, mad," though he added shrewdly, "but these were the temper of the times, when nearly every event was climactic and every utterance a shout of rage." In any case, so powerful a document was Walker's *Appeal* that it spread not only through the northern black community, but into the South as well. Southerners instantly became alarmed, and the Georgia legislature made the circulation of his pamphlet a capital offense. A price was set on Walker's head, and the mayor of Savannah attempted without success to persuade Harrison Gray Otis, the mayor of Boston, to punish Walker. But in June 1830, Walker died suddenly and mysteriously. It was rumored, without substantiation, that he was poisoned.

More important than his life was Walker's argument. Essentially his *Appeal* was an impassioned, evangelically inspired jeremiad—a fire-and-brimstone sermon to all Americans, black and white alike, in the great tradition of Jonathan Edwards and George Whitefield. Its main theme was the disparity between the preaching of principle and the practice of it in Christian, Enlightenment America and the awful retribution that would surely follow if Americans did not live up to their ideal. "I tell you Americans," he asserted, "that unless you speedily alter your course, *you* and your *Country* are gone!!!!! For God Almighty will tear up the very face of the earth!!!!"

Following Christianity, Walker stressed the unity and equality of all mankind in the sight of God. He also stood hard on the Declaration of Independence and its proclamation that "all men are created equal." "See your Declaration Americans!!! Do you understand your own language? Hear your language, proclaimed to the world, July 4, 1776," he cried out. As Walker saw it, neither Christians nor Americans really believed or acted upon their own doctrines. Instead, the English were "the best friends the coloured people have upon the earth." Thus he reversed the common myth of the contrast theme where America was the moral experiment and Europe was decadent. This was a stand that virtually every black intellectual would take, as more and more of them were received well in Europe and could see for themselves the status of men of color, such as Alexandre Dumas and Alexander Pushkin.

Throughout the *Appeal*, Walker directly assaulted as many major American political figures as he could. Thomas Jefferson was his favorite target because the lines concerning his belief in blacks' inferiority in the *Notes on Virginia* belied his lofty sentiments in the Declaration of Independence. Walker also attacked Henry Clay, the American Colonization Society, and John Randolph, who freed his slaves only at his death. The main burden of his arguments, however, was carried along three lines: (1) the wretchedness of blacks caused by ignorance, fostered by whites; (2) wretchedness in consequence of the preachers of religion of Jesus Christ, who, in a sense, duped blacks into being docile while they waited patiently for the hereafter; and (3) wretchedness in consequence of the colonization plan. He portrayed blacks as a once-mighty people, the builders of Egypt and Carthage and tutors of the Greeks, who were now brought low through ignorance fastened on them by white tyrants and preachers, but also by their own lack of drive. In all history no one, not even the Israelite in bondage, had been so badly treated as blacks. The only answer was God's retribution in the form of black activism and revolt. Black men must be the instrument of God's vengeance. "I assure you that God will accomplish it—if nothing else will answer, he will hurl tyrants and devils into atoms and make way for his people. But O my brethren! I say unto you again, you must go to work and prepare the way of the Lord." In 1831, inspired by such messianic visions, Nat Turner indeed prepared Walker's "way of the Lord," in his ill-fated Virginia rebellion.

Even to ardent emancipationists, Walker's *Appeal* seemed somewhat extreme. William Lloyd Garrison wrote: "We have had this pamphlet on our table for some time past, and are not surprised at its effect upon our sensitive Southern brethren. It is written by a colored Bostonian and breathes the most impassioned and determined spirit. We deprecate its circulation, though we cannot but wonder at the bravery and intelligence of its author." Later he added, "The circulation of this 'seditious' pamphlet has proven one thing conclusively—that the boasted security of the slave States, by their orators and writers, is mere affectation, or something worse." Garrison, however, was a pacifist, as were many black intellectuals and church leaders; consequently, many of them ultimately rejected the Walker line in favor of the doctrine of nonresistance and moral suasion.

After Walker, however, the abolition movement organized itself rapidly. In 1831, under Garrison's direction, the New England Anti-Slavery Society came into being and began sending agents out across the country. In

1833, in Philadelphia, the American Anti-Slavery Society was formed, financed by white merchant Lewis Tappan, buttressed by the Quakers, and populated with numerous black clergymen from in and around New York and Philadelphia. This society's manifesto was a paraphrase of the Declaration of Independence suggesting that their main theme was the unfulfilled promise of American revolutionary ideals, just as it had been for Walker.

Eventually three main centers for abolitionist activity developed. The New England movement was led by Garrison, Thomas Wentworth Higginson, Wendell Phillips, and Theodore Parker, and centered on the New England Anti-Slavery Society. The New York–Philadelphia societies extended beyond the American Anti-Slavery Society and the Quakers to capture virtually the whole of the Protestant evangelical movement as it was spearheaded by Charles Grandison Finney in upstate New York's "Burned-Over District." Finney's impact on audiences helped spread the movement to Ohio, where, under the leadership of Theodore Dwight Weld, it built upon the foundations laid by Quakers Charles G. Osborn, Elihu Embree, and Benjamin Lundy between 1817 and 1830. As historian Benjamin Quarles has pointed out in *Black Abolitionists*, black men were prominent figures in all of these groups and were instrumental in forming innumerable spin-off groups. One needs only to recall the names of James Forten, Absalom Jones, Richard Allen, Henry H. Garnet, John Gloucester, James McCune Smith, Samuel Cornish, James McCrummell, Robert Purvis, James G. Barbadoes, David Ruggles, Jehiel Beman, George Vashon, John Remond, Sojourner Truth, and William Whipper to get some idea of black people's own prominence in the movement. Most significantly, just as most white Protestant churches were dividing into "Old Side" and "New Side" sects, the black churches began to split off from the white parent organizations in a repudiation of discriminatory Christianity. Thus black people formed, for example, the Bethel Methodists and the Zion Methodists, the Temple Street African Church in New Haven, Connecticut (Congregationalist), St. Thomas' African Episcopal Church in Philadelphia, the Abyssinia Baptist Church of New York, and Cincinnati's Zion Baptist Church. Each of these churches and the hundreds like them formed centers for welding evangelical Christianity to the bandwagon of abolitionism. In effect, they put into practice the black muscular Christianity Walker had demanded.

IV

No black intellectual or leader had a greater impact on the American mind than Frederick Douglass, who represented the black Southern mind at its keenest. Born a slave about 1817 on a plantation in Talbot County in the backwater Eastern Shore of Maryland, Douglass spent the first twenty-one years of his life experiencing the continuous shocks of slave life. His separation from his mother, and then his grandmother; his horrible realization that he was not a boy like his master's son, with whom he played, but something different, a slave; his witnessing of the continual degradation of black authority figures; the whippings of women; the murders of recalcitrant coworkers, all caused his early life to become a continuous series of cinemalike "dissolves." In something akin to the experience of Henry Adams, though on a far different, though no less sensitive level, Douglass lived in a world where reality continually faded and nothing was as it seemed to be or seemed it should be for a young black man. Nothing illustrates the culture shock commonly experienced by the black slave better than the rude awakenings Douglass recorded in his moving *Narrative of Frederick Douglass*. Nothing, however, also illustrates better the black man's potential for surviving these culture shocks through inherent strength of character and mental capacity. When he escaped to the North in 1838 and began to lecture on the platform for William Lloyd Garrison's New England Anti-Slavery Society in 1841, Douglass quickly became a living example of what the motivated slave could do. A rather tall, robust man with a powerful face and head in an age that admired phrenological signs of genius, Douglass, after a few trial speeches, quickly began mesmerizing his audiences by his simple, forceful, and sincere method of delivery and excellent speaking voice. In the years 1845 to 1847, when he toured England, he was an even greater success, not only because of his forensic abilities, but because by that time he had published his famous narrative. More than anyone else, it was Douglass who rallied British antislavery sentiment during the late 1840s. He had become a cosmopolitan and his was a message of worldwide humanitarianism.

In 1847 he settled in Rochester, New York, and began to publish an abolitionist newspaper, the *North Star*, which became the most famous of its day, though not so famous as Douglass himself, and eventually its name was changed to *Frederick Douglass' Paper*. It was an ironic moral parallel to such widely distributed white papers as *Frank Leslie's Illustrated Weekly*.

Although he was a militant antislavery advocate, Douglass did not preach revolution. Rather, whenever he could, he insisted upon the extension and enforcement of the principles of the Declaration of Independence and the Constitution for all people. He believed in working through the American political system, and when Garrison burned the Constitution and refused to participate in the political process, Douglass turned away from him and consistently supported Liberty Party, Free Soil, and Republican candidates as the only effective means of helping black people. He advocated the doctrine of black self-help and lauded the efforts of black churches. "What we, the colored people, want, is *character*, and this nobody can give us," he declared in 1848. "It is a thing we must do for ourselves." He added in a passage somewhat reminiscent of Russell Conwell's *Acres of Diamonds*, "There is gold in the earth, but we must dig it—so with character." This was the voice of the self-made, self-taught black man who was advocating assimilation of black men into the white man's world in America. He believed it could be done because he had experienced it in Europe. Again he declared:

> Never refuse to act with a white society or institution because it is white or a Black one, because it is Black. But act with all men without distinction of color. By so acting, we shall find many opportunities for removing prejudices and establish the rights of all men.

Foreshadowing the ideas of Booker T. Washington, on whom he had a great impact, Douglass continually asserted the importance of economic improvement:

> Every blow of the sledge hammer, wielded by a sable arm is a powerful blow in support of our cause. Every colored mechanic is by virtue of circumstances, an elevator of his race. Every house built by black men is a strong tower against the allied hosts of prejudice. It is impossible for us to attach too much importance to this aspect of the subject. Trades are important. Wherever a man may be thrown by misfortune, if he has in his hands a useful trade, he is useful to his fellowman, and

will be esteemed accordingly; and of all the men in the world who
need trades we are the most needy.

Thus Douglass, unlike many abolitionists, did not advocate class or
racial struggle. Rather, in a traditional but forceful way he stood upon the
Christian doctrine of the unity of mankind and insisted upon adherence to
the principles of the Founding Fathers in the economic and social spheres
as well as the political. Moreover, while he was staunchly contending
against slavery in the South, he just as fiercely fought prejudice, segrega-
tion, and discrimination in the North. He contended against separate black
schools, black galleries in white Philadelphia churches, and segregated
compartments on packet boats and railroads. Because his approach was so
eminently practical and because he did not really threaten the American
system, Douglass was the most effective of all black intellectuals.

And yet not only was Douglass a strategist and purely practical thinker,
but he also had a more philosophical side, which reached out into science,
theology, history, and other learned disciplines. In a striking commence-
ment address to the students of Ohio's Western Reserve College in 1852 titled "The Claims of the Negro Ethnologically Considered," Douglass
turned his scorn on the racist science of S. G. Morton, George Gliddon,
Josiah Nott, and Louis Agassiz. In so doing he assaulted the current methods of science directly as a means of comprehending reality. "This is, you
know, an age of science, and science is favorable to division," he declared.
"It must explore and analyze until all doubt is set at rest." Then he proceeded in the same way James Fenimore Cooper had effectively lampooned
the specialist Dr. Obed Bat in *The Prairie* to show that the "dividers" in science were wrong, that their Linnaean hairsplitting provided them with
only a partial and unrealistic picture of man. Douglass insisted upon the
scriptural basis for a belief in the unity of mankind and then grafted upon
this the thesis that the physical and mental differences perceived in men
were the result of their environmental situation rather than a simultaneous
separate creation by God. Given this, adaptability was the most important
key to improvement or even to judging a group of men. That is, ethnologically, how well have they adapted to whatever conditions in which they
have found themselves? On this relativistic scale, the black man was among
civilization's leaders.

The poor bondsman lifts a smiling face above the surface of a sea of agonies, *hoping on, hoping ever.* His tawny brother, the Indian dies, under the flashing glance of the Anglo-Saxon. *Not So* the Negro; civilization cannot kill him.

In all ages, from the biblical to the days of ancient Egypt through the rise of Greece and Rome and western Europe and America, he has stood forth a man—a man of supreme adaptability who has endured and, so Douglass believed, would prevail.

It would be seven years before Darwin brought this kind of synthesis to the fore and his American disciple Asa Gray used it to shatter America's foremost scientist, the special creationist Louis Agassiz. In the early 1850s, Douglass, product of slavery, part of the "mind of the Old South," stood ready to absorb the great naturalist's principles and his correspondingly new view of science and reality. Without all of the data, or even the announced hypothesis in *On the Origin of Species*, Douglass was already applying it to the ascent of black men.

V

Still another ex-slave representative of the Southern black mind was William Wells Brown, the first American black novelist and playwright as well as the foremost black historian of the mid-nineteenth century. Brown was a fascinating person. Brown was born a slave in Lexington, Kentucky, and his mother was black but his father was a member of one of the "first [white] families" of Kentucky, and Brown often laughingly claimed descent from the aristocratic Higginses and Wycliffes.

In 1834 he escaped north to Ohio, where for years he worked on a Lake Erie steamboat, and in this role participated in the underground railroad into Canada. He soon learned to read, write, and speak with great skill, and from 1843 to 1849 he was an agent for the Western and Massachusetts antislavery societies. With the passage of the Fugitive Slave Law as part of the Compromise of 1850, Brown fled to England, where he was immediately lionized and remained, except for a grand tour of Europe and a visit as a delegate to the Peace Congress in Paris, for six years, until his freedom was purchased. He was especially proud of his friendship with Dumas, who was one-quarter black. This was appropriate because, in addition to racial affinities, the two men also belonged to the international fraternity of professional writers.

Brown wrote many books. First he published his *Narrative of William W. Brown, a Fugitive Slave* in 1847. Then he wrote *Three Years in Europe* (1852), a more or less standard travel book, though the first by an American black. His most sensational book, however, was his novel *Clotel, or the President's Daughter: A Narrative of Slave Life in the United States*, a story he rewrote in even more militant fashion as *Miranda, the Beautiful Quadroon* (1860–1861). Packed with enough plots and subplots to fill a hundred volumes, *Clotel* was, except for its black theme, a characteristic specimen of the rambling, romantic, sentimental novel. So characteristic was it that parts of the book were taken from a similar novel by the white author Lydia Maria Child. What was most interesting about Brown's book was that it was based upon the widespread legend that President Jefferson had fathered several female mixed-race children and then callously sold them down the river into degrading slavery. The central characters of the novel are Currer, Jefferson's fictional mistress, and her two daughters, Clotel and Althesa. Just as Brown regarded himself as a somewhat refined gentleman for having been descended from the Kentucky gentry, so too does he portray Clotel and Althesa as ladies of refinement. As such, however, they are subjected to the entire spectrum of black degradation—auction blocks, slave pens, cruel white overseers with seduction on their minds, breathless chases, and for good measure, participation in the Nat Turner Rebellion and the New Orleans yellow fever epidemic. It thus comes as something of a relief when Clotel, too refined for all this, finds herself trapped on the Long Bridge across the Potomac between Washington marshals eagerly enforcing the Fugitive Slave Act and slathering Southern slave catchers on the Virginia side, and jumps to her death before suffering further dishonor. The moral of the story is clear. If something like this could happen to a Founding Father's daughter, what of all the other daughters of "liberty"—white and black? To emphasize this point, Brown introduced a subplot based upon an actual occurrence in New Orleans in which a young white French girl was sold into slavery because, being taken for black, she could not, of course, testify on her own behalf.

Brown's point was that if it could happen to our black daughters it could happen to white daughters as well. This is a point Abraham Lincoln grasped when he declared in a speech at Chicago during his famous debates with Stephen A. Douglas: "I should like to know if taking this old Declaration of Independence, which declares that all men are equal upon principle, and making exceptions to it, where will it stop? If one may say it does not mean a Negro, why may not another say it does not mean some other man?"

Following the publication of *Clotel,* Brown became interested in Santo Domingo and its achievement of black independence. *In St. Domingo: Its Revolution and Its Patriots,* published in 1855, he, like many others of his day, held up Santo Domingo as a successful model of the black state. By this time, following the pioneer paths of William Nell, James W. C. Pennington, and A. Mott, he had become extremely interested in the global history of colored peoples. In 1863, just after the Emancipation Proclamation, Brown published perhaps his best book, *The Black Man: His Antecedents, His Genius, and His Achievements.* This was the first really important work in black history. He intended his work to "aid in vindicating the Black character, and show that he is endowed with those intellectual and amiable qualities which adorn and dignify human nature."

The book opened with a short autobiography, then in a kind of overview, Brown devoted twenty pages to "the Black Man and his Antecedents." He traced the black heritage back to Ethiopia, Egypt, Minerva, Jupiter, Tertullian, St. Augustine, Hanno, Hamilcar Barca, and Hannibal, thus historically emphasizing the timeless and extensive nature of the cosmopolitan black community and, by implication, the essential unity of all mankind. In this section he used his data to refute current political assertions, including some by Lincoln, that the black, though a man, was inferior. The remainder of the book was devoted to a series of fifty-seven biographies of famous black historical figures, including Benjamin Banneker, Nat Turner, Toussaint L'Ouverture, Crispus Attucks, Alexandre Dumas, Denmark Vesey, Martin Delany, Frederick Douglass, James W. C. Pennington, Sir Edward Jordan, and John S. Rock.

Later, in 1874, Brown wrote a more extensive work, *The Rising Son, or the Antecedents and the Advancement of the Colored Race,* in which, taking advantage of the archaeological enthusiasms of the day and the rise of historicism, he was much more effective in relating the American black to ancestors in the ancient world. Brown and his fellow black historians of the antebellum period might well be considered another early branch of the usable-past school of history, which has dominated American historiography since the Progressive Era.

As he searched for identity and his role in antebellum America, the black intellectual took on a triple orientation that, in a sense, mirrored the weaknesses and strengths of the whole of American culture. He was first and foremost a black man and, as such, a member of the world's colored community. He was also an American with deep ties to American soil and an astonishingly strong belief in American political values as articulated by the Founding Fathers, and finally, whether he enjoyed the role or not, he was a product, in some sense, of the Southern past and part of the whole complex that made up the tortured Southern mind. Though he shared nothing at all with the planter or even the poor white and the "Southern dream," the black intellectual did partake, sometimes actually and sometimes vicariously through affinity to his enslaved black brethren, of a racial memory that strangely always brought him back to the Old South and its problems. Despite all his tribulations and his hatred of slavery, for example, William Wells Brown titled his last book, written in 1880, *My Southern Home: Or the South and Its People.* The black, like the white American, was a man of many loyalties, though in contrast to the white Southerner he did not seek to particularize them and so divide himself from the rest of mankind. Instead, like most Americans, he attempted in the white heat of the slavery controversy to fuse them all into one—to absorb everything into one great cosmopolitan synthesis that he shrewdly saw was the only hope for the American and the American nation.

A simple catalogue reveals just how much the American black intellectual shared with American and western civilization. He believed in Christianity, usually Protestant evangelical Christianity. He believed in the Protestant ethic and subscribed to the idea of success through hard work. He believed in capitalism. He believed in the idea of the nation-state. But he also believed in the cosmopolitan ideals of the Enlightenment. He believed in the idea of community and in the ultimate great community, the unity of all mankind. He believed in the common descent of man as opposed to the special creationism held by a few select members of the scientific community. He believed in the power of nature, sometimes mystically and transcendentally, though he did not hold American nature over against Europe as the source of moral superiority. He did, however, believe in America's mission and did his best to bring American ideas to Africa and the Caribbean. He subscribed to all the values enunciated in the Declaration of Independence and asked only that they be fully extended to his race. He believed in the right of revolution against unjust laws, but he was also a pacifist and advocated, more often than not, nonviolent revolution. He believed in the usable past and romantic historicism. He believed in women's rights and temperance and, in general, in the idea that people's lives were not fixed in place but could be changed by reforming institutions and hence their conditions for living. In short, the American black intellectual, despite all his wretchedness and his tribulations, was an optimist. He believed, like Walt Whitman, in the future. In this he was quite different from his fellow white Southern intellectuals, who sought only to preserve the past—a task in which they waged a hopeless and tragic struggle, while the black man, looking ahead and listening hopefully, distinctly heard the trumpets of jubilee.

CHAPTER SIXTEEN

The Women's War

Next to abolitionism, perhaps the most spectacular and far-reaching reform crusade of the early nineteenth century was the militant campaign for
women's rights. Though for a time before the Revolution women had the
right to vote, the achievement of American independence meant a distinct
retrogression in their status. The heroic services and stature of Mercy Otis
Warren, first historian of the Revolution, and Abigail Adams, the first First
Lady to seriously give her husband advice as to how to govern the country,
notwithstanding, the Revolution was a setback for American women. Like
William Gilmore Simms, who wondered whether the South had actually
fought on the right side, and such black intellectuals as William Nell, who
wondered the same thing for his people, the American woman—especially
when she listened to English independents, such as Frances Trollope, Harriet Martineau, and Fanny Wright—began to wonder just what her stake in
America might be.

The law considered a woman essentially a minor, with no right to vote
or hold property in her own name. Married or unmarried, she was invariably subject to a male guardian. Divorce was unthinkable except by special
acts of the legislature and then only for extreme cause. For good measure,

as late as 1850 "a reasonable instrument" for wife beating was defined by one judge as a "stick no thicker than my thumb."

Even before the turn of the nineteenth century, however, people began to concern themselves with the status of women. Abigail Adams admonished her husband, "In the new code of laws which I suppose it will be necessary for you to make, I desire you to remember the ladies, and be more generous to them than your ancestors—If particular care and attention are not paid to the ladies, we are determined to foment a rebellion and will not hold ourselves bound to obey the laws in which we have no voice or representation." In another vein, in 1798, America's first male novelist, Charles Brockden Brown, published *Alcuin, A Dialogue*, which was concerned primarily with women's rights, and in *Arthur Mervyn* a major theme follows Mervyn's efforts to secure the inheritance of an orphaned country lass with whom he is in love. Mervyn also concerns himself with the enslavement of women and with divorce. As the story's hero he ultimately marries the only really liberated woman in the book.

Brown's interest in the question of women, like that of many others in the early nineteenth century, arose not only out of an interest in her status in the abstract, but out of a practical legal concern. As the adaptation of English law was taking place and the codification movement was building to high tide, the whole question of women's place in the legal code must have been such a common question as to make for a daily groundswell of discontent in every hamlet and town in America. In such a state of legal flux, women were bound to move to the fore.

The chief bulwark against them, however, was the Protestant Church. Ministers, following the Bible literally, persisted in seeing women as Adam's rib and therefore, by Christian lights, distinctly inferior. Moreover, it was by listening to women that Adam lost his innocence and was cast out of the Garden of Paradise. For a long time in Christian and fundamentalist America, such proof was conclusive. In the 1840s, when Sarah and Angelina Grimke attempted to deliver antislavery orations from the pulpits of New England, they succeeded only in splitting the abolitionist movement itself as the clergy indignantly rejected William Lloyd Garrison and Wendell Phillips, their sponsors, and withdrew its support from the New England Anti-Slavery Society. The same sentiments were echoed throughout the country and in England as well, where a delegation of women was overwhelmingly excluded from the World Anti-Slavery Convention in 1840. They sat in a curtained-off section of the gallery accompanied by Garrison, who refused to participate in the convention unless his female delegates were seated. During the proceedings he glowered down upon the "enlightened" British. Only rarely did a woman, such as Antoinette Brown, who was ordained a minister at Oberlin College, virtually in secret, break the barrier of discriminatory Christianity.

Considering the impact of the Scottish philosophy upon the United States, the religious sanctions against women must have seemed logical to most nineteenth-century Americans. Not only did a literal reading of scripture assign woman a lower place, but science did so as well. The Common Sense philosophy held that all of God's creatures were created for some purpose, hence they were supremely adaptable to their particular environmental sphere unless disturbed by some catastrophe or unless they wandered out of that sphere. In his benevolence, God had in effect adapted the earth to the wants and needs of his creatures in their proper environments. Clearly, then, it followed that woman, a very specially created creature, mentioned specifically in scripture, had a special place in the system of creation. This was, of course, as the lesser companion of Adam, which could thus be philosophically demonstrated to be a domestic role.

Following the principles of faculty psychology, women's faculties were different from those of men. They had to be, because their anatomy and biological functions were different. This could be demonstrated by the latest research into the nervous system. Dr. William Cullen of Edinburgh saw the brain and the nervous system as the central functioning organs of the body and excessive "excitement" as the chief cause of disease. His theory was carried on by Dr. John Brown, also of Edinburgh, who linked disease, from fevers to vapors, to an imbalance in the "excitability" quotient. Dr. Benjamin Rush, who had studied with both men, like many early American physicians tried to combine the Cullen-Brown nervous excitability thesis with a vascular theory in which excitement or excessive stimuli affected the blood vessels, expanding or contracting them, caused disease, and, in many cases, so disrupted the natural mental faculties as to cause insanity.

Woman, being created for a special domestic purpose, was not made to withstand the onslaughts of excitability generated by the strains and stresses of the competitive world of war, commerce, and politics. Participation in such events could and would disrupt her whole body and her mind. No less an authority than Dr. Amariah Brigham, superintendent of the Utica, New York, State Hospital and the first editor of the *American Journal of Insanity*, testified to this danger. In his authoritative book, *Remarks on the Influence of Mental Culture and Mental Excitement Upon Health* (1833), Brigham, concerned about the relative prevalence of insanity in the United States, cited four chief causes for the phenomenon. The first cause was "too constant and too powerful excitement of the mind, which the strife for wealth, office, political distinction, and party success produces in this free country." The fourth cause was most specifically related to women's situation. Calling attention to "the physiological difference of the sexes," he declared a major cause of insanity to be "the general and powerful excitement of the female mind." He went on to assert very positively that in women

> the nervous system naturally predominates; that they are endowed with quicker sensibility; and far more active imagination, than men; that their emotions are more intense, and their senses alive to more delicate impressions; and they therefore require great attention, lest this exquisite sensibility, which, when properly and naturally developed, constitutes the greatest excellence of women, should either become *excessive* by too strong excitement, or suppressed by misdirected education.

He deplored excessive education for females because it rendered their natural sensibility "excessive." By the same token he scorned the lack of exercise among upper-class American women and their participation in the activities of parties and even religious sects. The strong emotions generated by the latter activities could have dire consequences for women's minds, he concluded, and "deplorable effects upon their offspring." Such logic was evident in the "Old Side" orthodoxy's disapproval of female participation in the frenzies of revivalism, where it was patent that scores of women not only swooned but in many cases lost their minds and dignity as women—and sometimes their virginity. If this could happen in religious exercises it would be a possibility all the more exaggerated in the harsh secular world.

The fashionable blush, the swoon, and the vapors so common to nineteenth-century women, not to mention the exaggerated mental crises they suffered in deciding to go for life in the "outside" world, suggests that the vast majority of women subscribed to this religio-scientific theory of the "delicate woman." It was very real to them and hence a mental fact. Moreover, the "excitability" theory, as Brigham suggested, could be extended to men, who, though stronger, also were vulnerable and hence needed the calmness and sanctity of the good home, which women saw as their duty to provide. After all, besides dreaded insanity, apoplexy, heart failure, and tuberculosis were common causes of early death that could easily be attributed to the "excitability" theory.

Before one judges too harshly the comparative submissiveness of women in the nineteenth century, their failure to come to grips with the "hard questions" of cosmic reality, and their penchant for the domestic novel, it is important to see that, for them, orthodoxy in religion and the discoveries of science and medicine had made any venture outside the domestic sphere a distinct risk. This risk, and the fears it engendered, was reinforced by the spate of gothic novels that rapidly rose to fashion in the period and that women read assiduously in the sanctuary of the home. For many the perils of Charlotte Temple and the horrors of the gothic nightmare awaited them should they venture outside what social wisdom and their female "betters" considered their proper sphere. And they looked upon those women who did so as either "fallen angels" or unnatural beings. In penning the domestic novel, in celebrating the home, the female scribbler, herself living on the brink of disaster as a professional writer, was only promoting spiritual, mental, and physical health according to the lights of current religious doctrine and current scientific enlightenment. In her eyes she was a heroine herself.

I

Women, however, as Nathaniel Hawthorne suggested by his testy reference in 1855 to "a damned lot of scribbling women," did gain their greatest success in literature. For fifty years Sarah Josepha Hale was editor of *Godey's Lady's Book*, whose circulation ran to 150,000. She not only helped to popularize Amelia Bloomer's famous costume, but Hale also set the consumer style of female bourgeois America. Lydia Sigourney, the "Sweet Singer of Hartford," outsold all male poets and had her imitator way out west, the "Sweet Singer of Michigan," whom some erroneously thought to be a man attempting to cash in on her success. Mrs. E. D. E. N. Southworth, Susan Warner, Maria Cummins, Caroline Lee Hentz, Catherine Maria Sedgwick, Emily Judson, Caroline Kirkland, Mary Jane Holmes, and Fanny Fern were best-selling authors when Edgar Allan Poe, Hawthorne, and Herman Melville were esteemed in the smallest of circles. Maria Cummins's *The Lamplighter* sold seventy thousand copies in one year. Susan Warner's *The Wide, Wide World* went through thirteen editions and five hundred thousand copies in two years. Mrs. E. D. E. N. Southworth's *Ishmael* sold two million copies, which must have produced something worse than "a damp and drizzly November of the soul" in the defeated author of *Moby Dick*. Year after year the "scribbling women" poured out their "domestic novels," which ran as serials in magazines and newspapers, then sold by the hundreds of thousands in book versions.

Basically the "domestic novels" penned by female authors were derived from European models going back to the Englishman Samuel Richardson's *Pamela* and *Clarissa*, the latter of which was imitated by Susanna Rowson, America's first successful novelist, in the cautionary *Charlotte Temple* (1791). Plots and characters were also lifted or adapted from Walter Scott, Charles Dickens, the Bronte sisters, Jane Austen, Anthony Trollope, William Makepeace Thackeray, Honoré de Balzac, Eugène Sue, Edward Bulwer-Lytton, and Johann von Goethe's *Wilhelm Meister* and *The Sorrows of Young Werther.* This was because the female writers' best-selling works depended largely upon sentiment that in turn derived from such archetypes as Dickens's Little Nell, Emily Brontë's Catherine Linton, or Walter Scott's pious, submissive Rowena. In many ways the writings of the female scribblers were absurd, with their cardboard figures, "Perils of Pauline" plots, sunny-side views of hearth and home, and their extreme coyness and cloying religiosity. And yet they represented, first of all, a breakthrough into professions for women, and secondly they were vehicles for carrying both overt and covert cultural messages of supreme importance. What the Puritan sermon or jeremiad was to old New England, the sentimental novel was to antebellum America.

The overt message was more than clear, since by virtue of its endless repetition in hundreds of novels it hardly could have been overlooked. This was the dramatic expression the "Cult of True Womanhood," in which woman was a "hostage in the home." Almost all the sentimental novels embodied what historian Barbara Welter has called "the cardinal virtues—piety, purity, submissiveness, and domesticity." The novels were cultural stabilizers at a time when American culture as a whole was in the throes of rapid, violent change, financial panics, unpopular wars, division over slavery, and the whole broad spectrum of discontents that arose in the 1840s and 1850s on the tide of a democratic revolution of expectations. As stabilizers the novels provided reassurance, especially to women, who were largely the victims of sudden change in America. Christian piety had given way to secularism and gross materialism, according to some female writers. But pious Christianity was still the guiding star of the virtuous, who, being good Christians, would triumph in the end. Purity—chastity—too was still largely intact despite the temptations of a rising and almost certainly wicked urban civilization. But most important, despite the crusades of Susan B. Anthony and the large pretensions of Margaret Fuller, the American woman need have no confusion as to her sex role. As the Bible proclaimed, she must be submissive to the male, and her place, her true joy, was in the home. The home itself almost became a character in some of the novels because it was the only place of true refuge in a wide and tremendously confusing world. Because they were reassuring to women and men alike, because they upheld the old values and cultural roles, sentimental novels became one of the most potent moral forces of midcentury. Along with schoolbooks, they represented the tradition in such a way as to bring just enough fantasy, just enough adventure, just enough familiar, identifiable realism to the reader. This formula tapped the "common sensibilities" as a successor to the "common sense" reason of a previous generation. This change was symbolic of a new generation lost in emotionalism.

Covertly, however, though the novels were all written by "good women," they carried a slightly different message. For one thing, not Oliver Twist, but Little Gerty or Rosa Lee stood at center stage in these melodramas. By sheer quantity these novels called attention to the "woman question," if not the centrality of women in the nineteenth century. Secondly, by stereotyping the male—making him the kindly uncle, the filthy lecher, the weak father, the chaste brotherlike suitor, the callow minister—the female scribblers ever so subtly put men in their place. The qualities they admired in men were largely feminine—projected self-images derived from a rich childhood fantasy life usually learned at a doting father's knee. The message was unmistakable for the many male readers of their novels—if males wished refuge from the storm and stress of a rude world, the only way they could obtain it was by playing house. Thus the female scribblers aided the women's movement by a process of prestidigitation. Looking one way with fascinating protests about the value of "true womanhood," they created solidarity among women and a sense of identity in a changing world, while at the same time, through pathos and piety, seducing the male into supporting their cause. The incestuous sentimental novel was a monument to age-old "womanly wiles."

The most seductive of the female scribblers was of course Harriet Beecher Stowe, whose *Uncle Tom's Cabin* became the best-selling American novel of her time. According to Stowe, the idea for the story came to her while sitting in church in Cincinnati one February day in 1851. The central scene where saintly old Tom is flogged to death by Simon Legree and his henchmen burst upon her romantic imagination all of a sudden like a Charles Grandison Finney sudden conversion. Though she carefully collected information on visits to plantations in Kentucky, Stowe always declared that the story came to her directly from God. "It all came before me in visions," she said over and over.

Uncle Tom's Cabin, or *The Man That Was a Thing,* first appeared in serial form in Dr. Gamaliel Bailey's *Washington National Era* on March 20, 1852. Stowe, like Dickens, rose and fell in spirits with the fortunes of her characters, taking to bed in mourning at the death of Little Eva. So successful was the performance of the author and the serial that public demand in the hundreds of thousands arose for the book in the North, while the South made it an even greater cause célèbre by banning it south of the Mason-Dixon Line.

Uncle Tom's Cabin was, however, something more than a propaganda tract for the antislavery movement. It revealed to its multitude of readers the details of a way of life they knew nothing about. It showed the South in its domesticities as well as its atrocities. In fact, its chief horror was derived from the fact that otherwise good people in the South, rural folks like those found on every farm in the land, acquiesced in the whole dehumanizing process of slavery. She subtly suggested that such a disease could be contagious, thereby striking the fears, as well as the sentiment, of free Americans. The skill with which she utilized the suspenseful action quality of the romantic novel to keep her story moving, to develop the personalities of her striking characters, and to illustrate a broad Dickensian panorama of American "life among the lowly" can best be appreciated by comparing it to the digression-filled, confused social novels of James Fenimore Cooper. Stowe had a powerful theme shot through with romantic religiosity and she knew how to exploit it. It was not her intention, however, to start a civil war; rather, she sought to appeal to the universal good in every man to right a wrong and head off impending disaster. *Uncle Tom's Cabin* was a fictionalized restatement of the original principles upon which she presumed the republic to have been founded.

II

While the popular women writers held center stage, a no less serious band followed Margaret Fuller in a search for the true status of woman as an intellectual. Fuller's *Woman in the Nineteenth Century* was a climactic book, but other women intellectuals arose to express themselves as well. Their problem was complex, however, because society at large, including the average American woman, regarded a female intellectual as something of a sport, a freak, a contradiction in terms. On the other hand, those women who might be expected to offer understanding if not sympathy, those who were fighting politically for the cause of women's rights, seemed almost the epitome of Jacksonian anti-intellectualism. If the activity of the would-be female intellectual was not politically practical or monetarily productive, she became something of an outcast, as much a failure as a geological surveyor who neglected to look for gold.

Lydia Maria Child, Margaret Fuller's early "kindred spirit," felt this dilemma most acutely. Well-read and steeped in the continental philosophies of the day, she nonetheless wrote such popular novels as *Habomok* (1824), one of the first about an American Indian, *The First Settlers of New England* (1829), and *Philothea* (1836). When she tried to turn to serious issues, she was invariably drawn into the abolitionist crusade by her husband. In fact, one of her greatest successes was *An Appeal in Behalf of That Class of Americans Called Africans* (1833), which moved Wendell Phillips, William Ellery Channing, Charles Sumner, and Thomas Wentworth Higginson into the ranks of the abolitionists. And her *Correspondence Between Lydia Maria Child and Governor Wise and Mrs. Mason of Virginia* (1860) sold three hundred thousand copies.

Yet while Child ardently sympathized with abolitionists, she had glimpsed just enough of romantic intellectualism to want something more. She sought to define her own role as woman and culture heroine. The best way to do this was not, she discovered, in writing novels, tracts, or handbooks such as *The Frugal Housewife* (1829), however well they were received. Instead, she turned, like Fuller and like many black intellectuals of the day, to history, in search of herself. In 1833, for the *Ladies' Family Library*, she wrote *Good Wives*, which was a historical collection of the lives of women who had stood behind great men. It was a failure. She kept on with this theme, however, and published an even more ambitious work, *The History of Women in All Ages and Nations* (1835), and then a twin biography of her two favorite historical personages: the heroine of the French Revolution, Pauline Roland, and Madame de Stael. Of the two, Child more readily identified with Roland, who had worked with her husband on the great *Encyclopedia* before they both went to the guillotine.

The History of Women in All Ages and Nations was, in a sense, a product of the anthropological concerns of the Second Great Age of Discovery. It examined the lives of prominent women in all ages from all cultures, including South Sea islanders, attempting to understand their respective mores and ideals. It was an eclectic, rather unsystematic but empathetic book that aimed toward the same vision of the free society expressed by Fuller. The United States would, in Child's view, be the final melting pot of all the best feminine ideals culled through time in the world-museum.

History, however, especially history concerned with woman's role in time, seemed to be the main refuge of intellectual women, if they did not turn to literary criticism, translation, or schoolteaching. Elizabeth Ellet wrote three impressive works celebrating the "creative spirited" woman: *The Women of the American Revolution* (two volumes, 1848), *Pioneer Women of the West* (1852), and most important, *Women Artists in All Ages and Coun-*

tries (1859). In these works, she traced the origins of a true artistic culture to domestic handicraft and the feminine mystique, positing a law that culture is most artistic when it spawns the greatest number of female artists. Ellet was soon joined by Elizabeth Oakes Smith, wife of comic "downeastern" writer Seba Smith, creator of the Major Jack Downing burlesques of Andrew Jackson. In *Woman and Her Needs* (1851), Elizabeth Oakes Smith celebrated the new machine age in contrast with the chivalric age of handicraft. The machine culture had at long last freed women to be "women of thought"—true intellectuals—if only society would sanction it. She declared, "The idea of a true noble womanhood is yet to be created. It does not live in the public mind."

Other paths toward intellectual womanhood were those taken by Elizabeth Peabody, whose bookstore formed the Transcendentalists' salon and whose translations from French and German were crucial conduits for continental thought as it flowed into America, and Sarah Whitman of Providence, Rhode Island, who proved to be the shrewdest literary critic of the day. Whitman, a strikingly handsome woman, was once engaged to the beguiling Edgar Allan Poe. But his infidelity, drunkenness, profligacy, and penchant for creating an abusive scene in public soon canceled plans for the wedding. Instead, she sought fulfillment by producing some of the most lucid and insightful critical essays on the literature and philosophy published in the entire era. Her essay on Ralph Waldo Emerson, published in June 1845 in the *United States Magazine and Democratic Review*, not only provided the best analysis of Emerson's philosophy, an elusive subject at best, but also supplied a comprehensive account in detail of the whole German romantic movement from Immanuel Kant through Johann Fichte, Friedrich von Schelling, and Baruch de Spinoza.

III

Complete women's rights were not even approached in the nineteenth century, though some states, such as New York, altered their unjust laws in the antebellum period. Even the Nineteenth Amendment, giving women the vote in 1926, did not really redress the balance, nor did it make for the "unity of all mankind." It simply carried forth a revolution of rising expectations that by the twenty-first century has brought women's prospects to the point of dominance. This revolution of rising expectations had its beginnings over a whole range of activities in the early nineteenth century, but in none so characteristic as the exchange of tea parties between Lucretia Mott and Elizabeth Cady Stanton, in Seneca Falls and Auburn, New York, in the summer of 1848. Their teatime tête-à-têtes represented the latent power of women out of which came the first Women's Rights Convention, appropriately in July 1848, in which the women issued their own Declaration of Independence. It was the beginning of the end of male chauvinism. Soon the women became organized and institutionalized along political lines.

The pathbreaking Women's Rights Convention met July 19–20, 1848, at the Wesleyan church in Seneca Falls, New York. It included approximately three hundred people, including Frederick Douglass and James Mott, who presided over the convention. Its Declaration of Sentiments and Resolutions, written by Elizabeth Cady Stanton, began by paraphrasing the Declaration of Independence.

> We hold these truths to be self-evident: that all
> men and women are created equally: that they are
> endowed by their creator with certain inalienable
> rights: that among these are life, liberty and the
> pursuit of happiness.

She later added, "The history of mankind is a history of repeated injuries and usurpation on the part of men towards women, having as a direct object the establishment of and absolute tyranny over her." Then followed sixteen bills of particulars against men and twelve resolutions. Only one hundred of those present signed the Sentiments and Resolutions, but an organized women's rights movement had begun that took until 1926, and an amendment to the Constitution, to gain women the right to vote.

IV

Equal rights were not the only political issues that preoccupied American women in the nineteenth century. One of the most remarkable, if now half-forgotten, American women was Jane Storm McManus, who was interested in American expansionism. In the course of her public career—which she seems to have had little difficulty fashioning, in contrast with the self-conscious angst of Margaret Fuller—McManus was a female filibuster, impresario, land speculator, spy, confidential agent of the U.S. government, revolutionary, reformer, newspaper editor, foreign correspondent, author, and perhaps the most active woman of intrigue in North America.

Born near Troy, New York, in 1807, the daughter of an Irish Catholic lawyer, McManus seems to have grown up with the Albany Regency and Jacksonian politics. In 1823 she married her father's legal assistant, William Storm, with whom she had a child. But somewhere along the line both husband and child dropped out of her life, and in 1825 she turned up in Washington with her father, who had been elected to Congress. Since she was quite beautiful, McManus made political contacts easily. The most influential of these was Aaron Burr. A man of advanced age, Burr still burned with Texas schemes, and in 1832 he convinced McManus to go to Texas as his agent in a plan to settle German immigrants on a Mexican land grant. In November of that year, she sailed for New Orleans with her brother, a surveyor. They were bound for Texas by another ship. Something of Burr's enthusiasm for her is reflected in a letter of introduction he sent to Judge James Workman in Texas. He wrote, "She will be able to send out one or two hundred substantial settlers in less time and with better selection than any man or half a dozen men whom I this day know."

In the following year, McManus turned up in Matagorda Bay with the German immigrants who promptly deserted her and set up a colony of their own. While in Matagorda, McManus, who was traveling as Mrs. McManus, met William Cazneau, a Bostonian who would someday change her life. In the meantime, back in New York, McManus had become something of a celebrity. She had been named as correspondent in Eliza Jumel's spectacular divorce proceedings against Burr, then in his late seventies. McManus was implicated because a servant girl claimed to have caught her and the aged warrior in flagrante delicto, to which McManus, according to testimony, exclaimed, "Oh la! Mercy we are undone!" McManus was in Texas at the time, but Jumel won her divorce suit anyhow. She also made McManus a notorious woman. In 1838 in Texas, Colonel Ira Lewis was forced to challenge six men to duels on her behalf.

By 1835 McManus had returned to New York to raise funds for the Texas independence movement. "I would with joy contribute my mite to purchase arms for her brave defenders," she wrote Joseph Powers in October 1835. Soon thereafter she became a correspondent for the *Washington Star* and shortly afterward for Moses Yale Beach's *New York Sun*, the most militant expansionist paper of the day. In her articles for the *Sun*, McManus urged the immediate annexation of Texas. Her many articles appeared under the pen name "Cora Montgomery." During this period she maintained her friendship with Colonel Cazneau, who had fought alongside her brother at San Jacinto, and she became fast friends with the romantic third president of Texas, Mirabeau B. Lamar, who not only called upon her during a visit to Washington, but also dedicated his first published book of poems to her. Shortly afterward, she memorialized Lamar and deprecated his archrival, Sam Houston, in an article, "The Presidents of Texas," which appeared in John L. O'Sullivan's *United States Magazine and Democratic Review*. She also coined the term Manifest Destiny.

The Mexican War proved to be a high point in McManus's career of intrigues. From William Cazneau she learned that the Catholic Church interests in Mexico were willing to make a separate peace. This news she communicated to Archbishop John T. Hughes and then to Moses Yale Beach. James K. Polk, anxious to end the war on his terms (rather than those of his Whig generals), commissioned Beach as a secret envoy to the defectionists in Mexico. When Santa Anna learned of Beach's secret meetings in Mexico, McManus, as a spy, was forced to flee through enemy lines to General Winfield Scott's camp at Veracruz, where she urged him to continue fighting and told him the dictator planned to make a stand at Cerro Gordo. In the meantime, both she and Beach had developed a strong interest in the annexation of Cuba and the acquisition of a canal route across the Isthmus of Tehuantepec. In addition, possibly through her connection with Cazneau, she favored the detachment of the north Mexican provinces from that country and the creation of the Republic of the Rio Grande. In her dispatches to the *New York Sun*, which were a regular feature, she urged all these causes and was highly critical of Polk's conduct of both the war and diplomacy. For example, she wrote in July 1846:

The President has two paths, each leading to mighty results. . . . He may hew Mexico to fragments with the edge of his sword and take what share he pleases of the pay, or he may cease to war on the helpless and unoffending portion of the Confederacy and plant deep and strong the tree of liberty in the midst of a new and grateful republic. It is certain we would have had no war if our army had not been sent to look it up; but since we have one we must make its conclusion such as will prove to the world the resistless energy of republicanism. . . . This new republic of the Rio Grande would be of high advantage to the United States.

But Polk did not heed her words, and a State Department clerk named Nicholas P. Trist concluded a not altogether satisfactory treaty with Mexico in 1848—the Treaty of Guadalupe Hidalgo—that secured California, Texas, New Mexico, Arizona, Utah, and Nevada for $14 million in claims against Mexico.

By this time, McManus had begun to concentrate more and more on Cuban annexation. She stepped up her propaganda barrage in the *Sun* and issued two pamphlets extolling Cuba's virtues and their value for Americans, titled *The King of the Rivers* and *The Queen of the Islands.* The juxtaposition of the Mississippi with the "pearl of the Antilles" was not accidental, though it may also have entailed a Freudian slip. Beyond these efforts McManus became editor of *La Verdad,* a Spanish-language paper printed by Beach, whose sole purpose was to propagandize for Cuban annexation.

Then suddenly, in 1850, McManus abandoned her Cuban schemes, left for Texas, married William Cazneau, and went to live in an adobe and sod house on the Rio Grande at Eagle Pass, Texas. It seems clear that she and Cazneau had not abandoned their plans to promote a "republic of the Rio Grande." She had become a female Aaron Burr, and as with Burr, her plans did not work out. They had some promise, however, because at that time the U.S. Boundary Commission, in surveying the treaty line between the two countries, learned that in his treaty Trist had bargained away the only feasible southern transcontinental railroad route. Three years of negotiations ensued, but no north Mexican revolution was forthcoming, and instead aging General James Gadsden purchased what he erroneously believed to be the necessary railroad right of way from Santa Anna, who pocketed the money. McManus published a book, *Eagle Pass or Life on the Border* (1855), lamenting that the government had been so blind. "Here is the great track," she wrote, "to the Pacific which the government, with the grave and solemn blindness of an owl is looking for everywhere else." This was an obvious reference to the great Pacific Railroad Surveys of 1853–1855.

Disappointed with the failure of the north Mexican scheme, the planned annexation of Cuba, and failure to secure the rights to Tehuantepec, Mc-Manus left Texas and fastened her hopes for the rest of her life on securing Santo Domingo. At the same time, she was an ardent supporter of William Walker in Nicaragua. The Santo Domingo affair was her longest one, however. Several times she and her husband almost secured the establishment of a coaling station there, or even annexation, only to fail, right up through the Grant administration, when she worked hand-in-glove with the cunning Orville Babcock to annex Santo Domingo. In the end the Cazneaus were disappointed, and all McManus had to show for her efforts were three more books: *Our Winter Eden: Pen Pictures of the Tropics* (written in the 1850s but published in 1878), *In the Tropics by a Settler in Santo Domingo* (1863), and a novel, *The Prince of Kashna: A West Indian Story* (1865). The latter was the story of a young African chieftain illegally kidnapped by British slavers and brought to Jamaica. She heard the story from the boy himself, in what amounted to an earlier version of *Roots*.

McManus's dreams were not like those of most scribbling women of her time. Her three years in a sod house in Eagle Pass seem the closest she ever came to domesticity. Instead, the "excitability" of the harsh world of politics, commerce, war, and chicanery seemed to fascinate her and to drive her on. She was a unique person for any time, not least her own. She believed firmly in the Manifest Destiny of the United States. She was an ardent republican who did not believe in slavery, despite her support of William Walker. She considered herself a reformer who not only would bring free republican institutions to the tropics and to Mexico via annexation, but also would reform the Catholic Church by turning it from autocracy and greed to republicanism and Americanization. She was quite unlike Margaret Fuller—clearly more at home in the world—yet she found a strangely similar fulfillment. It was thus appropriate that she came to a strangely similar end. She went down with the steamer *Emily B.*

Souder in a hurricane off Cape Hatteras in December 1878. By that time she was forgotten and not lamented as was the mighty Fuller. Instead she appeared in a New York newspaper's list of casualties as "Mrs. William Cazneau, resident of Jamaica."

The infinite potentialities of nineteenth-century women are perhaps best illustrated by the colorful careers of the lively and beautiful Claflin sisters of Ohio, whose activities stretched out over the nineteenth century and into the farthest reaches of international mass revolution. Born the daughters of Reuben Claflin, who was run out of Hamer, Ohio, for committing arson, Victoria and her sister, Tennessee Celeste Claflin (who changed her name to Tennie C. Claflin), began their careers as professional spiritualists who regularly conferred with Demosthenes and other figures of the past. At age sixteen, Victoria married Dr. Canning Woodhull and he traveled with the family through the South putting on mesmeric shows, selling the Elixir of Life and "curing" cancer. In time Victoria and Tennie C. became the most famous clairvoyants in the country, and Dr. Woodhull was abruptly replaced by a gentleman named James C. Blood. The sisters and their entourage soon caught the eye of Cornelius Vanderbilt, for whom they recalled lost spirits while he set them up in a successful stock brokerage business. This led them quite unnaturally to socialism, and in 1870 they launched the socialist journal *Woodhull & Claflin's Weekly*, which advocated equal rights for women, free love, and a common standard of morality for men and women. The *Weekly* also proposed Woodhull as the first female candidate for president in 1870, and by 1872 she was the official Equal Rights Party candidate for that office. At the time, she gained added publicity by exposing the sordid affair between New York's most famous clergyman, Henry Ward Beecher, and the wife of a young reporter, Henry Tilton. Beecher, of course, was ruined, while Woodhull managed to carry on her own affair with Henry Tilton for at least six months.

Meanwhile, *Woodhull & Claflin's Weekly*, though financed by Vanderbilt, pioneered the publication of the works of Karl Marx and Friedrich Engels in the United States. Soon after, Woodhull was admitted as an official delegate to the first Communist International, where she was expelled as a result of the strenuous efforts of the chauvinist Marxist leader Frederick Sorge at the Hague Congress of the International Working Men's Association. Thus after a time she symbolized the International to workers all over

America, joyously leading parades of French Communards up Fifth Avenue. Then Vanderbilt died, and the commodore's family paid off the sisters. They sailed for England where, by coincidence, one married a titled banker and the other a Portuguese viscount. Nevertheless, by the end of the century they were still fighting for women's rights. In 1892, aided by her daughter Zulu Maud Woodhull, Victoria Woodhull launched the *Humanitarian*, another journal dedicated to the unity of all mankind. As far as women's rights and potentialities were concerned, the Claflin sisters provided a fascinating link between the early days of freedom's bitter ferment and women's more or less permanent liberation.

CHAPTER SEVENTEEN

Utopian Ideas

In the nineteenth century, Utopianism and Romantic social experimentalism ran at high tide. Many Americans were impatient with the workings of established institutions, especially government. They looked upon the new republic as the land of social experimentation, establishing their own self-contained Utopian communities that ran counter to many traditional and individualistic values. Immense tracts of unsettled, inexpensive land beckoned to the visionary reformers of Europe and the oppressed peoples they represented. Throughout the colonial period, beginning with the German pietists who settled the backcountry of Pennsylvania in the seventeenth century, Utopians of one sort or another saw America as the land of the future. Rarely, however, were these new communities inspired by native settlers; rather, they were primarily projections of European visionaries, with the exception of Joseph Smith's large-scale success in Mormonism. Thus, in one sense, the social upheavals of Europe, the desperate dreams of the persecuted and downtrodden, were projected onto nineteenth-century America. This increased the social ferment of the period and heightened the tendency to think in terms of grandiose models, symbols, large generalizations, climactic events, and a coming millennium that was so characteristic of the days of Jonathan Edwards and the First Great Awakening, which preceded the American Revolution. The rhythm and lifestyle of the Utopians were anything but pragmatic. They were usually out to change the world in one bold stroke—in the spirit and very often the strident tones of Tom Paine and the French revolutionaries or the high-flying German Romantics.

As early as 1683, almost a century before the American Revolution, Francis Daniel Pastorius, one of the most learned men of his time, led a colony of German immigrants to America, where they settled down together in Germantown, Pennsylvania. He was followed by Johann Jacob Zimmerman, a former Lutheran preacher famous for his astrological knowledge. Zimmerman had convinced his followers that the stars indicated the end of the world was coming in 1694, so they set off for America in a pious community to await that glorious event in Edenic surroundings. Magister Johannes Kelpius, a friend of Zimmerman's, believed that the true church was symbolized by a woman, so he took his followers to Wissahickon, Pennsylvania, where they built a tabernacle and scanned the sky for signs of a woman descending from heaven on the wings of an eagle. The colony came to be called the Woman in the Wilderness. In 1719, German Baptists under Peter Becker and Alexander March founded the Dunker, or Dunkard, community, while in 1735 Johann Conrad Beissel, Becker's assistant, moved off to found a celibate colony called Ephrata. The Ephratans practiced extreme self-denial, eschewed the use of metal, worked like draft animals from dawn till dusk, refrained from unnecessary conversation, and awaited the millennial coming of the Lord. All of these groups, however, did produce folk art, music, and even creative religious tracts, including a Mennonite martyrology, the *Ninety-nine Mystical Sentences* (1730), printed at Ephrata, and Beissel's *Godly Chants of Love and Praise* (1730). That the millennium did not come seemed not to discourage the early German pietists, and sects such as the Dunkards and Mennonites persist even today. Perhaps symbolic of one sort of millennium, however, a Dunkard church stood at the strategic center of the swirling, desperate combat at Antietam, a turning point of the Civil War.

The most important figure of early American Utopianism was Mother Ann Lee—the founder of the United Society of Believers in Christ's Second Appearing. Born in Manchester, England, in 1736, Lee was forced early into marriage by her family. She found the sex act revolting and saw four children die at birth. From the beginning her life was traumatic. In addition to her sexual problems, she and her family belonged to a revivalistic offshoot of Quakerism that was given to frenzied manifestations of God's divine grace. They came to be called Shakers. Lee herself commenced to see visions and to communicate with God and the spirits. This made her a special holy personage or prophet of the group and the target of abuse from her orthodox neighbors in England. She was stoned, jailed, and stood trial before a court of the Church of England, where it is said she confounded her accusers by speaking in seventy-two languages.

Lee had two important visions while in England. One traced original sin to the sexual relations between Adam and Eve in the Garden of Paradise and therefore moved her to declare celibacy the only moral way of life; the other, a vision of a tree, inspired her to take her followers to America, which she did in 1774. Settling first in Watervliet, New York, the Shakers began to seek converts. Between 1781 and 1783, following the trauma of the Revolutionary War, Lee and other Shakers traveled up and down the East Coast gaining many converts. The converts came at great price, however, as mobs abused them wherever they went. Lee died as a result of a mob in 1784.

Lee did, however, inspire Jemima Wilkinson, who also had visions and styled herself the "Universal Public Friend." Wilkinson introduced even more spiritualism into the Shaker religion because she believed she had died and returned to earth as a spirit. Ever afterward the Shakers believed they lived in a world of spirits and that they could call back the spirits of the dead. They themselves were not certain whether they were dead or alive. In short, they introduced extraordinary mystery into the religious revivalism of the Second Great Awakening. The Shakers also believed in the bisexuality of God—that is, both male and female were created in his image, as was everything in the world's animal and vegetable kingdom. Christ himself had entered Lee's body, while John the Baptist inhabited the flesh of another Shaker seer, Jane Wardly. Further, they believed the Day of Judgment had already taken place, thus they were living in a world already redeemed. The Shaker Church, it was said, was "upstairs above the rudimental state of men," one of the lower plateaus of heaven itself. But to maintain the ecstasy and privacy of this state they had to band together in a holy community free from the corruptions of the world. They espoused a doctrine of Christian communism. By 1830, when it reached its zenith, the Shaker religion had some five thousand members grouped in fifty-eight "families" living in eighteen separate communities.

Although they were given to ecstasy, wild dances, and trancelike frenzy as the spirits descended upon them, the Shakers normally lived a plain and frugal, even tranquil life in their communities. This is clearly indicated by the sunny, well-lit, yet unadorned and calm style of the architecture of their commune buildings. It is also evident in their spare but elegant furniture. Each Shaker craftsman took his time in an age that was otherwise given to haste. He was living in a kind of continuous present—an already resurrected state, something like Adam and Eve in Paradise—so time was not a factor. Death itself was a scarcely noticeable change since the world of departed spirits freely intermingled with those of the people temporarily inhabiting the earthly communes. As one writer put it, "All the Patriarchs, Prophets and Martyrs came to the Shakers, announcing that they had joined the Shaker Church. Alexander, Napoleon, Washington, and Franklin—to mention only four men of a different calibre—were frequent visitors." The Shakers' Utopian communities were to them but outward signs of a spirit world—a part of heaven where they enjoyed serenity and ecstasy in equal measure, and enormous power over life as we know it. They could perform miracles, heal the sick, foretell the future, and experience surprisingly beautiful visions. However, because of their commitment to celibacy, they found it difficult, if not impossible, to perpetuate themselves or their religion.

In 1804, more German communitarians started to arrive in America, thus beginning a phenomenon that continued throughout most of the nineteenth century. George Rapp, a pietist, brought six hundred followers, and Joseph Baumeler came with two hundred Separatists in 1817. Rapp and his people were farmers and not intellectuals who wished to pursue as closely as possible the social life in the New Testament. They settled first north of Pittsburgh on five thousand acres and in 1805 organized themselves into the Harmony Society, which featured patriarchal government and community property. The latter was adopted because many of their members were too old to work. By 1807 they adopted a rule of celibacy. However, harmony was a good term for the Rappites. They lived and worked hard together while at the same time enjoying the good plain

things of life, especially wine, food, and music. Rapp himself was a benevolent dictator who took great interest in the everyday details of the community and set its tone with his jolly humor.

The community prospered. In 1814 it acquired thirty thousand acres of
land in the Wabash Valley of Indiana, and by 1815 the whole community
had moved. Harmony, Indiana, became an important frontier trading center for nearly ten years before the Rappites sold it to the English Utopian
Robert Dale Owen. Its only drawback was its unhealthy malarial climate.
So in 1825 the Rappites again moved to a new community, which they
called Economy, north of Pittsburgh, but on the Ohio River, where again
they prospered until 1831, when Bernhard Muller arrived and created a
great schism. Muller, who called himself Count Maximilian de Leon,
sowed seeds of discord and eventually drew off one-third of the Rappites to
a disastrous end in a Utopia near Natchitoches, Louisiana. The "Count"
died and his followers scattered. In the meantime, Rapp was succeeded by
his able adopted son, Frederick, and the original Rappite community lasted
until the end of the nineteenth century.

The Rappites' doctrines were not really very esoteric. A pietistic and
fundamentalist offshoot of Lutheranism, the sect aimed toward harmony
by doing away with the invidiousness of hierarchical government in both
church and civil state. Rather, they were like an extended family ruled by
such patriarchs as George Rapp. Communal ownership was a necessity
forced upon them by demographic circumstance. What they had really
done was establish a plain, pious German dukedom in America's land of
abundance.

Joseph Baumeler, who established the Zoar Community in Ohio, was far
less easygoing than George Rapp. From the beginning, solemnity prevailed
over Zoar. Baumeler was constricted by a bureaucracy of his own making as
Zoar was incorporated like a company under a board of trustees who administered all property in common. The Zoarites seemed much more concerned with the organization of people and property than they did with
their religion, which had so few doctrines as to be almost invisible. They
had no clergy and did not practice audible prayer or recognize any sacra-
ments. Their only religious books were the Bible, a few hymnals, and 2,574
pages of discourses by Baumeler, who did not claim to be a prophet. In
short, there was no mysticism to their religious experiments. Rather, it

seemed corporate and economic in nature, yet by comparison with the Rappites' Harmony and Economy, it fared relatively badly even though it, too, lasted until the end of the century. At Zoar something new had happened. Instead of transplanting completely a German social unit to America, the Zoarites came to the new country and adopted many of the emerging business practices of the day. This came to be characteristic of many Utopian ventures.

For example, onetime Rappite Peter Kaufmann adopted a modified capitalism in his "labor-for-labor" store in Philadelphia in the 1820s. Instead of using money, however, he kept records of the labor expended in making certain items and used these labor measurements for the standards of exchange value. Later he moved west and, taking his labor-store concept with him, founded a colony near Cincinnati based on the idea called the United Germans of Teutonia. It was a short-lived community due to the fact that its members soon were integrated into the bustling city of Cincinnati, but it was fondly remembered by that city's German pioneers. In similar fashion, Henry Brokmeyer, one of the founders of the St. Louis Hegelian movement in 1858, sketched out a German Lutheran Utopia in his *Mechanic's Diary*, in which new settlers would be placed on land Brokmeyer loaned them. For a number of years, much of this land would be held in common by the farming community and administered by the local Lutheran minister. Brokmeyer's Utopia—a post–Civil War vision—had gradually moved almost completely into capitalist mode.

Not only the Germans, but the English and Scots as well were interested in America as a possibility for experiments in living. As early as 1795, Samuel Taylor Coleridge and his friend Robert Southey met at Cambridge to plan a community in America—hopefully on the Susquehanna, because Coleridge the poet liked the melodious name. They called their venture Pantisocracy, and it embodied the lofty principal of "aspheterism." The former meant democratic government, while the latter meant the community of property. For a time the two Romantic poets were captivated by the idea—twelve idyllic couples in the wilderness on the shores of the sweetly flowing Susquehanna, sharing everything in common, but nobody working too hard in nature's abundance. Such a life would leave time for study, contemplation, and poetry. Their dream gradually faded, however. Coleridge did not like Sarah Fricker, the mate his partners had picked out for him. He became sensitive to the fact that his friends and relatives thought him mad and would contribute no support for the venture. He began to hedge and suggested a tryout in Wales instead—a kind of Walden Pond experience—but to no avail. Finally, however, Southey burst the Pantisocratic bubble by secretly eloping with Edith Fricker and his uncle to Lisbon, Portugal, in November 1795.

In the 1820s the English radical Fanny Wright also tried to launch an American Utopia. She settled in Nashoba, a Tennessee Utopia designed to educate and emancipate black slaves. For a while she made the racially mixed venture work through sheer force of her formidable personality. But when she left it for a time, the newspapers delighted their readers with details of communal interracial free love. It was more than public opinion could stand, and after 1827 Nashoba, hacked out of the swamps and wilderness with such high hopes, collapsed. Clearly the energetic Wright had too many Utopian reforms operating at once with too little public support.

The most ambitious, if not pretentious, of the English reformers was wealthy philanthropist Robert Dale Owen. Flush with success after organizing Scottish workers communities at New Lanark, Owen proposed to reform rude America and then the world in the same way. He was ever a man for the grand generalization, the grand plan, the mere utterance of which seemed aimed to stun the House of Commons if not the czar of Russia and the Congress of Sovereigns at Aachen, to whom he addressed his lofty plans on behalf of humanity. By the spring of 1825 he had purchased George Rapp's community at Harmony, Indiana, and christened it—New Harmony! In the great hall there he announced pretentiously, "I am come to this country to try and introduce an entire new system of society; to change it from an ignorant, selfish system to an enlightened social system which shall gradually unite all interests into one, and remove all causes for contest between individuals." He felt that in three years he could reform America. In fact, he had carefully explained his plan to the president of the United States.

Owen's plans were primarily architectural. With his vast wealth he planned to house his ideal communities in structures of Romantic design built around courtyards, 1,000 feet on either side. The buildings would include a chapel, a library, lecture halls, laboratories, a ballroom, committee rooms, reading rooms, common rooms, and recreation rooms along with the usual kitchens, stables, laundries, and living apartments. Such structures sounded suspiciously like the colleges at Oxford or Cambridge, as if Owen wished to project on America the cloistered environments of those institutions of learning on a grand scale. This was, of course, possible in his view because environment made the man or woman, and what better environment than those hallowed temples of learning could be found for the training of rational citizens? The architectural drawings of Stedman Whitwell clearly reveal Owen's "collegiate" vision. But first Owen started with New Harmony. A vague constitution was drafted, and the doors were thrown open to the "industrious and well-disposed of all nations." Then the founder departed for Europe while the ragtag and bobtail of America poured in to sample his largesse. Generally they were subject to a board of directors or committee of control and ordered to begin building the celestial city. Immediately a newspaper, the *New Harmony Gazette*, sprang into being to propagandize the climactic venture.

In the winter of 1826, Owen returned with a company of scholars to staff his "college" in the wilderness. This group included Thomas Say, the Philadelphian who had discovered the principle of fossil dating, and who was now America's foremost entomologist. It also included the Scotsman William Maclure, a founder of American geology and president of the Philadelphia Academy of Natural Sciences; Charles Alexander Lasueur, a French naturalist who had been to Australia; Dr. Gerard Troost, who later conducted the State Geological Survey of Tennessee; three Pestalozzian teachers; and the eccentric naturalist Constantine Rafinesque. As a college faculty it may have been one of the best in America for its time, but a Utopian community on the edge of civilization was hardly an ideal working milieu. Almost immediately the testy Maclure broke with Owen and attempted to start his own Utopian venture geared solely toward Pestalozzian education, while Owen was aiming at changing the whole environment.

Between 1825 and 1830, though New Harmony was the focus, more than a dozen Owenite communities were formed. Few of them were successful, however, because there really was no master plan beyond Owen's vague environmental philosophy. Various classes of people did not mix well with one another. Few cared to indulge in the harder tasks, such as farming, and even more were simply opportunists hoping to live off the philanthropist's largesse. Owen never succeeded in replacing American

competitive individualism with the harmony and cooperation of communi-
tarianism. He had simply shifted the marketplace to his pocketbook. Thus,
as suddenly as they sprang into being, the Owenite communities collapsed
and were done by 1830. "The most ambitious and inclusive" Utopian experiment seen in America up to that time, Owen's achievements were nil in
the social realm. America was not New Lanark. His primary achievements,
however, were in the fields of education, as one might expect. Owen helped
introduce the Pestalozzian and kindergarten teaching methods to America.
He also developed the self-governing, or "free," school later made popular
by the St. Louis Hegelian Denton J. Snider, and he promoted Indiana's
public school system. Finally, he contributed to the cause of women's rights
as a member of the Indiana legislature, changing the divorce laws and le-
galizing property ownership for women. This, too, was a form of education. It was clear, however, that the projection of the English manor or the
British university onto a teeming, opportunity-filled America that was just
beginning to move west would not do. The tide of competition in Jacksonian America ran too strong and Owen had not even a religious principle or
a mystical philosophy with which to meet it. He had underestimated the
challenge of America.

Next it was the turn of the French, who brought to America a philosophy of true Utopianism—the sweeping mystical cosmology of Charles
Fourier. The son of a wealthy merchant and impoverished by the French
Revolution, Fourier had a grand global dream for reorganizing mankind.
Day and night in garret rooms or meager dens he dreamed his dream,
which, when published as his collected writings, ran to six volumes. "I
alone comprehend the true plan and the means of fulfilling it," he repeatedly asserted. Fourier's plan worked on the principle of gravity. Newton's
laws suggested to him that there must be a law of attraction for everything
in the universe, hence the universe must be innately harmonious. Moreover, if for every action there is an equal and opposite reaction, then among
men social roles despised by some will be relished by others. Also the human personality oscillates, and tasks that at one time are deemed repellant
will another time seem pleasant as the personality rights or balances itself.
All preferences are controlled by the passions, and Fourier made an exhaustive catalogue or taxonomy of these in the true spirit of the Second
Great Age of Discovery.

The organization and harnessing of the passions was the key to successful reform of the world. The idea was to organize all people so they took pleasure in everything they did. To accomplish this, people had to be broken down into groups of seven. In a group would be two wings of two each, representing respectively "ascending" and "descending" tastes and preferences. The middle three provided equilibrium. These groups were then related to all human occupations in a great organized division of labor. They clustered to form a larger number called a Series. Then the Series were in turn clustered to form the optimum social unit—the Phalanx, numbering exactly 1,750 persons covering a living area of about three square miles divided between all the major occupations like a planned greenbelt town. Dominating the landscape was a large building, balanced with a center and two wings, called a Phalanstery. This structure, reminiscent of a monastery, would house the entire Phalanx. The visionary Frenchman pictured Phalanxes spread out over the whole earth to number exactly 2,985,984. The capital of the world would be Constantinople, the ruler an Omniarch assisted by 3 Augusts, 12 Caesarians, 48 Empresses, 144 Kalifs, and 576 Sultans. Clearly, Fourier's mind was swayed by the appeal of Oriental exoticism as much as by the balanced concepts of Isaac Newton. This extraordinary combination of extreme "ratiocination" and exotic visions is somewhat reminiscent of the fevered mind of Poe. It further suggests that the paradoxes generated by the "information revolution" were by no means confined to America alone. They were endemic to western civilization.

The Fourier Phalanxes were not totally communal ventures as far as property was concerned. Rather, they were joint stock subscription enterprises. One did not even need to be a member or a resident of the Phalanx to hold shares in it. Accounts were kept of work done, and at the end of the year profits were divided according to a ratio of five-twelfths to labor, four-twelfths to capital, and three-twelfths to skill or talent. All resident members of each Phalanx could change work roles whenever they chose lest life become too monotonous. Thus work became, in a sense, play. Children who scavenged among the refuse heaps and led cleanup campaigns were to be celebrated in true Rousseau fashion as the culture heroes. They led all of the many parades scheduled and received the Salute of Esteem in Fourier's child-worshipping society.

Fourier's cosmology was equally interesting, if bizarre. Nothing better illustrates the confusion over scientific information that dominated the period than does the fantasizing of his fevered pseudoscientific imagination. Everything in the universe Fourier saw in anthropomorphic terms. Everything, even the stars and the planets, had passions, could fall in love, and could even reproduce. They passed through human stages of growth and even died. The moon, he insisted, contracted a fever from the earth just before the Great Flood and died. Planets had an average life of eighty thousand years, composed of thirty-two subdivisions, of which the earth was in the fifth period. In the eighth period, docility and harmony would reign. The earth would be suffused with perfumed dew. New moons would appear. The oceans would turn to lemonade. Men would grow tails with eyes, and wild animals would suddenly become loving "anti-beasts." In short, the optimistic Fourier envisioned the future of the earth as one "big rock candy mountain." On October 10, 1837, he was found dead in his miserable room, kneeling at his bedside, hopefully praying for this wonderful cosmillennium.

It is a commentary on the times that his fantasy was taken seriously by hundreds. Phalansteries were set up outside Paris. A newspaper, *Le Phalanstere*, emerged overnight and became a daily with thousands of readers. Fourier's doctrine spread to America through his chief disciple, Englishman Albert Brisbane. In 1840 this dour reformer published a treatise outlining Fourier's ideas titled *The Social Destiny of Man*. He converted the gullible Horace Greeley, whose *New York Tribune* seemed to thrive on fads, and Brisbane became a regular columnist for the paper. He captured the imagination of many of America's leading intellectuals and enlisted their support for what he called his "associationist" philosophy. Phalanxes began to spring up all over the country—principally as a protest against the exploitation of man by man in a work-oriented industrial society. More than anything else they seemed to be a protest against the Protestant work ethic and indeed everything about the common American way of life. The Utopians' superior knowledge would show the way. Clemont, Ohio, saw the planting of a Phalanstery. So, too, did upper New York state, Raritan Bay, Wisconsin, and Red Bank, New Jersey. But the most famous and disastrous Fourier commune was Brook Farm. In April 1844 it became a Phalanx,

which led to its demise in 1846 when the almost-completed grand Phalanstery burned to the ground, leaving the Brook Farmers so hopelessly in
debt as to end the whole venture. George Ripley, who had engineered the
transition to Fourierism, spent most of the rest of his life paying off the
debt. In all, no Fourier experiment lasted longer than twelve years.
Fourier's ideas blazed like a rocket across the western imagination and fiz-
zled out just as quickly. They represented a cosmological and social fire-
works exhibition enjoyed least of all by the genteel souls at Brook Farm.

Fourier's splendid imagination could hardly have been matched, but Eti-
enne Cabet, another Frenchman, rather reluctantly entered the lists in
1839 when he published *Un Voyage en Icarie*. Here was a Utopian novel that
like Fourier's fantasies caught the popular imagination of a France that was
soon to produce Jules Verne. Cabet's book, however, was a vehicle for criti-
cizing the excesses of a capitalist culture and appealed to the emerging
Paris Communards who preferred removal to Utopia than life at the barri-
cades. Reluctantly Cabet was cuffed into glory and persuaded to seek support for an Icarian community in America. In London, a Texas sharper sold
him one million acres of land in the new country for almost nothing. Under the ringing slogans "Travailleurs, allurs en Icarie" and "C'est au Texas"
a party set out for the promised land. When they reached Texas after great
hardships they found the land to be only an unpromising one hundred
thousand acres distributed in alternating squares like a checkerboard.

Certainly it was no place to found Utopia. Giving up on Texas, the ex-
hausted, disappointed Icarians turned north and purchased the deserted
Mormon city of Nauvoo, Illinois, where they flourished for a time under
Cabet's direction. Dissention finally overtook them, however, and the
Icarians split into several factions. Some moved to St. Louis, where Cabet
died of an apoplectic fit. Others settled north of that city at Cheltenham,
while the Nauvoo remnants moved to Corning, Iowa, where the high demand for their glass products generated by the Civil War saved them.
Icaria, strangely enough, survived in one form or another until nearly the
close of the century and it finally reached that mecca of all cults, California, in 1883.

Not all Utopias were products of the European imagination. Oneida, a
religious community dedicated to the gospel of perfectionism, was founded
under interesting circumstances in 1845 in Putney, Vermont, by John

Humphrey Noyes, a graduate of Dartmouth and Yale who had been an unsuccessful traveling minister. Sometime before 1845, Noyes, his wife, his brother, two sisters, and their respective spouses had all settled together in Putney in a family community, hoping to avoid the cruel competition of the marketplace in a bucolic setting. Eventually the community grew and in 1845 they drew up a constitution. The Oneida constitution made all property communal, but the bedrock of the community was its theory of love. To begin with, there was to be no selfishness regarding marriage partners. People were not to be held as property, hence legal marriage, which made women property, was abolished. Variety in sexual partners was encouraged. This was based upon the dual doctrine of love. One kind of love was amative—pleasure. The other kind was propagative—duty. Only through free, amative love could everyone be joined in true harmony. Under the doctrine of what Noyes called "complex marriage," there could be no permanent or "selfish" attachment among partners. All had to circulate freely. Selfishness was punished, though no one quite remembers how. Noyes himself boldly launched the practice of complex marriage when he publicly entered into relations with handsome Mary Cragin, the wife of a fellow Oneidan. Such behavior was frowned upon in bluestocking Vermont, however, and the whole community had to move to Oneida in upstate New York. Some years later, overflowing with success, Noyes opened a second community at Wallingford, Connecticut.

The other aspect of Noyes's gospel, propagative love, was also interesting. Having divorced the propagation of children from everyday sexual activity, the Oneidans decided on a plan for selective breeding called stirpiculture. This doctrine was to have a wide influence. As late as 1888, Victoria Woodhull published a ringing tract on its behalf titled *Stirpiculture, or the Scientific Propagation of the Human Race*. Employing strictly scientific criteria, Noyes and a casting committee matched up couples from some thirty-eight male and fifty-three female volunteers who in Noyes's words, "put aside all envy, childishness, and self-seeking to become martyrs to science and to offer themselves living sacrifices to God and true communism." Noyes added, "Laissez-faire in propagation as in economic affairs is a social wrong." In all, the Oneidans produced some fifty-eight "stirpicults" who were never allowed to have particular parents, but were kept in nurseries or day care centers and schooled by the community.

The government of the community was essentially left to chairman Noyes as a kind of benevolent dictator. He was advised by a number of standing committees representing workers in forty-three separate occupations. These committees were modeled on traditional guild socialism. In addition, mutual criticism or sensitivity sessions were held frequently to break down the ego and any "cult of personality" that might promote competition and selfishness and hence destroy the group's harmony.

Economically, politically, and socially Oneida was successful. The people manufactured beaver traps used by the mountain men, silver, tools, and many useful articles, thus overcoming the main problem of all other Utopian communities—economic insecurity. In addition, members were not disposed to leave the community, perhaps because of religious conviction and the peace it afforded them, or perhaps because they had been so thoroughly integrated into the community through complex marriage that they had difficulty changing their lives even if they wanted to. Some index of the loyalty and conviction that Oneida commanded can be gained from the comment of one female member: "We believed we were living under a system which the whole world would sooner or later adopt." The Oneida community lasted until 1879, a "city on a hill" to those daring idealists who wished to purge the world of selfishness and competition in all things.

One final variety of Utopianism was the combined brainchild of two rather strange American geniuses, Josiah Warren, an orchestra leader and inventor out of Cincinnati, and Stephen Pearl Andrews, an abolitionist and general reformer who styled himself the "Pantarch." Together these two men gave birth to a Utopia of pure individualism. Established in 1851 and finally extinguished in 1857, their anarchistic Utopia—Modern Times— was probably a fitting symbol for the underlying emotions of America on the eve of civil war.

Warren first sparked the idea. Possibly borrowing the concept from Johann Kaufmann, he opened an "equity" store in Cincinnati very similar to Kaufmann's "labor store." Soon it came to be called a "time store" and Warren became the apostle of "equitable commerce." His motto was "Cost the Limit of Price," by which he meant that an article was worth the cost of its materials plus the labor, or time spent making it. He even carried this principle into running his store, since when a customer entered he would set a large time clock and calculate the minutes he spent in the course of his transaction with the customer. This method proved to be so successful in bringing down prices *and* attracting customers that Warren opened another store in New Harmony. Around 1850 he met Stephen Pearl Andrews in New York.

Andrews was immediately taken with Warren's concept and termed him the "Euclid of the Social Sciences." Everywhere he went, even to séances, Andrews proselytized Warren's idea. He joined the Cincinnatian's phrase, "Cost the limit of price," to his own ringing slogan, "The Sovereignty of the Individual," and took to the lecture platform and the printing press. Soon he had published Warren's *Practical Details in Equitable Commerce* and his own *The Science of Society* (1851), which became the first American treatise on anarchy. On the platform he spoke wherever he was invited, especially at Working Men's and Mechanics' institutes, and sometimes where he was not invited. At the Industrial Congress of Working Men, one writer observed, "every time he rose to speak the chairman adjourned the meeting."

Speeches and treatises were not enough, however. Soon, under Andrews's dynamic leadership, the two men planned and laid out a Utopia in the pine barrens of Long Island, New York, near Islip in Suffolk County. The streets were surveyed "square to the meridian." Both men purchased lots and Warren opened still another time store. Andrews became a real estate promoter, and soon a village arose. The first inhabitants were able craftsmen, dissatisfied with their pay and working conditions in New York, so the community was able to quite easily construct the houses and other buildings it needed. Eventually, these sober settlers were joined by a glorious company of cranks—vegetarians, anti-tobacco men, clairvoyants, a phrenologist dentist, a Quaker who believed he was Johnny Appleseed, and one Theron C. Leland, who was hung up on the subject of Pitman's pot hooks. All the while, Andrews insisted on the sacred value of extreme individualism.

Soon more people joined them: Moncure Conway, an abolitionist clergyman who had been one of Georg Wilhelm Friedrich Hegel's prophets in America; Henry Edger, a staunch follower of Auguste Comte and positivism; and Dr. Thomas Low Nichols and his common-law wife, Mary Gove Nichols. The latter particularly intrigued Andrews because they seemed to believe in still another individualistic doctrine he was developing, the defense of free love. In addition to propagating the idea in *New York Tribune* debates with Horace Greeley and Henry James Sr., Andrews published a book titled *Love, Marriage, and Divorce, and the Sovereignty of the Individual* (1853). This book was used by the Nicholses as a text in their American Hydropathic Institute at Port Chester, New York, and they planned Desarrollo, a school at Modern Times. Shortly afterward, Modern Times became the mecca of free love on the eastern seaboard. As one observer declared, "Privacy was general; it was not polite to inquire who might be the father of a newly-born child, or who was the husband or wife of anyone." As Andrews's biographer has explained, Modern Times became a refuge not of "lovers of equity and freedom but of the bizarre," climaxed perhaps by the blind German who regularly walked naked through the streets and the "single-minded woman" who "insisted upon living on beans until she died."

It was by no means Bohemia, or Greenwich Village, or Paris of the 1920s, though perhaps it resembled latter-day Soho. The bizarre did not spawn creativity but rather reflected a certain sense of panic that had come over America in the throes of industrial change. In the late 1850s, as the financial crisis of 1857 indicated, the country, like Modern Times, seemed to lose its poise. The merely absurd rose more and more to the surface as people reached for definitions of not only the Union but also man and the self. Meanwhile, Modern Times as an experiment collapsed into a bourgeois town named Brentwood and most of the whole mad original crew, in the words of actor, singer, and playwright Noël Coward, "sailed away."

Clearly, most Americans were not really ready to accept European models of planned societies. Individualism and the "rage for chaos," or at least the illusion of liberty, dominated the great majority of intellectuals, artists, and common people alike. They were fascinated with the self and its seemingly infinite potential in America—so fascinated that even church, party, government, and union seemed something less than uppermost in their minds. Instead, each had his or her own cause, chosen from the vast smorgasbord of personally gratifying delights culled from the world-museum of infinite experience. Some, such as Andrews or Walt Whitman, espoused every cause. Others narrowed their sights to one. And increasingly in the 1850s, the one cause or question that loomed gigantically over all was that of slavery. Upon this dilemma, postponed improvidently for so long, rested the fate of the Union as a model for world freedom.

CHAPTER EIGHTEEN

Battle Hymns:
Abolition and/or Union

The prime symbol of Northern reform movements, and indeed to most Southerners the very symbol of Northern civilization itself, was William Lloyd Garrison, the sword and shield of abolitionism. Though he was disliked by vast numbers of his cohorts, Garrison in many ways epitomized militant Northern humanitarianism. For one thing, he was an enthusiast for all reforms—supporting peace, temperance, and women's rights, while opposing slavery, tobacco, capital punishment, gambling, theater, Sabbatarianism, and imprisonment for debt. At one time he even investigated the possibility of joining Noyes's Oneida Community. For another thing, he was an internationalist, gaining his first great fame as the antislavery delegate to the 1833 World Anti-Slavery Convention in London and forever afterward maintaining close contacts with European abolitionist thinkers. He was as fanatically dedicated to uncompromising abstract principle as any reformer in America, and yet at the same time he was familiar with the manipulation of organizations for his own purposes. His rhetoric, which some thought excessive, was really the capstone of reform invective against which all others, except perhaps Wendell Phillips and Theodore Dwight Weld, could measure theirs on a descending scale.

Whatever outspoken things needed to be said, Garrison usually said them first and most pointedly. If Sergeant S. Prentiss was the beau ideal of the Southern cavalier, then the gaunt, thin-faced, bespectacled, balding, intense Garrison was certainly the symbol of the crusading Yankee militant.

Garrison was born in 1805 in the seacoast town of Newburyport, Massachusetts, the son of a Baptist mother and an out-of-work, hard-drinking sea-captain father. One day, when Garrison was only three years old, his father deserted the family, leaving the mother and four children in extreme poverty—a poverty from which the members of the family never really recovered. Soon the family was divided, with Garrison's mother and brothers moving to Baltimore while he lived with a Baptist preacher who apprenticed him to the editor of the Newburyport *Herald*. There Garrison learned the newspaper trade, which was his basic profession for the rest of his life.

After failing in a newspaper venture of his own, in 1833 Garrison met the veteran Quaker abolitionist Benjamin Lundy and joined forces with him on the *Genius of Universal Emancipation* abolitionist newspaper. Garrison gave his first antislavery speech on July 4, 1829, at the fashionable Park Street Church in Boston. Two years later he parted company with Lundy in Baltimore when his penchant for outspoken invective involved him in a lawsuit with a slaveholder. To save the paper, Lundy left the city. Garrison remained behind in jail. He was finally rescued by the New York abolitionist silk mogul Lewis Tappan and became his protégé. It was principally Tappan who financed the *Liberator* when Garrison and his partner, Samuel Knapp, began publishing it in Boston in 1831. At first the *Liberator*'s circulation was extremely small, the main body of subscribers being a group of Philadelphia blacks. But Garrison was fortunate. As he exchanged papers with Southern editors, his fiery rhetoric soon came to the attention of opinion-makers all over the South. They were of course outraged, and Georgia placed a $5,000 price on his head. Thus hotheaded Southern editors made him famous—so famous that he quickly became the most prominent man in the antislavery movement and hence appeared in England at the 1833 antislavery convention.

From the outset, Garrison was not above self-advertisement. He knew that, as early as 1831, Tappan had plans to form an American antislavery organization and had already formed a New York organization, but Garrison quickly formed the New England Anti-Slavery Society, and when the national group came into being claimed credit as its founder, though he had nothing to do with it. Besides fighting for reform of all kinds and against Southerners, Garrison also fought continuously to maintain his position as the power in the antislavery crusade, packing meetings with his supporters whenever a showdown appeared imminent. And so it went until his health broke in 1855, though he lived through the Civil War he had helped cause and died in 1870.

Gradually, however, despite his sincerity and energy, Garrison came to seem something of an impediment to the antislavery crusade. His espousal of women's rights split off the whole movement from the clergy, who did not wish women to speak from their pulpits. This forced Garrison and his friend Frederick Douglass to continually attack the churches and the evangelical clergy who would have been their allies. But so sincere was Garrison about including women in the antislavery movement that in 1835 he attended, indeed instigated, the first Boston Female Anti-Slavery Society meeting and suffered for it. He was captured by vigilantes while hiding in a second-floor flat down the street from the meeting, hustled unceremoniously out the second-floor window and down a ladder in full public view, then paraded through the streets with a rope around his neck and lodged in jail. Glad to be alive, he proselytized his cause in prison and wrote on the cell wall:

> William Lloyd Garrison was put in this cell on Wednesday afternoon, Oct. 21, 1835, to save him from the violence of a "respectable and influential" mob, who sought to destroy him from preaching the abominable and dangerous doctrine that "all men are created equal," and that all oppression is odious in the sight of God! Hail Columbia! Cheers for the autocrat of Russia and the Sultan of Turkey!

In 1844 he lost further support among antislavery forces when he refused to back the Liberty Party or any other group that wished to abolish slavery by working through the political system. The Constitution, according to Garrison, was "a covenant with death and an agreement with hell." In 1854 he publicly burned a copy of it in the streets of Boston. By this time he had lost the crucial support of James Birney, Douglass, and thousands of others who wished to use the American political system as a means of terminating the evil of slavery. But Garrison was consistent up until the Civil War. He did not believe in the U.S. government, and, being a pacifist, he was certain that the only way to bring about the end of slavery was through invective, the pressure of public opinion, and the hammer blows of endless exhortation and moral suasion. Though he admired him, he did not even support John Brown and was never informed of the plot by his close friends Thomas Wentworth Higginson and Theodore Parker, who conspired with Brown. Given his inflexible moral principles, Garrison could not support Brown, just as he could not really approve of David Walker's revolutionary *Appeal* back in 1829. And so, after 1850, Garrison began to be less and less important to the abolitionist cause except as a symbol, just as the deceased John C. Calhoun took on a different and greater meaning for the South after 1850. Instead, real leadership shifted to others—Douglass, Birney, Theodore Dwight Weld, Charles Sumner, Higginson, and, most of all, Phillips, who on the eve of the Civil War wrested control of the American and even the New England Anti-Slavery Society from Garrison. The movement had grown too broad for one-man control. The Fugitive Slave Law, part of the Compromise of 1850, did more than all of Garrison's speeches to dramatize to Northerners the aggressive potentialities of slavery and the Southern slave bloc. As they saw poor harassed slaves chased through their towns and villages, as they put up with villainous marshals and bounty hunters, as they read about or even witnessed the murder of abolitionist editor Elijah Lovejoy in Alton, Illinois, the people of the North shifted their opinion, for they realized, as Birney astutely put it, "the question has become not only one of freedom for the African American, but freedom for the white as well." Perhaps the symbolic high tide of this kind of sentiment came in Boston in 1854, when the people had to stand by and watch the sad capture and deportation back to the South of the slave Anthony Burns. It was at this point that Phillips took command.

Other events twisted the knife ever deeper into the Northern conscience. The passage of the Kansas-Nebraska Act in 1854 canceled the 36°30' line between slavery and freedom. And the Dred Scott Decision of 1857, with its inflammatory obiter dicta, made clear that slavery could, and perhaps would, spread to every part of the land.

Meanwhile, though the Liberty Party had failed, the new Free Soil or Republican Party of 1856 stood a chance of success. However, neither Garrison nor Phillips supported it. Nor did they support Abraham Lincoln. Garrison remarked to Oliver Johnson that Lincoln, "if he is six feet four inches high . . . is only a dwarf in mind." And Phillips irrationally called Lincoln the "Slave Hound of Illinois." But strangely, after Lincoln's election, and when the war came, though Phillips continued to assail Lincoln, Garrison did not. He had favored secession of the free states from the Union, and he had favored allowing the "erring Southern sisters to depart in peace." He had been opposed to war and violence in any form and believed the Union was not worth the price. But when the war came he, like so many others, struggled with what Professor George Fredrickson has called an "inner civil war" and ultimately decided to wholeheartedly support the Union cause. Garrison's "inner civil war" was obviously not a casual thing. It meant that, like so many other Northern individualist intellectuals, he finally had to espouse and support the system, even though it went against one part of his divided conscience. Ralph Waldo Emerson, Oliver Wendell Holmes, Horace Greeley, John Greenleaf Whittier, Gerret Smith, and a whole host of Northern intellectuals had to shift their stand from pacifism and the right of peaceful secession to a stand for war and the Union. The consequence was ultimately their long-sought goal—the abolition of slavery.

The lesson Garrison had learned from the Civil War was that it was necessary to have faith in the ultimate goodness of the people. New England elitism and a "dropout" strategy was in the long run ineffective. However, the alacrity with which sizable numbers of New Englanders adopted the idea of secession by one or the other elements of the Union—the slave or the free states—indicates the extreme fragility of the state of American nationalism all over the country right up to the eve of the Civil War. It seems clear that if the South had not seceded, at least some parts of the North might well have done so. If America's Utopian experiment were to have any future at all, by 1861 the Union at last needed clear definition. The millennial future promised in 1787 would take place then or never. Compromise could no longer be achieved by combination, nor union and nationalism by postponing issues until some future date. The Day of Judgment was at hand. What was needed in 1861 was a clearly acceptable annunciation of the nation's overarching moral purposes. This task fell on Lincoln, whose oratory and steadfastness ultimately saved the Union—at the cost of one of the bloodiest wars in history.

I

By the 1850s, as many historians have pointed out, stereotyped sectional views of each other had grown up in both the North and the South. These stereotypes connoted many things that each section believed represented fundamental differences in the respective natures of their individual civilizations. They provided targets for invective from the opposition and therefore heightened emotionalism to a fever pitch, and they provided self-images that were rallying points for allegiance within each of the sections that drew them further and further away from allegiance to the nation-state as a whole.

But what has been overlooked in discussions of the relationship of cultural stereotypes—the Puritans and the Cavaliers—to the rise of sectional nationalism was the fact, evident from the birth of the republic, that at best only the most fragile of nationalistic feelings ever existed. Misled by the outburst of nationalist rhetoric after the War of 1812, some historians have concluded from the evidence that a strong and genuine nationalistic sentiment did in fact exist in the country. Generally, it might be argued that just the opposite was the case. The deliberate creation of anthems and political symbols, of military heroes and monuments, the frantic Fourth of July rhetoric, the calls by intellectuals for a national literature, a national art, and a national language were necessary *because* at the time there existed no true national spirit among the people, and also because they didn't reflect the existence of one. The contrived search for a monumental architecture in public buildings, such as the plan for Washington, D.C., and the deliberate fashioning of every significant institutional building, such as banks, churches, water works, etc., into the image of a Greek or Roman temple was obviously meant to imply the official quality of such institutions and hence their permanence. The Southern planter, when he built his grandiose Greek-pillared farmhouse, dramatically reflected this tendency. It represented role-playing derived not from security but from insecurity. Societal leaders in America had to prove to the masses that there was a nation, there was a culture, there was still a moral New World mission, there were lasting institutions, and that they—politicians, businessmen, and intellectuals alike—were the leaders who should be followed. Even in using nature, American intellectuals and cultural leaders desperately, over and over again, exploited the contrast theme. America was still the favored child of nature. Europe, the metropolis, was growing more corrupt and evil every day. They all protested too much for a nation created by cosmopolitanism.

As early as the Missouri crisis in 1820, Thomas Jefferson, who, trying vainly to form a consensus after an extremely bitter campaign, had even earlier said, "We are all Republicans. We are all Federalists," heard the divisive "fire bell in the night." Fundamentally America was a loosely organized eclectic country whose own history was world history and whose people were free to choose almost any style, tradition, allegiance, occupation, party, or cause they wished. And in most cases their personal choices, on a relatively microcosmic level, took precedence over their emotional commitment to the nation. Even the attempted monumentalism of the Capitol at Washington brought nothing but derision from people who failed to see it as an aid to national cohesion in any sense.

The history of early America in intellectual occupations all across the board is the history of men trying to fashion a uniform, visible national culture and failing by all standards of conventional judgment. America was something new. It was a global and timeless nation—more like an electromagnetic field that attracted billions of highly varied particles in a pattern that constantly shifted with the currents of energy than it was like an enduring monolithic traditional structure. When Whigs, such as Henry Clay with his American System, attempted to structure America in balanced Newtonian fashion according to a very definite theory of regional comparative advantage—the North as manufacturers and merchants, the South as growers of staples, and the West as food producers—the whole system failed because it was too perfect, too structured, and hence confining to American desires. The essence of American culture was not individualism per se, nor "an excess of democracy," but a militant vagueness and an extraordinary receptivity to novelty generated out of the scientific rhythm of the American experience in the Enlightenment period of its founding coupled with the continual fashionstorm of ideas from Europe that America, in contrast with such countries as China and France, never resisted but endlessly welcomed. In a very real sense, it was Lincoln's task, as the crisis leading to civil war mounted, to define a nation that had never really defined itself—a nation whose two great state documents, the Declaration of Independence and the Constitution, were mutually contradictory in principle, and a nation whose political impulse had habitually been compromise by combination, the melding of all points of view into a vague consensus, and the postponement of hard decisions to some future generation. The latter option, so casually espoused by Jefferson, who believed a revolution every generation was a good thing so long as it was not in his own state, was not available to Lincoln. When he came to power in 1861 the revolution, which had rolled on coolly since 1776, was hot and here and now.

II

It is too simple, of course, to assert that Lincoln gave focus to American culture in one short battlefield speech or even a series of public statements. Rather, his whole career as a complete political man seems to have been pointed toward saving the Union. From the time early in his career when he addressed the Young Men's Lyceum of Springfield and spoke of "some man possessed of the loftiest genius, coupled with sufficient ambition," who might possibly rise to lead America, Lincoln seems to have been pre-occupied with giving shape to the country. Even his Whig Party preference suggests that he favored national ordering—an American System—over the frontier disorder he saw all about him. He worshipped Henry Clay, the system-builder and "Great Pacificator." In nearly every one of his speeches, he also hearkened back to the traditionalism and prescriptive wisdom and symbolism of the Founding Fathers.

More than this, Lincoln invariably espoused the cause of the working man and denied that any culture needed "a mudsill class." In 1856, speaking of the John Calhoun–George Fitzhugh "master class" theory, Lincoln asserted:

> They insist that their slaves are far better off than Northern freemen.
> What a mistaken view do these men have of Northern laborers! They

think that men are always to remain laborers here—but there is no
such class. The man who labored for another last year, this year labors
for himself, and next year he will hire others to labor for him.

He further coupled this idea with the demand that the frontier must be
kept open and free for the settlement of free laborers. Slavery could not
spread to Kansas and Nebraska into territory north of 36°30' because it
would threaten free white labor, which could not compete with the slave.
This point formed one of his prime appeals to voters throughout the West.
It was the strength of the Free Soil Party in 1856 and later became a central
Republican tenet. All avenues of economic opportunity for the free white
laborer must be kept open at any cost. Failing to do so would create a class
struggle and with it a true "mudsill class." Lincoln joined the Protestant
work ethic with the cult of success into an assault on the idea of a class
struggle, thus approaching something fundamental in the common American emotion.

The Lincoln-Douglas debates in 1858 gave him a chance not only to
sharpen these views and his own image but also to formulate a gospel of
moral nationalism as opposed to selfish localism. Stephen Douglas, author of
the Kansas-Nebraska Act, espoused the idea of "squatter sovereignty," or the
doctrine that each territory or state should itself locally determine whether it
would be free or slave, which is, of course, just what Southerners were arguing. This fit in well with the loosely defined quality of American attitudes toward national government. It placed Douglas in a position to form a
coalition of Southern Democrats, Northern Democrats, and anti-abolitionist
moderates that in the 1860 presidential election would give him if not a majority at least the necessary plurality of votes to win the presidency.

Lincoln's problem was to create an image of Douglas that would make
such a coalition fail and, at the same time, create an image of himself that
would stamp him as a leader who could not only win but also morally and
justly define the Union and hence save it. To this end, Lincoln made the
following points:

1. Slavery was an evil and ought not to be extended but, as the
   Constitution implied, it should be put on "the path to ultimate
   extinction."

2. The Constitution must be respected. It was the bulwark of the Union and the finest work of the Founding Fathers. Therefore, where slavery was guaranteed by the Constitution, that is, in the Southern states, it must be guaranteed by the national government. But it must not be allowed to spread.

3. Squatter sovereignty was undemocratic because the people in the new territories could vote to enslave a man.

4. If they could vote to enslave a black man, one day they could vote to enslave a white man as well.

5. Slaves in the territories would ruin the territories for free white labor.

6. It was fundamentally undemocratic for a relatively small group of men in a territory to legislate in such a way as to disrupt the whole congressional balance of power in the rest of the country by bringing in a new slave or free state.

7. Though Lincoln favored political equality, he did not favor social equality for blacks.

8. In contrast, Douglas was a moral equivocator. He was the man who "did not care whether slavery was voted up or down." This was ultimately a proslavery position.

In the Freeport Doctrine, Lincoln succeeded in getting Douglas to respond to the Dred Scott Decision by saying that regardless of how the Supreme Court ruled, in the territories "slavery cannot exist a day . . . unless it is supported by local police regulations," thereby making the South suspicious of Douglas as well. He seemed likewise a man of expediency to the North.

Conversely, Lincoln's "House Divided" speech in June 1858 accepting the senatorial nomination made him seem more radical than he really was. Douglas, by continually playing on this speech, swung more and more abolitionists to Lincoln's side. And though he won the senatorial race, Douglas split the fragile parties. In 1860 Lincoln won the four-cornered presidential race because he kept the Northern vote together.

Philosophically he stood on the principles of the Declaration of Independence, declaring repeatedly, "The principles of Jefferson are the definitions and axioms of free society." And he squared the Declaration of Independence with the Constitution in a legalistic way by asserting that nowhere in the Constitution was slavery specifically protected by name. Rather, by terminating the African slave trade after twenty years, the Constitution-makers had actually intended to put slavery on the "course of ultimate extinction."

Though he had won the presidency and, in effect, defined the Union to his own satisfaction, Lincoln had by no means achieved a national consensus for his position. He worked hard and skillfully, however, to fashion a position where national consensus was possible and, in so doing, made clearer a feasible basis for national unity. He, of course, appealed to the prescriptive tradition of the Founding Fathers whenever he could, hoping, in a romantic age, to play sentimentally upon the "mystic chords of memory." He used the tradition of the law built up from the days of John Marshall, asserting that the federal government was sovereign over the states, that the Union was perpetual since nothing in the Constitution provided for its termination, and that no contract (sacred to lawyers and businessmen everywhere) could be broken except by the consent of both parties.

He played on common cultural ties, and he played on practicality. If the South espoused the principle of minority secession, what would prevent endless division among themselves? Moreover, since the states could not physically separate, what problems could better be solved by two nations than one? But ultimately Lincoln, though his principles were sound, failed to keep the Union together for one very simple reason: a true Union had never really existed.

New England had preached secession in the days of the Hartford Convention in 1814–1815. Jefferson and James Madison's *Virginia and Kentucky Resolutions* and Calhoun's *South Carolina Exposition and Protest* had asserted the right of virtual secession in the doctrine of nullification. On several occasions the West threatened to split off in a separate Mississippi Valley republic. Texas, with its own tradition of independence, was but loosely bound to the Union. Jefferson himself saw many sister republics springing up west of the Appalachians to the Pacific. Indeed, the Mormons had already established the kingdom of Zion out west. And the New England and Ohio abolitionists had already sent a constant barrage of appeals for secession to their respective legislatures. Even large numbers of free blacks wanted to secede in one way or another. And, as earlier indicated, many intellectuals began to wonder whether their ancestors had fought on the right side in the American Revolution—whether Europe did not have more promise, more moral grandeur, than "nature's nation."

To a man or woman, with the exception of Walt Whitman and occasionally Emerson, the major writers of the country saw the culture as split, fractured, and essentially tragic, while artistic taste and the art marketplace looked far more to Europe than to America. The new nation had been the creature of a generation of dedicated men, but their successors cared only sporadically for its benefits and traditionally believed "that government is best which governs least." Secession was thus not as traumatic as the bloody Civil War. The Civil War, however, made secession seem much more traumatic. In fact, large numbers of people favored letting the South depart in peace, and if a token war had to be fought, they believed the war would almost certainly be a short one—a kind of honorable joust, almost a sporting event—to decide a matter that was fundamentally of no great consequence in the long run anyhow. Fire-eating Edmund Ruffin, on Charleston's picturesque battery, pulled the lanyard of the cannon aimed at Union Fort Sumter in "high good spirits," and ladies in carriages with picnic baskets drove out to Bull Run in Northern Virginia to see the issue decided in an afternoon. It seems that for a moment of suspended time, only the frantic president, Lincoln, grasped what was really at stake—the potential destruction of a noble world-cultural dream of the perfect society.

And so he consistently refused to recognize that the Southern states had ever seceded, that the experiment in cosmotopian republicanism had ended. Even his victory plans, when he could see the end of the war through the long, dark tunnel, included bringing the Southern states back into the Union virtually as if nothing had happened, except for the emancipation of the slave. For the horror and the bitter, drawn-out fury of the war had pushed Lincoln into a clearer focus on the real nature of America better than anyone had yet achieved since the Revolution. It must indeed be an experiment in freedom—"the birthday of a New World." As such, the Emancipation Proclamation freeing the slaves on January 1, 1863, though imperfect due to the limitations of the president's powers as Commander in Chief, and timed with an eye to political strategy, was inevitable. The conflict was at base truly a moral crusade.

Lincoln made this clear at a short, solemn speech at Gettysburg on November 19, 1863. The war was the final test whether "a new nation, con-

CHAPTER NINETEEN

Centennial Vistas, 1876:
Toward the Twentieth Century

Eleven years after the black-shrouded funeral train carrying the body of President Abraham Lincoln passed through Philadelphia, the city of brotherly love, now resplendent in red, white, and blue bunting, was the scene of America's Centennial celebration. The republic had survived for one hundred years and seemed, as Walt Whitman wrote in his preface to the Centennial edition of *Leaves of Grass*, "only now and henceforth . . . to enter on its full democratic career." The Civil War, the tragic martyrdom of the president, the struggles and indecencies and failures of Reconstruction, even the recent scandals of the Grant administration, Whitman saw as "but passing incidents and flanges of our unbounded impetus of growth . . . weeds, annuals, of the rank, rich soil—not enduring perennial things." For Whitman, America, despite its trials, remained a "prophecy."

To the people of the nation, if the Centennial Fair of 1876 was any indication, America was indeed a prophecy, but it was also a past that demonstrated the toughness, the resiliencies, the glories of a land of liberty—"a teeming nation of nations" that, like Whitman himself, "contained multitudes." The Civil War had been fought so the Declaration of Independence and hence true liberty might prevail as the enduring basis of a new civilization that pointed toward the future. Now, at Philadelphia in May 1876, with the opening of the Fair, the glories of past, present, and future were displayed in a cultural congress of nations and American states from across the whole broad expanse of a continental union, symbolically reunited and renewed in its quest for identity as a nation of and among nations.

At dawn on May 10, 1876, the Liberty Bell commenced to ring. The Governor of Pennsylvania took his place at the head of a troop of silver-helmeted cavalry and began the procession to the Fair. Soon he was joined by President Ulysses S. Grant and his cabinet and countless other dignitaries including, incongruously, Emperor Dom Pedro of Brazil. Passing through the mud-spattered streets of Philadelphia, they entered Fairmont Park through the main gate opposite Belmont Avenue and took their places on a broad plaza between the enormous Main and Machinery halls. There a platform for four thousand people had been constructed facing a stage that held more than a thousand musicians. Grant's entrance was signaled by the playing of the "Centennial Grand March," specially composed for the occasion by Richard Wagner. Then followed the "Centennial Hymn," written by abolitionist John Greenleaf Whittier and John H. Paine, the "Centennial Cantata," written by Confederate soldier-poet Sidney Lanier, a Centennial prayer led by a Methodist bishop, and eighteen national anthems, sixteen for the foreign nations represented and two for the United States. The speeches lasted until noon, with that by Grant, the now scandal-ridden and hence fallen hero of the republic, receiving the least applause. Doggedly, however, with Pedro at his side, Grant proclaimed the Fair open and proceeded to the Hall of Machines, where he threw the switch on the giant Corliss steam engine, thus symbolically setting the Centennial and perhaps the next century in motion.

The America of the 1876 Centennial had undergone vast changes since Lincoln's death. The South during Reconstruction was subdued and reintegrated into the Union after ratifying the Thirteenth, Fourteenth, and Fifteenth amendments abolishing slavery and guaranteeing freedom and the vote to blacks, who nonetheless continued to be exploited victims of racism. The North, as a result of efficiencies learned in the Civil War, had become industrialized and the seat of Wall Street, thus dominating the culture. A new machine age had begun with inventors and entrepreneurs and crooked congressmen hard at work. The country had barely survived the crudities of many of these entrepreneurs, emerging as the Union Pacific Crédit Mobilier scandal; the unseemly battle between Commodore Cornelius Vanderbilt and Jay Gould for control of the Erie Railroad; the discovery of the Indian Ring and the Whiskey Ring, which resulted in the dismissal of Orville Babcock and William Belknap, Grant's personal secretary and the Secretary of War, respectively; the infamous Black Friday in 1869 when Gould and Jim Fiske tried to corner the gold market; and the 1873 collapse of the country's leading financial house, which led to a national panic and the demise of some five thousand businesses, which was to be repeated in 1893, when the nation would be rescued by none other than J. P. Morgan.

The voters had seen the campaign of the first female Communard candidate for president in 1872, and before the summer of 1876 was out, it would see the massacre at Little Bighorn of General George Armstrong Custer, one of the nation's still-untarnished "heroes." By the 1880s, Frederic Remington, the most popular artist of his day, was picturing with great verve, in a Darwinian and masculine way, the last conquest of the far western frontier, which by 1890 the U.S. Census Bureau declared no longer existed, even though in 1893 Wisconsin historian Frederick Jackson Turner declaimed it the key to the American character. In Cleveland, John D. Rockefeller had already begun to take control of the burgeoning oil industry. In Chicago, George M. Pullman was manufacturing fancy railroad cars to span the country over the transcontinental railroad, completed in 1869, while Philip Armour began butchering hogs for the world. Joseph McCoy had established the railhead cattle towns of Kansas—Abilene, Ellsworth, and Dodge City—to which saddle-sore Texas cowboys drove longhorns a thousand miles to market. Christopher Scholes had invented his typewriter, which would revolutionize office work and bring more and more women out of the home. Elisha Graves Otis had introduced the elevator, which made the skyscraper possible, especially in Chicago, rebuilding after the great fire of 1871, and by 1874 Samuel Gliddon had sold eighty million bales of his invention, barbed wire, to farmers who were moving in droves out onto the High Plains, which once had been called the "Great American Desert."

John Wesley Powell had shot the rapids of the mighty Colorado all the way through the Grand Canyon and in so doing had discovered the last unknown river and last unknown mountain range in the continental United States. As a result of his experiences, he became a pioneer of ecology when he began to protest farmers' moving out onto the arid lands of the West. Barbed wire or no barbed wire, the lack of rainfall made the region unsuitable for farming. But America was the land of the future and no one could stop the march of industrial progress. Not even the Grangers or the Populists, who protested exploitation by railroads and grain-elevator operators, not the Women's Christian Temperance Union, nor the Molly Maguires, who dynamited their way to oblivion in futile protests against the exploitation of labor.

James Eads's great iron bridge had at last spanned the Mississippi. *New York Herald* founder James Gordon Bennett had dispatched journalist Henry Morton Stanley to "find" Scottish missionary-explorer David Livingstone in darkest Africa, Captain William Reynolds on the USS *Lackawanna* had seized the Midway Islands, gateway to the Pacific, while William Seward had convinced Congress to purchase Alaska and the Virgin Islands, though President Grant had been frustrated in his attempts to acquire Santo Domingo. The United States, feeling the power of its industry and agriculture, was looking out across the far Pacific toward the status of a world power, which it would achieve in 1898, with Theodore Roosevelt's world-spanning "Great White Fleet," along with the defeat of Spanish Cuba and its Philippines fleet across the world.

Meanwhile, Montgomery, Ward, and Company had begun to send out its mail-order catalogs. Alexander Graham Bell had proved his telephone successful in a memorable conversation, "Mr. Watson, come here. I want you"; Cyrus Field had laid two Atlantic cables, bringing Europe even closer to the United States; Horatio Alger had published *Ragged Dick*, the first of his long series of newsboys' success stories; Ward McAllister had begun his career as the social arbiter of New York; and James Gordon Bennett had introduced polo at Newport. Charges of treason against Jefferson Davis had long since been dropped; Robert E. Lee had become a college president; and Boss Tweed of New York had spent a year in jail, which in no way diminished the rise of machine politics throughout the nation's cities. Tennis had been imported from England. Arc lamps made city streets "safer" for citizens. Thomas Edison and Eadweard Muybridge, the photographer of people and horses in various stages of motion, working with the brothers Auguste Marie Louis and Louis Jean Lumière and Étienne-Jules Marey's invention of the zoetrope in France, began organizing the whole process of moving pictures, which by the early twentieth century would begin to change the world anew. And at a small quiet gathering of the Connecticut Academy of Arts and Sciences, Professor Josiah Willard Gibbs articulated his phase rule of physical chemistry, which explained the states of matter, and would change the course of scientific thinking. Almost no one in the audience knew what he was talking about, and besides, the struggle over Darwinism still dominated science and religion. Thomas Huxley's visit to the United States in 1876 was *the* scientific event of the Centennial year. Booker T. Washington founded Tuskegee, the first black college, and W. E. B. DuBois became the intellectual voice of the black community.

The decade since Lincoln's assassination had indeed been turbulent and exciting. Much of this excitement was displayed at the Philadelphia Fair in the 194 temporary classical buildings, most of which were dismantled by November 1876 even as Rutherford B. Hayes and Samuel J. Tilden were disputing who would run the United States, and Grant prepared to set off on a tour around the world. But intellectually, at least four new philosophies, which owed to some foreign inspiration, clashed throughout the nineteenth century and looked toward the twentieth century.

By 1876, Englishman Herbert Spencer, influenced by Darwin, was America's philosopher. Beginning in 1851 with *Social Statics*, in which he coined the phrase "survival of the fittest," he had espoused evolutionism. After Charles Darwin's *On the Origin of Species* (1859) he became the prophet of social Darwinism, harnessing science to the cause of survival of the fittest. His heavy volume *Synthetic Philosophy* was a best seller in American intellectual circles as he espoused the cause of progress through extreme—some would say reckless—individualism. In his work, Spencer described a world unfolding progressively and teleologically according to Darwinian laws of evolution. A comprehensive thinker whose work synthesized almost all scientific developments in the nineteenth century, Spencer dwelt especially on a Lamarckian (vitalism and inheritance of acquired characteristics) version of pre-Darwinism and Lord Kelvin's physical laws of conservation of energy (matter and energy can be neither created nor destroyed, and the universe is heading toward entropy, or the transformation of energy into inert matter). For Spencer, however, all life on the planet, through a struggle for existence, was evolving for the better until at last a stage he called "equilibration" would be reached, in which there would be a perfect balance between matter and energy, and everything surviving would be perfectly adapted to its environment.

Spencer's philosophy made good sense to readers of E. L. Youman's *Popular Science Monthly,* and he spawned a whole school of formidable intellectual followers. The popular historian John Fiske, in *Outlines of Cosmic Philosophy* (1874) and countless other works, rendered concrete Spencer's thought in the details of human history, which he saw evolving through time according to God's laws recently discovered by Spencer. William Graham Sumner, a dynamic, rugged sociologist at Yale, in book after book reiterated the Spencerian philosophy, at the same time assailing all governmental interference in the laissez-faire economy of the Gilded Age. He positively reveled in the slogan "root hog or die" until at the end of his career, in the great classic *Folkways* (1906), he saw at last that Spencer's formula had not worked out—that the world was far less certain than the Englishman had led him to believe.

In 1877 Lewis Henry Morgan, a self-taught Indian expert, founded scientific anthropology in America with *Ancient Society,* a Spencerian tract that traced the rise of all mankind through successive stages of "savagery," "barbarism," and "civilization." Each stage or substage within his large framework was the result of a technological innovation until at last the highly specialized, industrial stage of civilization—clearly visible in the Centennial exhibits where, for instance, the Pyramid Pin Company displayed a machine that enabled a little girl to package 180,000 pins a day—was reached. When this last stage was reached, the process of realizing equilibration would begin and eventually government, the state, that "badge of lost innocence," would wither away, even after all the blood of the Civil War had been spilled to maintain it.

Social Darwinism spread like a disease through popular intellectual circles in Victorian America. It could be applied in unlimited ways. It helped foster a military policy of "survival of the fittest," which led to an arms buildup toward the end of the century, especially the Great White Fleet advocated by Captain Alfred Thayer Mahan, adviser to Navy Secretary Theodore Roosevelt. The Fleet could be used to justify a comparison of the world's peoples according to racial stock. In the latter case it was clear that "inferior" races were gradually but certainly losing out to the superior, especially Anglo-Saxon, races in the world struggle for survival. Josiah Strong, one of the great evangelical preachers of the day, made this abundantly clear in his widely distributed classic, *Our Country* (1885), which preached a gospel of immigration restriction. On many levels of American thought, Sumner, Spencerism, and Social Darwinism were powerful and persuasive. As laissez-faire philosophies, they represented a beguiling possibility of freedom to those individualists who dreamed of a free and open country or a financial empire like that of Carnegie.

But Social Darwinism had spawned an important offshoot—reform Darwinism. This led to an age of Progressivism toward the end of the century. A leader of Reform Darwinism was one of explorer John Wesley Powell's expert assistants, sociologist Lester Frank Ward. Bolstered by an influx of young men and minister reformers, as well as the followers of Jane Addams's settlement house movement and Charles Loring Brace's newsboys' lodging houses, touted by the popular success novels of Horatio Alger (*Ragged Dick* and *Mark, the Match Boy*), Darwinism underwent an about-face. Most of the Progressives based their new philosophy on the idea that man (or woman) had evolved to the point where he was not subject to the "iron law" of monism but could control his destiny through better government, which he did in such acts as the Sherman Antitrust Act in 1890. When one considered Darwin's "chance universe" and the ability of new species to adapt to or *choose* a better environment, it was clear that Reform Darwinism represented a much deeper understanding of the great naturalist's discovery. Even while the tycoons and railroad men, as well as the "robber barons" and "money men," seemed to dominate the road to the twentieth century, the age became one of reform that would culminate years later in the New Deal.

Populism and free silver, touted by presidential candidate William Jennings Bryan, was the farmer's reform. It owed little to foreign thought. On the other hand, labor unions, spearheaded by Samuel Gompers and many European immigrants, formed the American Federation of Labor, based on an urban and foreign conception of syndicalism that sometimes very nearly led to class war, as in the Pullman Strike of 1894. Nonetheless, this was an example of people thinking for themselves and breaking the "iron law of wages" that went back to eighteenth-century English economist David Ricardo and was carried through by Spencerism and Sumnerism.

Much of the reform movement—indeed the "age of reform" itself—was due to the massive wave of immigration from Europe toward the latter half of the nineteenth century. Self-conscious ethnic cultures striving to be American and at the same time maintain their old-world cultures made Americans, as historian Michael Kammin put it, a "people of paradox," and they remained so in the twentieth and twenty-first centuries.

Still another aspect of reform was launched by Oliver Wendell Holmes Jr.—legal realism, which sought to look less at time-honored legal traditions and more closely at the facts of a case. Such reasoning reached legal popularity in the cases of foreign-born judge Louis D. Brandeis, who in 1908 ruled that washerwomen could bargain collectively.

Legal realism as well as the rapid rise of photography must have borne some influence on literary and artistic endeavors as they dominated the nineteenth century. In literature, Rebecca Harding Davis's *Life in the Iron Mills* was perhaps the first such realistic novel, while John W. De Forest's *Miss Ravenel's Conversion from Secession to Loyalty* and Stephen Crane's *Red Badge of Courage*, together with Walt Whitman's recollections of his service in a Washington Civil War hospital, carried over the brutal realities of the bloody Civil War, clearly documented in Matthew Brady's gruesome photographs of battlefield scenes. Hamlin Garland reminded people of the crudities of frontier farm labor, "under the lion's paw" of capitalism, while one of the giants of the age, William Dean Howells, in such novels as *The Rise of Silas Lapham* and *A Modern Instance*, practically defined the precarious realities of everyday life in his time.

The two giants of realism were Mark Twain and Henry James. Twain, coming out of the tradition of southwestern frontier humor, wrote for the masses rather than the elite, and despite the mythical yet vernacular quality of his two greatest works, *Tom Sawyer* and *Huckleberry Finn*, he strove always for "authenticity." The Missouri frontier town of Hannibal (population five hundred) produced *Tom Sawyer*, while the magic of the wide Mississippi, where Twain had been a steamboat captain, provided the milieu for the immortal *Huckleberry Finn*, which also confronted the problem of slavery as Tom and Huck rescue Jim, a black slave, then "light out for the territory" that Twain knew so well from his newspaper days in Virginia City, Nevada Territory, and San Francisco. He dramatized the typical western journey in *Roughing It*, a mostly humorous book. Later, clad in his trademark white suit, Twain became a widely traveled humorist lecturer himself, taking his southwestern humor across America. Ernest Hemingway once declared that "all American literature came from Mark Twain," which is nonetheless something of an exaggeration, or "stretcher," as Twain would have it. But his profound mythical realism produced some of the best known works of American literature.

A new standard for realism was upheld in the great works of Henry James, *Washington Square, The Ambassadors, The Golden Bowl,* and many others that dealt with European fortune hunters in exquisite detail. But unlike those of Twain, James's subtle works were an acquired taste, better understood in Europe then America. James's complex, profound works were not written for the masses.

As for the continuing story of the realistic novel, Theodore Dreiser practically lived his novels, such as *American Tragedy* and *Sister Carrie*, while San Franciscan Frank Norris brilliantly pictured corrupt California life in *The Octopus* and *McTeague*, as well as Chicago in *The Pit*.

Meanwhile, new European ideas continued to define the growing American industrial giant. The fashionable French writer Émile Zola, drawing on other French writers, coined the naturalism approach to writing, which portrayed people in the grip of inexorable natural forces from which they could not escape. Given the confusing rapidity of American industrial and urban growth, concomitant with vanishing pastoral culture, naturalism seemed to fit the gospel of Darwinism. So such writers as Norris, Stephen Crane, Dreiser, and Jack London took their stories down to the basic scenario of "tooth and claw," which carried on into the twentieth century in such books as James T. Farrell's *Studs Lonigan*, William Faulkner's *Sanctuary*, and Cormac McCarthy's *Blood Meridian*.

Out in St. Louis, and among the German settlements from Cincinnati to Milwaukee and Chicago, people had another idea of reality. A small, determined

band—Henry Brokmeyer, William Torrey Harris and Denton J. Snider—
who had brought Hegelianism to St. Louis began to have a marked impact
on American thought. In 1867, in an effort to "transcend transcendentalism" and make Georg Wilhelm Friedrich Hegel "talk English," they
founded the *Journal of Speculative Philosophy* and organized Hegel societies
across the country. The focus of their efforts was to translate Hegel's
Larger Logic, an extremely difficult and abstract book, which they regarded
as the German philosopher's greatest work and the key to all knowledge.
Hegel's philosophy derived directly from the work of Immanuel Kant and
was influenced by the work of Johann Fichte, and especially Friedrich Wilhelm Joseph von Schelling, with whom he had worked at Jena. For Hegel,
as for the other post-Kantians, the problem of philosophy was to recognize
the world as mind or phenomena but at the same time find a way to transcend the division Kant had created between the worlds of the phenomena
and the noumena. Unless they could do this, Kantian metaphysics seemed
to bear little or no relevance to the everyday world of reality as experienced. Metaphysics, instead of being the key to human happiness, would
thus appear to be some esoteric game playable only by amateur logicians
and college professors who had been to Germany.

Hegel cut through this Kantian dualism. He began with the question of
the "self" and the "other," or the "noumena" and the "phenomena," and
concluded that there was really no self at all—unless defined by the "other."
The self could be determined only by what it was not at any moment in
time. But the more the self came into contact with others, the more completely defined it became, like the experience of the United States of America. Thus, to realize himself, of necessity man had to come into contact with
ever-widening groups of people—in the family, the work group, the community, the state, and the whole world. As he did so, the full dimensions of
his true potential gradually became realized in the web of global interrela-
tionships that made the United States the most powerful nation on the earth
by 1900. Moreover, as this process took place, God himself, expressed
through man, became more and more fully realized. As God, or "the Concrete Universal," as Hegel called him, revealed himself through the developing relationships of men and nations and great stages of history called
civilizations, the true principle of freedom was realized, men became more
godlike, and the world evolved toward potential perfection.

The particular process by which the self related to the other was a dialectic. In examining Kant, Hegel became fascinated with the concept of the "antimonies," or opposites in life that Plato also had observed. Hegel translated these into a special dialectic of thesis, antithesis, and synthesis that was, he insisted, the way mind, God's and man's alike, really worked. Thus the thesis, or self, confronted the antithesis and out of this inevitable confrontation came a larger and more complete self—the synthesis of opposites or the "me" and the "not me," in the case of mankind. This process went on endlessly as the world unfolded through time. To think correctly, men must translate every experience into these logical terms. Only then could analysis begin. Thus in analyzing the Civil War, in which they found themselves, the St. Louis Hegelians saw the struggle as an inevitable clash between law (the South) and principle (the North), out of which had emerged a new synthesis—a Union based upon new laws that expressed the true principles of freedom.

The Hegelian movement in America provided a philosophy of socialization—one that could be applied to ever-larger masses of people as urbanization accelerated. In fact, the city became the chief focus of the Hegelians, who prophesized that St. Louis itself would become "the future great city of the world." When it did not so become, Hegelians such as Harris, Brokmeyer, and Snider were not daunted. Harris and Snider focused on education and the arts. They brought in the Froebelian kindergarten and Karl Rosenkrantz's Idealist method of pedagogy to train a future generation of Hegelians. Harris went on to become the first U.S. Commissioner of Education, where his Hegelian ideas colored every phase of American educational development. Snider went on to write some forty-eight books, which he gave away freely, and participated in "free school" movements throughout the country as well as in settlement house projects, such as Jane Addams's Hull House, a refuge for the destitute in Chicago. Brokmeyer become governor of Missouri for a time, then went off to teach the Indians in Oklahoma and complete his translation of *Larger Logic*, which he failed to do and gave up. A half century later, it was found tossed in an attic, unfinished.

Other figures in the Hegelian movement rose to prominence in education, law, and even departments of philosophy. George Holmes Howison became a great figure in philosophy at Berkeley while George Herbert

Palmer at Harvard fashioned one of the great philosophy departments in the world, based on the Hegelian principle of the combination of opposites. No two men in his great concentration of talent held the same beliefs. Nothing could have been more opposite than the philosophical positions of, for example, Josiah Royce, an Idealist from California, William James, a Harvard Pragmatist and psychologist, Hugo Munsterberg, a psychologist of the new cinema, and George Santayana, a modern metaphysician, yet they formed perhaps America's most formidable community of philosophers.

Another direction in which Hegelianism turned, however, was toward the "dialectical materialism" of Karl Marx. In Germany, Marx, Ludwig Feuerbach, Friedrich Engels, and August Willich had adopted Hegel's dialectical analysis of history as the clash of opposite forces and his view of evolving civilizations, but they concentrated their analyses upon the enduring clash between the proletariat and capitalist classes, espousing the cause of the proletariat, which they believed would inevitably be victorious. In addition, they dropped God and the "concrete Universal" out of their thinking as being mystical superstition of no practical value. When Willich, one of Marxism's chief theoreticians, fled to America in 1850, he brought Marx's dialectical materialism with him to German Cincinnati. There he organized workingmen's unions and defied the churches. When he was condemned from the pulpits, his answer was a war cry for the masses. If he and the workingmen must go to hell, they would "make of hell a well-organized union foundry." Willich, who had fought heroically as a Union general in the Civil War, was only one of many Marxists who became endemic to industrializing nineteenth-century America. Others who would become famous were Joseph Weydemeyer, Friedrich Sorge, and Joseph Dietzgen, as well as Victoria Woodhull, in whose magazine, *Woodhull & Claflin's Weekly*, Marx's writings first appeared in America. As industrialism and violent labor strife grew throughout the latter half of the nineteenth century, so too the Marxist movement grew, though, as Lincoln had said, the abundant opportunity for an upwardly mobile individual in America seemed always to blunt its proletarian thrust and was outpaced by an age of government reform in almost every field. Nonetheless, it was one more philosophy behind the Centennial facade that looked forward to a future in the twentieth century.

Almost unobtrusively, however, the great revolution in American thought was taking place in part in 1871 at a small, informal gathering in Cambridge, Massachusetts, which someone called ironically the "Metaphysical Club." The principle participants were gruff gadfly Chauncey Wright; Charles S. Peirce, semiologist; William James, philosopher-psychologist; Oliver Wendell Holmes Jr., lawyer; two other lawyers, Nicholas St. John Green and Joseph Brand Warner; plus John Fiske, the most prominent historian of his day. Wright, who discovered the idea of consciousness, appeared as the leader of the group—"Our boxing master," James called him.

Wright's essay on the "Evolution of Self-Consciousness," though evidently much in debt to German philosophy, suggested a different path to discovering the self. Wright instantly accepted Darwin's doctrine of evolution and, in his essay, traced the evolution of the self-conscious in Darwinian rather than vitalist terms. Wright's real contribution, however, formed a kind of turning point in American thought. He was the first to clearly recognize the implications of Darwin's theory of chance mutations for any description of the universe. Wright, Peirce, James, Holmes, and St. John Green built upon the Darwinian concept of "the chance universe" and a new legal philosophy of expediency, part of which was derived from Scottish Realist Alexander Bain. Whereas Spencer, Hegel, and Marx had been teleologists, seeing the course of the unfolding cosmos as proceeding according to fixed laws, Peirce and most of his cohorts saw biological development, human behavior, everything in the universe as uncertain and subject to chance, though Peirce spent his life trying to chart chance. The lawyers abandoned the concept of truth for a belief that truth was what judges and juries decided. Philosophy, then, was merely a construct, a hypothesis, a statement of probability, not certainty or absolute truth. Philosophies that posited the latter, James saw as philosophies of the "bloc universe," or monism. To the Pragmatists, as they eventually called themselves—with the exception of Peirce, who believed they had stolen his word—the universe was governed by "cosmic winds" of chance that could change direction anytime, with any mutation or situation. The Pragmatists were the grandfathers of "situational ethics." What was needed, they believed, was a flexible philosophy that could ride and perhaps even guide the winds of chance.

In Pragmatism they developed such a philosophy, one that governs much of our behavior and certainly the politics and courts of the twentieth and twenty-first centuries in America. Even Royce, the Idealist, made his metaphysical structure into a Pragmatic ethic. He called for self-reliant decision-making that was socially oriented and hence aimed toward the maximum good for the whole community. This meant that the more people who could be brought into the decision-making process, the better it was for both society and the individual. This assumption lay at the heart of the "ethic of means." The highest good, for a democratic nation, was the maximum involvement of its citizens in their collective destiny. Theory could not be separated from practice. Intelligent man was not merely a spectator in the universe. The scientific practical method was the supreme instrument for organizing "social intelligence" in such a way as to slough off the past and cope with the ever-pressing problems of the present and future. It was a doctrine that educationist John Dewey made central to his philosophy.

The chief significance of Pragmatism, in its many forms, was its shift in emphasis from metaphysics, ontology, and system-building to epistemology or method. The Pragmatists eventually found a flexible way to cope with an ever-changing universe and everyday life and its problems in a practical yet scientific way. They created no moral structure meant to stand against the shockwaves of new information, hence the moral guides to behavior began to decline and had almost disappeared by the twenty-first century. The Pragmatists were not frightened by the new. By 1890, in his *Principles of Psychology*, James had discovered the "stream" of consciousness, where man could choose to focus on whatever became a problem or novelty and bring about his own satisfactory result or situation. James had created an instrument and codified a method that perfectly suited the new possibilities that had opened to the Americans in their quest for the perfect society. After 1876, these basic philosophies that came to preoccupy the late nineteenth and early twentieth centuries formed a subtle new thought that overcame Spencerism but curiously still revered the Constitution.

By the turn of the century, John Dewey had organized a famous experimental school at the new University of Chicago that gave direction and purpose to what would be called progressive education, which dominated

American education in the twentieth century. In so doing, Dewey had managed to mate Hegelianism with Pragmatism.

At a New World's Fair, the Columbian Exposition of 1893 in booming Chicago, America had reached a plateau of self-definition, a lofty vista where science, progress, and patriotism went hand in hand in the dynamic Chicago Centennial "birthday of the New World." Only a few must have suspected that the process of cultural self-definition, like that of the individual, was endless as long as the culture was alive and populated with "man thinking."

By the time America reached the twentieth century, the historian of ideas, Henry Adams, "maundering among the magnets" of the 1900 Paris Exposition, was still puzzled. Was the future the dynamos that hummed before him and hence science? Or was it the Virgin of Chartres, which is to say religious morality rather than the aimless vicissitudes of science? Over the years he had mastered the best ideas of European and American scientists and philosophers. He had studied Lord Kelvin's three laws of thermodynamics and found no future for humanity except what entropy produced, freezing to death, in a global cooling. It never occurred to him that mankind might perish through an excess of energy inherent in the atom of which he could have no knowledge. Instead he had pitted progressive evolution against Kelvin's laws and came out with Yale chemist Josiah Willard Gibbs's theory of the Rule of Phases. He had called Gibbs the greatest American intellect since Benjamin Franklin, but where had Gibbs left him? Looking at science, he saw only conflicting thought and all that was left was paradox, soon to be replaced by the confusions of twentieth-century European Modernism and Psychoanalysis.

AUTHOR'S NOTE ON BIBLIOGRAPHY

When I started this book some years ago, I did not intend to include fo
a bibliography because of the book's large, extensive scope, which ver
cludes foreign thinkers as well as Americans. I took pains to iden
sources in the text and the authorities from which I took many of
the frequent mention of scholar historians in the text.

Now, upon second thought, I have decided to include a bibli
thorities upon which I have depended, rather then mention all
text. It is not an exhaustive bibliography. I have included only
tated my writing of this book and those that might engage pe
the cosmopolitan sources of American thinking as the country
ued to be what I have defined in my introduction—a civiliza
cluded many Native Americans because they tended to be
civilizations, though our government has spent hundred
blood to "civilize" them, and they hold great interest for
and scholars.

In this afterword I do want to remind readers of my
"cultures" and "civilizations," a distinction that, to n
been made before. This distinction defines my story a
liography. I regret only that the circumstances of ag
doing another volume on the twentieth century, whe
flowered, despite numerous wars and a fast dividing

BIBLIOGRAPHY

Chapter 1: Tom Paine's Vision

Fast, Howard. *The Selective Work and Citizen Tom Paine*. New York: Modern Library, 1945.

Foner, Erie. *Tom Paine and Revolutionary America*. New York: Oxford University Press, 1976.

Foner, Phillip. *The Complete Writings of Tom Paine*. New York: Citadel Press, 1943.

Nelson, Craig. *Thomas Paine, Enlightenment, Revolution, and the Birth of Modern Nations*. New York: Viking Press, 2006.

Harmar, Harry. *Tom Paine: The Life of a Revolutionary*. London: Haus Ltd., 2006.

Paine, Thomas. *Common Sense*. Pamphlet, 1776.

Chapter 2: The Complex Road to an Independent Civilization

Bailyn, Bernard. *The Ideological Origins of the American Revolution*. Cambridge, MA: Harvard University Press, 1967.

Becker, Carl Lotus. *The Declaration of Independence: A Study in the History of Political Ideas*. New York: Vintage, 1970.

Berkin, Carol. *A Brilliant Solution: Inventing the American Constitution*. New York: Harcourt, 2002.

Bowen, Catherine Drinker. *Miracle at Philadelphia*. Boston: Little, Brown, 1986.

Burns, Eric. *Infamous Scribblers: The Founding Fathers and the Rowdy Beginnings of American Journalism*. New York: PublicAffairs Press, 2006.

Cerami, Charles. *Young Patriots (Madison and Hamilton)*. Naperville, IL: Sourcebooks Inc., 2005.

Chernow, Ron. *Alexander Hamilton*. New York: Penguin, 2004.

Corwin, Edward Samuel. *John Marshall and the Constitution, a Chronicle of the Supreme Court.* New York: Glasgow, Brook & Co., 1970.

Elliott, Emory. *Revolutionary Writers: Literature and Authority in the Early Republic, 1725–1810.* New York: Oxford University Press, 1982.

Elkins, Stanley M., and Eric McKitrick. *The Age of Federalism.* New York: Oxford University Press, 1993.

Ellis, Joseph J. *After the Revolution: Profiles of Early American Culture.* New York: W. W. Norton, 1979.

_____. *American Sphinx, the Character of Thomas Jefferson.* New York: Vintage, 1998.

_____. *Founding Brothers, the Revolutionary Generation.* New York: Alfred A. Knopf, 2002.

_____. *His Excellency, George Washington.* New York: Alfred A. Knopf, 2004.

_____. *American Creation.* New York: Alfred A. Knopf, 2007.

Epstein, David F. *The Political Theory of "The Federalist."* Chicago: University of Chicago Press, 1984.

Ferguson, Robert A. *The Enlightenment of America, 1750–1820.* Cambridge, MA: Harvard University Press, 1997.

Ferling, John. *A Leap in the Dark: The Struggle to Create the American Republic.* New York: Oxford University Press, 2003.

Hook, Andrew. *Scotland and America: A Study of Cultural Relations.* Glasgow, Scotland: Blackie, 1975.

Jensen, Merrill. *The Founding of a Nation, 1763–1776.* New York: Oxford University Press, 1968.

Kammen, Michael. *A Season of Youth, the American Revolution and the Historical Imagination.* Ithaca, N.Y.: Cornell University Press, 1978.

Labaree, Benjamin, and Ian R Christ. *Empire or Independence 1760–1776.* New York: W. W. Norton, 1976.

Lloyd, W. B., and Gordon Allen, eds. *The Essential Antifederalist.* New York: University Press of America, 1985.

Madison, James, Alexander Hamilton, John Jay. *The Federalist Papers.* New York: Penguin, 1987.

Main, Jackson Turner. *The Antifederalists: Critics of the Constitution, 1781–1788.* Chapel Hill: University of North Carolina Press, 1961.

McCullough, David. *John Adams.* New York: Simon & Schuster, 2001.

Morris, Richard Brandon. *The Forging of the Union, 1781–1789.* New York: Harper & Row, 1987.

Nye, Russel Blaine. *The Cultural Life of the New Nation, 1776–1830.* New York: Harper & Row, 1963.

Rakove, Jack N. *Original Meanings: Politics and Ideas in the Making of the Constitution.* New York: Alfred A. Knopf, 1996.

Randall, William Sterne. *Alexander Hamilton, a Life.* New York: HarperCollins, 2003.

Silverman, Kenneth. *A Cultural History of the American Revolution.* New York: Columbia University Press, 1987.

White, Morton. *The Philosophy of the American Revolution.* New York: Oxford University Press, 1978.

Wills, Gary. *Inventing America: Jefferson's Declaration of Independence.* New York: Oxford University Press, 1978.

_____. *Explaining America: "The Federalist."* Garden City, NY: Doubleday, 1981.

Wood, Gordon. *The Creation of the American Republic, 1776–1787.* Chapel Hill: Published for the Institute of Early American History and Culture at Williamsburg, Va., by the University of North Carolina Press, 1969.

_____. *Radicalism of the American Revolution.* New York: Vintage, 1993.

_____. *Revolutionary Characters: What Made the Revolution Different?* New York: Penguin, 2006.

_____. *The American Revolution, a History.* New York: Modern Library, 2003.

Wright, Esmond. *Causes and Consequences of the American Revolution.* Chicago: Quadrangle Books, 1966.

Chapter 4: The Scottish Enlightenment and the Minds of Early America

Ahlstrom, Sydney. *A Religious History of the American People.* New Haven, CT: Yale University Press, 1972.

Broadie, Alexander. *The Tradition of Scottish Philosophy.* Edinburgh: Polygon, 1990.

Bruce, Duncan. *Mark of the Scots.* New York: Carol Publishing Group, 1996.

Butterfield, I. H. *John Witherspoon Comes to America.* Princeton, NJ: Princeton University Press, 1959.

Cayton, Mary Kupiec, and Peter W. Williams, eds. *Encyclopedia of American Cultural & Intellectual History.* New York: Scribner, 2001.

Collins, Varnum. *President Witherspoon, a Biography.* Princeton, NJ: Princeton University Press, 1959.

Corwin, Edward Samuel. *John Marshall and the Constitution.* New Haven, CT: Yale University Press, 1970.

Grave, S. A. *The Scottish Philosophy of Common Sense.* Oxford, UK: Clarendon Press, 1960.

Herman, Arthur. *How the Scots Invented the Modern World.* New York: Crown, 2001.

Hook, Andrew. *Scotland and America: A Study of Cultural Relations.* Glasgow, Scotland: Blackie, 1975.

Hovencamp, Herbert. *Science and Religion in America, 1800–1860.* Philadelphia: University of Pennsylvania Press, 1978.

Howe, Daniel Walker. *The Unitarian Conscience: Harvard Moral Philosophy, 1805–1861.* Cambridge, MA: Harvard University Press, 1970.

Jaffe, Bernard. *Men of Science in America: The Role of Science in the Growth of Our Country.* New York: Simon and Schuster, 1944.

Koch, Adrienne. *The Philosophy of Thomas Jefferson.* New York: Columbia University Press, 1943.

Leyburn, James. *The Scots-Irish: A Social History.* Chapel Hill: University of North Carolina, 1969.

Lovejoy, Arthur. *The Great Chain of Being: A Study of the History of an Idea.* Cambridge, MA: Harvard University Press, 1970.

Martin, Terence. *The Instructed Vision: Scottish Common Sense Philosophy and the Origins of American Fiction.* Bloomington: University of Indiana Press, 1961.

McCosh, James. *The Scottish Philosophy.* Oxford, UK: Clarendon Press, 1960.

Sloan, Douglas. *The Scottish Enlightenment and the American College Ideal.* New York: Columbia University Press, 1971.

Chapter 5: Nationalism and the Varieties of Capitalistic Experience

Appleby, Joyce Oldham. *Capitalism and a New Social Order: The Republican Vision of the 1790s.* New York: Oxford University Press, 1984.

Boorstin, Daniel. *The Americans: The National Experience.* New York: Random House, 1965.

Burstall, Aubrey Frederic. *A History of Mechanical Engineering.* Cambridge, MA: MIT Press, 1965.

Bush, Clive. *Dream of Reason: American Consciousness and Cultural Achievement from Independence to the Civil War.* New York: St. Martin's Press, 1978.

Corwin, Edward. *John Marshall and the Constitution.* New York: Glasgow, Brooke & Co., 1970.

Coulson, Thomas. *Joseph Henry: His Life and Work.* Princeton, NJ: Princeton University Press, 1950.

Dalzell, Robert F. Jr. *Enterprising Elite: The Boston Associates and the World They Made.* Cambridge, MA: Harvard University Press, 1987.

Dorfmann, Joseph. *The Economic Mind in American Civilization 1606–1933*. New York: Viking Press, 1959.

Dunlap, William. *History of the Rise and Progress of the Arts of Design in America*. 2 vols. New York: Dover Press, 1969.

Faulkner, Robert K. *The Jurisprudence of John Marshall*. Princeton, NJ: Princeton University Press, 1968.

Ferguson, Robert A. *American Enlightenment, 1750–1820*. Cambridge, MA: Harvard University Press, 1997.

Hobson, Charles F. *The Great Chief Justice: John Marshall and the Rule of Law in American Political Thought*. Lawrence: University Press of Kansas, 1996.

Horwitz, Morton, J. *The Transformation of American Law*. Cambridge, MA: Harvard University Press, 1977.

Hunter, Louis C. *Steamboats on Western Rivers: An Economic and Technical History*. Mineola, N.Y.: Dover Books, 1993.

James, Henry. *William Wetmore Story and His Friends*. New York: Grove Press, 1957.

Kaplan, A. D. H. *Henry Charles Carey, A Study in American Economic Thought*. Baltimore: Johns Hopkins University Press, 1931.

Marx, Leo. *The Machine in the Garden: Technology and the Pastoral Idea in America*. New York: Oxford University Press, 1967.

McCloskey, Robert G. *The American Supreme Court*. Chicago: University of Chicago Press, 1994.

McCoy, Drew. *The Elusive Republic, Political Economy in Jeffersonian America*. Chapel Hill: University of North Carolina Press, 1980.

Miller, Perry. *The Legal Mind in America from Independence Day to the Civil War*. Garden City, NY: Doubleday, 1962.

_____. *The Responsibility of Mind in a Civilization of Machines: Essays*. Amherst: University of Massachusetts Press, 1979.

Morrison, Rodney J. *Henry C. Carey and American Economic Development*. Philadelphia: Transactions of the American Philosophical Society, 1986.

Nye, Russel Blaine. *The Cultural Life of the New Nation, 1776–1830*. New York: Harper, 1960.

Chapter 6: Reform, New Religions, and Nativism

Ahlstrom, Sydney. *A Religious History of the American People*. New Haven, CT: Yale University Press, 1972.

Billington, Ray Allen. *The Protestant Crusade, 1800–1860: A Study of the Origins of American Nativism*. New York: Macmillan, 1938.

Brodie, Fawn McKay. *No Man Knows My History: The Life of Joseph Smith, The Mormon Prophet.* New York: Alfred A. Knopf, 1957.

Hawes, Joseph M. *Children in Urban Society.* New York: Oxford University Press, 1971.

Hirshson, Stanley P. *Lion of the Lord: A Biography of Brigham Young.* New York: Alfred A. Knopf, 1960.

Lee, John. *Mormonism Unveiled: Including the Remarkable Life and Confessions of the Late Mormon Bishop, John D. Lee.* Albuquerque: Fierra Blanca, 2001. First published 1881 by Moffat Publishing.

Morris, Charles S. *American Catholic.* New York: Times Books, 1997.

Mulder, William, ed. *Among the Mormons: Historic Accounts by Contemporary Observers.* New York: Alfred A. Knopf, 1958.

Tyler, Alice Felt. *Freedom's Ferment; Phases of American Social History to 1860.* Minneapolis: University of Minnesota Press, 1944.

Watts, Edward. *In This Remote Country: French Colonial Culture in the Anglo-American Imagination, 1780–1860.* Chapel Hill: University of North Carolina Press, 2006.

Welter, Rush. *Mind of America, 1820–1860.* New York: Columbia University Press, 1975.

West, Elliott. *Growing Up with the Country: Childhood on the Far Western Frontier.* Albuquerque: University of New Mexico Press, 1989.

Widmer, Edward L. *Young America: the Flowering of Democracy in New York City.* New York: Oxford University Press, 1999.

Wright, G. Frederick. *Charles Grandison Finney.* Salem, Ohio: Schmul Publishing Co., 1996.

Chapter 7: *The Diffusion of Education*

Ambrose, Stephen E. *Undaunted Courage.* New York: Simon & Schuster, 1996.

Chase, Gilbert, *America's Music.* Urbana: University of Illinois Press, 1987.

Crane, Diana. *Invisible Colleges: Diffusion of Knowledge in Scientific Communities.* Chicago: University of Chicago Press, 1972.

Curti, Merle. *The Social Ideas of American Educators.* Totowa, N.J.: Littlefield Adams, 1966.

Elston, Ruth Miller. *Guardians of the Tradition: American Schoolbooks of the Nineteenth Century.* Lincoln: University of Nebraska Press, 1972.

Flexner, James T. *First Flowers of Our Wilderness.* Boston: Houghton Mifflin, 1947.

———. *America's Old Masters.* New York: Dover Publications, 1967.

409

bibliography
Harris, Neil. *The Artist in American Society: The Formative Years, 1790–1860.*
   New York: G. Braziller, 1966.
Hawes, Joseph Milton. *Children in Urban Society.* New York: Oxford University
   Press, 1971.
Hunter, Louis C., and Beatrice Jones Hunter. *Steamboats on the Western Rivers:
   An Economic and Technological History.* Cambridge, MA: Harvard University
   Press, 1949.
Kasson, John F. *Civilizing the Machine: Technology and Republican Values in
   America, 1776–1900.* New York: Penguin, 1977.
Lawrence, Cremin. *American Education: The National Experience, 1783–1876.*
   New York: Harper & Row, 1980.
Miller, Perry. *The Legal Mind in America: From Independence to the Civil War.*
   Garden City, NY: Doubleday, 1962.
_____. *The Life of the Mind in America from the Revolution to the Civil War.* New
   York: Harcourt, Brace & World, 1965.
Nye, Russel Blaine. *The Cultural Life of a New Nation, 1776–1830.* New York:
   Harper Torchbooks, 1960.
_____. *Society and Culture in America, 1830–1860.* New York: Harper & Row,
   1974.
Rudolph, Frederick. *The American College and University.* New York: Alfred A.
   Knopf, 1962.
Struik, Dirk J. *Yankee Science in the Making.* Boston: Little, Brown, 1948.
Westerhoff, John H. *McGuffey and His Readers: Piety, Morality, Education in
   Nineteenth Century America.* Nashville, Tenn.: Abingdon Press, 1978.

Chapter 8: The Writer and the Republic

Note I. The most indispensable introduction to American literature is Spiller, Robert, Willard Thorpe, and Henry S. Canby. *Literary History of the United States.* New York: Macmillan, 1958.

Note II. For people who read for pleasure and the spirit of the times, I recommend: Brooks, Van Wyck. *The World of Washington Irving.* New York: E. P. Dutton, 1944; *The Flowering of New England, 1815–1865.* New York: E. P. Dutton, 1986. *The Times of Melville and Whitman.* New York: E. P. Dutton, 1947; *New England: Indian Summer, 1865–1915.* New York: E. P. Dutton, 1948; *The Confident Years, 1885–1915.* New York: E. P. Dutton, 1952. These are old, but good narratives, which one seldom sees in literary studies in the twenty-first century.

Axelrod, Alan. *Charles Brockden Brown, an American Tale*. Austin: University of Texas Press, 1983.

Barlow, Joel. *The Vision of Columbus: A Poem in Nine Books*. Hartford, CT: Hudson and Goodwin, 1787.

———. *The Columbiad, a Poem*. London: R. Phillips, 1809.

Barth, John. *The Sot Weed Factor*. London: Panther, 1963.

Bartram, William. *Travels of William Bartram*. Ed. Francis Harper. Athens, GA: University of Georgia Press, 1998.

Brown, Charles Brockden. *Arthur Mervyn, Memoirs of the Year, 1793*. New York: Holt, Rinehart and Winston, 1962.

Burstein, Andrew. *The Original Knickerbocker: The Live of Washington Irving*. New York: Basic Books, 2007.

Calhoun, Charles. *Longfellow*. Boston: Beacon Press, 2004.

Charvat, William. *The Profession of Authorship in America, 1800–1870*. New York: Columbia University Press, 1992.

Davidson, Cathy N. *Revolution and the Word: The Rise of the Novel in America*. New York: Oxford University Press, 1986.

Douglas, Ann. *The Feminization of America Culture*. New York: Farrar, Straus and Giroux, 1998.

Ellis, Joseph J. *After the Revolution: Profiles of Early Americans*. New York: W. W. Norton, 2002.

Earnest, Ernest Penney. *John and William Bartram, Botanists and Explorers, 1699–1777, 1739–1823*. Philadelphia: University of Pennsylvania Press, 1940.

Grossman, James. *James Fenimore Cooper: A Biographical and Critical Study*. Stanford, CA: Stanford University Press, 1967.

———. *James Fenimore Cooper*. New York: Hesperides Press, 2006.

Hedges, William. *Washington Irving*. Baltimore: Johns Hopkins University Press, 1965.

Hoffman, Nancy, and John C. Van Horne, eds. *America's Curious Botanist: A Tercentennial Reappraisal of John Bartram, 1699–1777*. Philadelphia: American Philosophical Society, 2004.

Home, Henry, Lord Kames. *Sketches of the History of Man, Vol. IV*. New York: Twayne Publishers, 1970.

———. *Elements of Criticism*. Honolulu, HI: University Press of the Pacific, 2002.

Howard, Leon. *The Connecticut Wits*. Chicago: University of Chicago Press, 1943.

Irving, Washington. *History of New York by Diedrich Knickerbocker*. New York: Inskeep & Bradford, 1809.

_____. *The Rocky Mountains*, 2 vols. Phladelphia: Carey Lea and Blanchard, 1837.

_____. *Astoria*. New York: Thomas Y. Crowell & Co., 1954.

_____. *Adventures of Captain Bonneville, or, Scenes Beyond the Rocky Mountains of the Far West*. Kila, MT: Kissinger Publishing, 2004.

Lehmann, William C. *Henry Home, Lord Kames and the Scottish Enlightenment*. The Hague: Martinus Nijhoff, 1971.

Lewis, R. W. B. *The American Adam: Innocence, Tragedy and Tradition in the Nineteenth Century*. Chicago: University of Chicago Press, 1955.

Long, Robert E. *James Fenimore Cooper*. New York: Continuum Press, 1990.

Magee, Judith. *Art and Science of William Bartram*. Philadelphia: Pennsylvania State University Press, 2007.

McDermott, John Francis, ed. *Before Mark Twain: A Sampler of Old Times on the Mississippi*. Carbondale: Southern Illinois University Press, 1968.

McGuinness, Arthur E. *Henry Home, Lord Kames*. New York: Twayne Publishers, 1970.

Miller, Perry. *Nature's Nation*. Cambridge, MA: Harvard University Press, 1967.

Miller, Perry, ed. *Major Writers of America*. New York: Harcourt, Brace & World, 1963.

Nevins, Allan, ed. *James Fenimore Cooper, the Leatherstocking Saga*. New York: Modern Library, 1966.

Ringe, Donald A. *James Fenimore Cooper*. New Haven, CT: Yale University Press, 1962.

Rourke, Constance. *American Humor: A Study of the National Character*. Garden City, NY: Doubleday and Co., 1953.

Rowson, Susanna. *Charlotte Temple: A Tale of Truth*. New Haven, CT: Yale University Press, 1964.

Rubin, Joan Shelley. *Songs of Ourselves, the Uses of Poetry in America*. Cambridge, MA: Belknap Press of Harvard University, 2007.

Slaughter, Thomas. *The Natures of John and William Bartram*. New York: Alfred A. Knopf, 1996.

Todd, Edgeley W., ed. *Adventures of Captain Bonneville, U. S. A., in the Rocky Mountains and the Far West*. Norman: University of Oklahoma Press, 1961.

Tomkins, Jane. *Sensational Designs*. New York: Oxford University Press, 1985.

Williams, Stanley T. *Life of Washington Irving*. New York: Oxford University Press, 1935.

Chapter 9: Americans Join the Second Great Age of Discovery

Much of the story of America and the Second Great Age of Discovery can be found in three volumes by its conceptualizer. They are:

Goetzmann, William H. *Army Exploration in the American West, 1803–1863.* New Haven, CT: Yale University Press, 1959.

———. *Exploration and Empire: The Explorer and the Scientist in the Winning of the West.* New York: Alfred A. Knopf, 1966.

———. *New Lands, New Men.* New York: Viking Press, 1986.

The volumes expand American exploring activity from that of one army corps, Volume I, to the whole West, Volume II, to Americans and world exploration, Volume III.

Ambrose, Stephen. *Undaunted Courage, Meriwether Lewis, Thomas Jefferson and the Opening of the American West.* New York: Touchstone, 1996.

Beaglehole, J. C. *The Life of Captain James Cook.* Stanford, CA: Stanford University Press, 1974.

Botting, Douglas. *Humboldt and the Cosmos.* New York: Harper and Row, 1975.

Chaffin, Tom. *Pathfinder: John Charles Frémont and the Course of American Empire.* New York: Hill and Wang, 2002.

Conaway, James. *The Smithsonian: 150 Years of Adventure, Discovery and Wonder.* Washington, DC: Smithsonian Books, 1995.

Eiseley, Loren. *Darwin's Century: Evolution and the Men Who Discovered It.* Garden City, NY: Doubleday Anchor Books, 1961.

Goetzmann, William H., and Glyndwr Williams. *The Atlas of North American Exploration.* New York: Prentice Hall, 1992.

Goetzmann, William H., William Orr, David C. Hunt, and Marsha Gallagher. *Karl Bodmer's America.* Lincoln: University of Nebraska Press, 1990.

Goode, G. Brown. *Account of Smithsonian Institution, Its Origins, History, Objects and Achievements.* Washington, DC: Smithsonian Institution, 1904.

Helferich, Gerard. *Humboldt's Cosmos.* New York: Gotham Books, 2004.

Hudson, Linda. *Mistress of Manifest Destiny: A Biography of Jane McManus Storm Cazneau, 1807–1878.* Austin: Texas State Historical Association, 2001.

McCorkle, Barbara B. *America Emergent: An Exhibition of Maps and Atlases in Honor of Alexander O. Vietor.* New Haven, CT: Beinecke Rare Book and Manuscript Library, Yale University, 1985.

Morison, Samuel Eliot. *"Old Bruin": Commodore Matthew C. Perry, 1794–1858.* Boston: Atlantic Monthly Press, 1967.

Nasair, Abraham. *Before Lewis and Clark, Documents Illustrating the History of the Missouri, 1785–1804.* Lincoln, NE: Bison Books, 1990.

Philbrick, Nathaniel. *Sea of Glory.* New York: Penguin, 2003.

Quattrocchi, Anna Margaret. *Thomas Hutchins, 1730–1789.* PhD diss., University of Pittsburgh, 1944.

Quilley, Geoff, and John Bonehill, eds. *William Hodges, the Art of Exploration.* New Haven, CT: Yale University Press, 2005.

Rhodes, Richard. *John James Audubon: The Making of an American.* New York: Alfred A. Knopf, 2004.

Ross, Marvin C. *The West of Alfred Jacob Miller.* Norman: University of Oklahoma Press, 1968.

Smith, Bernard. *European Vision and the South Pacific, 2nd ed.* New Haven, CT: Yale University Press, 1985.

Smithsonian Institution. *The Smithsonian Experience: Science History, the Arts . . . the Treasures of a Nation.* Washington, DC: W. W. Norton, 1977.

Stanford, Alfred. *Navigator: The Story of Nathaniel Bowditch.* New York: William Morrow, 1927.

Stebbins, Theodore E., Jr. *The Life and Works of Martin Johnson Heade.* New Haven, CT: Yale University Press, 2006.

Tyler, Ron, ed. *Alfred Jacob Miller, Artist on the Oregon Trail.* Fort Worth, TX: Amon Carter Museum, 1982.

_____. *Audubon's Great National Work.* Austin: University of Texas Press, 1993.

Von Hagen, Victor. *South America Called Them.* Norman: University of Oklahoma Press, 1945.

_____. *Maya Explorer, John Lloyd Stephens and the Lost Cities of Central America and Yucatan.* Norman: University of Oklahoma Press, 1947.

Williams, Frances Leigh. *Matthew Fontaine Maury, Scientist of the Sea.* New Brunswick: Rutgers University Press, 1963.

Wolfe, Harry. *The Transit of Venus: A Study of Eighteenth Century Science.* Princeton, NJ: Princeton University Press, 1959.

Chapter 10: I Am *"Part or Parcel of God"*: The Romantic Search for the Self

Ahlstrom, Sydney. *A Religious History of the American People.* New Haven, CT: Yale University Press, 1972.

Cameron, Kenneth Walter, ed. *The Course of Transcendentalism During the American Nineteenth Century*. Hartford, CT: Transcendental Books, 1999.

Conrad, Susan P. *Perish the Thought: Intellectual Women in Romantic America, 1830–1860*. New York: Oxford University Press, 1976.

Flower, Elizabeth, and Murray Murphey. *A History of Philosophy in America. 2 vols*. New York: Putnam, 1977.

Hankins, Barry. *Second Great Awakening and the Transcendentalists*. Westport, CT: Greenwood Press, 2004.

Howat, John K. *American Paradise: The World of the Hudson River School*. New York: Metropolitan Museum of Art and Harry N. Abrams, 1987.

Howe, Daniel Walker. *Making the American Self: Jonathan Edwards to Abraham Lincoln*. Cambridge, MA: Harvard University Press, 1997.

Hutchison, James M. *Poe*. Jackson: University Press of Mississippi, 2005.

McKinsey, Elizabeth R. *Western Experiment: New England Transcendentalists in the Ohio Valley*. Cambridge, MA: Harvard University Press, 1973.

Miller, Perry. *The American Transcendentalists: Their Prose and Poetry*. Garden City, NY: Doubleday, 1957.

_____. *Nature's Nation*. Cambridge, MA: Belknap Press of Harvard University Press, 1967.

Peckham, Morse. *Man's Rage for Chaos: Biology, Behavior, and the Arts*. New York: Schocken Books, 1973.

Stebbins, Theodore E. *The Lure of Italy: American Artists and the Italian Experience, 1760–1914*. Boston: Metropolitan Museum of Fine Arts, 1992.

Tyler, Ron. *Audubon's Great National Work: The Royal Octavo Edition of the Birds of America*. Austin: University of Texas Press, 1993.

Vance, William Silas. *Carlyle and the American Transcendentalists*. Chicago: n.p., 1944.

Vogel, Stanley M. *German Literary Influences on the American Transcendentalists*. New Haven, CT: Yale University Press, 1955.

Wayne, Tiffany K. *Woman Thinking: Feminism and Transcendentalism in Nineteenth Century America*. Lanham, MD: Lexington Books, 2005.

Chapter 11: The Romantic Writer as Cosmopolitan Seer

The most insightful work on Hawthorne is Cowley, Malcolm, ed. *Introduction: The Viking Portable: Nathaniel Hawthorne*. New York: Viking Press, 1948, 1955 reprint.

Melville is a literary industry; for a large biography see Larant, Laurie Robertson. *Melville, a Biography*. New York: Clarkson, Potter, 1996; Miller, Edwin. *Melville*. New York: Perseus Books, 1975, is a medium-size book; and Delbanco, Andrew. *Melville, His World and Work*. New York: Vintage, 2006.

Amid the wasteland of Melville criticism, the three books I found interesting are
Vincent, Howard P. *The Trying Out of Moby Dick*. Boston, Houghton Mifflin Co.,
1949; Rogin, Michael. *Subversive Genealogy: The Politics and Art of Herman Melville*.
Berkeley: University of California Press, 1985; and Bercaw, Mary K. *Melville's
Sources*. Evanston, IL: Northwestern University Press, 1987.

Audubon, Maria. *Audubon and His Journals*. New York: Dover, Reprint
    paperback, 1986. Originally published 1897 by Scribner's Sons.
Brown, Lee Rust. *The Emerson Museum: Practical Romanticism and the Pursuit of
    the Whole*. Cambridge, MA: Harvard University Press, 1997.
Busick, Sean R. *A Sober Desire for History: William Gilmore Simms as Historian*.
    New York: Columbia University Press, 2005.
Charvat, William. *The Proliferation of Authorship in America, 1800–1870*. New
    York: Columbia University Press, 1992.
Dunlap, William. *History of the Rise and Progress of the Arts of Design in America
    Vol. II, Part 1*. New York: Dover Press, 1969.
Fiedler, Leslie. *Love and Death in the American Novel*. Cleveland: World
    Publishing Co., 1962.
Fuller, Margaret. *Margaret Fuller, American Romantic; A Selection from Her
    Writings and Correspondence*. Ed Perry Miller. Ithaca, NY: Cornell
    University Press, 1970.
Hale, William Harlan. *Horace Greeley: Voice of the People*. New York: Harper &
    Bros., 1950.
Hutchison, James. *Poe*. Jackson: University of Mississippi Press, 2005.
Kaplan, Justin. *Walt Whitman, a Life*. New York: Bantam Books, 1982.
Kaul, A. N. *The American Vision*. New Haven, CT: Yale University Press, 1962.
Matthiessen, F. O. *American Renaissance*. New York: Oxford University Press,
    1949.
Miller, Edwin. *Salem Is My Dwelling Place: A Life of Nathaniel Hawthorne*. Iowa
    City: University of Iowa Press, 1991.
Miller, Perry. *The Raven and the Whale: The War of Words and Wits in the Era of
    Poe and Melville*. New York: Harcourt, Brace, 1956.
_____. *American Transcendentalists: Their Prose and Poetry*. Garden City, NY:
    Doubleday, 1957.
_____. *The American Quest for a Supreme Fiction: Whitman's Legacy in the
    Personal Epic*. Chicago: University of Chicago Press, 1979.
Mott, Frank. *A History of American Magazines, 1741–1850*. Cambridge, MA:
    Harvard University Press, 1957.

Peckham, Morse. *The Triumph of Romanticism.* Columbia: University of South Carolina Press, 1970.

Reynolds, David S. *Beneath the American Renaissance: The Subversive Imagination in the Age of Emerson and Melville.* Cambridge, MA: Harvard University Press, 1989.

_____. *Walt Whitman's America.* New York: Alfred A. Knopf, 1995.

Rhodes, Richard. *John James Audubon: The Making of an American.* New York: Alfred A. Knopf, 2004.

Shapiro, Michael Edward. *George Caleb Bingham.* New York: Harry N. Abrams, 1993.

Silverman, Kenneth. *Edgar A. Poe, Mournful and Never-Ending Remembrance.* New York: HarperCollins, 1991.

Simms, William Gilmore. *The Letters of William Gilmore Simms.* Vol. 1. Columbia: University of South Carolina Press, 1952–1956.

Streshinsky, Shirley. *Audubon, Life and Art in the American Wilderness.* New York: Villard Books, 1991.

Taylor, William. *Cavalier and Yankee: The Old South and American National Character.* New York: Oxford University Press, 1993.

Walsh, John Evangelist. *Midnight Dreary: The Mysterious Death of Edgar Allan Poe.* New York: Minotaur, 2000.

Widmer, Edward L. *Young America: The Flowering of Democracy in New York City.* New York: Oxford University Press, 1999.

Wilson, Charles. *Encyclopedia of Southern Culture.* Chapel Hill: University of North Carolina Press, 1989.

Wilson, Forest. *Crusader in Crinoline.* Philadelphia: Lippincott, 1941.

Wolf, Bryan Jr. *Romantic Revision, Culture and Consciousness in Nineteenth Century American Painting and Literature.* Chicago: University of Chicago Press, 1982.

Woodberry, George E. *The Life of Edgar Allan Poe.* 1909. Reprint, New York: Biblo and Tanner, 1965.

Chapter 12: The Wild Jacksonian Age

Bauer, Karl Jack. *The Mexican War, 1846–48.* Lincoln: University of Nebraska Press, 1974.

Bender, Thomas. *Toward an Urban Vision: Ideas and Institutions in Nineteenth-Century America.* Lexington: University Press of Kentucky, 1975.

Benson, Lee. *Concept of Jacksonian Democracy: New York as a Test Case.* Princeton, NJ: Princeton University Press, 1961.

Blau, Joseph L., ed. *Social Theories of Jacksonian Democracy.* New York: Liberal
     Arts Press, 1954.

Bloch, E. Maurice. *George Caleb Bingham: The Evolution of an Artist.* Berkeley:
     University of California Press, 1967.

———. *The Paintings of George Caleb Bingham.* Columbia, MO: University of
     Missouri Press, 1986.

Bode, Carl. *Antebellum Culture.* Carbondale: Southern Illinois University Press,
     1959.

———. *American Life in the 1840s.* Garden City, NY: Doubleday Anchor Books,
     1967.

Borneman, Walter. *Polk.* New York: Random House, 2008.

Bowers, Claude Gernade. *Making Democracy a Reality: Jefferson, Jackson, and Polk.*
     Memphis: Center for American History, 1954.

Brands, H. W. *A Biography of Andrew Jackson.* New York: Bantam-Dell Group,
     2005.

———. *The Life and Times of Andrew Jackson.* New York: Doubleday, 2006.

Burstein, Andrew. *The Passions of Andrew Jackson.* New York: Alfred A. Knopf,
     2003.

Chaffin, Tom. *Pathfinder, John Charles Fre'mont and the Course of American
     Empire.* New York: Hill and Wang, 2002.

Chambers, William Nisbet. *Old Bullion Benton, Senator from the New West:
     Thomas Hart Benton, 1782–1858.* Boston: Little, Brown, 1956.

Cohen, Patricia, et al. *The Flash Press: Sporting Male Weeklies in 1840s New York.*
     Chicago: University of Chicago Press, 2008.

Davis, David Brian, ed. *Antebellum American Culture.* Lexington, MA: Heath, 1979.

Eisenhower, John S. D. *So Far from God: The U.S. War with Mexico, 1846–1898.*
     New York: Random House, 1989.

Erickson, Paul Joseph. *Welcome to Sodom: The Cultural Work of City-Mysteries:
     Fiction in Antebellum America.* PhD diss., University of Texas, 2005.

Goetzmann, William H. *When the Eagle Screamed: The Romantic Horizon in
     American Expansionism, 1800–1860.* New York: Wiley, 1966.

———. *Army Exploration in the American West, 1803–1863.* Austin: Texas State
     Historical Association, 1991.

———. *Exploration and Empire: The Explorer and the Scientist in the Winning of the
     American West.* Austin: Texas State Historical Association, 1994.

Haddad, John. *The American Marco Polo: Excursion to a Virtual China in U.S.
     Popular Culture, 1784–1912.* PhD diss., University of Texas, 2002. Now
     available online as Guttenberg Prize winner.

Hale, William Harlan. *Horace Greeley, Voice of the People*. New York: Harper & Brothers, 1950.

Herr, Pamela. *Jessie Benton Fremont, American Woman of the Nineteenth Century*. New York: Franklin Watts, 1987.

Holt, Michael F. *The Rise and Fall of the American Whig Party: Jacksonian Politics and the Onset of the Civil War*. New York: Oxford University Press, 1999.

_____. *The Fate of Their Country: Politicians, Slavery Extension and the Coming of the Civil War*. New York: Hill and Wang, 2004.

Howe, Daniel Walker. *What Hath God Wrought*. New York: Oxford University Press, 2007.

Hudson, Linda. *Mistress of Manifest Destiny*. Austin: Texas State Historical Association, 2001.

James, Marquis. *The Life of Andrew Jackson*. New York: Bobbs-Merrill, 1938.

Kohn, Hans. *The Age of Nationalism: The First Era of Global History*. New York: Harper, 1962.

_____. *The Idea of Nationalism: A Study in Its Origins and Background*. New York: Macmillan, 1968.

Lehuu, Isabelle. *Carnival on the Page: Popular Print Media in Antebellum America*. Chapel Hill: University of North Carolina Press, 2000.

Marks, Paula M. *Precious Dust: The American Gold Rush Era, 1848–1900*. New York: W. Morrow, 1994.

McKenney, Thomas L. *Memoirs, Official and Personal: With Sketches of Travels Among the Northern and Southern Indians*. New York: Paine and Burgess, 1846.

Meyers, Marvin. *The Jacksonian Persuasion, Politics and Belief*. New York: Vintage, 1960.

Monaghan, Gary. *The Great Rascal: The Exploits of the Amazing Ned Buntline*. Boston: Little, Brown, 1951.

Nevins, Allan, ed. *Polk: The Diary of a President 1845–1849*. New York: Capricorn Books, 1968.

Nye, Russell Blaine. *Society and Culture in America, 1830–1860*. New York: Harper & Row, 1974.

O'Connor, Stephen. *Orphan Trains: The Story of Charles Loving Brace and the Children He Saved and Failed*. Boston: Houghton Mifflin, 2001.

Pessen, Edward. *Jacksonian Panorama*. Indianapolis: Bobbs-Merrill, 1976.

Philbrick, Nathaniel. *Sea of Glory: America's Voyage of Democracy, The U.S. Exploring Expedition*. New York: Penguin, 2003.

Read, Georgia Willis, and Ruth Gaines, eds. *Gold Rush: The Journals, Drawings and Other Papers of J. Goldsborough Bruff*. New York: Columbia University Press, 1949.

Remini, Robert. *Martin Van Buren and the Making of the Democratic Party*. New York: Columbia University Press, 1959.

_____. *Andrew Jackson*. New York: Twayne Publishers, 1966.

_____. *Andrew Jackson and the Bank War: A Study in the Growth of Presidential Powers*. New York: W. W. Norton, 1967.

_____. *Andrew Jackson and the Course of American Democracy, 1833–1845*. New York: Harper & Row, 1984.

_____. *Legacy of Andrew Jackson: Essays on Democracy, Indian Removal and Slavery*. Baton Rouge: Louisiana State University Press, 1988.

_____. *The Life of Andrew Jackson: 3 Volumes in 1*. New York: Harper & Row, 1988.

_____. *Henry Clay: Statesman for the Union*. New York: W. W. Norton, 1991.

_____, ed. *The Jacksonian Era*. Wheeling, IL: Harlan Davidson, 1997.

_____. *The Battle*. New York: Viking, 1999.

_____. *Andrew Jackson and His Indian Wars*. New York: Viking, 2001.

_____. *John Quincy Adams*. New York: Henry Holt, Times Books, 2002.

_____. *Joseph Smith*. New York: Viking, 2002.

Reynolds, David, ed. *George Lippard, Prophet of Protest: Writings of an American Radical, 1822–1854*. New York: Peter Lang, 1986.

_____, ed. *Beneath the America Renaissance: the Subversive Imagination in the Age of Emerson and Melville*. Cambridge, MA: Harvard University Press, 1988.

_____. *The Quaker City, or The Monks of Monk's Hall*. Amherst: University of Massachusetts Press, 1995.

Rozwenc, Edwin Charles, ed. *Ideology and Power in the Age of Jackson*. Garden City, NY: Doubleday Anchor Books, 1964.

Sandweiss, Martha, Rick Stewart, and Ben W. Huseman. *Eyewitness to War: Prints and Daguerreotypes of the Mexican War, 1846–1848*. Fort Worth, TX: Amon Carter Museum; Washington, DC: Smithsonian Institution Press, 1989.

Schlesinger, Arthur M. Jr. *The Age of Jackson*. Boston: Little, Brown, 1946.

Seigenthaler, John. *James K. Polk*. New York: Times Books, 2004.

Sellers, Charles Grier. *James K. Polk, Jacksonian 1795–1843, Vol. I; James K. Polk, Continentalist, 1843–1846, Vol II*. Princeton, NJ: Princeton University Press, 1957.

Smith, Justin. *The War With Mexico*. 2 vols. New York: Macmillan, 1919.

Smith, Henry Nash. *Virgin Land: The American West as Symbol and Myth*. Cambridge, MA: Harvard University Press, 1960.

Somkin, Fred. *Unquiet Eagle*. Ithaca, NY: Cornell University Press, 1967.

Stanton, William. *The Great United States Exploring Expedition of 1838–1842.*
	Berkeley: University of California Press, 1975.

Stout, Janis P. *Sodoms in Eden: The City in American Fiction Before 1860.*
	Westport, CT: Greenwood Press, 1976.

Starr, Kevin. *Americans and the California Dream.* New York: Oxford University
	Press, 1973.

Unruh, John D. Jr. *The Plains Across: Emigrants and the Trans-Mississippi West,
	1840–1860.* Urbana: University of Illinois Press, 1979.

Temin, Peter. *The Jacksonian Economy.* New York: W. W. Norton, 1969.

Thompson, George. *Venus in Boston.* Amherst: University of Massachusetts
	Press, 2002.

Wishy, Bernard. *The Child and the Republic: The Dawn of Modern American Child
	Nurture.* Philadelphia: University of Pennsylvania Press, 1967.

Note: For those interested in the art of the period, I recommend the following
masterful works:

Hughes, Robert. *American Visions.* New York: Alfred A. Knopf, 1997.

Kelly, Franklin. *Frederick Edwin Church.* Washington, DC: National Gallery of
	Art, 1989.

Metropolitan Museum of Art. *American Paradise, the World of the Hudson River
	School.* New York: Harry N. Abrams, 1987.

Powell, Earl. *Thomas Cole.* New York: Harry N. Abrams, 1990.

Stebbins, Theodore. *The Lure of Italy: American Artists and the Italian Experience,
	1760–1914.* Boston: Metropolitan Museum of Fine Arts, 1992.

Chapter 13: The Imperial Mind: The West and the Future as Reality

Adeleke, Tunde. *Without Regard to Race: The Other Martin Robison Delany.*
	Jackson: University of Mississippi Press, 2003.

Bauer, K. Jack. *The Mexican War, 1846–1848.* Lincoln: University of Nebraska
	Press, 1974.

Bemis, Samuel Flagg. *John Quincy Adams and the Foundations of American Foreign
	Policy.* New York: Alfred A. Knopf, 1949.

Bremer, Richard G. *Indian Agent and Wilderness Scholar: The Life of Henry Row
	Schoolcraft.* Mount Pleasant, MI: Clarke Historical Library, 1988.

Brown, Charles. *Agents of Manifest Destiny: The Lives and Times of the Filibusters.*
	Chapel Hill: University of North Carolina Press, 1980.

Carr, Albert C. *The World and William Walker.* New York: Harper & Row, 1963.

Chamberlain, Sam. *My Confession, Recollection of a Rogue.* Ed. William H. Goetzmann. Austin: Texas State Historic Association, 1996.

Chambers, William N. *Old Bullion Benton.* Boston: Little, Brown, 1956.

Chase, Lucien Bonaparte. *History of the Polk Administration.* New York: G. P. Putnam, 1850.

Clokey, Richard M. *William H. Ashley: Enterprise and Politics in the Trans-Mississippi West.* Norman: University of Oklahoma Press, 1980.

Dippie, Brian. *Catlin and His Contemporaries: The Politics of Patronage.* Lincoln: University of Nebraska Press, 1990.

Eisenhower, John S. D. *So Far from God: The U.S. War with Mexico, 1846–1848.* New York: Random House, 1989.

Goetzmann, William H. *When the Eagle Screamed.* New York: Wiley, 1966.

_____. *Sam Chamberlain's Mexican War.* Austin: Texas State Historic Association, 1993.

Gregg, Josiah. *The Diary and Letters of Josiah Gregg, Southwestern Enterprises, 1840–1847.* Norman: University of Oklahoma Press, 1941.

_____. *Commerce of the Prairie.* Norman: University of Oklahoma Press, 1954.

Hafen, Le Roy R., and Ann W Hafen. *Journals of the Forty-Niners: Salt Lake to Los Angeles.* Lincoln: University of Nebraska Press, 1954.

Haynes, Sam W. *James K. Polk and the Expansionist Impulse.* New York: Longman, 1997.

Holliday, James. *And the World Rushed In: The California Gold Rush Experience.* New York: Simon & Schuster, 1981.

Hudson, Linda S. *Mistress of Manifest Destiny.* Austin: Texas State Historical Association, 2001.

Johannsen, Robert W. *To the Halls of the Montezumas: The Mexican War in the American Imagination.* New York: Oxford University Press, 1985.

Kames, Thomas. *William Gilpin, Western Nationalist.* Austin: University of Texas Press, 1970.

Leonard, Zenas. *Leonard's Narrative: Adventures of Zenas Leonard, Fur Trader and Trapper, 1831–1836; Reprinted from the Rare Original of 1839.* Ed. W. F. Wagner. Lincoln: University of Nebraska Press, 1978.

Manley, William Lewis. *Death Valley in '49.* Alexandria, VA: Time Life Books, 1982. First published 1894 by Pacific Tree and Vine Co.

Marks, Paula Mitchell. *Precious Dust: The North American Gold Rush Era.* New York: Simon & Schuster, 1984.

May, Robert E. *Manifest Destiny's Underworld: Filibustering in Antebellum America*. Chapel Hill: University of North Carolina Press, 2002.

_____. *The Southern Dream of a Caribbean Empire*. Gainesville: University of Florida Press, 2002.

Merk, Frederick. *Manifest Destiny and Mission in American History: A Reinterpretation*. New York: Vintage, 1966.

Morgan, Dale L. *Jedediah Smith and the Opening of the West*. Lincoln: University of Nebraska Press, 1953.

Mulder, William, and Russell Mortensen, eds. *Among the Mormons*. New York: Alfred A. Knopf, 1958.

Nelson, Anna Kasten. *Secret Agents: President Polk and the Search for Peace with Mexico*. New York: Garland Publishing, 1988.

Nevins, Allan, ed. *Polk: The Diary of a President, 1845–1849*. New York: Capricorn Books, 1968.

Owsley, Frank Lawrence Jr. and Gene A. Smith. *Filibusters and Expansionists: Jeffersonian Manifest Destiny, 1800–1821*. Tuscaloosa: University of Alabama Press, 1997.

Parkman, Francis Jr. *The Oregon Trail*. 1849. Reprint, New York: Penguin, 1982.

Pattie, James Ohio. *The Personal Narrative of James O. Pattie*. Ed. William H. Goetzmann. 1831. Reprint, Philadelphia: J. B. Lippincott, 1962.

Paine, B. Darwin. *Owen Wister, Chronicler of the West, Gentleman of the East*. Dallas: Southern Methodist University Press, 1985.

Prassel, Frank Richard. *The Western Peace Officer, a Legacy of Law and Order*. Norman: University of Oklahoma Press, 1972.

Porter, Joseph C. *Paper Medicine Man: John Gregory Bourke and His American West*. Norman: University of Oklahoma Press, 1986.

Scroggs, William O. *Filibusters and Financiers*. New York: Macmillan, 1916.

Seigenthaler, John. *James K. Polk*. New York: Holt & Company, 2003.

Sellers, Charles Grier. *James K. Polk, Jacksonian, 1795–1843. Volume 1*. Princeton, NJ: Princeton University Press, 1957.

_____. *James K. Polk, Continentalist, 1843–1846*. Vol. 2. Princeton, NJ: Princeton University Press, 1966.

Smith, Justin H. *The War with Mexico*. 2 vols. New York: Macmillan, 1919.

Smith, Henry Nash. *Virgin Land: The American West as Symbol and Myth*. Cambridge, MA: Harvard University Press, 1950.

Starr, Kevin. *Americans and the California Dream*. New York: Oxford University Press, 1973.

Unruh, John D. Jr. *The Plains Across: Emigrants and the Trans-Mississippi West, 1840–1860*. Urbana: University of Illinois Press, 1979.

Utley, Robert M. *A Life Wild and Perilous, Mountain Men and the Paths to the Pacific.* New York: Henry Holt, 1987.

Walker, William. *The War in Nicaragua, 1860.* Tucson: University of Arizona Press, 1985.

Wallace, Edward S. *Destiny and Glory: A Story of Filibustering in the Caribbean.* New York: Coward McCann, 1954.

West, Elliott. *The Contested Plains.* Lawrence: University Press of Kansas, 1998.

Winders, Richard Bruce. *Mr. Polk's Army: The American Military Experience in the Mexican War.* College Station: Texas A&M Press, 1997.

Chapter 14: The South and the Past as Reality

Bailey, Hugh C. *Hinton Rowan Helper, Abolitionist-Racist.* Tuscaloosa: University of Alabama Press, 1965.

Baldwin, Joseph Glover. *Flush Times of Alabama and Mississippi.* New York: Hill and Wang, 1976. See his chapter on Hon. S. S. Prentiss.

Bartlell, Irving H. *John C. Calhoun, a Biography.* New York: W. W. Norton, 1993.

Cash, W. J. *The Mind of the South.* New York: Alfred A. Knopf, 1941.

Coit, Margaret. *John C. Calhoun: American Portrait.* Englewood Cliffs, N J: Prentice Hall, 1970. First printed 1950 by Houghton Mifflin.

Clement, Eaton. *The Mind of the Old South.* Baton Rouge: Louisiana State University Press, 1967.

Davis, Richard Beale. *Intellectual Life in the Colonial South 1585–1783.* Knoxville: University of Tennessee Press, 1978.

Duff, John B. *The Nat Turner Rebellion: The Historical Event and the Modern Controversy.* New York: Harper & Row, 1971.

Eaton, Clement. *The Growth of Southern Civilization 1790–1860.* New York: Harper, 1961.

_____. *The Mind of the Old South.* Baton Rouge: Louisiana State University Press, 1967.

Ellis, Joseph. *American Sphinx: The Character of Thomas Jefferson.* New York: Alfred A. Knopf, 1997.

Faust, Drew. *A Sacred Circle.* Baltimore: Johns Hopkins University Press, 1977.

Fitzhugh, George. *Sociology for the South; or, The Failure of Free Society.* New York: B. Franklin, 1965.

Fitzhugh, George. *Cannibals All! or, Slaves Without Masters.* Ed. C. Vann Woodward. Cambridge, MA: Belknap Press of Harvard University Press, 1960.

_____. *Ante-bellum Writings of George Fitzhugh and Hinton Rowan Helper on Slavery.* New York: Capricorn Books, 1960.

Hafertepe, Kenneth. *America's Castle: The Evolution of the Smithsonian Building, 1848–1878*. Washington, DC: Smithsonian Institution Press, 1978.

Hofstadter, Richard. *The American Political Tradition and the Men Who Made It*. New York: Alfred A. Knopf, 1973. See especially his brilliant chapter "Calhoun, the Marx of the Master Class."

Holt, Michael. *The Rise and Fall of the American Whig Party*. New York: Oxford University Press, 1999.

Hubbell, Jay C. *The South in American Literature, 1607–1900*. Durham, NC: Duke University Press, 1954.

Lurie, Edward. *Louis Agassiz: A Life in Science*. Chicago: University of Chicago Press, 1960.

Lynn, Kenneth S. *Mark Twain and Southwestern Humor*. Boston: Little, Brown, 1960.

May, Robert E. *The Southern Dream of a Caribbean Empire, 1854–1861*. Athens: University of Georgia Press, 1989.

_____. *Manifest Destiny's Underworld: Filibustering in Antebellum America*. Chapel Hill: University of North Carolina Press, 2002.

McCardell, John. *The Idea of a Southern Nation: Southern Nationalists and Southern Nationalism, 1830–1860*. New York: W. W. Norton, 1979.

McPherson, James M. *Battle Cry of Freedom: The Civil War Era*. New York: Oxford University Press, 1988.

Niven, John. *John C. Calhoun and the Price of Union, a Biography*. Baton Rouge: Louisiana State University Press, 1988.

Oliphant, Mary Simms, Alfred Taylor Odell, and T. C. Duncan Eaves, eds. *The Letters of William Gilmore Simms. 5 vols*. Columbia: University of South Carolina Press, 1952–1958. See biographical sketch by A. S. Salley.

Osterweis, Rollin G. *Romanticism and Nationalism in the Old South*. New Haven, CT: Yale University Press, 1949.

Scroggs, William O. *Filibusters and Financiers*. New York: Macmillan, 1916.

Simms, William Gilmore. *The Yemanssee: A Romance of Carolina*. Boston: Houghton Mifflin, 1961.

Skipper, Ottis Clark. *J. D. B. De Bow, Magazinist of the Old South*. Athens: University of Georgia Press, 1958.

Stanton, William. *The Leopard's Spots: Scientific Attitudes Toward Race in America, 1815–59*. Chicago: University of Chicago Press, 1960.

Taylor, William Robert. *Cavalier and Yankee: The Old South and American National Character*. Cambridge, MA: Harvard University Press, 1979.

Trent, William Peterfield. *William Gilmore Simms*. Boston: Houghton Mifflin, 1892.

Woodman, Harold D. *King Cotton and His Retainers: Financing and Marketing the Cotton Crop of the South 1800–1925*. Columbia: University of South Carolina Press, 1990.

Wyatt-Brown, Bertram. *Southern Honor: Ethics and Behavior in the Old South*. New York: Oxford University Press, 1982.

Chapter 15: The Black Man as Intellectual

Adeleke, Tunde. *Without Regard to Race: The Other Martin Robison Delany*. Jackson: University Press of Mississippi, 2003.

Allen, Norm R. Jr. *The Black Humanist Experience: An Alternative to Religion*. Amherst, NY: Prometheus Books, 2003.

_____, ed. *African-American Humanism: An Anthology*. Buffalo, New York: Prometheus Books, 1991.

Banks, William. *Black Intellectuals: Race and Responsibility in American Life*. New York: W. W. Norton, 1996.

Barber, E. Susan. *One Hundred Years towards Suffrage: An Overview*. National American Woman Suffrage, http://memory.loc.gov/ammem/naw/nawstime.html.

Barbera, Donald R. *Black and Not Baptist: Nonbelief and Free Thought in the Black Community*. Lincoln, NE: Universe, 2003.

Brown, William Wells. *The Black Man: His Antecedents, His Genius, and His Achievements*. New York: Kraus, 1969. Originally published 1863 by T. Hamilton.

Cain, Rudolph A., ed. *The Critical Pragmatism of Alain Locke: A Reader on Value Theory, Aesthetics, Community, Culture, Race and Education*. Ed. Leonard Harris. Lanham, MD: Rowman & Littlefield, 1999.

Childs, John Brown. *Leadership, Conflict and Cooperation in Afro-American Social Thought*. Philadelphia: Temple University Press, 1989.

Conyers, James L., ed. *Black American Intellectualism and Culture: A Social Study of African American Social and Political Thought*. Stamford, CT.: JAI Press, 1999.

Cruse, Harold. *The Crisis of the Negro Intellectual*. New York: W. W. Morrow, 1967.

Delany, Martin Robison. *Condition, Elevation, Emigration, and Destiny of the Colored People of the United States*. New York: Arno Press, 1968.

Diedrich, Maria. *Love Across Color Lines: Ottilie Assing and Frederick Douglass*. New York: Hill and Wang, 1999.

Douglass, Frederick. *Life and Times of Frederick Douglass*. New York: Pathway Press, 1941.

_____. *Narrative of the Life of Frederick Douglass: An American Slave*. Cambridge, MA: Belknap Press of Harvard University, reprint, 1960.

DuBois, W. E. B. *The Souls of Black Folk*. New York: Signet Classics, 1995.

Franklin, John Hope. *The Militant South, 1800–1861*. Cambridge, MA: Belknap Press of Harvard University Press, 1970.

_____. *From Slavery to Freedom: A History of Negro Americans*. New York: Alfred A. Knopf, 1998.

_____. *Runaway Slaves: Rebels on the Plantation*. New York: Oxford University Press, 1999.

_____. *The Emancipation Proclamation*. Garden City, NY: Doubleday, 1963.

Fulmer, David. *Chasing the Devil's Tail*. New York: Harcourt, 2000.

Genovese, Eugene. *Roll Jordon Roll: The World the Slaves Made*. New York: Pantheon Books, 1974.

Greenberg, Kenneth S., ed. *Nat Turner: A Slave Rebellion in History and Memory*. New York: Oxford University Press, 2003.

Harlan, Louis R. *Booker T. Washington: The Wizard of Tuskegee*. New York: Oxford University Press, 1983.

Higginson, Thomas Wentworth. *Black Rebellion*. New York: Arno, 1969.

Huggins, Nathan Irvin. *Slave and Citizen: The Life of Frederick Douglass*. Boston: Little, Brown, 1980.

James, C. L. R. *Black Jacobins: Toussaint L'Ouverture and the San Domingo Revolution*. New York: Vintage, 1963.

Lewis, David L. *W. E. B. DuBois: Biography of a Race*. 2 vols. New York: Henry Holt, 1993.

Lofton, John. *Denmark Vesey's Revolt: The Slave Plot That Lit a Fuse to Fort Sumter*. Kent, OH: Kent State University Press, 1983.

Moses, Wilson Jeremiah. *Creative Conflict in African American Thought: Frederick Douglass, Alexander Crummell, Booker T. Washington, W. E. B. DuBois, and Marcus Garvey*. New York: Cambridge University Press, 2004.

Pearson, Edward A. *Designs Against Charleston: The Trial Record of the Denmark Vesey Slave Conspiracy of 1822*. Chapel Hill: University of North Carolina Press, 1999.

Quarles, Benjamin. *Black Abolitionists*. New York: Oxford University Press, 1969.

_____, ed. *Frederick Douglass*. Englewood Cliffs, NJ: Prentice Hall, 1968.

Russell, Dick. *Black Genius and the American Experience*. New York: Carroll & Graf, 1998.

Sekayi, Dia N. *African American Intellectual-Activists: Legacies in the Struggle.* New York: Garland, 1997.

Sinette, Elinor Des Verney. *Arthur Alfonso Schomburg: Black Bibliophile & Collector.* Detroit: Wayne State University Press, 1989.

Styron, William. *The Confessions of Nat Turner.* New York: Random House, 1967.

Watts, Jerry Gafio. *Heroism and the Black Intellectual: Ralph Ellison, Politics, and Afro-American Intellectual Life.* Chapel Hill: University of North Carolina Press, 1994.

Walker, David. *David Walker's Appeal to the Coloured Citizens of the World.* Ed. Peter P. Hinks. University Park: Pennsylvania State University Press, 2000.

Wright, W. D. *Black Intellectuals, Black Cognition and a Black Aesthetic.* Westport, CT: Praeger, 1997.

Chapter 16: The Women's War

Barry, Kathleen. *Susan B. Anthony, A Biography of a Singular Feminist.* New York: New York University Press, 1988.

Berkin, Carol Ruth, and Mary Beth Norton. *Women of America: A History.* Boston: Houghton Mifflin, 1970.

Brigham, Amariah. *Remarks on the Influence of Mental Cultivation and Mental Excitement Upon Health.* New York: Arno Press, 1955.

Carby, Hazel V. *Reconstructing Womanhood: The Emergence of the Afro-American Woman Novelist.* New York: Oxford University Press, 1987.

Charvat, William. *The Profession of Authorship in America.* Philadelphia: University of Pennsylvania Press, 1976.

Chodorow, Nancy J. *Feminism and Psychoanalytic Theory.* New Haven, CT: Yale University Press, 1989.

Conrad, Susan Phinney. *Perish the Thought: Intellectual Women in Romantic America, 1830–1860.* New York: Oxford University Press, 1976.

Cott, Nancy F. *A Heritage of Her Own: Toward a New Social History of American Women.* New York: Simon and Schuster, 1979.

_____. *The Grounding of Modern Feminism.* New Haven, CT: Yale University Press, 1987.

_____. *The Bonds of Womanhood: "Woman's Sphere" in New England, 1740–1835.* New Haven, CT: Yale University Press, 1997.

Davidson, Cathy N., et al. *The Oxford Companion to Women's Writing in the United States.* New York: Oxford University Press, 2005.

Douglas, Ann. *Feminization of the American Culture.* New York: Noonday Press/Farrar, Straus and Giroux, 1998.

Evans, Sara M. *Born for Liberty: A History of Women in America.* New York: Free Press, 1989.

Faragher, John Mack. *Women and Men on the Overland Trail.* New Haven, CT: Yale University Press, 1979.

Flexner, Eleanor. *Century of Struggle: The Woman's Rights Movement in the United States.* Cambridge, MA: Harvard University Press, 1975.

Friedman, Jean E., and William G. Shade. *Our American Sisters: Women in American Life and Thought.* Boston: Allyn and Bacon, 1973.

Fuller, Margaret. *Woman in the Nineteenth Century.* New York: W. W. Norton, reprint, 1971.

Gilbert, Sandra, and Susan Gubar. *The Norton Anthology of Literature by Women.* New York: W. W. Norton, 1985.

Glueck, Sheldon, and Eleanor Glueck. *Five Hundred Delinquent Women.* New York: Alfred A. Knopf, 1934.

Goldsmith, Barbara. *Other Powers: The Age of Suffrage, Spiritualism and the Scandalous Victoria Woodhull.* New York: Alfred A. Knopf, 1998.

Hedrick, Joan D. *Harriet Beecher Stowe, a Life.* New York: Oxford University Press, 1994.

Howard, Angela M., and Frances M. Kavenik, eds. *Handbook of American Women's History.* Thousand Oaks, CA: Sage, 2000.

Jensen, Joan M., and Gloria Ricci Lothrop. *California Women: A History.* San Francisco: Boyd & Fraser, 1978.

Jenkins, Melinda. *Gambler's Wife: The Life of Melinda Jenkins.* Ed. Paula Mitchell Marks. Lincoln: University of Nebraska Press: reprint. 1998.

Jacobs, Harriet A. *Incidents in the Life of a Slave Girl: Written by Herself.* Ed. Jean Fagan Yellin. Cambridge, MA: Harvard University Press, 1987.

Kelley, Mary. *Private Woman, Public Stage: Literary Domesticity in Nineteenth Century America.* New York: Oxford University Press, 1984.

Lerner, Gerda. *Grimké Sisters from South Carolina: Pioneers for Women's Rights and Abolition.* New York: Schocken Books, 1971.

_____. *A Majority Finds Its Past: Placing Women in History.* New York: Oxford University Press, 1976.

McCullough, David G. *John Adams.* New York: Simon and Schuster, 2001.

Myres, Sandra. *Westering Women and the Frontier Experience, 1800–1915.* Albuquerque: University of New Mexico Press, 1982.

Nagel, Paul C. *The Adams Women.* New York: Oxford University Press, 1979.

Rogers, Sherbrooke. *Sarah Josepha Hale: a New England Pioneer, 1788–1879.* Grantham, NH: Thompson & Rutter, 1985.

Schlissel, Lillian, ed. *Women's Diaries of the Westward Journey*. New York: Schocken Books, 1983. Thousand Oaks, CA: Sage Publications, 2000.

Sterling, Dorothy, ed. *We Are Your Sisters: Black Women in the Nineteenth Century*. New York: W. W. Norton, 1984.

Todd, Jan. *Physical Culture and the Body Beautiful: Purposive Exercise in the Lives of American Women, 1800–1870*. Macon, GA: Mercer University Press, 1997.

Tyler, Alice Felt. *Freedom's Ferment: Phases of American Social History from the Colonial Period to the Outbreak of the Civil War*. New York: Harper Torchbooks, 1962.

Wayne, Tiffany K. *Woman Thinking: Feminism and Transcendentalism in Nineteenth Century America*. Lanham, MD: Lexington Books, 2005.

Wolfe, Margaret Ripley. *Daughters of Canaan: A Saga of Southern Women*. Lexington: University of Kentucky Press, 1995.

Chapter 17: Utopian Ideas

Bellamy, Edward. *Looking Backward, 2000–1807*. New York: Signet, 2000.

Holloway, Mark. *Heavens on Earth: Utopian Communities in America, 1680–1880*. New York: Dover, 1966.

Klaw, Spencer. *Without Sin: The Life of the Oneida Community*. New York: Alan Lane, 1993.

Piltzer, Donald E., and Josephine Elliot. "New Harmony's First Utopians." *Indiana Magazine of History*, 100(3), September 1979.

Stern, Madeline B. *The Pantarch: A Biography of Stephen Pearl Andrews*. Austin: University of Texas Press, 1968.

Thomas, Robert David. *The Man Who Would Be Perfect: John Humphrey Noyes and the Utopian Impulse*. Philadelphia: University of Pennsylvania Press, 1977.

Tuverson, Ernest. *The Redeemer Nation*. Chicago: University of Chicago Press, 1974.

Vrheul, Jaap. *Dreams of Paradise: Visions of Apocalypse: Utopia and Dystopia in American Culture*. Amsterdam: VU University Press, 2004.

Chapter 18: Battle Hymns: Abolition and/or Union

Aaron, Daniel. *The Unwritten War, American Writers and the Civil War*. New York: Alfred A. Knopf, 1973.

Abzug, Robert H. *Passionate Liberator: Theodore Dwight Weld and the Dilemma of Reform*. New York: Oxford University Press, 1980.

_____. *Cosmos Crumbling: American Reform and the Religious Imagination*. New York: Oxford University Press, 1994.

Donald, David Herbert. *Lincoln*. New York: Simon & Schuster, 1995.

Duberman, Martin B., ed. *Antislavery Vanguard: New Essays on the Abolitionists.* Princeton, NJ: Princeton University Press, 1965.

Edelstein, Tilden G. *Strange Enthusiasm: A Life of Thomas Wentworth Higginson.* New Haven, CT: Yale University Press, 1968.

Filler, Louis. *The Crusade Against Slavery, 1830–1860.* New York: Harper & Row, 1960.

Forgie, George. *Patricide and the House Divided: a Psychological Interpretation of Lincoln and His Age.* New York: W. W. Norton, 1979.

Fredrickson, George. *The Inner Civil War: Northern Intellectuals and the Crisis of the Union.* New York: Harper & Row, 1965.

Gossett, Thomas F. *Uncle Tom's Cabin and American Culture.* Dallas: Southern Methodist University Press, 1985.

Holt, Michael. *The Fate of Their Country.* New York: Hill and Wang, 2004.

Jaffa, Harry V. *Crisis of the House Divided: An Interpretation of the Issues in the Lincoln-Douglas Debates.* Garden City, NY: Doubleday, 1959.

Merrill, Walter McIntosh. *Against Wind and Tide: A Biography of Wm. Lloyd Garrison.* Cambridge, MA: Harvard University Press, 1963.

Oates, Stephen. *With Malice Toward None: The Life of Abraham Lincoln.* New York: Haper & Row, 1977.

Quarles, Benjamin. *Black Abolitionists.* New York: Oxford University Press, 1969.

Thomas, Emery. *The Confederate Nation.* New York: Harper & Row, 1978.

Trudeau, Noah Andre. *Like Men of War, Black Troops in the Civil War.* Boston: Little, Brown, 1998.

Tuttleton, James W. *Thomas Wentworth Higginson.* Boston: Twayne Publishers, 1978.

Wilson, Edmund. *Patriotic Gore: Studies in the Literature of the American Civil War.* New York: Oxford University Press, 1962.

Yellin, Jean Fagan, and John C. Van Horne, eds. *The Abolitionist Sisterhood: Women's Political Culture in Antebellum America.* Ithaca, NY: Cornell University Press, 1994.

There are a great many books on the American Civil War and the events leading up to it, and at least one stunning television series. To save the reader time, out of this plethora of books, the following Pulitzer Prize winners are recommended:

McPherson, James M. *Battle Cry of Freedom: The Civil War Era.* New York: Oxford University Press, 1988.

Nevins, Allan. *Ordeal of the Union.* 2 vols. New York: Macmillan, 1992.

_____. *The War for the Union*. 2 vols. New York: Macmillan, 1992.

Potter, David. *The Impending Crisis, 1848–1861*. New York: HarperCollins, 1976.

Chapter 19: Centennial Vistas, 1876: Toward the Twentieth Century

Adams, Henry. *The Education of Henry Adams*. New York: Modern Library, reprint, 1931.

_____. *The Degradation of the Democratic Dogma*. New York: Macmillan, 1947.

Asbury, Herbert. *Gangs of New York*. New York: Thunder's Mouth Press, 2001.

Anderson, Nancy. *Thomas Moran*. Washington, DC: National Gallery and New Haven, CT: Yale University Press, 1997.

Barzun, Jacques. *A Stroll with William James*. New York: Harper & Row, 1983.

Beatty, Jack. *Age of Betrayal: The Triumph of Money in America, 1865–1900*. New York: Random House, 2007.

Borus, Daniel H. *Writing Realism: Howells, James and Norris in the Mass Market*. Chapel Hill: University of North Carolina Press, 1989.

Brands, H. W. *Masters of Enterprise: Giants of American Business from John Jacob Astor and J. P. Morgan to Bill Gates and Oprah Winfrey*. New York: Free Press, 1999.

_____. *The Money Men: Capitalism, Democracy and the Hundred Years' War Over the American Dollar*. New York: W. W. Norton, 2006.

Brent, Joseph L. *Charles Sanders Peirce*. Bloomington: Indiana University Press, 1992.

Brian, Denis. *Pulitzer: A Life*. New York: John Wiley, 2001.

Brown, Dee. *The Year of the Century: 1876*. New York: Scribners, 1966.

Bush-Brown, Albert. *Louis Sullivan*. New York: G. Braziller, 1960.

Claris, Carol. *Thomas Moran: Watercolors of the American West*. Austin: University of Texas Press, 1980.

Clark, Thomas D., and Albert Kirwan. *The South Since Appomattox: A Century of Regional Change*. New York: Oxford University Press, 1967.

Clegg, Brian. *The Man Who Stopped Time: The Illuminating Story of Eadweard Muybridge: Pioneer Photographer*. Washington, DC: Joseph Henry Press, 2007.

Cochran, Thomas, and William Miller. *The Age of Enterprise: A Social History of Industrial America*. New York: Macmillan, 1942.

Collier, Lincoln. *The Making of Jazz*. Boston: Houghton Mifflin, 1978.

Crunden, Robert Morse. *Ministers of Reform: the Progressives' Achievement in American Civilization, 1889–1920*. New York: Basic Books, 1982.

Curti, Merle Eugene. *The Social Ideas of American Educators.* Totowa, NJ: Littlefield, Adams, 1974.

Davis, Allen F. *Spearheads for Reform: The Social Settlements and the Progressive Movement 1890–1914.* New York: Oxford University Press, 1967.

Diggins, John Patrick. *Bard of Savagery: Thorstein Veblen and Modern Social Theory.* New York: Seabury Press, 1978.

Dippie, Brian, ed. *Charles M. Russell, Word Painter.* New York: Harry N. Abrams, 1993.

Downey, Fairfax. *Richard Harding Davis: His Day.* New York: Scribner, 1933.

Egbert, Donald Drew. *Socialism and American Art in the Light of European Utopianism, Marxism and Anarchism.* Princeton, NJ: Princeton University Press, 1988.

Feinstein, Howard M. *Becoming William James.* Ithaca: Cornell University Press, 1984.

Fisch, Max. *Classic American Philosophers.* New York: Appleton Century Crofts, 1961. This is the best book on pragmatism.

Foner, Eric. *Politics and Ideology in the Age of the Civil War.* New York: Oxford University Press, 1980.

_____. *Reconstruction, America's Unfinished Revolution, 1863–1877.* New York: Harper & Row, 1988.

_____. *Forever Free: The Story of Emancipation and Reconstruction.* New York: Vintage, 2006.

Foner, Philip S. *Women and the American Labor Movement: From Colonial Times to the Eve of World War I.* New York: Free Press, 1979.

Francis, Mark. *Herbert Spencer and the Invention of Modern Life.* Ithaca, NY: Cornell University Press, 2007.

George, Henry. *Progress and Poverty: An Inquiry into the Cause of Industrial Depressions and of Increase of Want with Increase of Wealth; the Remedy.* New York: Modern Library and Random House, 1942.

Goetzmann, William, ed. *The American Hegelians.* New York: Alfred A. Knopf, 1973.

_____. *Exploration and Empire.* New York: Alfred A. Knopf, 1966.

_____ and Kay Sloan. *Looking Far North: The Harriman Expedition to Alaska, 1899.* New York: Viking Press, 1982.

Goldman, Eric. *Rendezvous With Destiny: A History of Modern American Reform,* rev. ed. New York: Vintage, 1955. This is an important book for reform definitions.

Goodwyn, Lawrence. *Democratic Promise: The Populist Movement in America.* New York: Oxford University Press, 1976.

Gordon, John Steele. *An Empire of Wealth: The Epic History of American Economic Power.* New York: HarperCollins, 2004.

Gross, Linda P. *Philadelphia's 1867 Centennial Exhibition.* Charleston, SC: Arcadia, 2005.

Hacker, Louis M. *World of Andrew Carnegie: 1865–1901.* Philadelphia: Lippincott, 1968.

Hales, Peter Bacon. *Silver Cities: The Photography of American Urbanization, 1839–1915.* Philadelphia: Temple University Press, 1984.

Harlan, Louis R. *Booker T. Washington.* New York: 1972.

Hartsfield, Larry K. *The American Response to Professional Crime 1870–1917.* Westport, CT: Greenwood Press, 1985.

Hendricks, Gordon. *Albert Bierstadt: Painter of the American West.* New York: Amon Carter Museum and Harry N. Abrams, 1974.

Hines, Thomas. *Burnham of Chicago, Architect and Planner.* New York: Oxford University Press, 1974.

Hochman, Barbara. *The Art of Frank Norris, Storyteller.* Columbia: University of Missouri Press, 1988.

Hofstadter, Richard. *Social Darwinism in American Thought.* Boston: Beacon Press, 1944.

_____. *The Age of Reform; from Bryan to F. D. R.* New York: Alfred A. Knopf, 1955.

_____. *Anti-Intellectualism in American Life.* New York: Alfred A. Knopf, 1963.

James, Henry. *William Wetmore Story and His Friends: From Letters, Diaries and Recollections.* Whitefish, MT: Kessinger Publishing, 2006.

James, William. *Psychology: The Briefer Course.* New York: Harper Torchbooks, 1961.

Jenkins, Reese V. *Images and Enterprise: Technology and the American Photographer, 1839 to 1925.* Baltimore: Johns Hopkins University Press, 1975.

Johns, Elizabeth. *Thomas Eakins: The Heroism of Modern Life.* Princeton, NJ: Princeton University Press, 1983.

Josephson, Matthew. *The Robber Barons: The Great American Capitalists, 1861–1901.* New York: Harcourt, Brace, 1934.

_____. *The Politicos, 1865–1896.* New York: Harcourt, Brace, 1938.

_____. *Edison, a Biography.* New York: McGraw-Hill, 1959.

Kazin, Michael. *A Godly Hero: The Life of William Jennings Bryan.* New York: Alfred A. Knopf, 2006.

Klein, Maury. *The Life and Legend of Jay Gould.* Baltimore: Johns Hopkins University Press, 1986.

_____. *The Life and Legend of E. H. Harriman.* Chapel Hill: University of North Carolina Press, 2000.

Kohn, Hans. *The Age of Nationalism: the First Era of Global History*. New York: Harper & Row, 1962.

Kuklick, Bruce. *The Rise of American Philosophy, Cambridge, MA, 1860–1930*. New Haven, CT: Yale University Press, 1997.

———. *Puritans in Babylon: The Ancient Near East and American Intellectual Life, 1880–1930*. Princeton, NJ: Princeton University Press, 1998.

———. *A History of Philosophy in America, 1720–2000*. New York: Oxford University Press, 2001.

Lewis, David Levering. *W. E. B. DuBois: Biography of a Race, 1868–1919*. 2 vols. New York: Henry Holt & Co., 1923.

Lewis, R. W. B. *Edith Wharton: A Biography*. New York: Harper & Row, 1975.

———. *The Jameses: A Family Narrative*. New York: Farrar, Straus and Giroux, 1991.

Lynn, Kenneth. *William Dean Howells, an American Life*. New York: Harcourt Brace Jovanovich, 1971.

Martin, Jay. *The Education of John Dewey: A Biography*. New York: Columbia University Press, 2002.

McCracken, Harold, ed. *Frederic Remington's Own West*. New York: Promontory Press, 1994.

McCullough, David. *The Path Between the Seas: The Creation of the Panama Canal, 1870–1914*. New York: Simon and Schuster, 1977.

McElrath, Joseph R. Jr., and Jesse S. Crisler. *Frank Norris: A Life*. Urbana: University of Illinois Press, 2006.

McFeeley, William S. *Grant: A Biography*. New York: W. W. Norton, 1981.

Menand, Louis. *The Metaphysical Club*. New York: Farrar, Straus and Giroux, 2001. A recent popular book that erroneously sees Pragmatism as the product of Oliver Wendell Holmes Jr.'s Civil War experiences.

Miller, Perry, ed. *American Thought, Civil War to World War I*. New York: Holt, Rinehart and Winston, 1964.

Montgomery, David. *Beyond Equality: Labor and the Radical Republicans 1862–1872*. New York: Alfred A. Knopf, 1967.

Morand, Anne. *Thomas Moran*. Norman: Oklahoma University Press, 1996.

Morris, Edmund. *The Rise of Theodore Roosevelt*. New York: Modern Library, 2001.

Morrison, Hugh. *Louis Sullivan, Prophet of Modern Architecture*. New York: W. W. Norton, 1988.

Muybridge, Eadweard. *The Human Figure in Motion*. New York: Bonanza Books/Crown, 1989.

Myers, Gustavus. *History of the Great American Fortunes.* New York: Modern Library, 1936.

Naef, Weston, James Wood, and Therese Heyman. *Era of Exploration: The Rise of Landscape Photography in the American West, 1860–1885.* Boston: Graphic Society, 1975.

Nasaw, David. *Andrew Carnegie.* New York: Penguin, 2006.

Mott, Frank Luther. *A History of American Magazines.* 6 vols. Cambridge, MA: Harvard University Press, 1938–1968.

Oriard, Michael. *Reading Football: How the Popular Press Created an American Spectacle.* Chapel Hill: University of North Carolina Press, 1993.

Orvell, Miles. *The Real Thing, Imitation and Authenticity in American Culture, 1880–1940.* Chapel Hill: University of North Carolina Press, 1989.

Persons, Stow, ed. *The Selected Essays of William Graham Summer, Social Darwinist.* Englewood, NJ: Prentice Hall, 1963.

Peckham, Morse. *Man's Rage for Chaos: Biology, Behavior and the Arts.* Philadelphia: University of Pennsylvania Press, 1965.

Powers, Ron. *Mark Twain: A Life.* New York: Free Press, 2005.

Reynolds, Davis S. *Walt Whitman's America.* New York: Alfred A. Knopf, 1996.

Richardson, Robert P. *William James: In the Maelstrom of American Modernism.* Boston: Houghton Mifflin, 2006. This is the most recent biography of William James.

Rogosin, Donn. *Invisible Men: Life in Baseball's Negro League.* New York: Atheneum, 1983.

Ryan Alan. *John Dewey and the High Tide of American Liberalism.* New York: W. W. Norton, 1995.

Sandweiss, Martha. *Print the Legend: Photography and the American West.* New Haven, CT: Yale University Press, 2001.

Samuels, Ernest. *Henry Adams: The Major Phase.* Cambridge, MA: Belknap Press of Harvard University Press, 1964.

Samuels, Peggy, and Harold Samuels. *Frederic Remington: A Biography.* Garden City, NY: 1982.

Sante, Luc. *Low Life.* New York: Vintage, 1992.

Schuller, Gunther. *Early Jazz.* New York: Oxford University Press, 1968.

Seager, Robert II. *Alfred Thayer Mahan: The Man and His Letters.* Annapolis, MD: Naval Institute Press, 1977.

Secrest, Meryle. *Frank Lloyd Wright.* New York: Alfred A. Knopf, 1992.

Simon, Linda. *Genuine Reality, a Life of William James.* New York: Harcourt, Brace, 1998.

Sloan, Kay. *The Loud Silents: Origins of the Social Problem Film.* Urbana: University of Illinois Press, 1988.

Smith, Henry Nash, ed. *Popular Culture and Industrialism 1865–1890.* Garden City, NY: Doubleday, 1967.

Solnit, Rebecca. *River of Shadows, Eadweard Muybridge and the Technological Wild West.* New York: Viking, 2003.

Spiller, Robert, Willard Thorp, Thomas H. Johnson, and Henry Seidel Canby. *A Literary History of the United States.* New York: Macmillan, 1948.

Stallman, R. W. *Stephen Crane: A Biography.* New York: Braziller, 1968.

Stamp, Kenneth. *The Era of Reconstruction.* New York: Alfred A. Knopf, 1967.

Starr, Paul. *The Creation of the Media: Political Origins of Modern Communications.* New York: Basic Books, 2004.

Swafford, Jan. *Charles Ives, A Life with Music.* New York: W. W. Norton, 1996.

Swanberg, W. A. *Dreiser.* New York: Bantam Books, 1967.

Taft, Robert. *Photography and the American Scene.* New York: Dover, 1964.

Thayer, H. S. *Meaning and Action: A Critical History of Pragmatism.* Indianapolis: Bobbs-Merrill, 1966.

Veblen, Thorstein. *The Higher Learning in America.* New York: Sagamore Press, 1937.

Vorpahl, Ben Merchant. *Frederic Remington and the West, With the Eye of the Mind.* Austin: University of Texas Press, 1978.

Weiner, James. *Evolution and the Founders of Pragmatism.* Cambridge, MA: Harvard University Press, 1949.

White, G. Edward. *The Eastern Establishment and the Western Experience.* Austin: University of Texas Press, 1989.

White, Morton. *Social Thought in America, the Revolt against Formalism.* New York: Viking Press, 1949.

Wilkins, Thurman. *Thomas Moran, Artist of the Mountains.* Norman: University of Oklahoma Press, 1966.

Winks, Robin W. *Frederick Billings, a Life.* New York: Oxford University Press, 1991.

Zabel, Morton D., ed. *The Portable Henry James.* New York: Penguin, 1968.

ACKNOWLEDGMENTS

This book never would have come into being without the tireless help of my wife, Mewes, and her sister, Charlene McCarthy, my agent, James Hornfischer, and my editor, Brandon Proia, plus fifty years of teaching American intellectual and cultural history to thousands of very interested students at Yale and the University of Texas. None of my colleagues read parts or all of my manuscript except the eminent black historian, the late Henry Bullock. And finally I wish to thank the Social Science Research Council for granting me a wonderful year at the Stanford Center for Research in the Social Sciences. This and another book and a prize-winning television series were the result of this largesse.

INDEX